MUSEUMS, ETHICS A___ ___ ____
HERITAGE

This volume provides an unparalleled exploration of ethics and museum practice, evaluating the past, present and future of self-regulation in museum activities following ever-increasing controversy and debate around issues of collections, provenance, ownership, repatriation, human rights, environmental sustainability, 'difficult' heritage, social engagement and cultural identity. Using a variety of case studies that reflect the internal realities and daily activities of museums as they address these issues – from exhibition content and museum research to education, accountability and new technologies – *Museums, Ethics and Cultural Heritage* enables a greater understanding of the role of museums as complex and multifaceted institutions of cultural production, identity-formation and heritage preservation.

Benefiting from ICOM's unique position internationally in the museum world, this collection brings a global range of academics and professionals together to examine museum ethics from multiple perspectives. Providing a more complete picture of the diverse activities now carried out by museums, *Museums, Ethics and Cultural Heritage* will appeal to practitioners, academics, students, cultural policy makers and commentators on the changing roles of museums today.

Bernice L. Murphy is the former National Director of Museums Australia (Canberra), and served as Chair of the ICOM Ethics Committee (2004–2011); nine years (six as Vice-President) on ICOM's Executive Council (1995–2004); and three years as a founding member of ICOM's Legal Affairs Committee (2001–2004). She worked for fifteen years with a small team developing what became Australia's first museum of contemporary art, serving as Curator, Chief Curator and finally Director of the MCA Sydney (1984–1998). She has published since the 1970s on historical art and exhibitions, museum architecture, artists' training, art museums, and contemporary art (including indigenous art) from many countries. She is currently Editor of *Museums Australia Magazine* (a quarterly journal).

MUSEUMS, ETHICS AND CULTURAL HERITAGE

Edited by Bernice L. Murphy

INTERNATIONAL COUNCIL OF MUSEUMS
CONSEIL INTERNATIONAL DES MUSEES
CONSEJO INTERNACIONAL DE MUSEOS

LONDON AND NEW YORK

First published 2016
by Routledge
2 Park Square, Milton Park, Abingdon, Oxon OX14 4RN

and by Routledge
711 Third Avenue, New York, NY 10017

Routledge is an imprint of the Taylor & Francis Group, an informa business

General Editor: Bernice L. Murphy
Managing Editor (ICOM): Aedín Mac Devitt

British Library Cataloguing-in-Publication Data
A catalogue record for this book is available from the British Library

Library of Congress Cataloging-in-Publication Data
Names: Murphy, Bernice L., editor.
Title: Museums, ethics and cultural heritage/edited by Bernice L. Murphy.
Description: New York, NY: Routledge, 2016. | Includes index.
Identifiers: LCCN 2015050862| ISBN 9781138676329 (pbk.: alk. paper) |
ISBN 9781315560151 (ebk)
Subjects: LCSH: Museums–Moral and ethical aspects. | Museums–
Standards. |
Cultural property–Protection–International cooperation. | International
Council of Museums.
Classification: LCC AM7 .M8837 2016 | DDC 069–dc23
LC record available at http://lccn.loc.gov/2015050862

ISBN: 978-1-138-67632-9 (pbk)
ISBN: 978-1-315-56015-1 (ebk)

Typeset in Bembo
by Wearset Ltd, Boldon, Tyne and Wear

Printed and bound by CPI Group (UK) Ltd, Croydon, CR0 4YY

CONTENTS

PART IV
Heritage care and ethics through the lens of multiple cultures and regions   **129**

PART V
Evolving issues: Collaboration, provenance research, deaccessioning, social responsibility and public participation in museums   **191**

FIGURES

TABLES

CONTRIBUTORS

Vojtěch Blodig is a lecturer at the Jan Evangelista Purkyně University in Ústí nad Labem, Czech Republic and an active member of ICOM's International Committee, IC MEMO, which he chaired in the period 2007–12. Since 1990 he has been working in the Terezín Memorial, specializing in the research of the history of the Terezín Ghetto, also taking part in the institution's educational activities. His publications include a work called *Terezín in the 'Final Solution of the Jewish Question' 1941–1945*, while he has also been involved in the preparation for and publication of several books written by a team of authors on the issue of the Holocaust and the history of Terezín.

Stephanie de Roemer works with Glasgow Museums as a conservator for sculpture: medieval polychrome sculpture, nineteenth- and twentieth-century European sculpture, architectural, public sculpture and Installation Art, on display and in storage. She joined ICOM-CC in 2003 and is currently acting as the group coordinator for the working group on Sculpture, Polychromy and Architectural Decorations (Triennial 2014–17). She also worked as conservation intern and conservation officer in the artefacts conservation department at the National Museums of Scotland, Edinburgh, specializing in the conservation of marine archaeological artefacts in general and waterlogged organics specifically.

France Desmarais has been Director of Programmes and Partnerships at ICOM since 2010. In 2012, she created the only International Observatory on Illicit Traffic in Cultural Goods, thanks to the financial support of the European Commission. She is also Permanent Secretary of ICOM's Disaster Relief Task Force for Museums (DRTF) and an active member of the International Committee of the Blue Shield (ICBS). Prior to joining ICOM, she was head of strategic development at the McCord Museum in Canada.

Eric Dorfman is Director of the Carnegie Museum of Natural History in Pitts-burgh, Pennsylvania, USA. He is also President of the International Council of Museums Committee for Museums and Collections of Natural History (ICOM NATHIST) and serves on the ICOM Ethics Committee. In this capacity he led the drafting of the *ICOM Code of Ethics for Natural History Museums*, which is in the process of being translated into ten languages. Dr Dorfman has also published a number of books on natural heritage and climate change, including his most recent book *Intangible Natural Heritage* (Routledge, 2011).

Gary Edson is Professor Emeritus at the Center for Advanced Study of Museum Science and Heritage Management, Museum of Texas Tech University. He was Executive Director of the Museum of Texas Tech University and Director of the Center for Advanced Study of Museum Science and Heritage Management for twenty-five years. Edson is an active member of the International Council of Museums; he served on the Executive Council, and the ICOM Ethics Committee, Executive Council and was Secretary of the International Committee for Training of Personnel (ICTOP). He also served on the ICOM US board for fifteen years and was Chair of the American Association of Museums Committee on Museum Professional Training.

Dorota Folga-Januszewska is an art historian, art critic and museologist. She received her PhD in 1982 from Warsaw University. She worked at the National Museum of Poland from 1979 to 2008, starting as curator in 1991, becoming Director of Collections in 1995 and Director General in 2007. She is also a pro-fessor of museum studies at Wyszynski University in Warsaw. She has been Chair of ICOM's National Committee in Poland since 2012. Her work has appeared in more than 300 publications, and she has curated fifty-four exhibitions.

Michael M. Franz serves as Deputy CEO of the Stiftung Deutsches Zentrum Kul-turgutverluste at Magdeburg. He has also worked as an expert consultant for Ger-many's Federal Ministry of the Interior (*Bundesinnenministerium*) on legal and practical aspects of an Internet database on looted art. He was a lawyer at Unützer Wagner Werding, and in 2009 he advised the Austrian Federal Ministry of Science and Research (*Österreichisches Bundesministerium für Wissenschaft und Forschung*) on projects concerning looted art and trophy art in connection with the 'forMuse – Forschung an Museen'.

Amareswar Galla is an alumnus of Jawaharlal Nehru University, New Delhi, and is the founding Executive Director of the International Institute for the Inclusive Museum, India/Denmark/Australia (www.inclusivemuseum.org). He is also an Honorary Professor at the prestigious Global Change Institute, The University of Queensland, Australia. His publications range from *World Heritage: Benefits Beyond Borders* (Cambridge University Press and UNESCO Publishing, 2012), (2013, French and Korean) to *Heritage Curricula and Cultural Diversity* (Office of Multicultural Affairs, AGPS, Canberra, 1993). He is currently Curator of the Amaravati Ancient Town, A.P., and International Curator and Visiting Professor at the Don Bosco Centre for Indigenous Cultures, Shillong, India.

Alberto Garlandini is a museologist and expert in the management of cultural heritage. For the Lombardy region, he was Director-General of Culture, Director-General of Cinema, and President of Lombardy's Film Commission. He was appointed by the Italian Ministry of Cultural Heritage and Ministry of Foreign Affairs in the Commission for the Reform of State Museums and National Museum System, and in the Commission for the Promotion of Italian Culture Abroad. He is active in ICOM, as a member of its Executive Council, its Strategic Allocation Review Commission and its Strategic Plan Committee. He is also Chair of the Organising Committee of the 2016 ICOM General Conference in Milan. He is a lecturer in several Italian universities, and has been widely published on museums and heritage in Italian, English and French.

Nao Hayashi, a historian by training, has worked in the safeguarding of the built and movable heritage since 2002. Through operational projects in Africa, the Arab world, Asia and the Pacific, and Europe, she has designed and implemented programmes for building the capacities of museum professionals in developing countries and partnerships among institutions. Since 2014, she has been Museums Programme Coordinator at UNESCO, leading the elaboration of the new UNESCO *International Recommendation on the Protection and Promotion of Museums and Collections*.

Markus Hilgert is a specialist in Ancient Near Eastern Studies and the current Director of the Ancient Near East Museum (Vorderasiatisches Museum) at the Pergamon museum in Berlin (Staatliche Museen zu Berlin – Stiftung Preußischer Kulturbesitz). From 2007 until early 2014, Hilgert held a chair for Cuneiform Studies at Heidelberg University. Hilgert is a member of the European Academy of Sciences and Arts and has held visiting professorships at various universities in Europe and the United States.

Hans-Martin Hinz has been President of ICOM since 2010. He began his museum career as Advisor for the establishment of new museums for the Ministry of Cultural Affairs in West Berlin, Germany. From 2000 to 2001, he was Deputy Minister of Culture (Staatssekretär) for Berlin and has also occupied several positions in national and international museum institutions.

Emlyn Koster was a field geologist, university faculty member and research project manager before being at the helm of four major nature and science museums – Royal Tyrrell Museum of Palaeontology, Ontario Science Centre, Liberty Science Center, and since 2013 the North Carolina Museum of Natural Sciences – each on a journey of greater relevance to the needs of society and the environment. Past President of the Geological Association of Canada and of the global Giant Screen

Theater Association, immediate Past Chair of the Global Committee for the Association of Science-Technology Centers, he is currently also an Adjunct Professor of Marine, Earth and Atmospheric Sciences at North Carolina State University. A long-time proponent of relevancy in museums, he has recently contributed to the debate in the geological profession concerning the Anthropocene, and is a member of ICOM's new global working group to update the museum definition.

An Laishun is Vice-President and Secretary General of the Chinese Museums Association, Deputy Director of Luxun Museum, China, and a member of the Executive Council of ICOM. He is also Executive Editor-in-Chief, *Chinese Museum Magazine* since 2003. He teaches heritage studies and museology at three universities in China as guest professor. He has been a prominent thinker and innovator in the use of 'new museology' and ecomuseology for safeguarding the heritage of ethnic minority groups in China and promoted four founding community museums in China, developing a number of exhibitions on the culture of different communities in China. He has also published more than ninety papers on museological theory and management.

Eva Maehre Lauritzen is a botanist and Associate Professor Emerita at the Natural History Museum, University of Oslo. She is also former Chair of ICOM's National Committee in Norway.

Geoffrey Lewis was Chairman of the ICOM Ethics Committee (1997–2004), President of ICOM (1983–89) and Chairman of its Advisory Committee (1974–80). Currently retired, he was Director of Museum Studies in the University of Leicester (1977–89) and previously Director of Museums in the cities of Liverpool (1971–77) and Sheffield (1966–71), commencing his museum career at Worthing Museum & Art Gallery in 1950. Subjects of his publications have included the history of museums (including the centenary history of the UK Museums Association), museum management, museum ethics, museum training, and the computerized documentation of museum collections.

Aedín Mac Devitt has been Editor of ICOM's journals since 2010. Having worked in the publishing and press industries for several years, she joined ICOM in 2010 as Publications Officer, and was appointed Head of Publications and Documentation in 2015. She is also Managing Editor of *Museum International*.

Sharon Macdonald is Alexander von Humboldt Professor of Social Anthropology (with emphasis on Cultural Heritage and Museum Studies) in the Institute of European Ethnology at the Humboldt University, Berlin, where she is also Director of the Centre for Anthropological Research on Museums and Heritage (CARMaH). She also holds an Anniversary Professorship in Cultural Anthropology in the Department of Sociology at the University of York, UK, and in 2011–12 was Visiting Professor at Peking University.

François Mairesse teaches museology and cultural economics at the Université Sorbonne Nouvelle (Paris 3, CERLIS, ICCA). He also teaches museology at the École du Louvre. He is Chair of the International Committee for Museology (ICOFOM) and is former Director of the Musée royal de Mariemont (Morlanwelz) in Belgium. He is the author of several articles and books on museology.

Jane Milosch is founding director of the Smithsonian's Provenance Research Initiative in the Office of the Under Secretary for History, Art, and Culture, Smithsonian Institution. Previously she was Senior Program Officer for Art, directing pan-institutional art programmes, new interdisciplinary initiatives and strategic planning efforts for the arts at the Smithsonian. She completed the Getty's Museum Leadership Institute Training Program in 2009. Milosch was a curator at the Renwick Gallery of the Smithsonian American Art Museum, the Cedar Rapids Museum of Art in Iowa, and the Detroit Institute of the Arts. As Fulbright Scholar in Munich, she was managing editor for Prestel art books and consultant to art museums, galleries and other cultural institutions. Her research interests include modern and contemporary art, craft and design, especially the intersections of art, science, design and technology.

Eiji Mizushima was previously Vice-Chair of ICOM Japan and is currently a board member of ICOFOM (ICOM's International Committee for Museology), a member of the Disaster Relief Task Force of ICOM, an editorial board member of the *International Journal of Intangible Heritage* (IJIH), published by the National Museum of Korea, and a member of the editorial board of *Museum International*, published by ICOM. He has been actively involved in the management of a number of organizations: as President of JMMA (Japan Museum Management Academy), and President of MARC-ASPAC (Museum and Culture Advanced Research Center, Asia-Pacific). He has published more than fifteen books on museology and museum management, including Japanese translations of books in French and English.

Silvano Montaldo is Associate Professor of Contemporary History at the University of Turin, Italy, and Director of the 'Cesare Lombroso' Museum of Criminal Anthropology. He has published a number of papers on Italian nineteenth-century history. The main branches of his research activities demonstrate a particular focus on political, institutional, social and cultural phenomena, with specific regard to the cultural, formative and associative aspects of the initiatives, projects and activities of the nineteenth-century middle classes, as well as to the history of scientific culture.

Bernice L. Murphy is the former National Director, Museums Australia (Canberra) and Chair of the ICOM Ethics Committee from 2005 to 2011. She is also former Director of the Museum of Contemporary Art, Sydney (1984–2008). She served nine years (six as Vice-President) on the International Council of Museums Executive Council (1995–2004). She has published since the 1970s on exhibitions, art museums and contemporary art (including Indigenous art) and is the current editor of *Museums Australia Magazine*.

Bongani Ndhlovu is Executive Director: Core Functions at the Iziko Museums of South Africa. He was the Director of Ncome and Voortrekker/Msunduzi museums from 2004 to 2011. Before that he worked as a Ncome Museum Manager and as a Deputy Manager for the Ditsong: National Museum of Natural History. He started his museum career in 1996 as a cultural historian with the KwaZulu-Natal Museums Service. At ICOM he was formerly Secretary/Treasurer for ICOM's National Committee in South Africa.

Rina Elster Pantalony is Director of the Copyright Advisory Office at Columbia University and chairs the Legal Affairs Committee of the International Council of Museums. From 2002 to 2012, Ms Pantalony worked as principal intellectual property counsel to the Library and Archives of Canada, and her prior experience also includes an appointment as director of licensing for a joint Internet venture between The Tate, London and the Museum of Modern Art, New York, and legal counsel to the Virtual Museum of Canada, an online exhibition partnership between the Canadian Heritage Information Network (CHIN) and Canada's museums. From 2004 to 2014, she was faculty in the Moving Image Archive Preservation Program at the Tisch School of the Arts, New York University, where she taught courses in copyright law and policy.

Hermann Parzinger has thirty years of field research in many European countries as well as in the Near East and Central Asia. He was Director (1990–2003) and President (2003–08) of the German Archaeological Institute and since 2008 has been President of the Prussian Cultural Heritage Foundation, which is responsible for large cultural projects in Berlin including the renovation of the world-famous Museum Island and the reconstructed Berlin Palace. He has received several awards, among them the Leibniz Prize.

Marilyn Phelan has served as a Professor of Museum Science at Texas Tech University and has received numerous awards. Dr Phelan served for nine years on ICOM's Legal Affairs Committee, involved in preparing the mediation procedure for ICOM to recommend when individuals or countries make claims to stolen or illegally exported objects in museum collections. Her book on laws relating to museums was listed by the Smithsonian as one of a dozen books every museum should own.

Mónica Risnicoff de Gorgas graduated from the Argentine Institute of Museology as Museum Curator. She was director of the National Museum Estancia Jesuítica de Alta Gracia y Casa del Virrey Liniers, Córdoba, Argentina, for almost twenty-five years. At ICOM, she has been a member of the board of the National Committee in Argentina, a member of the ICOM Ethics Committee and a member of the board of ICOFOM (ICOM's International Committee for Museology). She is also Associate Professor of the Master of Museology, teaching museum management at the National University of Tucuman.

Anne-Catherine Robert-Hauglustaine is currently Director General of ICOM and an Associate Professor at the University Paris 1 – Sorbonne. She worked for nearly ten years at the Musée des Arts et Métiers in Paris, France, notably as the Director of the Exhibitions and Publications Department from 2000 to 2007 and as Editor in Chief of the museum's magazine from 2001 to 2008. During her term as board member (2007–10), then chairperson (2010–13) of ICOM's International Committee for Exhibition Exchange (ICEE), she was involved in various international exhibition projects.

Mechtild Rössler is Director of the Division for Heritage and the UNESCO World Heritage Centre at UNESCO. She has held different positions there including as Programme Specialist for Natural Heritage (1993–2001), Chief of Europe and North America (2001–10), Chief of the Policy and Statutory Meeting Section (2010–13) and Deputy Director (2013–14). In May 2014, she became the Deputy Director of the Heritage Division covering four UNESCO Conventions (1954, 1970, 1972 and 2001). She has published and co-authored thirteen books and more than 100 articles.

Martin R. Schärer is the current Chair of the ICOM Ethics Committee. He studied history, pedagogy and art history at Zurich University, specializing in historical research in Germany and Belgium. The initiator of the Postgraduate Studies Programme in Museology at Basel University (1992), he was also a lecturer of museology and the author of many articles on museology and food history. From 1979 to 1985, he spearheaded the creation of a new interdisciplinary museum on food (Alimentarium) in Vevey, opening in 1985, and was director of this museum until 2010.

Regine Schulz is Director/CEO at the Roemer and Pelizaeus-Museum in Hildesheim (Germany). She also teaches Egyptology at the Ludwig Maximilians University in Munich. She has been active for many years in the International Council of Museums, including her previous role as Secretary of the International Committee of Egyptology. She currently serves on ICOM's Executive Council and its Ethics Committee. She has curated, co-curated and consulted on many special exhibitions and has worked in the Egyptian Museums in Berlin and Munich and at the Walters Art Museum in Baltimore, as well as the Free University in Berlin, the Ludwig Maximilians University in Munich and Johns Hopkins University in Baltimore.

Michel Van-Praët was the former Conservateur général du patrimoine at the French Ministry of Culture. He was also a member of the Executive Council of ICOM and Emeritus Professor of the Natural History Museum (Muséum National d'Histoire naturelle), Paris.

W. Richard West, Jr. is President and Chief Executive Officer of the Autry Museum of the American West. He is also the Founding Director and Director Emeritus of the National Museum of the American Indian, Smithsonian Institution, Washington, DC (1990–2007). A former Board Chair of the American Alliance of Museums, he now serves on the board of directors of ICOM–US, and previously was a member of the Executive Council of ICOM (International Council of Museums, Paris), including as ICOM's Vice-President (2007–10). For six years he served as a member of ICOM's Ethics Committee (2005–11).

Sally Yerkovich is Director of the Institute of Museum Ethics at Seton Hall University and a consultant to numerous non-profit and educational institutions. She has over twenty-five years of leadership experience in high-profile American institutions including the National Endowment for the Arts, National Endowment for the Humanities, New Jersey Historical Society, South Street Seaport Museum, Museum for African Art and Tribute WTC, a grassroots visitor centre at the World Trade Center site. She has served on the board of the American Association of Museums and the US Committee for the International Council of Museums and was the President of the Council for Museum Anthropology and the Fund for Arts and Culture.

PART I

Introduction and context: ICOM's commitment to museum ethics

1

ICOM TURNS 70

Ethics and the value creation role of museums

Hans-Martin Hinz, President of ICOM

1946–2016: In 2016 the International Council of Museums commemorates seven decades of work for the global museum community, for the protection of cultural heritage in and outside of museums, and as a forum of international dialogue among museum professionals from all over the world. It is a timely review for ICOM in 2016 to analyze: what has been achieved over seven decades; what have been the most critical successes; and what can be done to build on the best of ICOM's potential in a new century.

Such an anniversary is also a timely opportunity to describe ICOM's present context and to map the organization's continuing contribution to the future development of museums, especially in their social service commitment to interpret, share, protect and develop nature and culture for a more peaceful global world.

In the twenty-first century, the role of museums in the service of society – a phrase that sits at the heart of ICOM's definition of a museum, and shapes its existence as an organization – must be continually discussed among museum professionals, politicians and owners or boards of museums, in order to ensure that museums strive to be front-runners in promoting knowledge and dialogue about history, culture and nature, as well as fostering sustainable practices and ongoing educational enrichment through use of their resources. Responding to social change around them, museums have for several decades been developing their skills and harnessing their resources to act as forums for reconciliation between communities.

This has long been a core task for museums, especially in countries that have experienced the historical burden or indeed been active participants in colonialism in all its forms. However, recent years have witnessed museums' innovation in programs that seek to build bridges of cultural and social understanding across differences in the fast-changing populations of modern cities globally. In addition to these serious social purposes, museums have also been steadily improving their programs and amenities to ensure they are welcoming to visitors, useful to their supporting communities and places of enjoyment and stimulation for all ages! In their key tasks of providing value through their resources and programming, museums aim to develop an inquiring consciousness that stimulates us all to understand the world and each other, and to share in the democratic values of our societies and diverse cultures.

As President of the International Council of Museums, I strongly support the international dialogue of the global museums community, which ICOM's many National and International Committees, Regional Alliances and Affiliated Organizations pursue year by year. This has a strong impact on our strategic thinking, our ethical behavior, our programs, and can advance the quality and variety of our daily work for museums of all kinds.

It is worth recalling that ICOM was founded only one year after UNESCO, and was envisaged as pursuing a key NGO role as a partner to UNESCO, at a time when the world was trying to repair the vast devastation after years of war and political conflict. Museum colleagues were among the first activists for meeting the challenges of the post-war era in rebuilding a better world.

ICOM began on a rather modest scale in November 1946, but with an expansive vision led by the American museum personality from Buffalo, Chauncey Hamlin (founding President of ICOM), supported by Georges Salles, then Director of French Museums (and later to become second President of ICOM). At a gathering in Paris chaired by Hamlin, representatives from fourteen countries first came together in a meeting at the Louvre Museum. This was the beginning of – what in terms of membership today has become – the largest international cultural organization, with its membership and networks including museum colleagues in almost 140 countries.

The founding purpose of ICOM was to create an international organization for cooperation among museums following the terrible period of militant nationalism, fascism, the Holocaust, multiple wars and their accompanying destruction on a previously unimaginable scale of global consequences. This international museum organization was conceived in its early years as a council of museum leaders from various countries, who would build a structure of professional interactions outside of governmental bodies representing the political sphere of international relations.

Museums were recognized as having specialized knowledge, unique cultural resources, trained staff and ethical values that could be coordinated to promote better understanding of an interconnected human history beyond nationalism, ideological divisions and militant politics, while also acting to protect a shared heritage internationally: the heritage of all humankind.

A fundamental aspiration of the founders of ICOM as an international museum organization was, and remains, the promotion of high standards of principled conduct in museums, including strong values of cooperative endeavor and public service. After years of intensive distortion of human values in many countries, museums after the Second World War wanted to revalidate ethical standards of heritage care and use of their resources in support of long-lasting values of an interconnected and shared heritage for all nations.

Museums all over the world were challenged to explain where we come from and our place in nature; to explore who we are, and how we can develop a shared future; to examine changes from inequality to equality in human history and our present relations; and to illuminate where and why human conduct failed or changed positively over time. Through international cooperation, this affirmative effort of museums was directed to assisting visitors to understand the past and advance society in its sustainable, democratic development, seeking a high degree of participation based on full respect for human values for all to share.

Seventy years of sustained international dialogue among museum professionals is a great record of success for ICOM. Today ICOM numbers more than 35,000 members (embracing both museums and individuals) all over the world. The common ground of ICOM's work is a strong moral purpose to maintain positive cooperation between diverse peoples and nations, to be valid everywhere and well recognized by individual societies and their political representatives, such as parliaments or governments.

The most important tool in advancing and protecting ICOM's shared goals is the *ICOM Code of Ethics for Museums*, which presents a set of base-standards for pursuing museum values and visions, as well as setting out clearly the responsibilities we have for preserving the cultural and natural heritage, both tangible and intangible.

FIGURE 1.1 Tenth ICOM General Conference opening at Copenhagen, performed by H.M. the Queen of Denmark ©ICOM.

These standards include clear principles for the governance and operation of museums and the preservation of their collections. They provide frameworks for mediation of conflicts concerning interpretation and ownership of cultural property. The standards also include principles of ethical behavior of employees, guiding the conduct of all people working in and for museums, which is increasingly understood as including all volunteers and supporters of museums' programs.

Ethical codes of professional practices on a national basis are much older than ICOM's code, and go back to the early twentieth century. What makes the *ICOM Code of Ethics for Museums* so distinctive, however, is its international, global reach. It aims to provide standards underpinning and linking all other national or more discipline-specific codes – some developed in recent years by ICOM's own specialist International Committees – and therefore providing a unifying framework for the protection of standards in museums everywhere. ICOM Code has also been accepted as the international reference document for museum work of various countries in their own museum laws, often acknowledged in the documents of parliaments and governments at a national level.

Guided by this international ethical standards framework, museums are increasingly taking an active role in protecting important parts of the global world heritage: in their collections and cooperative programs multilaterally; but also beyond museums, especially when cultural heritage is at risk – which is increasingly occurring as a result of social uprisings, armed conflicts and natural disasters.

I just want to highlight here the work of ICOM's Ethics Committee, which has met regularly since the late 1980s to deal with ethical matters of concern within and beyond ICOM, including disputes involving conflict between different parties about cultural property rights.

I also want to mention ICOM's programs developed in recent years against illicit trafficking in cultural goods – for example, the publication of the *ICOM Red Lists* since the year 2000, profiling significant objects at risk of being sold on the illegal market for art and antiquities. Similar efforts were carried forward with ICOM's *One Hundred Missing Objects* series in the 1990s (focused on regions), while these two series of publications, jointly, have resulted in a surprising number of identifications of stolen objects and restitutions to their countries of origin. Such programs and activities further demonstrate the ethical mission guiding us all as museum professionals in our global commitment to continuing care and protection of culture and heritage.

The discussion about museum values and standards within ICOM, which intensified in the late 1960s and gathered strength again in the 1980s leading to the first comprehensive ICOM Code, has never ceased. It continues today in many ICOM gatherings around the globe, including the long-standing discussion about updating the ICOM museum definition, and the continuing identification of new tasks that our institutions have today.

In our fast-changing world, the challenges facing museums in the digitally driven environment of communications today are also modifying the way museums carry out their work and engage multiple audiences. Museums compete with numerous media forces today, while themselves incorporating social media and new communications platforms in their aim to be inclusive in terms of broad content and target groups. This also means continuing to protect the public values of culture among minorities, and beyond solely market-driven forces in the arena of commercial exchange.

What is the perception of museums today, and how will they change tomorrow? What will make museums attractive to visitors and online audiences in ten or twenty years' time? What continuing and new roles will they play for local populations, for visitors and tourists, for regions, nations and international communities? For example, what kinds of programs will affirm museums as well-accepted places of dialogue and communication between disparate groups of society in the cause of social integration; in promoting reconciliation of differences after civil conflict; and in rebuilding respect and mutual understanding after armed conflicts internationally?

Over the past decades museum professionals have acquired many new skills and positive experiences through visitor-oriented museum policy in exhibitions and online presentations. Museums have become more participatory and inclusive institutions, producing multi-viewpoint explanations of nature, history and culture. ICOM and museums in many areas have strengthened links between groups, communities and nations through cross-border activities and international cooperative programs. Many new directions have been included in recent years, such as participating in the formation of the Blue Shield internationally, of which ICOM forms one of the four 'Pillar' organizations for global protection of heritage in the face of armed conflict and natural disasters.

Museums today are often among the first cultural stakeholders committing their institutions, knowledge and resources to take action when it comes to dealing with a tragic past – for example, fostering the new beginnings to be established for many nations after the end of the Cold War, or other far-reaching political changes in other continents over decades. Museums have crucial skills and resources for creating new dialogues among former enemy states or mutually estranged groups on a cultural level, as they did within the Balkans following the wars of neo-nationalist conflict and ethnic genocide during the 1990s. Even in more recent international political conflicts, museums are again renewing their best efforts and long-standing links to maintain international dialogue through their NGO networks, and to maintain cooperation around high ethical standards and heritage conservation goals binding us all to strive to overcome continuing difficulties and crisis points in international cultural relations.

ICOM can take heart and strength from so many positive achievements in recent decades, through cross-border projects that help people to understand differing viewpoints and multiple currents forming the background of conflicts that have occurred, and highlighting the strong actions needed to rebuild positive links between communities divided across diversity and difference.

What is different from earlier times, however – and we have to take this into sharpened consideration today – is the greater public awareness and media interest in museum work: in escalating prices for cultural objects and in governance of museums; in exhibitions and public programs interpreting culture, social history, science and the natural world; in museum collections and their provenance histories; and in heritage ideas and multiple values carried by culture in the world around us. The communications-driven environment of daily life now accelerates all discussions exponentially and challenges museums' work in all parts of the world.

Nevertheless some things have not changed. The plumb line for future development of our work will continue to be ethical values, and the ethical responsibilities we share in our work on behalf of the natural and cultural heritage of all. Affirming this durable framework of values, we must review, extend and renew the ethical framework of museum work as an ongoing responsibility.

This constant reprise and update of standards should be pursued in cooperation with all who are responsible for museums, especially governmental proprietors and leaders in the political sphere, in order to advance the cause of museums in their protection of unique, interconnected heritage collections and long cared-for resources for the ongoing understanding of human history and social development.

The International Council of Museums has acted collaboratively in the past, parallel to UNESCO's Conventions development – especially the pathfinding 1970 *Convention on the Means of Prohibiting and Preventing the Illicit Import, Export and Transfer of Ownership of Cultural Property*, at a time when the international museums community formulated its first shared ethical statement around the ethics of acquisition, in endeavoring to advance museums' awareness around international standards that should govern any continuing collecting of cultural objects, especially antiquities, cultural heritage jeopardized during armed conflicts, and the cultural heritage of formerly colonized peoples.

In partnership with UNESCO and others, ICOM continues to promote international guidelines and ethical standards for the work of museums in the twenty-first century. This ICOM publication on ethics is therefore a perfect opportunity for discussions about the intercrossing paths that will ensure museums continue to advance the strong history and legacy of values and cooperative action we have inherited, while recalibrating our best endeavors in a challenging, changing world.

As President of ICOM I take the opportunity to thank all ICOM members, in whatever roles they have played as supporters or in positions held as leaders, for their contributions to both ICOM and the international museums community over the past seven decades. And last but not least in these tributes, I thank the staff and the General Secretariat of ICOM in Paris, along with all who discharge honorary work for ICOM in its hundreds of committees and bodies active in program delivery every year throughout the world.

ICOM also could not have been so successful during the past seventy years without the cooperation of many other international organizations and supporters – extending its own networks into a host of other networks. ICOM looks forward to extending these many efforts, networks and wider partnerships in future decades.

2

THE ROLE OF MUSEUMS IN THE TWENTY-FIRST CENTURY

Anne-Catherine Robert-Hauglustaine, ICOM Director General

The world of museums is changing rapidly.

What will become of museums in the twenty-first century? What role can they continue to play in a world where culture, heritage and collections are being held to ransom, trafficked and in many cases destroyed?

It is a world where the historical value of cultural property must be defended, a world where profiteering has taken precedence over the accessibility of collections, a world where museums of all types and sizes and in all locations are in danger, due to a lack of financial resources needed to maintain them, to continue their educational activities in service of society, and to develop their research and training programmes.

In these times of uncertainty and fear, the International Council of Museums and its worldwide network of professionals are here to help those who defend museums, heritage, culture and the cause of peace.

On the other hand, museums remain vital sources and resource networks for affirmative interaction, affirming people's diverse histories, shared creativity and achievements and the collective heritage of all. In his latest work on the irreplaceable treasure of Palmyra, Paul Veyne reminds us that: 'Knowing or only wanting to know one culture, one's own, is condemning oneself to live at a standstill' (Veyne 2015: 141).

In a world where museums are being transformed – like the new Musée de l'Homme in Paris; being built against magnificent backdrops, like the Baksi Museum in Turkey; providing a meeting space for communities, like the MAS in Antwerp, Belgium; or being built by the hundreds, as in China – the International Council of Museums plays a unifying role.

For several years, museums have had to reflect increasingly on their ethical role. Restituting works of art has become a central issue for certain museums, and a diplomatic approach must be taken to ease tensions surrounding such requests.

The extremely sensitive question of the future exhibition and restitution of human remains is at the heart of our ethical considerations. The recent restitutions of the *Mokomokai* (preserved ancestral warrior heads of New Zealand's Māori people) by museums in Rouen and Oslo are just the start of a long process heightened by discussions of the issue of sanctity of ancestral remains.

Bringing culture back to a world suffering from the depleting effects of acculturation, in which entire generations have forgotten their past, is one of our greatest challenges. ICOM's drafting of a new standard-setting instrument for museums, in conjunction with UNESCO and at the request of its Member States, is a step in this direction (ICOM/UNESCO 2015). Adopted at the 38th General Conference of UNESCO in November 2015, this critical text, titled *Recommendation on the Protection and Promotion of Museums and Collections, their Diversity and their Role in Society*, marks a decisive step in the inter-governmental arena for upholding the importance of museums and collections, and affirming their integral contribution to social development.

The 37th General Conference of UNESCO in November 2013 recognised the need to establish a new normative instrument for museums, with the financial support of Brazil. This text was well received by our network. Our discussions focused on three areas: the integrity of collections; the importance of the role of professionals in museums; and the social role of museums on regional and community levels.

The integrity of collections includes the need for an inventory and for standardised tools to more effectively combat looting, determine the provenance of collections, and protect collections to ensure their role in promoting a better understanding of the world around us.

Specific recommendations on the social role of museums are outlined as follows:

III. Issues for Museums in Society
Social Role

16. Member States are encouraged to support the social role of museums that was highlighted by the 1972 Declaration of Santiago de Chile. Museums are increasingly viewed in all countries as playing a key role in society and as a factor in social integration and cohesion. In this sense, they can help communities to face profound changes in society, including those leading to a rise in inequality and the breakdown of social ties.

17. Museums are vital public spaces that should address all of society and can therefore play an important role in the development of social ties and cohesion, building citizenship, and reflecting on collective identities. Museums should be places that are open to all and committed to physical and cultural access to all, including disadvantaged groups. They can constitute spaces for reflection and debate on historical, social, cultural and scientific issues. Museums should also foster respect for human rights and gender equality. Member States should encourage museums to fulfil all of these roles.

18. In instances where the cultural heritage of indigenous peoples is represented in museum collections, Member States should take appropriate measures to encourage and facilitate dialogue and the building of constructive relationships between those museums and indigenous peoples concerning the management of those collections, and, where appropriate, return or restitution in accordance with applicable laws and policies.

The UNESCO text recognises the importance of museum professionals who are trained in different museum jobs and can fulfil their role of protecting knowledge and research, interacting with the public and managing collections. In this vein, in 2013, ICOM established the ICOM-ITC training centre in Beijing, in close collaboration with the Chinese Museums Association and the Palace Museum in Beijing. Two week-long sessions are held at the training centre every year, to provide specialised training and workshops in museum and heritage activities for around thirty young professionals drawn from around the world. This initiative has been complemented by a seminar held in Tanzania in 2015, and another to be held in Qatar in 2016. More programmes are also planned to take place in Algeria in 2016 and 2017.

Indeed, Africa is becoming increasingly active in the creation of permanent museums. While the continent continues to suffer from the devastating effects of illicit trafficking, as illustrated in the forthcoming ICOM *Red List* for South Africa and Mali, a discussion of tangible and intangible cultural heritage is gradually taking shape (El-Abiad 2014) with actions, seminars and training sessions taking place in Burkina Faso, Senegal and Tanzania. In reading the work of Yves Girault, Professor at France's Muséum national d'Histoire naturelle (National Museum of Natural History) in Paris, one can see the initial results of African experiments that highlight the issues of participatory museology being called into question; the important role of UNESCO World Heritage sites; and the need to develop these sites, particularly the infrastructure that will allow them to be visited regularly and open to the public, for example, the Loropeni ruins in Gaoua, Burkina Faso.

But let us turn to the definition of the museum proposed by ICOM at its Triennial General Conference in Vienna in 2007, thus articulated:

> A museum is a non-profit, permanent institution in the service of society and its development, open to the public, which acquires, conserves, researches, communicates and exhibits the tangible and intangible heritage of humanity and its environment for the purposes of education, study and enjoyment.
>
> *(ICOM 2007)*

The result of lengthy discussions within ICOM's Ethics Committee and the work of ICOM's International Committee for Museology (ICOFOM), this definition remains subject to necessary changes in order to keep up with current trends in museology, particularly in connection with recent discussions of the more reflexive notion of museum institutions versus museums; museums without collections; museums closed to the public; and those that are for-profit, an idea brought about in the CIMAM Annual Conference in Doha, November 2014.

In *La fin des musées*, Catherine Grenier (2013: 17) reminds us that since the 1980s, the definition of the museum has been extended to include all of the components of an arts centre. Nevertheless, how far can a museum change and metamorphose into new forms without losing its identity? This is a major issue for new museums, foundations and contemporary art exhibition spaces in search of new audiences. But what kind of audience? Audiences at the heart of our concerns as professionals? Or audiences that perceive museums mainly through visits to large artistic retrospectives, major temporary exhibitions and new buildings?

With the staging and media coverage of exhibition openings throughout the world, museums are growing and the number of temporary exhibitions is steadily rising. Yet is the increased pace and presence of exhibitions automatically a reflection of the health of our museums? Do exhibitions play the role of showcasing acquisitions and presenting the exceptional masterpieces that the public is so fond of? Are they addressing economic concerns, at a time when the large majority of our museum institutions are being affected by contracting government support and budget cuts? The diversification of resources remains critical, with the appearance in the last few years of new actors such as associations of friends of museums, foundations and endowment funds, which can play a crucial role in helping to fund museums and exhibitions. The proliferation of temporary exhibitions has been so successful in part thanks to a better understanding provided of the works presented, often staged as if in the theatre, in dedicated spaces, with a real consideration for the public experience and the quality of the visit. For example, exhibition lighting, which was long overlooked, has become an integral component of contemporary museography (Ezrati 2015: 20).

New economic models are emerging in line with the 'hybrid museum' described by François Mairesse, particularly in China, where hundreds of museums are being created, requiring the urgent training of professionals who will have to manage these new museum institutions (Mairesse 2010).

While the notion of participatory museology may make one wonder, it is spreading throughout the world as a possible solution to the diversification of resources, to modes of presentation and to selection processes. It highlights the role of communities in difficulty, like in Canada, where issues surrounding the First Nations require a complex museum approach.

Museums are *definitely* on the rise! It is now up to us to develop the tools they need for the future.

References

El-Abiad, J., 2014. *Le patrimoine culturel immatériel*. Paris: L'Harmattan.
Ezrati, J-J., 2015. *L'éclairage d'exposition*. Paris: Eyrolles.
Grenier, C., 2013. *La fin des musées*. Paris: Éditions du Regard.

ICOM, 2007. 'Development of the Museum Definition according to ICOM Statutes (2007–1946)', at: http://archives.icom.museum/hist_def_eng.html (accessed 18 December 2015).

ICOM, and UNESCO, 2015. *Recommendation on the Protection and Promotion of Museums and Collections, their Diversity and their Role in Society*. [Final Draft], May 2015.

Mairesse, F., 2010. *Le musée hybride*. Paris: La Documentation Française.

Veyne, P., 2015. *Palmyre, l'irremplaçable trésor*. Paris: Albin Michel.

3

THE WORK OF THE ICOM ETHICS COMMITTEE

Martin R. Schärer

The Ethics Committee of the International Council of Museums celebrated its 30th anniversary in 2016. It was created shortly after the adoption of the first comprehensive Code of Ethics by the General Assembly of ICOM in 1986.

Already in 1971 ICOM had adopted, in support of UNESCO's 1970 Convention, the first elements of a code (two resolutions which could be considered as a forerunner of the more complete Code developed in the following decade). These two resolutions dealt only with acquisitions, documentation of collections and field missions, and were mainly focused on illicit trafficking and illegal aspects of the international trade in antiquities. Adopting guidelines for museums was considered necessary by ICOM to protect the standards and good standing of museum professionals – and to ensure that museums lent their support to UNESCO's and other international efforts to protect the world's endangered heritage. ICOM maintained that a museum should not simply be a store – as later emphasized in broadcasting ICOM's new international standards statements in *ICOM News*:

> Let us have no illusions. Museums cannot make themselves respected, and the museum profession cannot retain its dignity, unless those who are proud to be part of the latter agree to submit, voluntarily and spontaneously, to principles which are scientifically and morally sound.
>
> *(ICOM News 1970: 49)*

And then followed the very important sentence: 'The laws of the market cannot become the laws which govern museums' (*ICOM News* 1970: 49). Published some forty-five years ago, this statement is still valuable – I would even say it is more valuable with respect to actual museum discussions on economic problems, fundraising, illicit traffic of cultural goods, and repatriation or the return of objects.

Within the general context of an increasing discussion based on *moral relativism* (and linked with similar issues concerning human rights), some important questions have to be raised: Is the ICOM Code (ICOM 2004), which has been adopted as a reference in many different countries' legislation, sufficiently representative of the diversity of today's world? Or should we adapt it to varying regional and cultural traditions? Do general principles of conduct need to be expressed according to multiple cultural frameworks? In other words: Should we defend principles of moral universalism or of moral relativism? I think this question remains open for further consideration, and inevitably controversial discussions! (Lukes 2008).

I have had the privilege to serve ICOM's Ethics Committee for nearly twelve years: two terms as a delegated member from the Executive Council and two terms as Chair. Through these years, the committee's main discussions have shifted from the treatment of concrete cases to a wider reflection on more general issues and basic topics of museum conduct and professional standards.

Over recent decades, the (museum) world has continued to change greatly. The relationship between museums and society is a complex and continuing theme, where many topics are involved with and have an ethical dimension: financing – collections – architecture – public(s) – society – leadership, first come to mind; and we could add: tourism – globalization – research – communication – marketing, and even more. In fact, many of these topics had already gained closer attention in the revision of the *ICOM Code of Ethics for Museums* (ICOM 2004), which a former Chair of the Ethics Committee, Geoffrey Lewis, explains in his essay on the Code's revision and reorganization, in Chapter 5 of this volume (Lewis 2016).

It goes without saying that the museum as an institution situated within the social web has to live in the present conditions of social evolution. But what conduct continues to be acceptable according to professional standards, and what is to be rejected? The *ICOM Code of Ethics for Museums* provides many (global) principles that frame answers to these questions; and it guides conduct that can also be interconnected around specific themes.

Should the Code be totally revised, simply because it was last revised more than a decade ago? There is reason for caution about this idea, since many regulatory matters and definitions in the ICOM Code have since become part of different countries' national legislation concerning museums or cultural heritage protection. For these reasons the Ethics Committee currently intends to elaborate guidelines around particular issues and evolving topics – to provide a series of annexes to the Code. The first two concern acquisitions and deaccessioning: two hotspots, not only for cultural history museums, but also for natural history collections (for example, agreed standards on the protection of endangered species); guidelines on the sponsorship of museums, and museum shops, may follow next. Another initiative of the Ethics Committee will be to improve and augment the glossary of relevant terms and definitions for museum activities, as currently annexed to the Code.

The *ICOM Code of Ethics for Museums* is considered in very different manners around the world. Some museum colleagues consider that it is good to have a

Code, but that it is insufficiently effective without legal power behind it. It is certainly the case that the Ethics Committee can give advice – but no more. We can never impose the results of our discussions, and – even less – can we prevent unethical behaviour, apart from the fact that ICOM has the power to exclude ICOM members who do not uphold the standards set out in the ICOM Code. As a tool, however, the ICOM Code continues to provide a clear (and binding) set of guidelines for member museums' and individual members' conduct and standards.

However, the majority of ICOM members have a very positive view of the Code's effectiveness, considering that each profession needs a code of ethics and that the sheer existence of both the Code and an Ethics Committee is of great value. The ICOM Code has long proved its effectiveness by providing an important framework of ethical principles to guide those working in and for museums.

It is of value to publicize the mission of the Ethics Committee:

> The Ethics Committee advises ICOM in all matters relating to museum professional ethics. The members of the Committee, whose mandate is renewed triennially, are appointed by ICOM's President. The Committee operates in parallel to the Legal Affairs Committee and the Finance and Resources Committee, and works under the authority of the Executive Council.
>
> The objectives of the Ethics Committee are as follows:
>
> •   Monitor the application of ICOM's Code of Ethics for Museums, inform the Executive Council of serious violations of the Code, and eventually request that certain recommendations be published in *ICOM News*;
> •   Recommend to the Executive Council, the Advisory Committee and eventually the General Assembly, any changes or additions to ICOM's Code of Ethics for Museums that may be found necessary;
> •   Review on behalf of ICOM other codes of ethics that may be developed by the subordinate bodies of ICOM concerning their specialized domains;
> •   Maintain awareness and advise the Executive Council on evolving ethical issues affecting museums and their work within the cultural heritage sector today; submit a general report on the Committee's work during the preceding triennium to each General Assembly coinciding with the General Conference of ICOM (see ICOM online).

The actual Committee has fourteen members drawn from all over the world, most recently appointed for the period 2014–16. The main general topics in the Committee's daily life are:

•   the illicit traffic of cultural goods
•   clandestine archaeological excavations
•   destruction of cultural goods
•   emergency actions and disaster relief

- claims for return of objects to their original communities
- claims for return of stolen/confiscated items to their rightful owner(s)
- mediation for contentious issues
- unethical behaviour of museum professionals
- deaccessioning, closure and financial pressures on museums
- revision and diffusion of ethics tools developed by international committees
- advice to ICOM members on specific cases or matters brought to the Ethics Committee for attention.

It goes without saying that ICOM collaborates internationally with other bodies – for instance, with UNESCO, UNIDROIT, INTERPOL, the World Intellectual Property Organization (WIPO), the World Customs Organization (WCO), and so on.

ICOM also publishes the well-known *Red Lists/Listes Rouges*, which classify highly endangered categories of archaeological objects or works of art in the most vulnerable areas of the world, in order to prevent them from being sold or illegally exported. There are, for example, several *Red Lists* concerning war zones in the Middle East region. With respect to cultural property disputes or claims for return of objects, ICOM has an established Mediation Programme in collaboration with WIPO to assist museums.

In overview, the Ethics Committee mainly observes, advises, informs and educates. Concerning the latter domain, a working group elaborates training programmes, including the highlighting of case studies that are useful for professional training and ethics education. Such documents are intended to enable trainers worldwide to establish locally adapted curricula and to promote the ICOM Code. In this context, there was a well-appreciated workshop on ethics issues, utilizing concrete case studies, during an ICOM Advisory Council meeting in 2014. Discussion also concentrated on recently created guidelines for basic texts and articles on ethics issues within and outside the ICOM context.

During the three decades of its existence, the Ethics Committee of the International Council of Museums has developed its activities over much territory concerning both individuals' and museums' ethical obligations, and the wider public's concern with standards of conduct by museums. Meanwhile, the Committee remains an important body serving ICOM and helping members and the wider profession to steer a course through the complicated and varied museum world today, in all its different forms and settings. The Committee is committed to its continuation of service to ICOM, and as a reference body for the international museum community more broadly.

References

ICOM News, 1970. Paris: International Council of Museums, 23 (2): 49.
ICOM, 2004 [2006]. *ICOM Code of Ethics for Museums*. Paris: International Council of Museums, at: http://icom.museum/fileadmin/user_upload/pdf/Codes/code_ethics2013_eng.pdf

(accessed 17 December 2015). The complete ICOM Code is also provided as Appendix I, this volume.

ICOM website, at: http://icom.museum/the-committees/technical-committees/standing-committee/ethics-committee/ (accessed 17 December 2015).

Lewis, G., 2016. 'The *ICOM Code of Ethics for Museums*: Background and objectives', in Bernice L. Murphy, (ed.), *Museums, Ethics and Cultural Heritage*. London and New York: Routledge, Chapter 5.

Lukes, S., 2008. *Moral Relativism*. New York: Picador.

4

CHARTING THE ETHICS LANDSCAPE FOR MUSEUMS IN A CHANGING WORLD

Bernice L. Murphy

Introduction

In 1996, Alpha Oumar Konaré (President of Mali, and a former President of ICOM) was interviewed, along with other former ICOM Presidents, for some personal reflections on ICOM's first half-century of history. This was in preparation for the 50th jubilee celebrations of ICOM, in November 1996 – celebrated during a private gathering on a closed day in the Louvre, where ICOM had first assembled in 1946. Alpha Konaré focused on the importance of ICOM's Code of Professional Ethics and stated: '[I]f we were to embody a single value, this [the Code of Ethics] would be the most important one for me.'[1] Two decades later, as ICOM marks the 70th jubilee of its existence (in 2016, in Milan), ethics and the ICOM Code[2] continue to be central to ICOM's existence and values as a world organization for museums. As Gary Edson emphasizes in his essay on museum ethics in Chapter 14 of this volume:

> The authority of the *ICOM Code of Ethics for Museums* cannot be overestimated. It has been and continues to be the most influential standards document produced by any organization for the international museums community.[3]

Today, there is an unprecedented interest by public media worldwide in ethical issues and museums. Ethical issues are no longer subjects for confined discussion in professional gatherings, academic teaching of museum studies, or seminars for those who work in museums. The professional conduct of museums has become mainstream news.

This interest has been aroused by many factors. One is the high-profile position and huge expansion in audiences and socially engaged programming that the most successful museums have attained in public consciousness since the 1970s. Another factor is a rising interest in governance and transparency applying to cultural institutions. A further factor has been the internationally networked media coverage of illicit trafficking, the fate of looted cultural property during armed conflicts and restitutions of expropriated property seized during the holocaust, together with ongoing, diverse repatriation claims mounted by colonized peoples who have experienced devastating loss of their heritage historically.

The general public today has strong expectations of museums. There are high standards of honesty and value attributed by visitors to the objects, knowledge and displays that museums present and circulate, linking them with other museums near and far. This gives a special character to the museum profession itself in public standing. At the same time, this situation obligates museums in new ways to honour the public expectations that underlie their position of social trust.

ICOM's Code of Ethics seeks to secure and uphold public trust in museums, which continues to be close to the core of its mission of social service. As former ICOM Ethics Committee Chair Geoffrey Lewis stresses, in his explanation of the background to the current Code: 'The care and interpretation of the cultural heritage places the museum in a special position of public trust.' Furthermore, the museum's duty of care and interpretation is unusually important: 'As humanity's inheritance, cultural property is no ordinary property.'[4]

The concept of humanity's inheritance transmitted in the forms, places, buildings, sites and interpretive activities through which museums carry out their work was a notion animating the founding of ICOM at the threshold of new international efforts for rebuilding damaged social and cultural institutions after World War II.

ICOM's 1946 founding shaped by a moral commitment to human heritage

Although ICOM today is a large international organization, it began very differently – principally as a small body of museum *representatives* from different parts of the world, with delegate members proposed from each country and restricted to a few persons. ICOM was born in an atmosphere tensioned by an acute awareness of the importance of collective effort on behalf of the world's cultural heritage, with a special mission in the historical context of the late 1940s, after World War II. The United Nations was established in October 1945 – and UNESCO shortly afterwards. Meanwhile ICOM was inaugurated within the same fortnight as UNESCO's first General Conference in Paris,[5] in November 1946.

The atmosphere at the time was marked by a scarred world consciousness and moral anxiety as to how to rebuild better relations between nations. A key statement from 1946 combining these two ideas may be found in the preamble to UNESCO's constitution, noting that: '[S]ince wars begin in the minds of men, it is in the minds of men that the defences of peace must be constructed'.[6] In 1945–46, after the trauma of devastating wars, there was a strong desire to pursue international mechanisms to create a more secure and equitable world. ICOM's founding was therefore shaped by the same context through which UNESCO was forged: 'in a spiritual undertaking and a moral effort … founded upon the intellectual [and] moral solidarity of mankind'.[7]

The inauguration of UNESCO favoured creation of a special partner body that could bring *museums* together internationally – as the institutions that housed the major physical collections forming a huge part of the world's cultural and scientific heritage. Thus, ICOM was founded as a non-governmental body (NGO), to pursue programmes of international cooperation directly through its professional networks on a museum-to-museum basis.

ICOM has always valued its NGO status as a *non-governmental organization*. This status enables ICOM to act outside the politically constituted channels occupied by IGOs (or *inter-governmental organizations*) such as the United Nations and UNESCO itself – while ICOM also supports collaborative programmes in partnership with such organizations. ICOM's NGO status and more informal, museum-to-museum networks have provided it with a flexible and responsive character in its international activities. Museums people can often act in direct consultation and positive cooperation, despite troubled relations at a political level; or act for what they know to be good objectives internationally and nationally, without any political position being adopted.

ICOM meanwhile values its increasingly significant collaborative actions with IGOs – as described in detail by France Desmarais,[8] including ICOM's International Observatory on Illicit Traffic in Cultural Goods. These varied relationships and partnerships emphasize how far ICOM has travelled in its commitment to caring for cultural heritage through international cooperation over the seven decades of its existence.

ICOM's longest-standing IGO relationship is with the pivotal world body for culture and heritage, UNESCO, which housed ICOM's Secretariat for more than six decades (and still accommodates the ICOM-UNESCO documentation centre and some ICOM services). ICOM's dialogue with UNESCO recently accomplished one of the most significant jointly achieved initiatives since 1960: in the UNESCO *Recommendation on the Protection and Promotion of Museums and Collections, their Diversity and their Role in Society*, adopted during the UNESCO General Conference on 17 November 2015. The background to the development of this crucial Recommendation over several years is provided by François Mairesse,[9] who also acted as a representative from ICOM and the museums field in the development of the text finally adopted by UNESCO. With ICOM's President and Director-General strongly involved in the final stages of steering this Recommendation to fruition as an internationally agreed platform for the importance of museums – both in world heritage care and also in cultural development policies for all Member States of UNESCO – ICOM's partnership with UNESCO for seven decades has achieved one of its most significant expressions.

The Director of Heritage within UNESCO, Mechtild Rössler, and her colleague Nao Hayashi, have provided a text for this volume[10] that performs a uniquely important service. It is imperative today that the museums community worldwide be well informed about the international legal instruments for heritage protection, especially UNESCO's many conventions for the safeguard of world cultural heritage since its landmark '1970 Convention'.[11] This was 'the first international legal framework concerning the illicit trafficking of cultural property and the movement of cultural property', and it 'provides an important guideline for museums to frame their ethical standards and acquisition policies'.[12] Meanwhile the significance of the 2015 UNESCO Recommendation on the value of museums is best expressed in UNESCO's own statement of the importance of museums' continuing role (since 1946) in 'many of the fundamental missions of the Organization':

> As the most prominent global institution for safeguarding heritage in all its forms, tangible and intangible, movable or immovable, museums play an ever increasing role in stimulating creativity, providing opportunities for research and formal and informal education, thus contributing to the social and human development throughout the world.[13]

ICOM as a worldwide organization

ICOM's membership today encompasses more than 35,000 members (many of which are individual museums numbering hundreds of individuals as well as tiny institutions in regional locations). ICOM's global representation extends beyond its National Committees through further networks, including Affiliated Organizations and Regional Alliances, reaching some 140 countries. In addition to ICOM's *c.*115 National Committees (NCs), the structure of the organization encompasses thirty International Committees (ICs). The ICs provide annual meetings and international networks for specialist museum work: from archaeology and history, natural history, fine arts, decorative arts and design, science and technology, ethnography, and museology, to Egyptology; from museums of glass, literature and musical instruments, to museums of money and banking, and arms and military history; from historic house museums, regional museums, university museums and memorial museums, to city museums. ICOM's ICs also specialize in broadly interconnecting activities such as collecting, training of museum personnel, exhibitions exchange, education and cultural action, conservation, documentation, architecture and museum techniques, museum management, audio-visual and new technologies, public relations and museum security.

Some International Committees have existed for decades in ICOM. Meanwhile more recent committees have been created as new needs or centres of attention arise in the activities of museums globally. Among these are ICMEMO (or the International Committee for Memorial Museums in Remembrance of the Victims of Public Crimes), which has highlighted how transcendent values of human justice, built on internationally shared ideals of human dignity and equality, have created new focal points in the ethical orientation of museum work today. Such concerns have also motivated the formation of a significant Affiliated Organization to ICOM,

FIGURE 4.1   The ICOM General Conference in Buenos Aires, Argentina, 1986 ©ICOM.

in the Federation of International Human Rights Museums (FIHRM), established in 2010.

Through all of these activities and touch-points with partner professional organizations at international, national and regional levels, the extent of ICOM's connections and influence on behalf of museums worldwide is incalculable in numerical terms. ICOM acts globally as a 'network of networks'.[14]

ICOM's 'mission-change' of the 1970s, forging a new commitment to social development

It is useful to provide a brief sketch of how the 1970s shaped ICOM in crucial ways, transforming it from a rather small and selective body into the more globally inclusive organization it is today. This sketch also highlights how ICOM's internal transformation involved an intensified and urgent consciousness of ethical issues in the 1970s, and the need for a comprehensive code of professional standards to be formulated by ICOM. Previously ICOM had left such issues to individual countries and their national bodies to decide on standards of professional conduct. Some countries took up ethics early through their own professional associations – as was the case with the American Alliance of Museums (AAM), founded in 1906, which was the first to establish a code of ethics, in 1925. However, the later twentieth century witnessed far-reaching changes to the social and political structures that had shaped the world in which ICOM was formed.

The political activist movements that erupted across the world in 1968 – particularly marked by the student rebellion that spread riotously through the streets of Paris in May – inevitably impacted upon ICOM, headquartered at the heart of these upheavals in France. Sharp critiques arose within ICOM about museums being anchored in the past and too focused internally on their collections. It was argued in activist circles that museums were conservative institutions created historically by social élites, and therefore poorly adjusted to addressing modern societies' needs and the realities of dramatically expanding urban communities; or responding to crucial issues for nations of the developing world.

Not surprisingly, as reformist energies intensified after May 1968, the 1971 ICOM preparatory meetings in Paris and ensuing General Conference in Grenoble were engulfed by political critiques of museum conservatism. There was a suspension of normal business of the ICOM General Assembly in Grenoble in 1971; new and younger voices erupted with challenges and demands, insisting on changing ICOM itself to include individuals and not simply representatives of museums; and there were calls for far-reaching reform of ICOM as an international organization to support all types of museums – not simply a selective 'Council' of museums representing the longest established and most privileged institutions.

The three years between the ICOM General Assemblies in Grenoble (1971) and Copenhagen (1974) marked a watershed in ICOM's history. This was a time when the organization's very survival seemed in crisis for a short while. However, important structural changes were accomplished that enabled ICOM to recommence its life on a much broader basis of representation of the museums sector internationally.

A group of 'mould-breaking' reforms[15] adopted in 1974 changed ICOM from a tightly regulated federation of national 'delegate' members from each country to a more participatory, membership-based organization – without further restriction of membership numbers permitted in each country or the joining of International Committees. This opened the way for ICOM's steady increase in size, geographical footprint, and the expanding work of its committees and networks in subsequent decades.

ICOM's definition of museums changed after 1974

There was a new ethical undercurrent to the changes that were accomplished by ICOM in the early 1970s. Most importantly, ICOM's definition of a museum (in the ICOM Statutes) changed in 1974 to include a new and singularly important phrase that signalled a museum's *social orientation* as a defining objective for its existence. A museum was not only a permanent, not-for-profit institution, distinguished mainly by a building or collections, but also an institution 'in the service of society and its development'.

This change redirected ICOM's orientation and mission in fundamentally important respects. In addition to redefining the character of a *museum* in the early 1970s, ICOM was also more precisely defining the character of the *museum profession*.

A slightly revised definition of the museum profession in 1974 (in Article 5 of the ICOM Statutes) now included reference to persons not only 'having received a specialised technical or academic training or possessing an equivalent practical experience' but also 'respecting a fundamental code of professional ethics'.[16] This was a crucial shift in strategic placement of ethical obligations. A commitment to ethical standards was now positioned as a central and *defining requirement* of belonging to 'the museum profession' itself.

Training alone was no longer sufficient for the good standing of a museum professional. Nor could formal history or institutional prestige be sufficient to honour public trust in a museum. The upholding of a code of ethical conduct, shaping all aspects of the life of museums, was required as an active, ongoing commitment. These changes in ICOM definitions in the 1970s – redefining both museums and the museum profession – have provided ICOM's public projection of museums and all who work for them (including boards and volunteers) with a more inclusive and encompassing ethical orientation towards social service and public value ever since.

One further outcome of the 1971–74 organizational reform in ICOM was a call for museums to become more vigilant in ethical issues concerning acquisitions – particularly in view of the 1970 UNESCO Convention against illicit trafficking of cultural heritage, touching directly on provenance questions and especially antiquities being acquired by the world's richest museums. The ICOM Executive Council's initiative in issuing its own parallel statement in 1970, on The Ethics of Acquisition, provided a clear expression of concern for greater vigilance in provenance matters. This was especially spurred by the archaeological community and other networks directly witnessing the ravaging of sites and irreparable loss of both heritage and knowledge through looting, illicit traffic and trading in cultural heritage.

ICOM became more actively engaged in *standards-setting internationally*, rather than relying on various codes existing at the national level in many countries. In the General Assembly resolutions of 1971 and 1974, ethical issues were prominent in the plans for change. ICOM was called on by its membership in 1974 to draft a comprehensive code of ethics as a point of reference for both ICOM and the sector at large.[17]

The ICOM *Code of Professional Ethics* (1986)

In 1986, a completed text – evolved through an ethics sub-committee coordinated by Patrick Boylan, who had led a comparative investigation of different national codes already in use – was successfully put before the ICOM General Assembly in Buenos Aires. The first ICOM *Code of Professional Ethics*,[18] providing a base-standard international reference tool, was thus ratified and later disseminated as a key ICOM document (and published jointly with the ICOM Statutes):

> It set forth the basic principles for museum governance, for acquisitions and disposal of collections, as well as rules for professional conduct and responsibilities vis-à-vis collections, the public and the profession.[19]

The 1986 Code became a touchstone document for ICOM's programmes, self-awareness and moral force as the international voice of museums in subsequent years. In its monitoring and application under an ICOM Ethics Committee established by the Executive Council in 1990, which continues to the present day,[20] the ICOM Code provided a framework through which new social needs and progressive changes in museum work could also be considered.

The rise of 'culture' and 'cultural diversity' in museum ethics since the 1980s

The importance of ethical questions within widening concerns for *cultural diversity* in the 1980s was also gradually gaining strength in ICOM. These issues had implications not only for museums but also for the heritage sector as a whole. Moreover, the work of museums was increasingly challenged by post-colonial critique, requiring museums to rethink a range of issues concerning the representation of knowledge and history – especially the representation of diverse social constituencies and cultural minorities whose agency in the interpretation of their own heritage had long been ignored.

One of the most important initiatives for a recasting of culture's role in social and economic progress occurred during the UN-declared World Decade for Cultural Development (1988–97). This involved the creation in the 1990s of a World Commission on Culture and Development, led through an initiative of the Nordic countries in UNESCO. The WCCD, through investigations coordinated by UNESCO, took representations from many countries and individuals in forums from 1993 to 1995. The process sought to gain comparable positioning for 'culture and development' in world consciousness as had been achieved through years of effort in the 1970s for the 'environment and development'.[21]

It was now culture's turn. It was emphasized that 'development' for any society was an issue to be understood first *in cultural terms*, since the cultural background of all groups making up a common society fundamentally shapes all other values about educational, economic and technological development. However, culture needed additional insights, and a more particularizing effort of differentiation, than the discourse on the environment had provided. It was recognized through WCCD investigation and submissions that global *cultural diversity* is not simply a precious resource comparable to *biodiversity*. Cultures are subject also to continual processes of cross-cultural interaction, mobility, reformation, adaptation, fusion and renewal in different ways from biological adaptation. In the final outcome report, *Our Creative Diversity*, published by UNESCO in 1995, in a section titled 'Culture in search of a global ethics', it was asserted that 'cultures overlap'; 'cultures usually do not speak with one voice'; and 'cultures do not form homogeneous units'.[22]

Amareswar (Amar) Galla was one of the participants and proponents of change in the UNESCO/WCCD forums of the 1990s, and arguments about culture's key role in development have consistently shaped his objectives since that time, as pursued in the mobile project of the Inclusive Museum and its travelling conferences. He continues to argue two decades after the WCCD's work that, while '[c] ritical museologists and heritage practitioners concur that the contextual frameworks for museums are diversifying despite the accelerated pace of all forms of globalization and homogenization', it remains 'necessary to ensure that deep research and cultural action inform the nexus between the four pillars of social, economic, cultural and environmental sustainability'.[23]

By the early 1990s, in addition to culture's 'pillar' role in development, it was also clear that what was at stake, and often jeopardized by social development models tied to economic progress, were the desirable continuities of value among and between peoples *in their cultural diversity*. Moreover, this diversity itself is historically one of the richest achievements of human culture. It is an absolute value and right, and − unlike other rights and freedoms − culture cannot be protected at an individual level alone. Rather, it is collectively shared by groups, even whole societies, and needs to be understood and secured through collective values and interconnected effort.

Along with this altering awareness in the political sphere about social and economic development, there was intensive work in academic arenas steadily expanding throughout the 1980s that comprehensively reinterpreted the history of *modernity*. Modernity was no longer understood as a single storyline, endlessly repeated at different *rates* in different countries. Rather, modernity has been an infinitely variegated and continuing *process*, both of adoption and adaptation, through which modernization has been embraced, resisted, extended and modified itself in different circumstances. Modernity has created its own variegated history of social adjustments to technological change, suggesting a complex map of *localized versions of modernity*, rather than a uniform global enterprise.

Tracing impacts in the museums sector: it is possible to observe, through these coeval movements of the 1980s and 1990s, important global shifts in consciousness that were steadily challenging and changing museum ethics, opening up more differentiated concepts of communities and the social obligations of museums − 'in the service of society and its development' (as first specified in the 1974 'Museum' definition of ICOM). These shifts were occurring in museum forums, in academic gatherings and publications, and finally in world cultural and political organizations at a governmental level. Cumulatively these changes disclosed the growing significance, particularization and refocused importance of culture and heritage issues in world affairs. Meanwhile culture and heritage now had to be supported directly *in their internal diversity* and mutual differences, as well as through common solutions to their preservation and communication globally.

In the same period, additional questions arising through recognition of cultural diversity were eroding further boundaries. Native American and Indigenous communities dispossessed by colonialism were pressing upon the museum profession and knocking ever more insistently at the doors of collections. For example, *repatriation and restitution claims* were becoming stronger and more varied in form. Museums in Australia had been taking their own initiatives to repatriate human/ancestral remains and secret-sacred items in the 1980s, and adopted a national policy in 1993, *Previous Possessions, New Obligations: Museums Australia Policy for Museums in Australia and*

Aboriginal and Torres Strait Islander Peoples,[24] locking these intentions into a collective set of protocols for remediation of past wrongs to Indigenous people (and without waiting for government impetus or directive). Meanwhile changes were also afoot in the United States, Canada and New Zealand. The forceful impact of new legislation in the United Sates – notably the Native American Graves Protection Act, 1990 – has been well articulated by the Founding Director of the National Museum of the American Indian, W. Richard West:

> [R]epatriation laws represented a seismic shift in museum paradigms and practice regarding 'authority' that reached far beyond the literal return of certain categories of objects from museums to Native communities.[25]

The expanding momentum of change demanded clearer recognition of museums' ethical obligations to what ICOM's (revised) Code in 2004 now acknowledged as *source communities*,[26] specifying ethical requirements as to how their cultural heritage is to be *cared for, interpreted and presented* by museums to public audiences. Furthermore, the gradual restoration of Indigenous peoples' *intellectual authority, voices* and *judgement* – concerning the knowledge that needs to be transmitted (and in some cases withheld) when interpreting or organizing displays and exhibitions of their heritage – required fundamentally altered practices within museums. Changed awareness also led to the forging of important *new ethical relationships with 'communities of origin'* (or *source communities*) that acknowledged centres of expertise beyond the mural boundaries of museums as institutions. This is strongly emphasized by Richard West:

> Repatriation . . . affirms the proposition that cultural authority, as a matter of the museum's social responsibility, may sometimes sit outside that institution, and in the hands of others not members of the priesthood in the temple on the hill.[27]

Such developments had different, but no less urgent, expressions of reformative intention as they spread to other continents and regions – especially in southern Africa. Repatriation, and a transformed regard for the long history of racialized treatment of human remains by museums as objects of research, was a pivotal issue for the new government of South Africa elected in 1994. This was publicly conveyed through the potent symbolism of President Nelson Mandela's appeal to the government of France for return of the remains of the cruelly abused woman of Khoi descent, Sarah Baartman, as analyzed in the essay on continuing repatriation issues within South Africa today by Bongani Ndhlovu: 'To a degree, the public debate around the return of Sarah Baartman's remains from France . . . became a focal-point and highlighted the role of museums in sordid practices of the past.'[28]

These changes, now internationally registered and determinedly voiced with new legal authority in the 1990s, fundamentally challenged the work of museums, and have continued to have important implications for museum programmes and ethical consciousness today. Many museums by the late twentieth century had developed critical resources, exhibitions and interpretive programmes to enable insight into the negative processes of politics and history, including critiques of damaged history – and its damaging effects on both individuals and human communities. In addition to the text by Bongani Ndhlovu, dealing specifically with South Africa, these issues are explored further in the present volume by Sharon Macdonald (discussing the representation of 'difficult history' in many national contexts)[29] and Mónica Risnicoff de Gorgas (analyzing the unacknowledged history of Afro-American heritage in Latin American museums).[30]

Changes in museums' treatment of the remains of *people* (in reality to their descendants, often venerated ancestors) and *things* (to dispossessed Native peoples, their former 'belongings') directly included ethical issues of the intellectual and cultural property rights vested in the living sources of authority in Indigenous communities. Such issues had already surfaced in ICOM's operational qualifications added to the *definition* of a museum. Since 2001, ICOM has recognized non-collecting institutions (art galleries showing contemporary art but not collecting) and community-based cultural centres and 'keeping places' (for example, in aboriginal, Native or Indigenous communities) as coming under its definition of a museum. However, the long-denied recognition of the direct intellectual property rights, as well as cultural authority embedded within tangible and intangible heritage collections recording Indigenous peoples' history (from 'artefacts' to ceremonial designs, dances, chants and songs), have only slowly been seeping into the challenged, ethical consciousness of the world's museum communities.

These diverse sites of activities interconnecting museums and collections provide a reminder of the different kinds of knowledge (as well as social, intellectual and aesthetic systems) at work in the interpretation of collections. They also point to wider contexts of culturally and historically shaped knowledge to which collections relate – or, in important senses, *to what, to whom and where things 'belong'* while held in the care of museums for carrying out their public mission as interpreters, custodians and bearers of human knowledge and heritage across generations and eras within the world's memory.

Ethics, cultural rights and human rights

When museums address issues of the cultural rights of communities, the basis upon which disputes are decided becomes complicated. There are sharp challenges for museums in a world where the concepts of human rights,[31] universal values, cultural heritage and justice – especially the complex concept of distributive justice underpinning democratic philosophy – have come to recast ideas of participation, ownership and control of cultural property.

The *Universal Declaration of Human Rights*, adopted by the General Assembly of the United Nations in 1948, guarantees, among other rights, the right to participate fully in cultural life. Cultural rights are complex to define, and are often regarded as the least developed aspect of the legal provision for protection of human rights.

Meanwhile, there is a fundamental tension between human rights discourse – which, by its very nature, mobilizes a transcendent morality grounded in *humanitas* and universal rights – and a communitarian rights discourse that moves in a contrary direction: towards the specificity of communities, and an upholding of their aspirations to maintain internally self-regulating values that sustain a unique cultural heritage, often in distinction from both other cultures and a dominant mainstream.[32]

However, it is important to find a bridge between these two apparently conflicting movements in the discussion of cultural property, human rights, cultural rights and disputes as to rightful ownership. The bridge may be found in a comparative analysis of culturally diverse solutions to common ethical issues found in all societies: for example, of recognized *collective good* and *the reciprocity of duties* that flows between individuals and communities in matters of conservation of knowledge, culture and the environment; and of the necessity of active care for the *interpretation and transmission of heritage* from one generation to the next. Although these often-contending dynamics of rights claims regularly create tensions to be worked through heuristically, the difficulties are never a reason for abandoning the challenge of understanding, or using them as an excuse for dismissal. It is necessary to dispel the myth that a call for more ethical action by museums in acquisitions or repatriation matters would entail a simplistic disentangling of the multiple cultural histories that configure long-held objects, or a revocation of the complex, layered history of collections built over centuries.

Nevertheless, cultural rights are clearly restricted if major items or parts of the continuing cultural heritage of peoples have been removed or alienated (for example, under colonialism), or are subject to continuing illicit traffic and looting from their source countries. When museums acquire cultural material (especially antiquities) without provenance, they support a situation of well-demonstrated abuse to archaeology and cultural heritage care, encouraging looting, forgery, illicit trafficking and wanton destruction of irretrievable knowledge and resources. Thus collectors may become 'the real looters', as stated in a 1993 issue of *Archaeology* by Ricardo J. Elia,[33] sparking a debate that has continued through ongoing public coverage of looting, illicit trading and museums' acquisition of antiquities with either no provenance at all or with a pseudo-history that is fraudulently constructed to elude scrutiny.[34]

Provenance research: an evolving front of new knowledge in museums

Provenance research is no longer the preserve of connoisseurship or pedantry. It is one of the most important, revitalized and progressive areas of museum work currently. This is not only from an ethical perspective but also through the new issues and expanding fields of knowledge being stimulated by intensified research into the complex itineraries that attend and illuminate understanding of the life of objects, and to whom or where they have 'belonged', or might ultimately belong today.

Provenance research thereby underpins museums' interpretive contract with the public, and feeds into the most innovative work of exhibitions and publications. It is as relevant to modern art as to antiquities, and should foreshadow the biographies of contemporary artworks brought to a public audience. In its potential for illuminating the histories and meanings of non-Western and Indigenous cultural works, and their very different repertoires of significance and 'belonging', provenance research is limitless.

The challenge now is for museums to utilize the unique advantages of their multiple resources, to conceive new measures of cooperative endeavour for the research and management of collections and continued care of cultural heritage today. This involves actively considering the relationship of collections to source-nations, source-cultures or source-communities (where identifiable). The possibilities of mutually beneficial relationships in heritage care and collection development are growing, as museums build links that forge new partnerships, exchanges and enriched knowledge through provenance research.

One of the significant international agencies for the tracing of lost works of art through looting and similar illicit activities is the Deutsches Zentrum Kulturgutverluste (German Lost Art Foundation), based in Magdeburg, Germany. This agency also strives to achieve, sometimes through mediation, 'just and fair solutions' to cultural property disputes associated with looting, and often concerning works seized during the holocaust, as highlighted in this volume in a text by Michael Franz.[35]

In the incisive and stimulating vision of new kinds of provenance research in archaeological collections today provided by Markus Hilgert, Director of the Pergamon Museum in Berlin, the challenges are laid out clearly:

> [W]e must take note of the fact that visitors to archaeological museums today are increasingly interested in the cultural and socio-political topic of 'provenance', and demand information accordingly.... [W]e can currently observe that objects are increasingly becoming the subject of practices and discourses that are located outside of academia and research, and by now have attracted a remarkable interest, a 'new sensitivity' within the sphere of society, politics, and culture.[36]

The remarkable scale and new collection relationships with source communities through the Humboldt Forum project and continuing research by the multiple institutions situated on the Museums Island in Berlin, of which the Pergamon Museum is one part, are set out by the President of the Prussian Cultural Heritage Foundation, Hermann Parzinger.[37] Meanwhile, the potential to build links between previous silos of expertise in a digitally supported research and access environment is compellingly demonstrated by Jane Milosch, heading a major provenance research initiative of the Smithsonian Institution in Washington:

> When, through human exchange and now, technology, we can network ... silos together, then the information and resources stored in each can be used

to create a richer, more globally extended understanding of human culture.[38]

It is not possible to do all things at one time. Nevertheless, how museums manage to care for these values of restored knowledge – as well as for their collections – vitally shapes their position as significant social institutions sustaining both communities and heritage simultaneously. This highlights how museums are today becoming both mediators and '(re)mediators': as they reinterpret their own histories, calling attention to the complex circumstances that forged both the institution of the museum itself and the collections constituted within. This imaginative and fertile self-questioning signals a new phase of greater ethical maturity on the part of the museums of the world. The fostering of many new kinds of conversations within and about museums, their collections and interpretive programmes, promises an exciting epoch of rich provenance researches and a new intellectual harvest of human knowledge and resources. It also signals a more active engagement by museums with the communities and societies they serve – and new narratives around collections being formed today.

Some remarks on the philosophy of ethics

Ethics entails a strong sense of *duty towards public good*. However, ethics involves more than a state of mind filled with high ideals and good intentions. A philosophy of ethics for museums involves a disposition towards *affirmative action* on matters of ethical principle, towards the exploration of good judgement in all manner of contexts in daily decision-making. It involves not only a commitment to good conduct itself, but also an accompanying recognition that good conduct is *a learned activity*, not naturally acquired through social training. It is therefore different from moral values. Moreover, museum ethics sometimes involves difficult choices between different options that might seem to have equally plausible reasons in their favour.

The easiest ethical decisions to make are between good and bad principles. More challenging and difficult – but demonstrating a needed *questing ethical disposition* – are the professional conduct decisions that require discrimination between two or more equally good principles that might point to conflicting paths of conduct or resolution. This can be demonstrated in the case of differing issues concerning *deaccessioning* or removal of objects from a collection – as discussed in an essay in this volume by François Mairesse.[39] For example, the general *presumption of permanence* (or 'inalienability') of public collections – which secures public trust and honours the modern history of museums as long-term institutions for public benefit – has traditionally required the most cautious approach to any proposal for *deaccessioning* or *disposal* of objects from museum collections.

In many countries, as explained in Mairesse's text, this is precluded by law, which regards public collections as the property of the state and by definition *inalienable*. However, this important long-term value and inalienable status of collections, whether by tradition or law, is challenged by a more recently framed exhortation the *ICOM Code of Ethics for Museums*. The revisions of 2004 include a clear statement that museums have an ethical obligation to consider in a transparent manner any credible claims from *communities of origin* (where these can be identified). Museums are now obligated to recognize and consult source communities, not only for involvement in the interpretation or treatment of collected material that they have produced, but perhaps even to address restitution or repatriation of collection items. As the ICOM Code specifies: 'requests for return' of 'sensitive materials' by source communities[40] should be treated 'expeditiously [and] with respect and sensitivity'.[41]

Meanwhile, even long-standing legal constraints on repatriation have been overturned in some cases in recent years. One example has been facilitated through the Human Tissue Act of 2004 in the UK, which enabled various repatriations of Australian Aboriginal and Torres Strait Islander ancestral remains from British museums. An early, notable example of this change in British law enabled two repatriations from the British Museum to the Tasmanian Aboriginal community in 2006,[42] which was later followed by some hundreds of further repatriations of ancestral remains from museums in the UK (notably from the Natural History Museum and others) in a continuing process that is today coordinated through the Australian government on behalf of all Australian Indigenous communities. Even in France, long-standing legal sanctions against repatriation were overturned in the case of the return to New Zealand in January 2012 – after a legal change in 2010 – of twenty mummified heads (or Toi moko), from Māori warriors killed in battle in the eighteenth or nineteenth centuries.[43]

Leadership in ethics

Most professions have codes of conduct or ethics by which they bind the actions of their members together in processes of internal self-regulation. There is in fact a considerable commonality of principle shaping such codes. However, the museum profession has a special standing in public trust, and a precious relationship to human knowledge, history and heritage, which it promises to protect and care for according to high ideals of responsibility, integrity and service to society.

A good code of ethics – of which the ICOM Code represents the international base standard – needs to set down clear principles for an individual museum, group of museums, or the museums sector more broadly. Its principles will be linked into a systematic statement of standards that bind together the conduct of all who work in or with museums. This includes volunteer staff and boards of governance, senior and junior employees, as well as all personnel in the most technically skilled areas or senior positions of responsibility inside a museum, and the consultant personnel whom a museum engages.

Good *leadership in ethical matters* meanwhile draws upon the most mindful conduct and capacities of all who work in or for museums. Leadership in ethics does not reside comfortably in the prestige of seniority; it is not wrapped in a protective banner of years of service; nor bolstered by the pride of needing to be 'right' in judgement or conduct. On the contrary, ethical judgement is aroused in the recognition of vexing choice. It is nurtured in often-difficult conditions of active exploration of *doubt* as to what is 'the right thing' to do in professional conduct, when that might not be easy either to determine or to carry out.

Leadership in ethical matters strengthens through *acquired knowledge and capabilities* to assist oneself and others to discern how subtly 'right' and 'wrong' judgements may seem to commingle innocently together in day-to-day situations of museum work. An ethical disposition is commensurate with the effort to probe and resolve such tensions. It ensures a demonstration of good faith in standards and ideals, even when it is not always easy to navigate the best solution between competing forces or principles. A colleague who has never experienced an ethical dilemma about conflicting principles or practical choice in daily museum work is possibly not the best leader of ethical teaching or debate.

Ethics training

Ethical training within and involving all who work for or in association with museums remains an important issue. There is almost universal respect for the ICOM Code of Ethics, but the Code is insufficiently utilized. Being of declared central importance, it needs demonstrative activation. An ethics code for museums cannot be treated like a medical dictionary, to be consulted only in a crisis for a specialized diagnosis of symptoms of disease; nor an arcane theological text to instruct troubled consciences; nor a sanitation document to ensure general cleanliness of public operations.

Within a framework of the urgency, and at times insurgency, of an ethical vision of the role of museums in social commitment and service today, the ICOM Code can never be 'left on a high shelf'. Ethical issues are connected to the thrust and throng and throb of daily life in museums. The Code's provisions need to be at the elbow of decision-makers, in the consciousness of curators and volunteers, known and referenced by museum educators and conservators, and energetically publicized to stakeholders, politicians and community representatives. The Code's articles need to be 'voiced' as reference points in ordinary work situations, and find a strong presence in museum policies.

Ethics and museum codes of ethics form a regular component of museum studies and museology courses today – and ethics has long been advanced through ICOM's International Committee for Training of Personnel (ICTOP). However, training also needs to be pursued in informal settings, with an action-orientation that enables exploring the ethical questions that lurk in the most ordinary and informal of daily settings in museum activities.

A fine model of training in museum ethics, and the use of the ICOM Code, has been developed by a former member of ICOM's Ethics Committee, Eva Maehre Lauritzen. This ethics-in-action model[44] utilizes fictional fables or 'tales', of which the seemingly artless simplicity disguises its almost infinitely extensible capacity for both social and cultural adaptation, as well as intellectual sophistication. First developed in Norway, and then applied in workshops in other countries, the ethics-in-action model seeks to promote ethical consciousness as daily, collaborative self-learning. It fosters an approach where all who work or volunteer in museums may discuss and cultivate good principles of conduct to guide decision-making. It also seeks to enable museum colleagues to connect the ICOM Code with local worlds. The model offers an important tool, in combination with case studies in museum ethics, for hands-on development of training and consciousness of museum ethics.

Meanwhile two essays in the present volume explore ethics training and the impact in Asian contexts: essays by An Laishun[45] concerning China, and Eiji Mizushima[46] concerning Japan. And four significant case studies that arose through the work of the ICOM Ethics Committee are analyzed at the conclusion of the present publication, forming its final section.

Differences between ethics and law

There are tensions in ICOM's Code of Ethics between what is often required of museums under national laws – which may restrain, for example, initiatives towards any repatriation of material in national collections[47] – and the principles requested to be upheld according to a code of professional ethics, which raise higher standards of professional conduct than those required by law.

ICOM's new Code of Ethics urges, for example, that *conversations* be established where substantial claims are made to material in museum collections, or dispute exists as to collections' proper interpretation, retention or appropriate use. For example, 'Museums should be prepared to initiate dialogues …' (ICOM Code, Article 6.2); and 'The possibility of developing partnerships with museums in countries or areas that have lost a significant part of their heritage should be explored' (Article 6.1).

ICOM does not predict the outcomes of such conversations or negotiation, but it clearly urges that they be undertaken. While the law may not require such moves on the part of museums, an expanding and changing ethical consciousness *does* require such a disposition towards action. The important distinctions highlighted here, between ethical principles and law, have vital implications for *mediation*,[48] which might produce a successful conclusion in a legal sense – whereby a dispute may be resolved or abandoned, even without recourse to law – but an unsatisfactory outcome may persist in terms of ethics. For example, resolving a dispute between two parties claiming cultural property, whether by formal judgement of a claim in court or through mediated resolution outside legal action, may not in itself address the violated ethical principles underlying the dispute.

It should also be noted that there may be multiple and even conflicting ethical issues in play in some situations of dispute as to ownership, control or use of cultural property in collections. An ethics code may not provide any simple or clear solution. This is where the *conversations* that are the lifelines of *learned judgement* in museums are vital for ethical conduct, for they reinforce scrupulous practice, nurture good decision-making and uphold public trust in museums as social institutions.

While highlighting and endorsing international legal instruments, such as the various UNESCO Conventions for the protection of cultural heritage internationally, ICOM signals in its Code that ethical standards for the museum profession involve a *higher* order of duty than is enshrined in law. Law generally lags behind ethics in expressing evolving standards or binding principles of self-regulative conduct. It can be said that ethics extends beyond the *quantitative limits* of the law by enlarging its *qualitative scope* and reach within the broader spheres of social conduct, promoting standards of respect for diversity and mutual care of heritage.

Ethics also directly advances ideas as to how human beings may interact reciprocally and positively around shared ideals, rather than be driven by divisive and destructive competition for resources (the context of the devastating world wars of the early twentieth century that had shaped UNESCO's and ICOM's founding in 1945–46).

Recovering the ethical connections between natural and cultural heritage

One of the most important challenges from an ethical perspective on museums' development, and the urgent issues of social service and public education today, points to the need to affirm our responsibilities to environmental systems and natural heritage that have sustained human development throughout its long history. Indeed the natural world is infinitely older than the rather brief period in which human beings have emerged and been nourished, sheltered and sustained by its resources. The threat to the sustainability of those resources today calls upon the most profound ethical attention and communicative action by museums. ICOM has produced a specialized code of ethics in the area of natural history museums, led by Eric Dorfman through a NATHIST Working Group over some years and adopted in 2013. Dorfman explains:

> The … differences between natural history museums and other types of heritage institutions were the catalyst for ICOM NATHIST in 2006 to form the Ethics Working Group and agree to draft a code that stood alongside the *ICOM Code of Ethics for Museums* as a specialist document addressing issues specific to the sector.[49]

However, the manifest signs of threatened biodiversity in a world of stressed natural systems are now so inescapable and urgent that intensified action is required in an outward orientation of public education around environmental jeopardy. As Eric Dorfman has proposed: '[N]atural history institutions engaging in best practice might well include biodiversity conservation in their core mission.'[50] A comprehensive analysis of natural history museums' historical development, and their crossover work today with science centres in interpreting the Anthropocene environment and public understanding of systems change, is provided in an essay by Emlyn Koster, who strongly asserts the responsibility of museums in public education and awareness: '[N]ature and science museums are at their most powerful when they also integrate social responsibility and unravel past-present-future trends.'[51] Koster also reminds us that the deteriorating conditions of Earth's biodiversity are eliciting an increasing number of public declarations sounding alarm from scientific analysis:

> February 2012, Washington, DC: Learning-focused representatives from mainly US natural history organizations issued the following declaration (Watson and Werb 2013: 260):

> 'Humanity is embedded within nature and we are at a critical moment in the continuity of time; Our collections are the direct scientific evidence for evolution and the ecological interdependence of all living things; The human species is actively altering the Earth's natural processes and reducing its biodiversity; As the sentient cause of these impacts, we have the urgent responsibility to give voice to the Earth's immense story and to secure its sustainable future.'[52]

Meanwhile Michel Van-Praët, another long-serving leader in the NATHIST community of ICOM, has provided a historical review of a crucial, integrative aspect of the formative 'cabinets' often nested within museum collections. He highlights important relationships nurtured through wonderfully diverse objects commingling as evidence simultaneously of humankind's history, the Earth's materials and the world's creatures – interrelationships that maintained close connections between natural and cultural heritage at the dawn of modern science. In his analysis, Michel Van-Praët makes a strong plea for new interdisciplinary research urgently needed today to re-examine the once-intimate connections in human and natural heritage that became critically separated through specializations in museums:

> The changes that societies must make will require greater sharing of available information: information that museums, and particularly natural science, archaeology, and anthropology museums, hold abundantly in their collections. This will require not only going beyond disciplinary approaches, including for museums, by questioning the typologies of collections, but also combining scientific approaches with societal questions, both to answer those questions and to identify issues to which societies should be alerted.[53]

New relationships and evolving work with communities

To Robert R. Janes, one of the most insightful and insistent critics of museums' current stewardship of their public duties of social service – with an urgent response to threatened environmental sustainability as a key topic in his test of performance – museums still remain very important and unusual institutions: 'There are simply no better social institutions than museums to help define a sustainable future, grounded as they are in a diachronic view of humankind's successes and failure.'[54]

Many museums today, sharply re-examining their former failings through a history shaped more by collecting and conserving than interpreting, communicating and public serving, have changed almost beyond recognition of connection with their former character. Museums have shifted from an emphasis on exclusivity of ownership and begun to act in ever more diverse ways according to values of shared custodianship and mutual stewardship of cultural and natural heritage. They have sought to build new kinds of partnerships in programme developments, exhibitions, research and heritage care – some taking on the challenge not only of protection but also of active maintenance and renewal of cultural traditions, especially in recognizing colonial historical contexts of rupture and loss. In so doing, many museums have found themselves to be the recipients of enlivening new resources and social as well as intellectual partnerships. They have become hosts to expanding knowledge, enlarged collections, innovative exhibitions and new kinds of extra-mural engagement and access to and of their remarkable resources by diverse communities.[55]

In addition, following innovative collaborative work with their social constituencies and co-responsive programmes and project developments, museums are transforming their performative social capabilities and service to local communities. As an essay by Sally Yerkovich demonstrates: 'For some museums, engaging with the community can become a central focus and lead to a realignment of mission and organizational values as well as organizational structure.'[56] Even the traditional preservation field of museum conservation may be turned outwards to a positive commitment to community education, in providing the tools for enhanced preservation of communities' own heritage. In an exposition by Stephanie de Roemer, conservation may move from a specialist domain, internally focused, to become 'the lubricant that ensures the dynamic museum facilitates cultural creativity, circulating many new forms of knowledge, ideas, values and experience as expressions of the intangible culture and the preservation of tangible cultural heritage in perpetuity'.[57] In a very differently calibrated analysis, the essay by Dorota Folga-Januszewska[58] provides a reflection not only on the ontological journey of the museum as a form and idea from Graeco-Roman antiquity to the present, but also on the special transformation that occurs to all objects upon entering the museum and later re-presented for human encounter – a process from which no shell or cell from nature is immune, no more than any object by an artist snatching raw material from the everyday world can avoid the transformative gaze of aesthetics. There are inflections of both ethics and neuroaesthetics in her intriguing exposition of the psychological challenge and pleasure afforded by engagement with objects in the transformative space of a museum.

All of the developments of museums' diversified services and increased commitment to social impact described through the essays in this volume are linked by an ethical dimension. Museums today are ever more active in recognizing the inescapable connectedness of their collections and knowledge, and of the interdependent resources they command. Museums are diversifying and extending their service to multiple cultural heritages and diverse social communities. They are also reinventing their stewardship of a shared understanding of nature and culture, of science and society, of progress and reversals in the world's histories and narratives. Museums are charged with a special public duty of probity of conduct in their comprehensive exploration of streams of difference in human knowledge, expressions and achievements, through the manifold activities they pursue today on behalf of human memory, history and heritage, and its transmission to all who deserve its safeguard and passing on as their shared inheritance.

Notes

1 Sid Ahmed Bagli, Patrick Boylan and Yani Herreman (eds), *History of ICOM, 1946–1996*. Paris: International Council of Museums, 1998, p. 79.
2 *ICOM Code of Ethics for Museums* (2004). Paris: International Council of Museums. The full text of the *ICOM Code of Ethics for Museums* is provided as *Appendix I* in the present publication. It is also available online for download from the ICOM website (with links to translations in French, Spanish, and some 40 other languages). The English version is accessible at: http://icom. museum/professional-standards/code-of-ethics/.
3 Gary Edson, 'Unchanging ethics in a changing world', in Bernice L. Murphy (ed.), *Museums, Ethics and Cultural Heritage*. London and New York: Routledge, 2016, Chapter 14.
4 Geoffrey Lewis, in 'The *ICOM Code of Ethics for Museums*: Background and objectives', in Bernice L. Murphy (ed.), *Museums, Ethics and Cultural Heritage*. London and New York: Routledge, 2016, Chapter 5. See especially section: 'The eight principles of the ICOM Code'.
5 UNESCO assumed its operational life at its first General Conference, held at the Sorbonne University, Paris, 20 November–10 December 1946. See Fernando Valderrama, *A History of UNESCO*. Paris: UNESCO, 1995, p. 24.
6 Ibid.
7 Ibid., p. 25.
8 See France Desmarais, 'Protecting cultural heritage at risk: An international public service mission for ICOM', in Bernice L. Murphy (ed.), *Museums, Ethics and Cultural Heritage*. London and New York: Routledge, 2016, Chapter 11.
9 François Mairesse, 'The UNESCO *Recommendation on the Protection and Promotion of Museums and Collections, their Diversity and their Role in Society*', in Bernice L. Murphy (ed.), *Museums, Ethics and Cultural Heritage*. London and New York: Routledge, 2016, Chapter 10.
10 Mechtild Rössler and Nao Hayashi, 'UNESCO's actions and international standards concerning museums', in Bernice L. Murphy (ed.), *Museums, Ethics and Cultural Heritage*. London and New York: Routledge, 2016, Chapter 9.
11 The full title of this ground-breaking convention is the *UNESCO Convention on the Means of Prohibiting and Preventing the Illicit Import, Export and Transfer of Ownership of Cultural Property, 1970*.
12 Rössler and Hayashi, 'UNESCO's actions and international standards concerning museums'.
13 Ibid.
14 Detailed information on all of ICOM's committees and networks is provided on the ICOM website, at: www.icom.museum.
15 Bagli *et al.*, *History of ICOM*, p. 51; see also pp. 27–29, and note the remark (by Patrick Boylan, author of this section, p. 27): 'From the legal standpoint, the eleventh General Assembly [in Copenhagen, 1974] held the very future of ICOM in its hands.'
16 From Article 5, Revised Statutes of ICOM, adopted at ICOM General Assembly, Copenhagen, 1974, as reported in Bagli *et al.*, *History of ICOM*, p. 28.

17 See Bagli *et al.*, *History of ICOM*, esp. pp. 29, 51. 'A decisive resolution at the General Assembly in Copenhagen launched the drafting of ICOM's Code of Professional Ethics' (Patrick Boylan, p. 29).

18 The development of ICOM's Code of Ethics, from 1971 to 1986 (when the first complete Code was adopted), and the revision of that Code (in two stages, 1998–2001; and 2001–04) to produce the revised Code of 2004, is thoroughly covered by Geoffrey Lewis, who guided that revision as Chair of ICOM's Ethics Committee. See Lewis, '*ICOM Code of Ethics for Museums*'.

19 Bagli *et al.*, *History of ICOM*, p. 33.

20 Presidents/Chairpersons of the ICOM Ethics Committee since its establishment: Hubert Landais (1990–97); Geoffrey Lewis (1997–2004); Bernice L. Murphy (2004–11); and Martin R. Schärer (2011–). See also the text on the continuing work of the Ethics Committee by current Chairperson, Dr Martin Schärer, 'The work of the ICOM Ethics Committee', in Bernice L. Murphy (ed.), *Museums, Ethics and Cultural Heritage*. London and New York: Routledge, 2016, Chapter 3.

21 See *Our Creative Diversity: Report of the World Commission on Culture and Development* (1995). Paris: UNESCO, 1996, p. 8.

22 'A new global ethics', *Our Creative Diversity*, Ch. 1: pp. 33–51: p. 35.

23 Amareswar Galla, 'In search of the Inclusive Museum', in Bernice L. Murphy (ed.), *Museums, Ethics and Cultural Heritage*. London and New York: Routledge, 2016, Chapter 29.

24 *Previous Possessions, New Obligations*, the founding Indigenous Policy adopted by Australian museums collectively in 1993, has been succeeded by the revised policy, *Continuing Cultures, Ongoing Responsibilities: Principles and Guidelines for Australian Museums Working with Aboriginal and Torres Strait Islander Cultural Heritage*, as adopted by Museums Australia in 2005, at: www.museumsaustralia.org.au/userfiles/file/Policies/ccor_final_feb_05.pdf.

25 W. Richard West, Jr. 'Native America in the twenty-first century: Journeys in cultural governance and museum interpretation', in Bernice L. Murphy (ed.), *Museums, Ethics and Cultural Heritage*. London and New York: Routledge, 2016, Chapter 26.

26 Lewis, '*ICOM Code of Ethics for Museums*'; concerning 'source communities', see paragraphs 4.3, 4.4, p. 8 and 6.7, p. 10, at: http://icom.museum/ethics.html.

27 West, 'Native America in the twenty-first century'.

28 Bongani Ndhlovu, 'Using the past to forge a future: Challenges of uniting a nation against skeletal odds', in Bernice L. Murphy (ed.), *Museums, Ethics and Cultural Heritage*. London and New York: Routledge, 2016, Chapter 27.

29 Sharon Macdonald, 'Exhibiting contentious and difficult histories: Ethics, emotions and reflexivity', in Bernice L. Murphy (ed.), *Museums, Ethics and Cultural Heritage*. London and New York: Routledge, 2016, Chapter 25.

30 Mónica Risnicoff de Gorgas, 'Afro-descendent heritage and its unacknowledged legacy in Latin American museum representation', in Bernice L. Murphy (ed.), *Museums, Ethics and Cultural Heritage*. London and New York: Routledge, 2016, Chapter 28.

31 The Universal Declaration of Human Rights (UDHR) was adopted by the General Assembly of the United Nations, resolution 217 A (III), 10 December 1948. The International Covenant on Economic, Social and Cultural Rights is one of two UN human rights covenants directly based on the UDHR – the other being the International Covenant on Civil and Political Rights.

32 For a comprehensive analysis of these tensions and their historical background, see Costas Douzinas, *The End of Human Rights: Critical Legal Thought at the Turn of the Century*. Cambridge: Hart, 2000.

33 See Ricardo J. Elia, 'A Seductive and Troubling Work', *Archaeology*, 46 (1), 1993, pp. 66–69.

34 See Peter Watson and Cecilia Todeschini, *The Medici Conspiracy: The Illicit Journey of Looted Antiquities from Italy's Tomb Raiders to the World's Greatest Museums*. Cambridge, MA: Perseus Books Group, 2006; and a later tracing of related narratives in Jason Felch and Ralph Frammolino, *Chasing Aphrodite: The Hunt for Looted Antiquities at the World's Richest Museum*. New York: Houghton Mifflin Harcourt, 2011.

35 Michael M. Franz, 'Advice and support in the recovery of lost art: The German Lost Art Foundation (Deutsches Zentrum Kulturgutverluste)', in Bernice L. Murphy (ed.), *Museums, Ethics and Cultural Heritage.* London and New York: Routledge, 2016, Chapter 13.

36 Markus Hilgert, ' "Definitely stolen?": Why there is no alternative to provenance research in archaeological museums', in Bernice L. Murphy (ed.), *Museums, Ethics and Cultural Heritage.* London and New York: Routledge, 2016, Chapter 20.

37 Hermann Parzinger, 'Remodelling shared heritage and collections access: The Museum Island constellation and Humboldt Forum project in Berlin', in Bernice L. Murphy (ed.), *Museums, Ethics and Cultural Heritage.* London and New York: Routledge, 2016, Chapter 15.

38 Jane Milosch, 'Advocating for international collaborations: World War II-era provenance research in museums', in Bernice L. Murphy (ed.), *Museums, Ethics and Cultural Heritage.* London and New York: Routledge, 2016, Chapter 19.

39 François Mairesse, 'Deaccessioning: Some reflections', in Bernice L. Murphy (ed.), *Museums, Ethics and Cultural Heritage.* London and New York: Routledge, 2016, Chapter 21.

40 *ICOM Code of Ethics for Museums* (2004; Paris: International Council of Museums, 2006), Articles 4.3 and 4.4, at: http://icom.museum/ethics.html.

41 *ICOM Code of Ethics for Museums*, Article 4.4.

42 See the British Museum's publication of the repatriation of Tasmanian Aboriginal cremation ash bundles, and full details for its decision in 2006, at: www.britishmuseum.org/about_us/management/human_remains/repatriation_to_tasmania.aspx.

43 See Tom Hunt, 'Toi moko arrive at Te Papa: Maori welcomed home after 200 years', *The Dominion Post*, 27 January 2012, at: www.stuff.co.nz/dominion-post/news/6322514/Toi-moko-arrive-at-Te-Papa.

44 Eva Maehre Lauritzen, 'Ethics in action: Situational scenarios turning the keys to the *Code of Ethics*', in Bernice L. Murphy (ed.), *Museums, Ethics and Cultural Heritage.* London and New York: Routledge, 2016, Chapter 34.

45 An Laishun, 'The Chinese museum: Transformation and change through ethics construction', in Bernice L. Murphy (ed.), *Museums, Ethics and Cultural Heritage.* London and New York: Routledge, 2016, Chapter 17.

46 Eiji Mizushima, 'Ethics, museology and professional training in Japan', in Bernice L. Murphy (ed.), *Museums, Ethics and Cultural Heritage.* London and New York: Routledge, 2016, Chapter 18.

47 Legislative restriction on the inalienability of British national collections was the case argued historically against repatriation claims by museums in the UK – until the introduction of the Human Tissue Act 2004; see: www.legislation.gov.uk/ukpga/2004/30/contents.

48 'The ICOM-WIPO Mediation Programme – a joint initiative of both organizations launched in 2011 – provides a feasible and appealing means to settle ownership questions without recourse to the often protracted and costly measures entailed in legal action.' See Marilyn Phelan, 'Stolen and illegally exported artefacts in collections: Key issues for museums within a legal framework', in Bernice L. Murphy (ed.), *Museums, Ethics and Cultural Heritage.* London and New York: Routledge, 2016, Chapter 12.

49 Eric Dorfman, 'Ethical issues and standards for natural history museums', in Bernice L. Murphy (ed.), *Museums, Ethics and Cultural Heritage.* London and New York: Routledge, 2016, Chapter 6.

50 Ibid.

51 Emlyn Koster, 'From Apollo into the Anthropocene: The odyssey of nature and science museums in an external responsibility context', in Bernice L. Murphy (ed.), *Museums, Ethics and Cultural Heritage.* London and New York: Routledge, 2016, Chapter 22.

52 Ibid. The internal reference in this quote is to B. Watson and E. Werb, 'One hundred strong: A colloquium on transforming natural history museums in the twenty-first century', *Curator*, Vol. 56, 2013, pp. 255–65 – as provided in Koster's list of references.

53 Michel Van-Praët, 'Reversing the de-realization of natural and social phenomena: Ethical issues for museums in a multidisciplinary context', in Bernice L. Murphy (ed.), *Museums, Ethics and Cultural Heritage*. London and New York: Routledge, 2016, Chapter 7.

54 Robert R. Janes, 'Museums and the end of materialism', in Janet Marstine (ed.), *The Routledge Companion to Museum Ethics: Redefining Ethics for the Twenty-First-Century Museum*. London and New York: Routledge, 2011, pp. 54–69: p. 66. See also Robert R. Janes, *Museums in a Troubled World: Renewal, Irrelevance or Collapse?* London and New York: Routledge, 2009.

55 This has strongly been the case in Australia, for example, where state and national art museums collect Aboriginal and Torres Strait Islander art as 'contemporary art', often have specialist Indigenous curators, and have their collections and research enriched through direct links with living artists and elders, and often long-term agreements or partnerships in heritage care undertaken with communities. All Australian natural history museums, meanwhile, have joined in a concerted effort at provenancing and repatriation of Indigenous ancestral remains to descendant communities – and often have established long-term relationships in the process.

56 Sally Yerkovich, 'Ethics in a changing social landscape: Community engagement and public participation in museums', in Bernice L. Murphy (ed.), *Museums, Ethics and Cultural Heritage*. London and New York: Routledge, 2016, Chapter 23.

57 Stephanie de Roemer, 'Conservation: How ethics work in practice', in Bernice L. Murphy (ed.), *Museums, Ethics and Cultural Heritage*. London and New York: Routledge, 2016, Chapter 24.

58 Dorota Folga-Januszewska, 'A museum triangle: Ethics, standards of care and the pleasure of perception', in Bernice L. Murphy (ed.), *Museums, Ethics and Cultural Heritage*. London and New York: Routledge, 2016, Chapter 16.

PART II

The ICOM Code and evolving issues for museums' conduct and care of heritage

5

THE *ICOM CODE OF ETHICS FOR MUSEUMS*

Background and objectives

Geoffrey Lewis

ICOM has been concerned with ethical matters for most of its seventy-year existence, and the *ICOM Code of Ethics for Museums* benefits greatly from this continuity. This period has seen profound changes both to museums and the museum idea, which are reflected in the three important stages that mark the development of the present Code.

Although there had been a conference resolution on the illegal excavation and exportation of items of cultural heritage a year after ICOM's founding in 1947, the first landmark in the preparation of an ICOM Code arose in parallel with the work towards the 1970 UNESCO convention on the illicit transfers of cultural property. An ICOM working group drew up twenty recommendations to reinforce the international effort against illicit trafficking. This was seen 'as a first step in establishing a professional ethical code regarding acquisition', and was endorsed at the 1971 ICOM General Assembly with resolutions on 'the ethics of acquisition' and the 'documentation of collections and field missions'. The resolutions as drafted referred to the reconstitution of cultural heritages and for collections and their associated documentation resulting from scientific fieldwork to be deposited in the country of origin. In support of this, ICOM prepared a handbook of national legislations relevant to cultural property, which was published in 1974.

As the result of an ICOM General Assembly resolution in 1974, a small working group was formed to prepare a comprehensive code of ethics. A draft was produced. The 1977 General Conference received a paper titled 'Eléments d'une éthique internationale'. At the 1980 ICOM General Conference, each of ICOM's international committees was asked to discuss 'professional ethics for museum personnel' and to report their conclusions. The outcome was a conference resolution seeking further study of the topic, and in 1981, an ad hoc committee was asked to prepare 'a code of ethics and professional practices'.

UNESCO supported ICOM in this work, and information was sought from some ninety nations about their ethical codes and practices. This, and the exhaustive analysis of existing national codes of ethics by the committee, provided an invaluable resource in developing the ICOM *Code of Professional Ethics*, which was approved unanimously at ICOM's General Assembly in 1986, and published the following year. This comprehensive document has been the base for subsequent revisions of the ICOM Code.

Following the adoption of the Code, ICOM's Executive Council appointed a small ad hoc Standing Committee on Museum Ethics to monitor its progress, and a few years later reconstituted this body as the ICOM Committee for Professional Ethics, giving it greater powers including the opportunity for individual members to contact the Committee directly on ethical concerns.

The third landmark in the development of ICOM's Code dates to 2004, when the current *ICOM Code of Ethics for Museums* was approved by the General Assembly. The need to revise the 1986 Code was driven principally by social and organisational change impacting on museums, rather than variations in curatorial practice. These influences included the changing scene in the provision of museums and their widening role linked to the care and protection of the natural and cultural heritage. Traditionally museums were associated with the movable cultural heritage but, with increasing conservation awareness, this came to include historic sites and buildings as well as significant habitats and aspects of the living heritage of humanity including the intangible cultural heritage.

The revised Code took account of many of the social and economic changes affecting museums as well as their widening purpose: new cultural concepts and more diverse value systems shaping museum programmes and the use of their collections; changing income sources and operational contexts; museums' growing reliance on commercial activities; and the increasing role of voluntary support organisations and membership bodies, and in some cases independent foundations dedicated to museum fund-raising.

In addition to such changes reshaping the museum environment, issues raised in new international conventions relevant to museums were addressed, together with matters concerning the acquisition, deaccessioning and disposal of museum collections.

The revision of ICOM's Code took place over two triennia (1998–2004) and included periods of consultation with the membership. Initially the 1986 Code was updated. This revision received General Assembly approval in 2001, and served as an interim Code until the next General Assembly in 2004 when the present, fully revised and reorganised *ICOM Code of Ethics for Museums* was adopted.[1]

The eight principles of the ICOM Code[2]

1 Museums preserve, interpret and promote the natural and cultural inheritance of humanity

Understanding the nature of the cultural and natural heritage is fundamental to museums and therefore to the ICOM Code. As humanity's inheritance, cultural property is no ordinary property. Furthermore, there are few enterprises where the key resource for success is not expendable – in the case of museums, the collection. Indeed, there is a perpetual internal tension in museums between the preservation and utilisation of this central resource; and a certain paradox at the heart of a museum's mission deepens when the maintenance and enhancement of the collection is also a key measure of success. An institution with such complex public responsibilities needs to be permanent, well-founded, resourced and managed, and to pursue a clear sense of purpose and direction. The heading to this first section of the ICOM Code sets the scene on the primary and enduring purpose of museums.

Changing philosophies in museum management also influenced this section. Some resulted from the adoption of new management theories, while others arose through association with other professions – for example, education, libraries, leisure and tourism. In addition, social change had seen an increase and diversification in museum stakeholders, each with varying perceptions and expectations of the museum. These included the governing body, donors, the communities served (visitor and non-visitor alike), the subject disciplines, 'Friends' and other cognate bodies, partner providers, sponsors, retail organisations and other interests. These had increased the expectations of museums and their services with varying values influencing the contributions these parties made to, or drew from, the museum.

The care and interpretation of the cultural heritage places the museum in a special position of public trust. However, in some cases the funding of this public trust had become increasingly dependent on the private or commercial sectors, or a combination of private and public sectors. Corporate sponsorship had tended to replace private patronage in financial support for museums; however, sponsorship is a two-way process – essentially an exchange of specified services rather than untied support. Meanwhile, museums cannot be viewed simply in terms of input/ output devices, and it is crucial to the social mission and public trust of museums that their resources do not figure as expendable items in their financial accounts. Taking stock of all these changes, the ICOM Code needed to make clear that museums have increased in complexity as multi-purpose institutions, and this raised new ethical issues to address in museum management.

2 Museums that maintain collections hold them in trust for the benefit of society and its development

This concerns the obligation of every member of the museum profession to ensure proper care of the collections. The aim should be to ensure the collections are passed on to future generations in as good and safe a condition as practicable. This affects the day-to-day usage of collections; it means establishing good working practices to ensure the security of the collection; it requires adequate precautions in place in the event of natural or man-made disasters. These factors also apply to material in transit or temporarily in the museum's care.

A particularly important element in museum risk management is preventive conservation, ensuring that collections are maintained in a protective environment in store, on display or in transit.

The museum's acquisitions or collections policy is a key document in collections management. It will have the agreement of both professional staff and the governing body and should also be in the public domain, to ensure transparency both of intent and practice. This document will have clear statements on most of the elements in this section of the ICOM Code.

Normally an active museum adds to its collection. It is necessary to establish the full history of any item before acquisition is considered. While a donor may have 'legal title' to an object, this does not rule out a previous illegal acquisition. For this purpose, the concept of due diligence was introduced in the 2004 Code. Any dealing with inadequately provenanced material is seen as condoning illicit trade and is therefore unethical. Museums are expected to assume a position of leadership in this area of conduct as a contribution to halting the extensive denudation of the world's natural, cultural and biological resources.

It follows that extensive records support the collections. Without documentation, an item has little value. This, however, goes further than recording the physical characteristics and associations of the item and its full history. It includes statements regarding its condition and any conservation or restoration treatment it may have received. There will normally be supporting documentation, not least that providing indisputable evidence of ownership, whether or not ownership is vested in the museum. Internet access has led many museums to make their catalogues available online. The ICOM Code draws attention to the need to control sensitive information, whether publishing online or by other means.

Sometimes it is necessary to stabilise an object or specimen, treat deterioration, make repairs or undertake restoration. It is particularly important to obtain the best available advice where such conservation is necessary, and this should only be undertaken by a qualified conservator-restorer.

Additional elements of collection care arise in the case of human remains and material of sacred significance. These should be appropriately and respectfully housed and will normally be maintained as archival collections in scholarly institutions, available for legitimate study on request. Usage of the material should be consistent with professional standards and the interests and beliefs of the originating community. Information relating to communities with interests in any material representing their heritage should be made available freely.

Finally, there must be a strong presumption of the permanence of museum collections. This means that deaccessioning or disposal will be rare. The situations where this is acceptable are indicated in the Code. However, where money or compensation arise from a disposal, this should be used solely for the benefit of the collection and normally for acquisitions to that collection.

Provision is made in the ICOM Code for museums to act as an authorised 'repository of last resort'. This affords support for housing recovered specimens or objects, which may be unprovenanced or derived from illicit activities that relate to the territory over which the museum has lawful responsibility.

3 *Museums hold primary evidence for establishing and furthering knowledge*

Museums have a special responsibility to scholarship and sharing of knowledge. In many areas of scientific knowledge, museums are the recognised custodians of the primary sources of material evidence, and field records on which certain knowledge is based. It is important to identify such material, and it may be necessary to restrict its usage in certain cases. This material, with its associated information, should be made available to scholars as freely as possible, unless there are confidentiality or security restrictions. This applies even if a request for access relates to a special field of interest of museum staff.

Most museums undertake research. This may relate to the collections, associated fieldwork, or to interpretive and publication activities. Such research should be related to the museum's mission and objectives, and be undertaken to the highest standards. The results of research should be published to further knowledge and make it available to the wider public and scholarly community. The rights to such work, when published, must be agreed with the museum.

Occasionally an outstanding item of primary evidence, contributing substantially to knowledge, becomes available to a museum but is of doubtful provenance. Such an item would not normally be acquired, but here the interests of the subject discipline become paramount, rather than the interests of the museum. Any decision to acquire such an item should be made independently by subject specialists in the discipline concerned, and not by particular curators or the governing body of the museum.

4 *Museums provide opportunities for the appreciation, understanding and management of the natural and cultural heritage*

In serving society, the museum's facilities should be physically and intellectually accessible regularly and during reasonable hours. Members of staff, the collections and documentation should also be available by appointment or other arrangement. Sharing knowledge and expertise with the public is fundamental to the social purpose of museums and should be conducted in a professional manner. Public involvement in supporting the museum, its goals and activities also brings mutual benefits. Interaction with a constituent or local community helps a museum develop its educational role and engage wider audiences. Specialist staff can greatly benefit this work and increase the museum's service to various communities. Certain communities, however, may find it inappropriate for aspects of their heritage to be displayed, particularly human remains and sacred items, and these views should be respected.

The public's main contact with the museum is through its interpretive work. This may be through display, exhibition or verbally; or via public programmes, visitor services, guided tours of collections or exhibitions, and various forms of publication including e-books and other internet access to museum resources. This interpretive work, while increasingly diverse in its forms, should maintain standards of accuracy, honesty and objectivity, and be well-founded academically.

5 Museums hold resources that provide opportunities for other public services and benefits

The specialist expertise of museum staff can lead to requests for advice on many matters that are not strictly within the museum's mission. These include planning, development impact studies or environmental conservation. Involvement in such work can provide useful feedback and extension of museum knowledge, but care should be exercised that the time involved in such activities does not compromise the museum's main mission.

Many museums offer appraisal or opinion services and, in the area of visual art, these may well be sought on artworks owned privately or by commercial organisations. This provides a public service and can also be an important source of information for museums. Information about such material should be treated as confidential, but if it contributes to knowledge, the owner should be encouraged to allow publication, if appropriate. Objects should only be valued for recognised public bodies. Where the museum might benefit financially or legally, or have some other interest in an item, appraisal must be undertaken independently.

Objects that might have been illegally or illicitly acquired, transferred, imported or exported should not be identified or otherwise authenticated. In such cases, the appropriate authorities should be notified.

6 Museums work in close collaboration with the communities from which their collections originate as well as those they serve

Items from the cultural and natural heritage acquire or carry associations with people, places and events, and these often give them significance and the *raison d'être* for their place in a museum collection. This distinguishes them from ordinary property. Nevertheless, such associations can give rise to tensions. For example, the geographical association of an item, particularly from an area where political boundaries have changed, may be deemed of supranational or national, regional or local significance, and therefore raise questions as to which museum should most appropriately house it. Such tensions are compounded when the item has ethnic, political or religious significance. This should provide opportunities to share information and exhibitions with museums in the communities concerned.

With regard to international collections, there may be opportunities to return material to the country or people where it originated. This is particularly relevant when an item might have been illicitly exported or transferred from its country of origin, or looted during a period of occupation. The display of such items gives the appearance of condoning such behaviour.

Collecting from contemporary communities and interpreting their heritage requires the closest collaboration with the community concerned and respect for their traditions and cultures. Items of sacred significance, including human remains, whether contemporary or earlier, need to be handled with sensitivity and respect for the community concerned. Particular sensitivities may arise in multicultural communities. Cooperation with relevant heritage and community bodies can bring benefits to both parties, as can the involvement of museum-based organisations such as 'Friends' or cognate volunteer associations.

7 Museums operate in a legal manner

Museums must conform to the laws of the territory in which they are situated and to their governing legislation, together with any trusts for which they are responsible. This also applies to any international or regional legislation and treaty obligations that may be in force. The law concerning the natural and cultural heritage varies considerably from country to country, and at times the ICOM Code may take on a quasi-legal role in providing standards for museum conduct where legislation is deficient or lacking. The Code uses certain international legislation as a guide to professional standards, and these legal instruments apply to ethical museum practice, whether or not these conventions or treaties have come into force in a particular state or country concerned.[3]

As enabling and employment laws vary considerably between nation states, ICOM does not promote a view at this level other than to give the general guidance listed in section 1 of the Code.

8 Museums operate in a professional manner

Maintaining, preserving and interpreting the people's heritage is a public service. The public has a right to expect this to be undertaken responsibly and in a professional manner, observing accepted standards and laws, and other necessary safeguards against illegal or unethical conduct. The employing authorities of museum staff should develop policies, procedures and conditions of employment consistent with these responsibilities to enable them to be undertaken in a professional and ethical manner. Loyalty to the employing authority and to colleagues is an important element in professional ethics, as is upholding the dignity and honour of the museum profession and promoting a better public understanding of its role in society.

Museum staff will have knowledge, experience and contacts which often provide external opportunities, such as advisory and consultancy services, teaching, writing and broadcasting, or personal requests for specialist opinions or evaluations of cultural, scientific and natural heritage material. Staff are also likely to develop relations with other specialists and with the commercial market and private interests.

Such associations can present conflicts of interest, which require prudent and principled assessment. Professional relationships should be conducted to the highest standards, respecting confidentialities and avoiding any situation where personal gifts or favours might compromise a professional relationship or the standards of the employing museum. Personal collecting by staff must not conflict with that of their institution. Profiting from buying or selling anything relating to the natural or cultural heritage is unethical for museum employees. Wherever a conflict arises or can be anticipated, the matter should be shared with the appropriate authority and the situation clarified and/or rectified.

The ICOM Code provides standards to which a museum professional may reasonably aspire, and membership of ICOM is an affirmation of the Code. These standards also serve as a statement of the standards that the public has the right to expect of museums and their staff.

Conclusion

Museum practitioners come from a variety of academic and operational backgrounds with diverse allegiances and loyalties. The *ICOM Code of Ethics for Museums* not only sets out minimum standards for museum conduct but also seeks to promote common bonds of service among members of a diverse profession with common strategic aims. It was important, therefore, that the restructured ICOM Code had the 'look and feel' of the profession it serves; that it could be identified directly with the principles that govern a museum's strategic aims; and that it used clear language that could be understood and translated into members' own languages.

The ICOM Code has continued to provide a professional standard and framework for museum work since its adoption in 2004. It is also recognised as a statement of good practice at a governmental level, and has recently been cited as such in the UNESCO *Recommendation on the Protection and Promotion of Museums and Collections, their Diversity and their Role in Society,* 2015.[4]

However, museums operate in a world of social, economic and technological change and are influenced by this environment. It will be important to continue to identify the museum's response to these issues. This particularly applies to the opportunities that digitisation, virtualisation and the increasing use of social media provide for the work of museums. However, museums are still fundamentally concerned with the 'real thing', whether in a tangible or intangible form. The relevance of the ICOM Code as an international base-standard guide to ethical museum practice remains while society respects and identifies with its cultural and natural heritage and seeks to learn from, preserve and value its continuity.

Notes

1 The full text of the *ICOM Code of Ethics for Museums* is provided in *Appendix I* to the present publication. It and is also publicly accessible on the ICOM website, along with other ethics guidelines adopted by ICOM (including the *Code of Ethics for Natural History Museums,* produced by ICOM-NATHIST – *Appendix II,* this volume; and the *CIMAM Principles for Deaccessioning,* produced for museums of modern and contemporary art – *Appendix III*).

2 Ibid. See the full text of the *ICOM Code of Ethics for Museums* as *Appendix I* in the present publication. The Code is also available online for download from the ICOM

website (with links to translations in French, Spanish, and many other languages). The English version is accessible at: http://icom.museum/professional-standards/code-of-ethics.

3 In addition to the UNESCO *Convention for the Protection of Cultural Property in the Event of Armed Conflict* (The Hague Convention, First Protocol, 1954 and Second Protocol, 1999) and the UNESCO *Convention on the Means of Prohibiting and Preventing the Illicit Import, Export and Transfer of Ownership of Cultural Property* (1970), the *ICOM Code of Ethics for Museums* takes account of and adopts as a standard the following legislation: the *Convention on International Trade in Endangered Species of Wild Fauna and Flora* (1973); the *UN Convention on Biological Diversity* (1992); the UNIDROIT *Convention on Stolen and Illegally Exported Cultural Objects* (1995); the UNESCO *Convention on the Protection of the Underwater Cultural Heritage* (2001); and the UNESCO *Convention for the Safeguarding of the Intangible Cultural Heritage* (2003).

4 UNESCO *Recommendation on the Protection and Promotion of Museums and Collections, their Diversity and their Role in Society*, 2015, Article 26. The full text of the UNESCO *Recommendation Concerning the Protection and Promotion of Museums and Collections, their Diversity and their Role in Society*, 2015, is provided as *Appendix V* in the present publication. See also François Mairesse, 'The UNESCO *Recommendation on the Protection and Promotion of Museums and Collections, their Diversity and their Role in Society*', in Bernice Murphy (ed.), *Museums, Ethics and Cultural Heritage*. London: Routledge, 2016, Chapter 10.

6

ETHICAL ISSUES AND STANDARDS FOR NATURAL HISTORY MUSEUMS

Eric Dorfman

Introduction

The operating context for natural history museums is changing. Many biological populations from which collections are assembled are declining catastrophically; 50 percent of the world's species have disappeared in the last forty years (McRae *et al.* 2014). Habitats are declining on a similar scale through changing land use practices and steadily destabilizing climate. At the same time, the global financial crisis has left many natural history institutions with reduced scientific staff balancing research and communication with an increasingly diverse and technically sophisticated audience.

Perhaps in recognition of this, the methods and motivations for managing natural history museums are being more closely reviewed, both from outside the field and from within it. For instance, collecting specimens of some taxa (e.g. birds; Winker *et al.* 2010) are coming under increasing scrutiny and cross-industry standards are being developed that contribute to the credibility which museums typically enjoy. The fact that traditional collecting for zoology collections most frequently requires animals' death ethically requires an associated data set to justify their demise:

> [Bird] specimens and associated data that result from [...] collecting benefit a wide variety of scientific studies and often serve as the basis for successful management and conservation of populations, species, and ecosystems [...]. However, a bird should be collected only when available information provides reasonable assurance that doing so will not imperil the species or biologically defined population, considering the life-history characteristics of that species or closely related ones.
>
> *(Winker et al. 2010: 690)*

Thinking in the sector about collecting has moved on substantially from the nineteenth century, when taking fauna for museum collections ushered species over the brink of extinction (e.g. the Huia Callaeidae: *Heteralocha acutirostris*; Morris and Smith 1995), or when individuals of easily-handled species were specifically bred by museums to be killed for dioramas – as was common practice until the mid-twentieth century.

Collecting specimens from nature is one of a number of issues that distinguishes natural history museum ethics from other branches of museology. Others include the fact that it can be considered an ethical responsibility of natural history museums to work to conserve the environments from which their collections are derived (see 'Taipei Declaration' below). Natural history museums also sometimes display or do research on live animals, in which care of these individuals is also a priority. Non-living material, both specimens of extant species as well as fossils, can represent more than their immediate value to science, which sometimes requires a shift in thinking from natural history curators. Adding to this complexity is the fact that many natural science institutions also collect and display human remains, which requires sensitivity to the beliefs and values of originating cultures and, one hopes, a collaborative approach.

The following are two examples which illustrate the degree to which natural history museums have ethical issues that are unique to them.

Big game hunting, land use and dioramas

One of the most widely publicized ethical issues in the natural history arena in recent times was the South West African lion 'Cecil' (*c*.2002–1 July 2015) that resided mainly in the Hwange National Park in Zimbabwe. The lion was an important feature of the park both for visitors and researchers. On 29 June 2015, Cecil was wounded with an arrow by Walter Palmer, an American recreational big game hunter. Over the next forty hours Palmer tracked the lion, ultimately killing him with a rifle. Cecil's considerable suffering and ultimate death sparked international outrage among animal rights activists, conservationists, politicians and celebrities, culminating in prosecution against Palmer and his associates (BBC News 2015).

Even though the lion was not destined for a museum, the general outrage over this episode raised serious questions about historic habitat dioramas, many of which were populated with specimens from big game expeditions in the late-nineteenth and early-twentieth centuries. The first habitat dioramas were developed during a burgeoning recognition that wild populations are not infinite, and values about species, both positive and negative, began to change (Carruthers 2005). Even today, dioramas are valued both as cultural heritage and for their ability to impart stories of nature and conservation (e.g. Wonders 1993; Hutterer 2014). Nevertheless, while Cecil was in the news, the public questioned museums about the origins of the taxidermy material on display.

The emotive component of big game hunting notwithstanding, the sport's impact on conservation is multifaceted, and many recreational game reserves protected for a single species serve to augment the preservation of entire biomes (Loveridge *et al.* 2007). For example, the Community Areas Management Programme for Indigenous

Resources (CAMPFIRE) scheme was developed by the Government of Zimbabwe in the late 1980s to promote the sustainable use and conservation of natural resources of the country through the generation of income for rural communities. In the scheme, participating Zimbabwean rural district councils set aside an estimated 36,000 km^2, augmenting land set aside as part of the country's national parks system (Campfire Zimbabwe 2015). Wildlife hunting is an important source of revenue across Africa, bringing in critically needed resources to desperately poor communities (Makombe 1994), and in many cases creating habitat that would otherwise be converted to farmland (Loveridge *et al.* 2007). In museums, specimens like elephants from old-time big game expeditions are even now being used to solve real-world environmental issues, such as contributing baseline data critical for interpreting the isotopic signatures of ancient ivory believed to have been exported from eastern Africa (Coutu 2015).

Much of the value of dioramas to a modern audience relies on the interpretation not only of the specimens but their contextualizing habitats, and what is said about them. As Winker *et al.* (2010) point out regarding the taking of wild birds for museum collections, the display of material already in those collections is an ethical issue that requires some sensitivity.

Biodiversity conservation: the Taipei Declaration

Collecting institutions have a connection with nature based on the wildlife they exhibit, their objects and associated research. In advancing their work and public programmes, they present their visitors with opportunities to engage meaningfully with the marvels of nature. Many of these institutions also emphasize a mission of conservation and contribute directly to conservation education and science. ICOM NATHIST considers doing so as an ethical responsibility, and in 2015 released the *Taipei Declaration on Natural History Museums and Biodiversity Conservation*. The text of the Taipei Declaration is focused on the notion that it is the ethical responsibility of natural history museums to 'give back' to the wild populations that have provided their collection objects:

> A major role of natural history museums is to collect and steward natural history objects, generating knowledge regarding these objects and disseminating this knowledge to the community. Natural history museums also engage the public to form deep bonds with the natural world and commit to its preservation.
>
> Increased human activities have created catastrophic declines in biodiversity. Both ethics and logic point to a mandate to conserve vulnerable habitats and species. To achieve best practice, natural history museums take action to conserve natural habitats and populations.

Exploring this further, natural history institutions engaging in best practice might well include biodiversity conservation in their core mission. Miller *et al.* (2004) suggested eight potential questions to evaluate actions towards that mission:

1. Does conservation thought define policy decisions?
2. Is there sufficient organizational funding for conservation activities?
3. Is there a functional conservation department?
4. Does the institution advocate for conservation?
5. Do conservation education programs effectively target children and adults?
6. Does the institution contribute directly to habitat protection locally and internationally?
7. Do exhibits explain and promote conservation efforts?
8. Do internal policies and activities protect the environment?

These questions were offered by Miller *et al.* (2004) as a place to begin discussion in the hope that they would encourage employees and administrators of collection-based institutions to promote conservation activities. In the years since these questions were posed, the natural history museums sector has not yet made great strides towards adopting conservation action as an industry standard, despite the exceptional work undertaken by some institutions.

ICOM Code of Ethics for Natural History Museums[1]

These differences between natural history museums and other types of heritage institutions were the catalyst for ICOM NATHIST in 2006 to form the Ethics Working Group and agree to draft a code that stood alongside the *ICOM Code of Ethics for Museums* to provide a specialist document addressing issues specific to the sector. The process of drafting the *ICOM Code of Ethics for Natural History Museums* was begun in 2007, and was ratified by the ICOM General Assembly on 17 August 2013. The aim of the ICOM NATHIST Ethics Working Group was to establish a minimum standard of practice, which can be built upon by individual institutions.

The document first sets out a position statement that explains the purpose of natural history museums and their responsibilities:

The multifaceted purpose of natural history museums is to:

*   Build and store natural history collections.
*   Conduct research and interpret the results.
*   Support the process of science and biological conservation.
*   Enhance public understanding and appreciation of the natural world.
*   Collaborate with the public in deriving their own meaning from the natural heritage they encounter in the museum and in nature.

> While differences among cultural milieux and personal opinions are respected, all dissemination of information – whether through display, publication or other means – should be well-founded, accurate and with a responsible consideration of the academic disciplines concerned. Members of ICOM NATHIST should take its published position statements into account when developing applicable policies.

The position statement serves to codify the perspectives of natural history museums who are members of ICOM NATHIST and reminds them of our agreement on critical issues. This was not always easy, as standards such as the ICOM NATHIST's *Moscow Statement on Natural History Museums and Evolution* were not at first universally accepted. While resolving issues such as these required lengthy negotiation, the end result is that the group's existing members are unanimously supportive of the approved statements of ICOM NATHIST.

The introduction concludes with the following statement:

> Natural history collections in museums are a three-dimensional archive of the natural world and relationships of societies with their environments. In many cases, they may document a world that no longer exists. As such, these collections should be treated with the care and attention merited by such an important resource.

Inclusion of this statement is important, because natural history collections can sometimes be underrepresented in legislation and conventions (e.g. UNESCO *Convention for the Safeguarding of the Intangible Cultural Heritage*; Dorfman 2012), but science curators can also look on natural history collections and objects purely for their research value, rather than their potential market value. Many specimens, especially extinct species and those such as rhinoceros and pangolin that contain large amounts of keratin, are frequently less secure within museums than they should be.

The NATHIST Code then focuses on the specific challenges of natural history museums in six sections:

1. **The care and display of human remains.** Although the ICOM Code of Ethics covers care and display of human remains, natural history institutions that include this in their collections can face complex and specific challenges. For instance, the fact that they are in a natural history museum at all raises questions about the place of colonial thinking in modern museums and the level of dignity with which human remains are displayed.
2. **The collection, display and storage of extinct and recently extinct organism specimens.** The section includes collecting, displaying and storing this material, as well as its associated data. Emphasis is placed on ensuring provenance, sharing data and dignity of display. Museums that display live specimens are covered by augmenting the standards set by the World Association of Zoos and Aquariums.
3. **The proper collection of rocks, minerals and fossils.** Fossil material is considered to be the traces or remains of plants, animals and other organisms preserved for geological timescales by virtue of their deposition conditions. It is argued that they should be treated appropriately within legislation. This includes minimising environmental impacts of collecting activities.
4. **The deposition and repatriation of natural history specimens, as well**

as data sharing and value-added activities such as object conservation and stabilisation. This section covers ethical considerations around deposition and repatriation of natural history specimens, as well as data sharing and 'value-added' activities such as object conservation and stabilisation. Repatriation can be complex, especially with natural history specimens, which usually have no 'maker'. Additionally, sharing data freely may be problematic with species threatened with poaching.

5. **The duty of care for people and objects, including occupational safety and health, the exchange of objects and best practice guidelines for storage and handling.** Standards for Duty of Care for People and Objects, which includes occupational safety and health, exchange of objects and best practice guidelines for storage and handling.

6. **The need for collected natural history data to be published in order to disseminate this work to the scientific community.** Publication is the final issue addressed in the document. It is considered an ethical issue to use and disseminate the data to justify the cost to the environment in obtaining the specimen or sample.

Appendix I to the NATHIST Code lists the ICOM NATHIST 2006 Ethics Working Group that contributed to the formation of this Code and Appendix II provides standards for taxidermy specifically.

In drafting the NATHIST Code, it was the goal of the ICOM NATHIST Ethics Working Group to create a tool that codifies the field a bit further with respect to ethical considerations for natural history museums. It is understood that many institutions have their own internal ethics systems and go much farther than our document on some issues. It is however hoped that the Code sets minimum standards and a common language that cuts across the size and capacity of institutions, their differing cultural milieux and the diverse strengths of specific collections.

Acknowledgements

I acknowledge the immense undertaking that the NATHIST Ethics Working Group took on in accepting this task. Adrian Norris, formerly of Leeds Museum, was especially active in bringing together disparate ethical topics. Bernice Murphy, former Chair of the ICOM Ethics Committee, was also a rigorous sounding board and provided considerable moral support during the lengthy process. Finally, I would like to thank all the people in the many natural history museums who devoted their time to thinking about how to strengthen our sector.

Note

1. The complete text of ICOM's NATHIST Code is provided as *Appendix II* of the present Routledge publication (while the ICOM Code forms *Appendix I*). The NATHIST Code is more widely available for download (also in French and Spanish translations)

from the website of ICOM at: http://icom.museum/professional-standards/code-of-ethics/code-of-ethics-for-natural-history-museums.

References

BBC News, 2015. 'Cecil the lion: Zimbabwe hunter bailed over killing'. *BBC News*, 29 July 2015. Archived from the original on 11 October 2015, at: www.bbc.com/news/world-us-canada-33699346 (retrieved 16 December 2015).

Campfire Zimbabwe, 2015, at: http://campfirezimbabwe.org/index.php?option=com_content&view=article&id=47&Itemid=54 (accessed 6 December 2015).

Carruthers, J., 2005. 'Changing perspectives on wildlife in Southern Africa, c.1840 to c.1914'. *Society & Animals*, 3 (3): 183–200.

Coutu, A., 2015. 'The elephant in the room: Mapping the footsteps of historic elephants with big game hunting collections'. *World Archaeology*, 47 (3): 486–503.

Dorfman, E., 2012. 'Intangible natural heritage: An introduction', in E. Dorfman (ed.), *Intangible Natural Heritage: New Perspectives on Natural Objects*. Oxford: Routledge, pp. 1–15.

Hutterer, R., 2014. 'Habitat dioramas as historical documents: A case study', in S.D. Tunnicliffe and A. Scheersoi (eds), *Natural History Dioramas: History, Construction and Educational Role*. Amsterdam: Springer.

Loveridge, A., Reynolds, J. and Milner-Gulland, E., 2007. 'Does sport hunting benefit conservation?', in D.W. Macdonald and K. Service (eds), *Key Topics in Conservation*. London: Blackwell Publishing, pp. 134–44.

McRae, L., Freeman, R. and Deinet, S., 2014. 'The Living Planet Index', in R. McLellan, L. Iyengar, B. Jeffries and N. Oerlemans (eds), *Living Planet Report 2014: Species and Spaces, People and Places*. Gland, Switzerland: WWF.

Makombe, K., 1994. *Sharing the Land: Wildlife, People and Development in Africa*. Harare: IUCN/ROSA and Washington, DC: IUCN/SUWP.

Miller, B., Conway, W., Reading, R.P., Wemmer, C., Wildt, D., Kleiman, D., Monfort, S., Rabinowitz, A., Armstrong, B. and Hutchins, M., 2004. 'Evaluating the conservation mission of zoos, aquariums, botanical gardens, and natural history museums'. *Conservation Biology*, Vol. 18: 86–93.

Morris, R. and Smith, H., 1995. *Wild South: Saving New Zealand's Endangered Birds* (2nd ed.). Auckland: Random House.

Winker, K., Reed, J.M., Escalante, P., Askins, R.A., *et al.*, 2010. 'The importance, effects, and ethics of bird collecting'. *The Auk*, 12 (3): 690–95.

Wonders, K., 1993. 'Habitat dioramas as ecological theatre'. *European Review*, Vol. 1: 285–300.

7

REVERSING THE DE-REALIZATION OF NATURAL AND SOCIAL PHENOMENA

Ethical issues for museums in a multidisciplinary context

Michel Van-Praët

The dissociation between collections that document nature and those dedicated to human societies reflects mankind's ambiguous position towards nature

From the sixteenth to the eighteenth centuries, Europe's cabinets of natural history collected and preserved all of nature's mineral and living resources together, and considered human beings part of their collections – not only in terms of their anatomy, but also including any of their technical and cultural achievements outside of the fine arts. While these cabinets gradually came to be called 'natural history museums' over the course of the eighteenth century, they continued to combine the study of nature and man. In addition to collecting and describing natural species, they also found themselves at the heart of research and collections concerning the origin of humankind, with the creation of the disciplines of archaeology and human palaeontology. At the same time, the natural history cabinets also participated in the great explorations that preceded and later accompanied European colonialism. They became enriched with a multitude of new species for scientific research and a wealth of evidence documenting the diversity of human societies. In addition to their nature-detailing collections, natural history museums preserved and promoted collections of prehistoric and ethnological artefacts for several centuries, and some even continue to do so today.

Historically, the family of natural history museums was at the heart of the development of science in Europe and contributed, in the nineteenth century, to the understanding of the dynamic phenomena that have led to permanent changes in the living world and human societies, both of which had previously been perceived in Western thinking as unchanging for nearly 2000 years. An analysis of an increasingly extensive collection of objects gathered from every continent and every ocean contributed to the abandoning of creationist ideas and the emergence of the theory of evolution. In *Philosophie Zoologique* (1809), Lamarck described how natural history museums and their collections had contributed to this new scientific concept. He wrote that the idea that plant and animal species do not evolve 'is refuted every day in the eyes' of those 'who have successfully consulted the great and rich collections of our museums' (Lamarck 1809: 54–55).

While these museums contributed to the development of new disciplines such as palaeontology, anthropology, ethnology, and others, they also encouraged the division between the natural and human sciences. This division reflects both the specialization of the different disciplines and the long-standing ambiguity of the relationship between mankind and nature, in which man gradually came to see himself as separate from – and in part superior to – the natural world.

The intensive specialization of scientific disciplines led to a new organization of collections, and was coupled with the development of most of the new disciplines that emerged both outside of museums and in competition with them. This was the case, for example, in the second half of the nineteenth century, when physiology emerged out of the natural sciences; and, later, when social anthropology grew out of the human sciences.

In some cases, when certain museums were renovated, their existing collections were reorganized and divided. This was the case, for example, at the British Museum in London in the late nineteenth century, when natural history collections were placed in a location separate from the original museum, which meanwhile retained the collections related to the history of humanity and its artistic achievements. Collections generally became more specialized during the gathering and sorting phases. This is what happened in Paris, for example, after certain archaeological digs in the early nineteenth century. Among the objects brought back from Egypt, sarcophagi were kept at the Louvre, while dozens of human and animal mummies were sent to the National Museum of Natural History – with the scientific community's disciplinary approach, and increasing compartmentalization of research, having the effect of breaking up the cohesiveness of an entire collection.

In the only exception to the extreme specialization of collections, some museum *exhibitions* (or displays) did pursue a multidisciplinary approach. However, it was not until the late twentieth century that some researchers began to move beyond related disciplines to combine the points of view of the human and natural sciences, generally in exhibitions on subjects such as the environment or the definition of humanity. Collections were sometimes classified more as a means to highlight a certain scientific discipline, rather than to provide an interconnecting analysis of the natural and cultural information they contain.

In 1948, writing about the Musée de l'Homme, which he founded, Paul Rivet stated that such divisions hinder our understanding of mankind and humanity.

> In giving it this name [the Musée de l'Homme], I wanted to indicate that anything concerning human beings, in their many different aspects, could and should find a place within the collections. In France and elsewhere, the compartmentalization of the science of mankind, ethnology, had run its

course and achieved its objective. It was time to bring together a broad synthesis of all of the results produced by specialists and force them to compare their conclusions, verify them, and use them to support one another. Humanity is an indivisible whole, not only in space, but also in time. The divisions that the enormity of their task forced scholars to make – physical anthropology, prehistory, archaeology, ethnography, folklore, sociology, linguistics – are as artificial as classifications based on political geography. […] It was time to break them down.

(Rivet 1948: 112)

While the creation of the Musée de l'Homme was a critical success worldwide, Paul Rivet's organization of collections using a multidisciplinary approach was jeopardized after his retirement by the reorganization of his Chair of Ethnology of Modern and Fossilized Man and its division into two, and later three, different chairs (Physical Anthropology, Ethnology and Prehistory). How to organize collections is a question yet to be fully explored, either inside or outside the human sciences, even though current societal issues require a multidisciplinary approach.

With the expansion throughout the world of the Western model of transmitting heritage – the museum – gathering pace just at the time when scientific disciplines began to specialize in the nineteenth century, the question of what the typology of museum collections should mean and indicate about the world also became international, including in cultural areas where the distinction between nature and culture is less pronounced, or at least different from the Western model.

In this respect, Krzysztof Pomian also pointed out the risk for all museums, not only those focused on the human sciences, of 'dividing their objects not according to what links them together, but according to divisions between disciplines, and of mutilating them to the point of making them unrecognizable' (Pomian 1987: 11).

Paul Rivet's and Krzysztof Pomian's convergent analysis is often cited, and seems particularly relevant today as part of a comprehensive analysis of the rapid changes occurring both in societies and the natural environment. However, the ethical issues surrounding the organization of collections are rarely raised, including in ICOM's Code of Ethics.[1]

While the issue of ethical conflicts is present in the Code, it is significant to note that the articles on *collections* (Articles in Chapters 2 and 3), *sharing knowledge* (Articles 3 to 9), and *professional practices* (Articles in Chapter 8) do not explicitly address the issue of *making collections more accessible*; neither do they mention conflicts of interest or *competition between scientists*, which could have the effect of causing the structuring of collections along strict disciplinary lines.[2]

The articles in the Code of Ethics present high standards for the accessibility of collections and their documentation; but they do less to address the professional and ethical issues of researching and promoting knowledge, through enabling the multidisciplinary accessibility of collections and their associated documentation.

In some ways, the evolution of the ICOM Code of Ethics has unintentionally made access to collections more restrictive, if one compares the version adopted in

2004 with the previous one adopted in 2001. Having participated in the drafting of both versions, I believe this had more to do with efforts to make the 2004 version more concise, rather than any desire to restrict the accessibility of collections. However, it was also the result of a lack of discussion from 1999 to 2004 on a broader issue, reaching beyond the contents of particular articles: namely, a proactive effort to articulate ways to address the ethical issues surrounding *multidisciplinary research*, which was a topic that has been arising with increasing urgency in academic work for many years.

In the 2004 Code of Ethics (the current Code), the issue of 'accessibility' mentioned in the heading of Chapter 2 is not addressed in any specific article; meanwhile, making collections available 'as freely as possible', as mentioned in Article 3.2, is limited by the phrase 'having regard to restraints arising for reasons of confidentiality and security' – a phrase that in the 2001 version mainly concerned documentation published on the Internet (Article 6.4 in the 2001 version). Similarly, in Article 2.20 in the 2004 version, access to documentation is granted to 'museum personnel and other authorized users', which normatively limits access, while the contrasting phrase in the 2001 version, 'staff and other legitimate users', took the necessary process of collaboration into consideration.

While the ethical principles mentioned in the headings of each chapter positively address issues such as 'accessibility' (Chapters 2 and 3), 'the promotion of [...] heritage' (Chapter 4), and 'the contributions of museums to society' (Chapter 8), the articles within these chapters do not address the ethical issue of providing *increased multidisciplinary access*. In addition, no article explicitly mentions the very real danger of conflicts of interest related to the fact that the person who manages a museum's collection is often a specialist in that collection's field, but must know whose support is necessary to enable colleagues working in related fields to have similar access (which is frequently the case arising through the multidisciplinary approach to a number of topics); or even become conflicted in the case of the same subject as him or herself, when free access to collections is sought (ICOM 2004).[3]

Whatever changes are made to the ICOM Code of Ethics in the future, there is a very strong case for addressing the issue of the *accessibility of collections* for multidisciplinary use in a modern context; this would be achieved by including new articles that encourage granting researchers access to collections, in addition to the current articles that deal mainly with the protection and preservation of those collections. The Code of Ethics could also explicitly state that while the increasing *digitization of collections* encourages their use and analysis within an institution, this should not in any way hinder their analysis and access by a variety of other researchers and for diverse purposes, including those working in related fields, as long as such research does not destroy any important references attached to the original information.[4]

This is an important and challenging time for research in natural history museums and collections. After seeing their usefulness to contemporary research questioned for many years, natural history museums now find themselves at the heart of research on global environmental changes, the loss of biodiversity and the role of mankind in the transformation of natural processes.

Referring again to the case of natural history museums' progress historically, the increasing division and compartmentalization of collections was not only detrimental to the development of certain aspects of knowledge, but also came to threaten their very existence in the second half of the twentieth century. As these museums gradually became more specialized in describing and inventorying the diversity of nature, and as new biological and geophysical disciplines emerged, some scientists within the new disciplines questioned the usefulness of historic collections in contemporary research and, consequently, even museum exhibitions of these collections themselves. Natural history and ethnological museums worldwide experienced a crisis of positioning and purpose that led to the loss of financial support for natural science museums, along with the wholesale closing of public exhibitions (long-term displays) of historically collected material collections; and for some ethnological museums, a retreat to aestheticism and sectarianism.

To appear more 'modern', some natural science museums anxiously developed exhibitions featuring educational or interactive components, making them more like science centres, while at the same time mobilizing less and less of their collections for interpretation and public use. It was only at the very end of the twentieth century that certain science museums began to reaffirm the modernity and 'relevance' of their collections, through the creation of new museums or extensive renovations of those existing. Rather than employing interactive or virtual components as a *substitution* for their collections, these museums used new communications technologies to help *interpret* their collections in more engaging ways. They now relied on the fact that their collections contained rich resources that reflected previous states of the natural world, and could be used to analyse how it has been transformed, and even to document mankind's responsibility for the extinction of many wildlife species. In addition to museums with large palaeontological collections, this was also the case with the opening of the Grande Galerie de l'Évolution (1994, in Paris), the creation of the Naturalis Biodiversity Centre (in Leiden), and the two phases in the creation of the Darwin Centre (opened in 2009) including a re-mobilization of collections within the Natural History Museum in London.

In general, natural and human science museums no longer have to justify the usefulness of their collections in contemporary research and public exhibitions. They have found new legitimacy in offering research programs and creating exhibitions that mobilize their collections around increasingly multidisciplinary subjects (biodiversity, climate, evolution, etc.) or multidisciplinary points of view on singular subjects of interest to society (whales, wolves, bears, etc., through the lens of multiple disciplines, such as biology, ethology, mythology, and even aesthetics). They now face a second major challenge, that of defining their role in social debate and their responsibility to sound the alarm in the face of the current global environmental crisis. Museums can no longer simply meet society's expectations. Sounding the alarm through creation and innovation has become a crucial challenge for natural and human science museums. It is now possible to reconsider the past approaches of researchers and curators by highlighting how they have both contributed to making considerable progress in scientific knowledge and at the same time also fragmented that knowledge, by heightening the disconnection between nature and culture. Today, studying and changing the perception of mankind's place in the living world is essential to limiting the consequences of changes to the world's environment and climate.

The increase in disastrous weather events has helped raise awareness of global environmental changes and their relationship to human activity. However, despite a growing number of warnings about the consequences these changes will have on human beings' health and living conditions, denial and reckless abandon still persist, hindering the development of a collective approach to prevention, as seen by the limits of the COP 21 conference (21st Session of the Conference of the Parties to the United Nations Framework Convention on Climate Change).

The changes that societies must make will require greater sharing of available information: information that museums, and particularly natural science, archaeology and anthropology museums, hold abundantly in their collections. This will require not only going beyond disciplinary approaches, including for museums, by questioning the typologies of collections, but also combining scientific approaches with societal questions, both to answer those questions and to identify issues to which societies should be alerted.

Sounding the alarm is central in order to bring museums of natural and human sciences together once again, both in terms of subject matter and also in terms of professional practice. The question now is: can an exhibition go beyond presenting a consensus to create a forum for debating conflicting points of view? Can an exhibition make the public aware of a new issue by mobilizing professional expertise (despite the fact that we know that the top-down communication model is limited)?

In Paris, at the National Museum of Natural History, we chose to go beyond presenting a consensus when we designed the Gallery of Evolution (La Grande Galerie de l'Évolution) in the late 1980s – or perhaps we anticipated a different consensus by a few years in dedicating, for example, several hundred square meters to presenting a number of specimens of wildlife species that had recently become extinct or were endangered due to pressure from human societies. This proved in the 1980s to be a real battle of ideas, because at that time there was no consensus regarding the loss of biodiversity among either scientists or public authorities. In addition, the Rio Conference (1992) had not yet encouraged people to think about sustainable development, and it was difficult to convince the project's scientific committee to accept the ethical choice of calling part of the exhibition *Man: A Factor in Evolution*.

Today, interpreting the global environmental crisis has given rise to even more ethical questions in designing exhibitions on topics that question progress, demographics, the diversity and unity of humanity, its place in the living world and similar topics.

Analysing the disastrous consequences of changes in the world's environment and climate for biodiversity and human health by mobilizing information contained in museum collections, presenting arguments that prove the responsibility of human societies for these changes, and highlighting the heightened vulnerability of the world's poorest people are all important ethical issues facing our museums.

At a time when the phenomenon of de-realization – based in part on a distorted use of new communication technologies – is growing and leading to irrational behaviours, like the belief in conspiracy theories, increasing violence in social responses to change, and similar disordering of the fabric of social relationships, the use of collections, their accessibility, and their broadest possible interpretation beyond the subjects of exhibitions are major ethical issues for all museums.

When it comes to questioning the relationship between mankind and nature, the phenomenon of de-realization is amplified by man's growing disconnection from nature due to urbanization, with the majority of the world's population now living in cities.[5] This gives museums with natural and human science collections documenting the evolution of the relationship between mankind and nature an even greater and more urgent social responsibility.

Museums must become socially engaged to combat de-realization and encourage the necessary paradigm shift in the relationship between mankind and nature so that future generations do not have to live on a more inhospitable planet. Such considerations were at the heart of the renovations of the Musée de l'Homme (Van Praët 2012).

For example, a topic as seemingly non-controversial as the Neolithic age, which could be presented by museums of anthropology, Egyptology, the history of civilizations or ceramics, illustrates the ethical questions that should be asked when designing exhibitions around topics as traditional as 'Where do we come from?', 'Who are we?' and 'Where are we going?', as was the case when the Musée de l'Homme in Paris was renovated and reopened in October 2015.

For 10,000 years, Neolithization has corresponded to the domestication of plant and animal species that remain essential to feeding humanity. It has been accompanied by the modifying of land for agriculture and the process of creating settlements that has led to today's mass urbanization movement. Over thousands of years, Neolithization has helped shape the current notions of well-being and progress. In every society, those notions have been associated with a controlled use of the immediate environment based on a variety of cultural practices that, thanks to the growth of knowledge, have made an increasingly effective use of natural resources possible, without considering – until very recently – the overall limitations of the planet, even though the world's population has grown from a few million to several billion people during this long period.

In most modern societies, well-being is therefore associated with a feeling of controlling nature, or at least its resources, for the benefit of humankind. This has contributed to today's positive image of engineering and the view that it can compensate for the changes that have occurred – that it has the capacity to protect the environment, and even repair the damage caused by humans.

Breaking with this thousand-year-old paradigm and getting out of what could be considered a late Neolithic age, without suggesting that humanity is condemned to regression, will require reorienting science, technology and, more generally, mankind's creativity – from controlling nature to evolving along with it – and taking natural phenomena into account.[6]

Museums play a key role in promoting and encouraging society to discuss the idea that mankind must evolve along with nature.

Faced with the need to change the perception of the place of human beings in the living world and, more generally, mankind's relationship to nature, natural and social science museums must play a major role not only to 'promote the natural and cultural inheritance of humanity' but also 'for the benefit of society and its development', as stated in the titles of the first two chapters of the *ICOM Code of Ethics for Museums*.

Museums must use their current and future collections to inform, at least in their area of expertise, the discussion on the future of humanity, including by questioning the meaning of the term 'development'. This term must be considered and re-sensitized from an ethical point of view: as being in solidarity with mankind and in harmony with natural processes.

These natural processes include, among other things, the loss of biodiversity, which has been abundantly documented by natural science museums, and functions performed by the biosphere that are essential to the well-being of human societies – from the fertilization of plants by insects to the regulation of the carbon and oxygen cycles by terrestrial plants and marine phytoplankton. The necessary understanding of these phenomena, which reflect mankind's evolution alongside nature, will also require increased research as the basis for more resourceful social communication. These conditions speak directly to imaginative as well as scientifically informed use of special resources: to challenges in which museums – particularly natural science museums – have a major role to play.

Notes

1 The full text of the *ICOM Code of Ethics for Museums* is provided as *Appendix I* in the present publication. It is also available online for download from the ICOM website (with links to translations in French, Spanish, and many other languages). The English version is accessible at: http://icom.museum/professional-standards/code-of-ethics.

2 These comments on the *ICOM Code of Ethics for Museums* are in no way a criticism of the collective efforts made from 1999 to 2004, which was an extremely rich undertaking for those of us who participated in the revision work of the ICOM Ethics Committee. The comments are simply meant to identify possible improvements that could be made, fifteen years later, to promote the preservation and accessibility of collections and their documentation, in the aim of sharing knowledge and encouraging the multidisciplinary approach made increasingly urgent by changes in society and the natural environment.

3 Collections that are the property of a museum or its supervisory authority, and not materials that have been collected and are still in the research, sorting and original publication phases prior to becoming permanent parts of a collection. Access to such materials is governed by research principles.

4 The digitization of collections can provide a better shared understanding of the existing collections in a given museum, and even in one's own museum, which is even more a reason why the indexing of collections must anticipate multidisciplinary approaches to facilitate access to them, rather than replacing them.

5 According to the United Nations, 54 per cent of the world's population, or 3.88 billion people, lived in cities in 2014, including an estimated 1 billion people living in slums.

6 Some authors classify the current period as the Anthropocene, a concept made popular by Nobel Laureate Paul Crutzen. The Anthropocene is considered a new geological period corresponding to the major transformation of the planet's environment following industrialization. It seems to us more appropriate here to consider the transformations related to the process of Neolithization (and hence, to use the term 'late Neolithic age' for the current period) and to consider the necessary changes not in terms of a crisis (or even a geological crisis, as the term 'Anthropocene' would suggest) but in terms of the adaptation of human societies to a natural world that has been partly modified but is not itself in danger. It is the health and well-being of future generations and the most fragile societies that are at considerable risk. Independent of climate change, the World Health Organization currently estimates the number of premature deaths due to pollution at eight million a year, and the International Monetary Fund estimates the cost of illnesses and environmental damage at $US4.9 billion, or more than the total of all annual public health expenditures worldwide.

References

ICOM, 2004. *ICOM Code of Ethics for Museums*. Paris: International Council of Museums, 2006, at: http://icom.museum/fileadmin/user_upload/pdf/Codes/code_ethics2013_eng.pdf (accessed 15 December 2015).

Lamarck, Jean-Baptiste, 1809. *Philosophie Zoologique*. Paris: Museum of Natural History.

Pomian, Krzysztof, 1987. *Collectionneurs, amateurs et curieux, Paris-Venise: XVIe-XVIIIe siècles*. Paris: Gallimard.

Rivet, Paul, 1948. 'Organisation d'un musée d'ethnologie'. *Museum*. Paris: UNESCO Publishing.

Van Praët, Michel, 2012. *Reinventing the Museum to Mankind: Museums in an Age of Migrations*. Milan: Mela Books, at: www.mela-project.eu/upl/cms/attach/20120524/194251494_2514.pdf (accessed 15 December 2015).

8

DANCES WITH INTELLECTUAL PROPERTY

Museums, monetization and digitization

Rina Elster Pantalony

In 2006, and again in 2013 in a second edition, I wrote an intellectual property management guide for museums, which was published by the World Intellectual Property Organization (WIPO). Part II, and in particular Chapter 6 (Pantalony 2013), were devoted to identifying potential business opportunities for museums in relation to defined museum-related intellectual property. Museums have tiptoed around this issue, and museum administrators have often asked that their points of view be held in confidence – and if made public at all, provided only anonymously. Representatives of various cultural heritage institutions have been known to speak about this issue in hushed tones, stating: 'You know, it's controversial …' Why does this subject cause such discomfort in the museum community, and amongst its professionals and scholars?

The issue of intellectual property in relation to museums or museum activity has given rise to much criticism over the past twenty years. The advent of new media technologies and the Internet in the 1990s revolutionized our ability to communicate, but it also gave rise to a revolution in commerce and commercial activity. Museums were eager to embrace new means of communication and embarked upon significant experimentation. Organizations such as the Museum Computer Network (MCN), and conferences such as Museums and the Web, were and continue to be devoted to the intersection of museums and digital media.

However, certain early adopters within the museum community, primarily in Britain and North America, were willing to experiment further in pushing the boundaries of 'acceptability' by examining the intersection between digital media production, traditional museum subject matter, and commercial activity.[1] As we are now well aware, digital media production, particularly in the online environment, can give rise to significant intellectual property issues. During these early years in the 1990s and following, rights management and licensing were seen as primary mechanisms by which museums could 'generate revenue'. In fact, they defined early business models propagated by various experiments in the early dot.com era. Moreover, the assumption in this era was that the principal intellectual property held by museums was vested in the photographic copyrights connected to museum collections. Thus the conclusion, held by many, was that if museums were going to experiment in the production of digital media, and engage directly in commercial activity and in the online environment, then the end results could only lead to commercialization of the museum collection.

The purpose of this paper is to examine the root of our discomfort with this subject. What causes those of us in the museum community to recoil with distaste when commercial activity and museum activities are mentioned at the same instance? What do we mean by the boundaries of 'acceptability', as referenced above? And finally, are there instances where museum intellectual property can be 'leveraged' and intermixed without causing such a visceral reaction? The argument being advanced in this essay is that the answer to many of these questions lies within our community's ethics and values that shape our community members' individual mandates.

What is museum intellectual property?

What is it that we are discussing, and do we adequately understand the interplay between intellectual property and museum activities? Is the initial assumption raised correct: that only photographic images of museum collections constitute museum intellectual property? In order to examine the subject with dexterity, it is necessary first to identify what we mean by 'museum-related IP'.

In 1999, the Canadian Heritage Information Network (CHIN), an agency of the Canadian government then responsible for experimentation with museum content and the Internet, surveyed museums and published a report identifying what was largely a list of collections-based intellectual property. CHIN's survey included photographic copyrights of images of artefacts and artworks in museum collections, audio recordings and audio-visual works, and various media productions related to collections (Pantalony 2013; CHIN 1999). However, there was little, if any, mention of the intellectual property developed by the museum for museum use. At the same time, the (then) American Association of Museums – now renamed American Alliance of Museums (AAM) – published a guide to copyright and trademarks, wherein its authors delineated distinctions between copyright-protected museum assets and trademarks as intellectual property held or managed by museums. In particular, AAM's guide listed the museum name and various identifying marks and logos, and the museum building – particularly where easily identifiable and iconic – as important museum intellectual property assets (Pantalony 2013; Shapiro and Miller 1999). The AAM publication also distinguished between intellectual property that was collections-based and intellectual property that was institutional.

Since that initial period of experimentation, the list of museum intellectual property items has been expanded to reflect the development of the Internet as a social media, educational and interactive communications tool. The list now includes many forms of intellectual property that are primarily institutional in nature: for example, new technologies designed and developed to manage and tag collections; mark-up language specifically designed for museums; conservation techniques and curatorial works; industrial designs developed for and by museums; domain names; the establishment and use of the .museum domain, and forms of proprietary identifiers related to social media; and proprietary information concerning donors, patrons, and fundraising (Pantalony 2013: 35–53, n. 3). It has therefore become abundantly clear that museum-related intellectual property no longer comprises, and likely never did comprise, only photographic images of artworks and artefacts. It is possible, however, that our initial attempts to define what museums hold as intellectual property, and our early preoccupations with images of artworks and artefacts, cause persisting misperceptions.

Museum ethics, digital media production and distribution

The International Council of Museums (ICOM) has formulated its own Code of Ethics for Museums that has codified a series of primary museum values. The *ICOM Code of Ethics for Museums* states, variously, that:

1. Museums preserve, interpret and promote the natural and cultural inheritance of humanity by enabling documentation, providing a statement of mission and objectives, and ensuring access to museums and their collections.
2. Museums that maintain collections hold them in trust for the benefit of society and its development by ensuring and promoting provenance, caring for a collection's continuity and documenting the collection, including a full identification and description at the item level.
3. Museums hold primary evidence for establishing and furthering knowledge and hold a particular responsibility for the care, accessibility and interpretation of the primary evidence collected and held.
4. Museums provide opportunities for appreciation, understanding and management of cultural heritage through their educational and outreach programs, interacting with their respective communities and promoting heritage as an integral part of their educational role.[2]

In each of the above-enumerated principles (four of the eight that organize the ICOM Code), there is a strong underlying public purpose and educational mission profiled, also establishing museums as having a fiduciary responsibility towards society in managing their collections. Museums are affirmed as having key ethical responsibilities of circulating and promoting the heritage that they collect, exhibit and preserve as part of their outreach mandates towards the communities that they serve. Under each of the above-enumerated principles, it is also clear that museums can achieve their stated objectives within the context of their own ethical standards by producing and communicating digital media. In all such instances, intellectual property plays a significant role. The question then arises: What happens within this ethical framework if properties attached to the collection are monetized?

Critical assessments of museum intellectual property and commercial uses

Curators and scholars have often been critical of attempts by museums to experiment in the field of digital media production and its monetization. One fairly well-known published assessment is found in Calvin Tomkins' essay titled 'The Modernist ... and the Tradition of the New', published in the *New Yorker Magazine* in November 2001. In his focus on New York's Museum of Modern Art and the tradition of modernism, Tomkins reports some of the frustrations experienced by curators in being expected to grapple with administrative responsibilities associated with digitization and the production of digital media that also connect the museum with 'entrepreneurial' endeavours. In his essay he profiles Kirk Varnedoe, MoMA's then-departing chief curator of painting and sculpture, commenting on museums as viable (money-earning) enterprises. While Varnedoe admitted that the Museum of Modern Art steadfastly resisted the trend, he nevertheless acknowledged the pressures as existing. Varnedoe had voiced grave reservations about the museum's then-recent decision to establish a website in collaboration with the Tate in London that had a commercial purpose at its core:

> The plan, as the marketing honchos explained it, would be to 'leverage the brand identity' of both museums in selling merchandise from their gift shops and providing other services, and Varnedoe, who gags at language like that, was very relieved when the Tate dropped out and the plan was put on hold.
> *(Tomkins 2001: 82)*

Varnedoe was a modern art scholar and educator. His view, admittedly purist and representative of a period now receded, strongly rejected the vision of a museum that concerned itself with business activities connected to primarily collections-based intellectual property.

Even contemporary views of collections-based intellectual property within the field continue to be problematic. In a recent essay as part of a 2014 publication, Jon Ippolito, Professor of New Media and Co-Director of the Still Water Lab and Digital Curation Program at the University of Maine, refers to intellectual property law as the death knell of contemporary culture. His view is that while copyright may assist the development of works in media worth collecting such as film, video and digital media, the increasing intrusion of intellectual property into the cultural *milieu* of creativity can have indirect effects that restrict or prohibit access to works, or inhibit their re-use in the future. He outlines in his essay, 'Death by Law', that there is a danger of rising emphasis on the value of profit over the value of preservation, which itself provides us with a history of what has already been created, and often the context in which it was created (Rinehart and Ippolito 2014: 151–52).

Ippolito's comments are telling, in that where values of profit dominate over values of preservation, he experiences a reaction similar to that of Varnedoe. That is, he becomes frustrated by the impact of intellectual property in not allowing him to carry out what he perceives to be his primary responsibilities based on ethical principles – those of preservation, experimentation and access – despite the fact that intellectual property plays a positive role initially in the creative process. Thus, the utilization of institutional-based intellectual property never enters Ippolito's framework since he perceives any commercialization of collections-based intellectual property as automatically in conflict with scholarship, experimentation and preservation.

The late Stephen Weil, an intellectual property lawyer and former deputy director of the Smithsonian Institution's Hirshhorn Museum and Sculpture Garden, argued in his highly influential book, *Making Museums Matter*, for an emphasis on the 'quality museum'. Weil's thesis is that a museum of quality will first and foremost be purposeful, accountable for its collection, able to manage itself well and effective in its objectives; and that efficiency, on the other hand, while an admirable trait, is not of primary importance (Pantalony 2013: 35–53). That is, the responsibilities of a museum pre-eminently relate to mission and mandate rather than activities that promote merely efficiency of operations, such as financial outcomes. Weil's judgement is one that places primary value on the underlying ethical standards associated with museums, while revenue generation is viewed mainly as a means of achieving efficiency. With respect to the intellectual property resources of collections, however, he pleads in his final chapter for the museum community to reconcile its ethical values of scholarship and public purpose with the need to monetize collections-based intellectual property.

Is there any further case to be made surrounding the monetization of collections-based intellectual property? What about sustainability of programming? Dr Kenneth Crews wrote a highly critical article in 2012 about museum policies and image licensing, arguing that museums have strained the limits of copyright control under US law that curtails the availability of art images far beyond any argument grounded in copyright law. The position taken in his article is that by supplying high-resolution images, museums engage in what can be an active and lucrative licensing service despite the copyright status of the photographic image; or, at the least, this is an activity where the museum, through copyright licensing, strives to cover its expenses. Crews states further that one of the issues motivating his analysis is the potential conflict of interest between a museum's policies and its educational and public interest objectives (Crews 2012: 796–97). However, questions that merit raising are: What about the lucrative nature of image licensing as an activity? And can museums afford to abandon this income source?

As early as 2004, it was recognized that the licensing of museum images generated little, if any, net revenues to museums (Pantalony 2013: 47, n. 1). In an Andrew P. Mellon Foundation-funded study, it was concluded that cultural heritage institutions do not carry out image creation or pursue rights and reproductions activities because of profitability. The costs, particularly where underlying rights are at play, are too high to yield a net profit or even to recover the full costs outlaid. Instead, museums respond to external market activities largely driven by the publishing and media industries, and they use the traditional vehicle – that is, the licence – to regulate the terms and conditions of use. In fact, there is some suggestion that museums are now moving towards a distinction between reproduction in commercial publications in contrast to scholarly uses, and in the latter case do not use licensing terms to limit re-use nor seek to charge a licensing fee for scholarly-related reproduction (Pantalony 2013: 47, n. 1).

In addition, there may be distinct scholarly reasons for a museum to require certain terms and conditions of access. If an image is going to be attributed to a museum, whether directly or indirectly, where the image is of a work in the museum's collection, the image result has to be one of museum quality. Additionally, apart from colour correction and exact likeness as standards expected of museum reproductions, there are scholarly reasons why, at a minimum, the attribution of the author or artist and the attribution of the source or collection are associated requirements for an image obtained from a museum. Regardless of whether a museum maintains a view of art imaging and licensing as a commercial activity, and uses licensing language to control access, it is nevertheless considered good scholarly practice and an expected form of citation to attribute any reproduced artwork to a particular artist; and to indicate the origins of such an image or work as residing within a museum collection. Museums, as educational institutions, must support research and scholarly practices that underlie particular disciplines and the expansion of knowledge.

Kenneth Crews was not incorrect, however, to call for a resolution of conflicting policies and activities concerning the access to images of artworks and artefacts in museum collections – albeit, perhaps for reasons other than those provided in his article. Museum licensing of art images may in fact be 'bad business'. Image licensing may be far worse than a loss leader. Given the complexities of potential underlying rights and the negative impact upon a museum of competing with artists for revenues garnered from licensing images of their art in copyrighted works, a museum might be better served by allowing unfettered access to their images – as long as such access is lawful, and as long as attribution of the respective artist and collection origin or source is provided.

As I suggested in my own publication in 2013, the key to financial sustainability may actually lie in allowing broad open distribution of museum images as a means to promote the collection and the museum as a whole. Museum images thus increase a museum's 'cultural capital' through profiling the overall breadth and scope of a collection. Admittedly a paradigm shift in resource use, this change in attitude can increase global awareness of the museum as an educational resource, amplifying its integrity and uniqueness as an institution and, as a result, enhancing the overall value of its institutional intellectual property – that is, its trademarks in general performance and public goodwill (Pantalony 2013: 47, n.1). Not only can unfettered access to museum images promote institutional intellectual property, but maximizing access for public benefit is itself in keeping with the principles and values enumerated in the ICOM Code of Ethics, as described previously.

Turning to the critical analysis of intellectual property and commercial activities described in this essay: Over the past sixteen years, frustrations have been expressed by museum scholars about instances where intellectual property issues have presented a barrier to preservation, or efforts to educate or carry out scholarly or programmatic activities. Such barriers have appeared to become particularly vexatious where collections-based intellectual property was at issue. Even Stephen Weil, in his theoretical analysis of what constituted a quality museum, as discussed earlier, specially cautioned against placing too much emphasis on efficiency as a way of potentially harming attention to overall quality. That is, museum mission and mandate – or purpose-driven activities – always hold the keys in Weil's scheme of values to ensuring quality and success for a museum.

With respect to the issue of image licensing as a commercial activity – that is, as an activity that leverages a museum collection directly for revenue purposes – most assessments have critiqued this tendency as not only antithetical to museum ethics concerning access to collections, inhibiting both preservation and public outreach, but also as reflective of poor business practice. The only terms and conditions deemed necessary in dictating access to images of a museum collection focus on lawful use of images and required attributions of author, artist, and source or origin, as necessary adjuncts to scholarly citation and good practice educationally.

There are instances where museum intellectual property can be leveraged without generating tension between museum ethics and the museum's need to generate revenue. In fact, if museum institutional intellectual property is managed by the museum purposefully, in keeping with ICOM's Code of Ethics for Museums, it may provide resources for a museum's greatest business opportunity.

Notes

1 In 1999, the Museum of Modern Art and the Tate Modern collaborated in an attempt to create an online commercial space about modern art and culture. The Guggenheim Museum also created an experimental online site called Guggenheim.com for similar purposes. Guggenheim.com launched in 2001 and soon after abandoned its dot.com initiative. MoMA/Tate disbanded its partnership without having created an online site.
2 See ICOM 2004. *ICOM Code of Ethics for Museums*. Paris: International Council of Museums, 2006; material highlighted represents Principles 1, 2, 3, and 4 of the ICOM Code structured around eight principles, and incorporates some of the supporting statements in each of those sections. The full text of the *ICOM Code of Ethics for Museums* is provided as *Appendix I* in the present publication. It is also available online for download from the ICOM website (with links to translations in French, Spanish, and many other languages). The English version is accessible at: http://icom.museum/professional-standards/code-of-ethics.

References

Canadian Heritage Information Network. *Like Light Through A Prism: Analyzing Commercial Markets For Cultural Heritage Content*. Ottawa: Government of Canada, 1999.
Crews, Kenneth D., 2012. 'Museum policies and art images: Conflicting objectives and copyright overreaching'. *Fordham Intellectual Property, Media and Entertainment Law Journal* 22: 795.

ICOM, 2004. *ICOM Code of Ethics for Museums*. Paris: International Council of Museums.

Pantalony, Rina Elster, 2013. *Managing Intellectual Property for Museums*. Geneva: World Intellectual Property Organization, pp. 10–53, at: www.wipo.int/copyright/en/museums_ip/ (accessed 17 December 2015).

Rinehart, Richard and Ippolito, Jon, 2014. *Re-Collection Art, New Media and Social Memory*. Boston, MA: MIT Press, pp. 142–53.

Shapiro, Michael and Miller, Brett I., 1999. *A Museum Guide to Copyright and Trademarks*. Washington, DC: American Association for Museums.

Tomkins, Calvin, 2001. 'The modernist Kirk Varnedoe, the Museum of Modern Art, and the tradition of the new'. *New Yorker Magazine*, 5 November 2001, pp. 72–83.

Weil, Stephen E., 2002. *Making Museums Matter*. Washington DC: Smithsonian Institution Press.

PART III

International action, treaties and benchmarks for protection of the world's heritage

9

UNESCO'S ACTIONS AND INTERNATIONAL STANDARDS CONCERNING MUSEUMS

Mechtild Rössler and Nao Hayashi

The Constitution of UNESCO, adopted on 4 November 1946 in the immediate aftermath of World War II as a means to realize its fundamental purpose of contributing to peace and security by promoting collaboration among the nations. It states the importance of the 'free flow of ideas by word and image' (2-[a]), of 'conserving and protecting works of art' (2[c]), and of the 'exchange of persons, artistic and scientific objects'.

André Malraux, the French Minister of Culture appointed in 1958, was not only one of the most vocal proponents of the international Nubian campaign of UNESCO but also the genitor of the notion of the '*musée imaginaire*' (Malraux 1947). The Nubian campaign was a milestone that later led the international community to the adoption of the 1972 World Heritage Convention. Furthermore, the concept of the imaginary museum is an idea that 'reverberated' in the post-war consciousness of the indivisibility of the world's heritage (Allais 2012).

The UNESCO project, 'Archives of Colour Reproductions of Paintings' (UNESCO 1981), carried out from 1949 to 1979, reflected Malraux's idea to facilitate access of the general public, who would not usually have the opportunity to experience original artworks. The project's main purpose was to build a collection of colour reproductions of paintings through contacts with publishers of reproductions of world-class masterpieces. The selection of prints was made by two expert committees based on the quality of the reproduction, the importance of the artist and the original piece. For more than thirty years of the project's duration, UNESCO published the catalogues consisting of more than 15,000 images. The project also promoted the advancement of technical standards and methods of art reproduction. The prints are still kept at UNESCO Headquarters today.

Malraux's idea, and the critical debates it triggered in subsequent decades, still have relevance when discussing initiatives relating to museums and collections today – notably the central idea of the power of works of art, or what is today more commonly enshrined in legal instruments as 'cultural property' that encompasses a broader range of objects, to transcend divergence and to unite in diversity. By relying on the progress of technology of reproduction, it also expressed an aspiration for the information society, another important aspect of UNESCO's work in promoting a more informed society, and equal access to education and knowledge (Smith 2005).

The UNESCO Recommendation of 1960 concerning the most effective means of rendering museums accessible to everyone

Until the adoption of the new UNESCO global *Recommendation on the Protection and Promotion of Museums and Collections, their Diversity and their Role in Society* in November 2015, the earlier recommendation adopted in 1960 remained the sole global instrument with museums as the subject matter. The General Conference deplored the low attendance of museums by the general public, even in countries with a diversity of museums, while museums 'represent a wealth of culture and human achievement' (UNESCO 1958). It instructed the Director-General to study the most effective means of enabling all segments of society, and especially the working classes, to have liberal access to the treasures of the past, bearing witness to people striving after beauty and culture. From one point of view, the main focus of the debates and final texts of the UNESCO 1960 Recommendation could be seen to complement Malraux's imaginary museum concept, the art reproduction project, and the great Nubian campaign, regarded by some as the summit of a high culture approach. The central theme of the 1960 Recommendation was to promote access of all classes of society to museums and their displays in light of the advancement of industrialization and increase in leisure time and new social conditions.

The importance of museums as a source for cultural advancement of all, as educational institutions and the cultural aspirations of workers, was stressed, and Member States were encouraged to take appropriate steps to ensure that museums are accessible to all without regard to economic or social status (UNESCO 1960: II General Principles). It also provided technical instructions to facilitate the understanding of displayed collections by different people, convenient opening days and hours to accommodate the workers' leisure time, and recommended free admission. The Recommendation also stressed the place and role of museums in the community, which should in turn take part in the activities and development of the museums. Regular and official liaison between museums and local educational institutions and leaders was encouraged.

Museums and collections in different UNESCO Conventions

While UNESCO advocated the importance of museums as institutions for education and peace-building, and implemented famous safeguarding campaigns for built heritage – for the temples of Abu Simbel, Mohenjo-Daro, Borobudur and Venice – a series of legal instruments in the field of culture were adopted from early 1950.

These instruments also refer to technical or functional aspects of museums and collections for the safeguarding of the world's heritage.

The *Universal Copyright Convention*, with Appendix Declaration relating to Articles XVII and Resolution concerning Article XI, adopted in 1952, was intended to provide legal protection to rights of authors, and explicitly mentioned that: 'Each Contracting State undertakes to provide for the adequate and effective protection of the rights of authors and other copyright proprietors in literary, scientific and artistic works, including writings, musical, dramatic and cinematographic works, and paintings, engravings and sculpture' (UNESCO 1952).

The UNESCO *Convention for the Protection of Cultural Property in the Event of Armed Conflict with Regulations for the Execution of the Convention* (1954) and its two protocols (the second established in 1999) includes museums and other cultural institutions as important subjects of protection, safeguarding and respect, being defined themselves as 'cultural property' containing movable cultural property (UNESCO 1954 [1999]: I-[a], [b] and [c]). In this Convention, the definition of cultural property refers to, irrespective of origin or ownership:

> (a) movable or immovable property of great importance to the cultural heritage of every people, such as monuments of architecture, art or history, whether religious or secular; archaeological sites; groups of buildings which, as a whole, are of historical or artistic interest; works of art; manuscripts, books and other objects of artistic, historical or archaeological interest; as well as scientific collections and important collections of books or archives or of reproductions of the property defined above.

The 1954 Convention also provides the guidelines to the High Contracting Parties concerning military regulations, the notion of special protection, immunity of cultural property, and transport of cultural property under special protection and in urgent cases. The first protocol provides guidance in controlling the removal and illegal export of cultural property from occupied territory. Importantly, the first protocol also stipulates the obligation of the High Contracting Parties to return cultural property deposited in the territory of another High Contracting Party (UNESCO 1954a: II-5).

The 1962 UNESCO *Recommendation concerning the Safeguarding of Beauty and Character of Landscapes and Sites* was an important step towards the enhancement and protection of landscapes in the broader sense. It also included:

> isolated small sites, whether natural or urban, together with portions of a landscape of particular interest, should be scheduled. Areas which provide a fine view, and areas and buildings surrounding an outstanding monument should also be scheduled. Each of these scheduled sites, areas and buildings should be the subject of a special administrative decision of which the owner should be duly notified.
>
> *(UNESCO 1962: Article 20)*

This concerned many museums which were located in historic buildings and surrounded by landscape parks. This Recommendation is further relevant for the topic of the 2016 ICOM General Conference on 'Museums and Cultural Landscapes'. The President of ICOM noted in the first announcement that:

> [t]he international museum community will gather together in Milan around the theme of 'Museums and cultural landscapes', which raises a number of issues dear to all of us, as museums around the world strive to redefine their roles and positions in relation to their communities and with respect to the cultural heritage that lies beyond their walls.[1]

The UNESCO *Recommendation on the Means of Prohibiting and Preventing the Illicit Export, Import and Transfer of Ownership of Cultural Property* (1964), a precursor of the 1970 Convention, defines the term 'cultural property' as:

> [...] movable and immovable property of great importance to the cultural heritage of a country, such as works of art and architecture, manuscripts, books and other property of artistic, historical or archaeological interest, ethnological documents, type specimens of flora and fauna, scientific collections and important collections of books and archives, including musical archives.
> *(UNESCO 1964: I-1)*

In 1968, the UNESCO *Recommendation concerning the Preservation of Cultural Property Endangered by Public or Private Works* was adopted, and extended its scope to the vestiges, sites and structures that are not yet excavated (UNESCO 1968: I-2).

The UNESCO *Convention on the Means of Prohibiting and Preventing the Illicit Import, Export and Transfer of Ownership of Cultural Property* was adopted in 1970 as the first international legal framework concerning the illicit trafficking and movement of cultural property. It provides an important guideline for museums to frame their ethical standards and acquisition policies. Its broader definition of cultural property includes most types of museum collections (UNESCO 1970: Article 1). It encourages the elaboration of national laws and legislations, the establishment of national special services for the protection of cultural heritage (Article 5), as well as the importance of establishing museums as institutions vital to the preservation and presentation of cultural property. The establishment and keeping up-to-date of a national inventory, of protected property, 'a list of important public and private cultural property whose export would constitute an appreciable impoverishment of the national cultural heritage', is explicitly mentioned as a provision to be respected by a State Party. It should also be noted that the 1970 Convention, while addressing the governments as State Parties, also encompasses private cultural property that is also important for a nation, though the enforceability on private collections remains difficult in the sphere of public international law, and requires a complementary instrument as mentioned further below.

The 1970 Convention also mentions an obligation of a State Party for:

> establishing, for the benefit of those concerned (e.g. curators, collectors and antique dealers) rules in conformity with the ethical principles set forth in this Convention; and in accordance with Article 5(e), taking steps to ensure the observance of those rules.
>
> *(UNESCO 1970)*

In general, the regulations on the circulation of cultural property, its import and export, are also included notably using an appropriate form of certificate that warrants the exportation, in accordance with Article 6 (UNESCO 1970). Provisions for States concerning the acquisition by their museums prohibit the acquisition of cultural property of another State Party when illegally exported after the entry into force of this Convention, in the States concerned, in accordance with Article 7 (UNESCO 1970). It further prohibits the import of stolen cultural property from a museum, a religious or secular public monument or similar institution in another State Party, provided that 'such property is documented as appertaining to the inventory of that institution' (UNESCO 1970). The possible return of illicitly imported or stolen cultural property is also guided concerning recovery and return, under the condition that 'the requesting State provides just compensation to an innocent purchaser or to a person who has valid title to that property' (UNESCO 1970).

The 1972 UNESCO *Convention concerning the Protection of the World Cultural and Natural Heritage* is a unique instrument that does not specifically mention museums. However, indirectly it also covers sites, which cover museums, such as the Plantin-Moretus House-Workshops-Museum Complex (Belgium), or include museums within World Heritage property, such as the Museum Island, Berlin (Germany). In its 1972 Preamble, the *World Heritage Convention* considered:

> that it is essential ... to adopt new provisions in the form of a convention establishing an effective system of collective protection of the cultural and natural heritage of outstanding universal value, organized on a permanent basis and in accordance with modern scientific methods.
>
> *(UNESCO 1972a)*

At the same time, the 1972 UNESCO *Recommendation concerning the Protection, at National Level, of the Cultural and Natural Heritage* covered such heritage at the national level, calling, among other items for Member States to 'cooperate with regard to the protection, conservation and presentation of the cultural and natural heritage, seeking aid, if it seems desirable, from international organizations, both intergovernmental and non-governmental' (UNESCO 1972b: Para. 66).

In the implementation of the 1972 *World Heritage Convention*, museums played an increasing role to make the public understand the site and its Outstanding Universal value of World Heritage places, in particular at archaeological sites, interpretation centres at large-scale sites, or properties which are of difficult access due to their location or transnational serial character. The ever-growing ecological or cultural heritage tourism, enhanced by the success of the UNESCO World Heritage programme, offers a framework for site-related museums to promote intercultural understanding and interpretation of the complex values at a given site. Collaboration with ICOM on museums for sustainable development, education and community programmes was crucial in many regions. About 8,000 museums or interpretation centres are located at or within the more than 1,000 World Heritage properties in 163 countries. The World Heritage Committee called in some cases directly upon the services of ICOM, such as in the case of Afghanistan: '[i]nvites the Director-General to organize actions similar to those undertaken in Angkor (Cambodia) with the International Council of Museums (ICOM) to increase the Afghan national capacity to prevent illicit trafficking of heritage' (UNESCO 2002).

UNESCO also adopted in 1976 the *Recommendation concerning the International Exchange of Cultural Property*, which promotes licit international exchange and circulation of cultural property among cultural institutions.[2]

> The circulation of cultural property, when regulated by legal, scientific and technical conditions calculated to prevent illicit trading in and damage to such property, is a powerful means of promoting mutual understanding and appreciation among nations, but also to correct some inequality in the legal international flow of cultural property, represented by loans and deposits, which were most often as an unilateral operations and phenomenon in industrialised countries and in large public institutions such as museums. Interestingly, this instrument promoted at that time the accession of '[...] some of these items, which are of only minor or secondary importance for these institutions because of their plurality, would be welcomed as valuable accessions by institutions in other countries' and encourages a systematic policy of exchanges among cultural institutions 'by which each would part with its surplus items in return for objects that it lacked, would not only be enriching to all parties but would also lead to a better use of the international community's cultural heritage which is the sum of all the national heritages'.
>
> *(UNESCO 1976)*

It is interesting to note that transfer of ownership or derestriction of cultural property belonging to a public body or a cultural institution was promoted as a means of intercultural exchange, while it draws the attention of cultural institutions to 'the opportunities for reassembling a presently dismembered work that would be afforded by a system of successive loans, without transfer of ownership, enabling each of the holding institutions to take its turn to display the work in its entirety' (UNESCO 1976: III-12-[4]). Moreover, it still maintains coherence with the 1970 Convention by stating that:

[t]he development of international exchanges should enable the cultural institutions of the different Member States to enlarge their collections by acquiring cultural property of lawful origin, accompanied by documentation
calculated to bring out their full cultural significance. Accordingly, Member
States should take all necessary steps, with the help of the international organizations concerned, to ensure that the development of such exchanges goes
hand in hand with an extension of the action taken against every possible
form of illicit trading in cultural property.

(UNESCO 1976: V)

Given the difficulties of dealing with the issues of private law facilitating the
movement of illegally acquired objects, a legal loophole where UNESCO, as an
intergovernmental organization, could not intervene, the UNIDROIT *Convention
on Stolen or Illegally Exported Cultural Objects* of 1995, a framework under private
law, has particular importance as a complement to the provisions provided by the
1970 Convention and other instruments relating to the ban on illicit trafficking in
cultural property, which should be initiated by governments. Elaborated at the
request of UNESCO, this instrument was developed for States to commit to
uniform treatment for restitution of stolen or illegally exported cultural objects and
enable restitution claims to be processed directly through national courts. The
UNIDROIT Convention covers all stolen cultural objects, unlike the 1970 Convention, which specifies that the objects should be inventoried and declared.

The UNESCO *Convention on the Protection of the Underwater Cultural Heritage*,
adopted in 2001, also recommends collaboration with museums for safeguarding
this category of heritage; it also gives room for new forms of museums, including
underwater museums, and using new technologies to provide access to the underwater cultural heritage located on the bottom of the oceans or inland water
bodies.

The operational directives of the UNESCO *Convention for the Safeguarding of the
Intangible Cultural Heritage*, adopted in 2003, defines museums as important institutions for collection, documentation and conservation data on intangible cultural
heritage and public information on it (109), as well as agents of dissemination of the
information on intangible cultural heritage in need of urgent safeguarding
(118 [b]).

In 2005, UNESCO adopted the *Convention on the Protection and Promotion of the
Diversity of Cultural Expressions*, thereby expanding its field of international standards-
setting from heritage to contemporary creativity and expressions. While without
directly mentioning the role of museums in achieving its principles, the Convention also seeks a subtle balance in the midst of an ever-increasing process of globalization, and, as a response to this challenge, an increase in the will of diversification
of cultures, of which museums are major agents of transmission and creation. Cultural and creative industries directly concern activities of museums, notably through
the development of local products.

Operational projects

Along with the standards-setting instruments, UNESCO's field operations have greatly contributed to promoting principles and ethics in safeguarding heritage and transmitting related knowledge. The Nubian campaign gave birth to the Nubia Museum in Aswan, inaugurated in 1997, to house the more than 3,000 objects found during the excavations carried out as part of UNESCO's International Campaign to Save the Monuments of Nubia. This campaign was converted, at the completion of the rescue operation and the opening of the Nubia Museum in 1980, into the ambitious project of the establishment of the National Museum of Egyptian Civilisation in Cairo (UNESCO 1980). UNESCO continues to assume the Secretariat of the Executive Committee, composed of Member States (UNESCO 2015a).

UNESCO was closely associated with the development of the State Hermitage Museum in the Russian Federation from 1993. The organization provided expertise in complementing the museum's Master Plan and established the Hermitage UNESCO project in 1994. The cooperation raised funds, and UNESCO provided expertise in specific areas of the repair and revitalization of the museum, both from managerial and physical reforms, for instance, for the restoration of the Rubens gallery and the new entrance through the Winter Palace courtyard (UNESCO 2003b).

With the establishment of the International Coordinating Committee for the World Heritage site of Angkor in 1993, UNESCO has also been closely associated with the management of cultural property in Cambodia, through continued assistance to the National Museum in Phnom Penh and the national authority in charge of the management of the Angkor site. The establishment of the artefact inventory in cooperation with École française d'Extrême-Orient since 1995 and the nationwide training for storage and inventories in the 2000s are the most notable examples of this collaborative support (UNESCO 2009). In addition, UNESCO provided support and expertise to facilitate the return of Khmer cultural property kept in foreign museum institutions. Its current support is aimed at revitalizing World Heritage site-related museums located in the three Mekong countries, that is, Cambodia, Viet Nam and Laos (UNESCO 2014) and establishing a centralized storage for all artefacts unearthed from the Angkor site and other major archaeological sites of the Khmer Empire, such as Koh Keh and Kulen.

In the 2000s, UNESCO played a central role in protecting and safeguarding the collections of the National Museum of Afghanistan, by coordinating international efforts to help restore its damaged collections that represent the intercultural influence through the Silk Road (UNESCO 2006; UNESCO 2010), as well as by mediating several operations of establishing 'safe havens' for priceless Afghan collections (UNESCO 2007), in cooperation with several national and international private institutions which ensured stewardship of these collections.

The National Museum of Iraq is another institution that UNESCO has been closely associated with for its rebirth. The total number of collections looted around

2003 was said to be approximately 15,000 items, and as of 2014–15, 28.6 per cent of these looted objects were returned to the museum. UNESCO has raised more than $US30 million to support the Iraqi heritage sector, notably through capacity building for museums (UNESCO 2005b) and World Heritage sites.

Training activities for museum professionals in all continents have been carried out through the network of UNESCO's field offices, as well as in collaboration with important partners such as the International Council of Museums (ICOM) and the International Centre for the Study of the Preservation and Restoration of Cultural Property (ICCROM), notably in the field of preventive conservation (UNESCO 2011a). According to the joint research conducted by UNESCO and ICCROM in 2011, the world's museum collections remain in an alarming situation where 25 per cent of 1,490 museum institutions in 136 countries surveyed did not have an object movement register, an accession register (or one that was up to date), location codes, or a main catalogue, neither in paper nor computerized format.

Since 2011, cultural heritage, including museums, has become a deliberate target or collateral victim in armed conflicts. While the field rescue operations remain impractical due to the absence of international mandate and security and safety provisions, UNESCO has made utmost efforts in mobilizing its network, in the concerned countries and abroad, to minimize the damage to cultural heritage and museums. Technical training was carried out with museum professionals in conflict zones for first-aid operations, risk preparedness and emergency documentation, which will soon be published in the form of practical guidelines to assist museum professionals conducting emergency operations under conflict. At the UN level, several resolutions directly and indirectly relating to cultural heritage protection were adopted, and UNESCO follows the implementation of Resolution 2199 relating especially to the prevention of illicit trade of looted objects from Iraq and Syria.

Towards the new international standards-setting instrument – the new UNESCO *Recommendation on the Protection and Promotion of Museums and Collections, their Diversity and their Role in Society*

The number of museums around the world has increased significantly, from 22,000 in 1975 to 55,000 in 2012 (Hudson and Nicholls 1975; Sauer 2004; De Gruyter 2012). Global tourism and regional development are boosting the museum sector with a more diverse and demanding public as a result of changes in their perceived role in societies. These changes have brought about new challenges for policy makers, stakeholders and professionals alike. In addition to a museum's historical role in heritage preservation and dissemination of related knowledge within society, defined by the three basic functions – preservation, research and communication – new, increasingly growing but potentially conflicting roles have emerged. A museum's social, educational and economic roles have new effects on its operation at multiple levels. The internationalization of museum institutions, triggered by globalization, offers opportunities for museums to benefit from greater openness to new endeavours, circulation of resources and cooperation perspectives, while the inequalities among museums worldwide remain important in terms of human, financial and institutional resources. The diversity in management models, collections to be preserved and functions is also an important factor when reflecting on the applicability of the policy guidelines. These inequalities and unevenness remain to be addressed through innovative mechanisms of cooperation.

The UNESCO General Conference in November 2011 initiated a discussion on the desirability of a new normative instrument that would acknowledge the new roles of museums (UNESCO 2011b: 36 C/Resolution 46). As a result, an international experts meeting was hosted in Rio de Janeiro in July 2012, co-organized by UNESCO and the Brazilian Institute of Museums (IBRAM) in consultation with ICOM. Upon debating the subject at that session in November 2013, the General Conference recognized the need for a new standards-setting instrument, by admitting that the existing international instruments in the field of museums do not sufficiently address contemporary challenges and larger contributions of museums to sustainable development and intercultural dialogue. It requested UNESCO, as the only United Nations agency with a mandate in the field of culture and as a global forum for multilateral collaboration, to establish the legal and policy standards for reinforcing the protection and promotion of museums and collections worldwide in the form of a Recommendation (UNESCO 2013: 37 C/Resolution 43).

An Intergovernmental Meeting of Legal and Technical Experts, held at UNESCO Headquarters on 27 and 28 May 2015, gathered nearly 170 experts, designated by eighteen observer organizations and a total of seventy-three Member States to discuss the draft Recommendation, prepared in cooperation with ICOM. A final draft text of a new UNESCO *Recommendation on the Protection and Promotion of Museums and Collections, their Diversity and their Role in Society* was adopted by the expert meeting (UNESCO 2015b).[3] The spirit that motivated the debates was to make possible the most useful text to Member States, by reflecting a wide variety of situations, approaches and value systems to provide general guidelines to be adapted to specific contexts.

The Recommendation provides guidance to Member States in a number of important areas such as supporting adherence to legal and professional standards, preserving the diversity of museums, stimulating national and international collaboration, private and public funding mechanisms and partnerships, compiling professional inventories, digitization and good practices. The subtle balance of the traditional role of museums with their new, notably economic role and necessity to multiply economic revenue, was maintained. Moreover, a very important paragraph on creating constructive dialogue with Indigenous peoples was agreed on.

Conclusion

UNESCO has a long-standing involvement in museums worldwide: through its legal instruments, but also through the journal *Museum* created in 1948, now run by ICOM as *Museum International*. In many of UNESCO's recommendations and declarations, museums are covered directly (notably the 1960 and 2015 Recommendations) or indirectly including in its Conventions, most prominently the 1970 and 1972 Conventions.

UNESCO and its Member States, by endorsing the provisions expressed in UNESCO's various legal instruments and notably by the adoption of the new global Recommendation in 2015, recognized the increasing significance of museums and collections in many of the fundamental missions of the organization. As the most prominent global institution for safeguarding heritage in all its forms, tangible and intangible, movable or immovable, museums play an ever-increasing role in stimulating creativity, providing opportunities for research and formal and informal education, thus contributing to social and human development throughout the world.

UNESCO will implement its new museum Recommendation by inviting Member States to adapt this instrument to their specific institutional and socio-cultural contexts, and will explore the modalities in adapting their legal, administrative and institutional frameworks, developing appropriate principles and guidelines through consultations with museum institutions and other partners at a national level.

It is equally important to integrate museums and collections into a wider framework of national and regional cultural policy development so that careful attention can be given to the planning, design and implementation of projects relating to museums and collections. International cooperation frameworks should be further developed to bridge the gaps among museums, in terms of technical and institutional expertise, especially to cope with the threat to cultural heritage in times of conflict.

Strengthening UNESCO's actions in preserving heritage and fostering the museum's role in social, educational and economic development will certainly complement the actions led by the museum community worldwide, for which ICOM provides the most important network.

Notes

1 For online access to the complete PDF document, see the ICOM website: http://icom. museum/fileadmin/user_upload/pdf/ICOM_2016/neu_final_First_Ann_2016–2.pdf (accessed 18 December 2015).

2 Herein, 'international exchange' shall be taken to mean any transfer of ownership, use or custody of cultural property between States or cultural institutions in different countries whether it takes the form of the loan, deposit, sale or donation of such property carried out under such conditions as may be agreed between the parties concerned.

3 The full text of the UNESCO *Recommendation Concerning the Protection and Promotion of Museums and Collections, their Diversity and their Role in Society*, 2015, is provided as *Appendix V* in the present publication. See also François Mairesse, 'The UNESCO *Recommendation on the Protection and Promotion of Museums and Collections, their Diversity and Role in Society*', in Bernice Murphy (ed.), *Museums, Ethics and Cultural Heritage*. London: Routledge, 2016, Chapter 10.

References

Allais, L., 2012. 'The design of the Nubian Desert: Monuments, mobility, and the space of global culture' in *Governing by Design, Architecture, Economy and Politics in the Twentieth Century*. Pittsburgh, PA: University of Pittsburgh Press.

De Gruyter, 2012 (19th edn). *Museums of the World*. Berlin: De Gruyter & Co.

Hudson, K. and Nicholls, A., 1975. *The Directory of World Museums*. New York: Columbia University Press, 1975.

Isar, Y.R., 2014. 'UNESCO, museums and development', in P. Basu and W. Modest (eds), *Museums, Heritage and International Development*. London: Routledge.

Malraux, A., 1947. *Musée imaginaire*. Paris: Skira.

Sauer, 2004 [1992] (11th edn). *Museums of the World*. Munich: K.G Sauer-Verlag.

Smith, D., 2005. 'The art of the grand project: Malraux's imaginary museum and its contemporary legacy', in J. Gratton and M. Sheringham (eds), *The Art of the Project: Projects and Experiments in Modern French Culture*. New York and Oxford: Berghahn Books.

Tissot, Francine, 2006. *Catalogue of the National Museum of Afghanistan 1931–1985*. Paris: UNESCO Publishing.

UNESCO, 1952. The *Universal Copyright Convention, with Appendix Declaration relating to Articles XVII and Resolution concerning Article XI*, at: http://portal.unesco.org/en/ev.php-URL_ID=15381&URL_DO=DO_TOPIC&URL_SECTION=201.html (accessed 15 November 2015).

UNESCO, 1954a. *Convention for the Protection of Cultural Property in the Event of Armed Conflict with Regulations for the Execution of the Convention*, at: http://portal.unesco.org/en/ev.php-URL_ID=13637&URL_DO=DO_TOPIC&URL_SECTION=201.html (accessed November 2015).

UNESCO, 1954b. *Convention for the Protection of Cultural Property in the Event of Armed Conflict with Regulations for the Execution of the Convention* [First Protocol], at: http://portal.unesco.org/en/ev.php-URL_ID=15391&URL_DO=DO_TOPIC&URL_SECTION=201.html (accessed 15 November 2015).

UNESCO, 1954 [1999]. *Convention for the Protection of Cultural Property in the Event of Armed Conflict* with *Regulations for the Execution of the Convention* [Second Protocol], at: http://portal.unesco.org/en/ev.php-URL_ID=15207&URL_DO=DO_TOPIC& URL_SECTION=201.html (accessed 15 November 2015).

UNESCO, 1958. 'Records of the General Conference (9C/DR/18Rev)', at: http://unesdoc.unesco.org/images/0011/001145/114585E.pdf (accessed 15 November 2015).

UNESCO, 1960. 'Recommendation concerning the most effective means of rendering museums accessible to everyone', at: http://portal.unesco.org/en/ev.php-URL_ID=13063&URL_DO=DO_TOPIC&URL_SECTION=201.html (accessed 15 November 2015).

UNESCO, 1962. *Recommendation concerning the Safeguarding of Beauty and Character of Landscapes and Sites*, at: http://portal.unesco.org/en/ev.php-URL_ID=13067&URL_DO=DO_TOPIC&URL_SECTION=201.html (accessed 15 November 2015).

UNESCO, 1964. *Recommendation on the Means of Prohibiting and Preventing the Illicit Export, Import and Transfer of Ownership of Cultural Property*, at: http://portal.unesco.org/en/ev.php-URL_ID=13083&URL_DO=DO_TOPIC&URL_SECTION=201.html (accessed 15 November 2015).

UNESCO, 1968. *Recommendation concerning the Preservation of Cultural Property Endangered by Public or Private Works*, at: http://portal.unesco.org/en/ev.php-URL_ID=13085&URL_DO=DO_TOPIC&URL_SECTION=201.html (accessed 15 November 2015).

UNESCO, 1970. *Convention on the Means of Prohibiting and Preventing the Illicit Import, Export and Transfer of Ownership of Cultural Property*, at: http://portal.unesco.org/en/ev.

php-URL_ID=13039&URL_DO=DO_TOPIC&URL_SECTION=201.html (accessed 15 November 2015).

UNESCO, 1972a. *Basic Texts of the 1972 World Heritage Convention*, at: http://whc.unesco. org/documents/publi_basictexts_en.pdf (accessed 15 November 2015).

UNESCO, 1972b. *Recommendation concerning the Protection, at National Level, of the Cultural and Natural Heritage*, at: http://portal.unesco.org/en/ev.php-URL_ID=13087&URL_DO=DO_TOPIC&URL_SECTION=201.html (accessed 15 November 2015).

UNESCO, 1976. *Recommendation concerning the International Exchange of Cultural Property*, at: http://portal.unesco.org/en/ev.php-URL_ID=13132&URL_DO=DO_TOPIC&URL_SECTION=201.html (accessed 15 November 2015).

UNESCO, 1980. 'Resolutions of the General Conference C21 Res. 4/11', at: http:// unesdoc.unesco.org/images/0011/001140/114029e.pdf (accessed 15 November 2015).

UNESCO, 1981. 'Catalogue of reproductions of painting, 1860–1979', with seventeen projects for exhibition, at: http://atom.archives.unesco.org/ag-13-archives-of-colour-reproductions-of-paintings (accessed 15 November 2015).

UNESCO, 2001. *Convention on the Protection of the Underwater Cultural Heritage*, at: www. unesco.org/new/en/culture/themes/underwater-cultural-heritage/2001-convention/ official-text (accessed 15 November 2015).

UNESCO, 2002. 'Implementation of the World Heritage Convention in Afghanistan', at: http://whc.unesco.org/en/decisions/915 (accessed 15 November 2015).

UNESCO, 2003a. *Convention for the Safeguarding of the Intangible Cultural Heritage*, at: www. unesco.org/culture/ich/en/convention (accessed 15 November 2015).

UNESCO, 2003b. 'The New Hermitage'. *MUSEUM International*, 1 (217): 4–7, at: http:// portal.unesco.org/culture/en/ev.php-URL_ID=14402&URL_DO=DO_TOPIC&URL_SECTION=201.html (accessed 15 November 2015).

UNESCO, 2005a. *Convention on the Protection and Promotion of the Diversity of Cultural Expressions*, at: http://en.unesco.org/creativity/convention/2005-convention/2005-convention-text (accessed November 2015).

UNESCO, 2005b. *Restoring Conservation Labs of the Iraq National Museum*, at: www.unesco. org/new/en/iraq-office/culture/museum-sector/conservation-labs/ (accessed November 2015).

UNESCO 2006, *Catalogue of the National Museum of Afghanistan 1931–1985*.

UNESCO, 2007. 'Museum-in-Exile: Swiss Foundation safeguards over 1,400 Afghan artefacts', at: www.unesco.org/new/en/culture/themes/museums/museum-projects/archive/ museum-in-exile-swiss-foundation-safeguards-over-1400-afghan-artefacts/#c167606 (accessed November 2015).

UNESCO, 2009. 'Training seminar for staff in charge of the Documentation and Inventory of Cambodian Museums', at: www.unesco.org/new/en/culture/themes/museums/ museum-projects/archive/training-seminar-for-staff-in-charge-of-the-documentation-and-inventory-of-cambodian-museums/#c163911 (accessed November 2015).

UNESCO, 2010. *The Museums of Ghazni, Afghanistan*. Paris: UNESCO Publishing, at: www.unesco.org/new/en/culture/themes/museums/museum-projects/archive/the-museums-of-ghazni-afghanistan/ (accessed November 2015).

UNESCO, 2011a. 'UNESCO-ICCROM Partnership for the Preventive Conservation of Endangered Museum Collections in Developing Countries (2007–2010)', at: www. unesco.org/new/en/culture/themes/museums/unescoiccrom-re-org/unesco-iccrom-partnership-for-the-preventive-conservation-of-endangered-museum-collections-in-developing-countries-2007-2010/ (accessed November 2015).

UNESCO, 2011b. 'General Conference 36 C/Resolution 46', at: http://unesdoc.unesco. org/images/0021/002150/215084e.pdf (accessed November 2015).

UNESCO, 2013. 'General Conference 37 C/Resolution 43', at: http://unesdoc.unesco. org/images/0021/002150/215084e.pdf (accessed 15 November 2015).

UNESCO, 2014. *Revitalising World Heritage Site Museums for a Better Interpretation of Living Heritage Sites in Cambodia, Laos and Viet Nam*, at: www.unesco.org/new/en/culture/ themes/museums/world-heritage-site-museums (accessed November 2015).

UNESCO, 2015a. 'International Campaign for the Establishment of the Nubia Museum in Aswan and the National Museum of Egyptian Civilization (NMEC) in Cairo', at: www. unesco.org/new/en/culture/themes/museums/museum-projects/international-campaign-for-nubia-museum-and-nmec (accessed November 2015).

UNESCO, 2015b. *Recommendation on the Protection and Promotion of Museums and Collections*, at: www.unesco.org/new/en/culture/themes/museums/recommendation-on-the-protection-and-promotion-of-museums-and-collections (accessed November 2015).

UNIDROIT, 1995. *Convention on Stolen or Illegally Exported Cultural Objects*, at: www.unid-roit.org/instruments/cultural-property/1995-convention (accessed November 2015).

Yusuf, A.A. (ed.), 2007. *L'action normative de l'UNESCO. Volume 1: Elaboration des règles Internationales sur l'Education, la Science et la Culture*. Leiden and Boston: UNESCO/ Martinus Nuhoff Publishers.

10

THE UNESCO *RECOMMENDATION ON THE PROTECTION AND PROMOTION OF MUSEUMS AND COLLECTIONS, THEIR DIVERSITY AND THEIR ROLE IN SOCIETY*

François Mairesse

Although the museum is often presented as a place dedicated to the enhancement of knowledge, of education and of enjoyment, it may also be constituted as a political instrument serving a governmental organization to which it is responsible. The museum might even be used to disseminate questionable ideas as well as contestable scientific theories; to celebrate bellicose or pacifist values; to either stir racial hatred or bring out togetherness. Fortunately, the positive dimension of the museum was largely consolidated through the creation of the International Museums Office in 1926 by the League of Nations, both of which were presented as '[established] institutions for intellectual cooperation', while international cooperation was deemed to be a cornerstone for advancing understanding between peoples – and hence for ensuring peace.[1]

From 1945 onwards, a similar mandate led to the creation of the United Nations Educational, Scientific and Cultural Organization (UNESCO); and the founders of ICOM were inspired by the same aspirations in the following year (1946). Undeniably, however, the diverse reasons that nowadays lead to the creation of museums have sometimes moved in different directions from the early ambitions guiding these post-war cultural organizations. Where they were motivated, for example, by shared concerns for the preservation of humanity's common heritage, for goals of universal education and mutual understanding, these ideals often seem forsaken today when museums espouse seemingly more trivial purposes, such as publicity, prestige, or local economic and touristic development that is not shaped by a cultural vision.

It was in the context of these many changes in the contemporary vision and purpose of museums, while the spectacular growth in their number and proliferation across countries and continents seems unflagging, that debates in UNESCO's General Conference meetings in 2013–15 led to the adoption of the UNESCO *Recommendation on the Protection and Promotion of Museums and Collections, their Diversity and their Role in Society* on 17 November 2015. This instrument for international intergovernmental policy development aims to emphasize the function of museums within society and their propensity to foster peaceful world relations, as museums dedicate themselves to the development of knowledge and the bringing together of peoples around the care of a shared heritage.

UNESCO and museums

UNESCO's role in support of heritage may be considered in this perspective of common cause. The emblematic campaign for the safeguarding of Nubian monuments, which began in the 1960s, was a key moment in the rising awareness that heritage outstrips borders, and that the responsibility for it falls to all of mankind.[2] This logic of protection and promotion, implemented by the many UNESCO-led actions, is embodied in the *Convention concerning the Protection of the World Cultural and Natural Heritage* adopted by the UNESCO General Conference on 16 November 1972, and then, some three decades later, in the *Convention for the Safeguarding of the Intangible Cultural Heritage*, in 2003.

UNESCO has always played a leading role in museum-dedicated programmes, in the development of museum teaching programmes and training seminars, as well as provision of financial support for museums leading to the creation of new institutions. From a legal standpoint, the instruments adopted by the General Conference have – in most cases – been conceived from a heritage perspective, which focuses on the preservation of tangible cultural objects and heritage, encompassing monuments and sites as well as museum collections. Thus the *Convention for the Protection of Cultural Property in the Event of Armed Conflict* (The Hague Convention) and its two protocols (of 1954 and 1999); the *Convention on the Means of Prohibiting and Preventing the Illicit Import, Export and Transfer of Ownership of Cultural Property* (1970); augmented by the UNIDROIT *Convention on Stolen or Illegally Exported Cultural Goods* (UNIDROIT 1995); the *Convention on the Protection of Underwater Cultural Heritage* (2001); and the *Recommendation on International Principles Applicable to Archaeological Excavations* (1956): altogether, this constitutes an important list of legal instruments adopted by UNESCO in the course of its existence, which have directly influenced museum collections in general, and movable objects in particular, in terms of the acquisition and preservation of collections.

Despite all these connections, the sole instrument dedicated exclusively to museums and adopted by a UNESCO General Conference dates back more than half a century: this is the *Recommendation concerning the Most Effective Means of Rendering Museums Accessible to Everyone* (1960). While its content remains relevant today, the document has been somewhat neglected, for a recommendation – as the term itself implies – cannot compel States to enforce it. By contrast, a convention, when it is ratified, requires a strict execution of its terms by signatory States.

Thus the question of drawing up a legal instrument specifically dedicated to museums and their different functions was highlighted progressively. It is worth pointing out here that such instruments – rather than being aimed at established museum professionals – are directed to Member States required (or, in the case of a recommendation, called upon) to translate in their national legislation a set of recommendations related to the activities and management of museums in their territory. The aim of these texts is to foster awareness of important matters affecting museums among States and society at large, while ICOM is charged to utilize its world networks to address museum professionals directly. A number of States already have legislation dedicated to the museum field, but it is far from the case for all of the 195 Member States of UNESCO. It is therefore necessary to consider the general framework for museums' activity and their many functions, all the more so since that the current context is *a fortiori* one of unprecedented change, related to globalization and transformations across all social conditions.

Accordingly, at the 36th session of the General Conference of UNESCO in 2011, a draft resolution on the protection and promotion of museums and collections – representing the work carried out by UNESCO as initiated and presented by Member States – was submitted by Brazil. The idea of heritage protection and promotion is at the very heart of previous conventions or recommendations on heritage and cultural diversity, but at this stage no document existed calling for the protection and promotion of museums *per se*, or more specifically their many functions and activities.

It is interesting to mention the characteristics of the country that brought forward the proposal, Brazil – then benefiting from a vibrant economy that enabled it to become one of the foremost developing countries of the early 2000s. As such, Brazil organized the ICOM General Conference in 2013 (in Rio), and many other major world events serving to develop its own museum networks while, at the same time, affirming a vision that would differ from that advanced by 'superstar museums' (Frey 1998) – such as the British Museum, the Louvre or the various Guggenheim museums. In many ways, the general model of the museum, as it emerged historically and through the activity of the most popular museums, is not universally acknowledged as the only reference model. Additional dimensions, especially the social role of museums or their political influence, are deemed just as critical. Brazil played an active part in enabling a number of collections not strictly related to museums (but in the eyes of some professionals, comparable in importance to museum heritage – for example, university collections, study and research collections) to merit equal recognition for their role in heritage protection.

And so the first international meeting of experts was organized in Rio de Janeiro in 2012, in partnership with ICOM and IBRAM (the Brazilian Institute of Museums), to discuss the goal of implementing an international standard-setting instrument for these issues.[3] Experts identified many needs in the museum field, highlighting: (1) the general importance of museums as agents of social change, forums of cultural diversity, formal and informal training centres and stimulators of economic development; (2) the goal of ratification by Member States of current legal instruments; (3) the enhancement of museum policies in terms of sustainable development, social inclusion, use of information and communications technology, etc.; (4) the development of international cooperation; and (5) highlighting measures specifically dedicated to museums.

A few months later, this first effort was complemented by two reports. The first was a legal report drafted by Patrick J. O'Keefe, exploring the current perimeter of existing instruments, as well as the scope of new instruments intended to answer the above-mentioned needs. Meanwhile the second report described in more detail the museological aspects that could be included in a new instrument – drafted later by the present author, in collaboration with ICOM.

The drafting of a recommendation on museums – rather than a convention – resulted from the dialogue between experts during the 2012 Rio meeting and the subsequent content of both reports. In many ways, a convention would have been too constraining: not only does it bind, by principle, Member States (for example, through organizational requirements or provision of minimum funding levels), but it also requires financial resources for monitoring, which are unavailable from UNESCO funds. The risk therefore was that Member States likely to ratify a convention would prove to be insufficient in number. A recommendation thus appeared to be more relevant and feasible to gain approval by the 37th General Conference in late 2013. UNESCO's mission was then to prepare, in close partnership with ICOM, the ad hoc document needed to advance this process.

Therefore ICOM – both its General Secretariat and network alike – was involved from the very beginning in formulating UNESCO's reflection on museums. UNESCO pursued the partnership initiated with ICOM in 2012, in a shared endeavour to prepare a first-draft text that would serve as a basis for the debate on the recommendation project. This was scheduled for an intergovernmental meeting of category II experts, whereby a final text would be elaborated and voted on by the 38th General Conference, in November 2015.[4] In a relatively short time and in collaboration with UNESCO, ICOM prepared a first-draft recommendation to be considered for comments of Member States, and then of experts.

The General Secretariat of ICOM commissioned a team which I had the honour to join – composed of France Desmarais and Raphaël Roig, supported by Anne-Catherine Robert-Hauglustaine – to prepare a draft text on museums. When the first draft was finished, the group sought the opinion of many members of the ICOM networks for their expertise. Meetings with UNESCO were organized (with Alfredo Pérez de Armiñán, Assistant Director General for Culture, Mechtild Rössler, Director of the Heritage Division, and Nao Hayashi, Museums Programme Coordinator, as well as other experts requested by UNESCO). Following these meetings, a document was in turn sent to Member States in January 2015, which was later amended by the UNESCO Secretariat according to comments provided by Member States. This was then debated on 27 and 28 May 2015, during the intergovernmental meeting of experts at the organization's headquarters in Paris, with several ICOM representatives present, including ICOM President Hans-Martin Hinz.

The two-day work session of May 2015, led by government experts during the intergovernmental conference, led to a quite substantial transformation of the original ICOM text, as several paragraphs were deleted and new elements added. Thus the concept of 'collection', which had previously been introduced by the Rio conference organizers in the original documents, was removed from the final versions – since it was deemed too difficult to define a collection in general terms without weakening the project's *museological* quality overall. However, reference to 'collections' was reintegrated in the recommendation's framing title as well as appearing throughout the body of the text.

More symbolically, however, the May 2015 meeting concluded the first phase of the work based on professional and academic expertise (essentially originating from the ICOM network) and was succeeded by the work of diplomatic interplay, with more than seventy-five countries submitting arguments during the intergovernmental conference of UNESCO. In addition, about twenty international organizations – such as ICOM and ICCROM – as well as the European Commission were also present, albeit as consultative voices but unable to submit amendment proposals to the text. Discussions were passionate but polite; sometimes twenty States would join in the analysis of a single paragraph. Different visions of the museum, as well as of related national or international policies, emerged. The geopolitical backdrop of the museum field – as the meeting highlighted when each paragraph was adopted following rules of consensus – led to the final adoption of a text that necessarily integrated compromises. Intergovernmental harmony, indeed, is given priority over imperatives of a more academic nature. This complex collective exercise, diplomatically and editorially, led to the final drafting and design of the text presented and adopted in Paris on 17 November 2015, during the 38th UNESCO General Conference.

A foundational text

A museum professional skimming through the text of the recommendation might come to the somewhat hasty conclusion that most of its elements are not really innovative, and might wonder about the merit of this instrument for the museum world. Yet the text is, in fact, of major importance, inasmuch as it defines the place of ICOM in the museum world along with the museum itself within society. As mentioned previously, the recommendation is the first instrument adopted by UNESCO that introduces, in general terms, the role of museums in the world, as well as the associated functions and activities they can provide in society. Moreover ICOM is acknowledged throughout by UNESCO Member States as a primary reference body in museum organizational matters. The definition of a museum utilized in the document is that formulated by ICOM (the 2007 version); and ICOM documents are also cited as the primary source in matters relating to heritage and collections issues. But above all, it is the *ICOM Code of Ethics for Museums*[5] that is given the importance it deserves, being presented as an authoritative reference for matters of good practice in museums and for the treatment of conflicts inherent in the activity of museums. This positioning of ICOM well reinforces its ties with UNESCO, which can only be of benefit to both institutions.

The document follows a classic structure for such an instrument: (i) a number of concepts are defined ('museum', 'collection' and 'heritage'); (ii) the functions of museums are recalled; and (iii) the challenges museums must address are described. Finally (iv) the general and functional policies to be implemented to meet these challenges are also detailed throughout. Insofar as the document is addressed to policy makers, a number of defining elements of the museum field are stated in the preamble, in particular the basic functions of the museum (preservation, research and communication; education was later, subsequent to the Conference, defined as a separate function). These functions must be upheld, and are not to be overlooked in favour of political strategies that tend to have a more direct impact (gaining prestige or enhancing tourism and economic outcomes).

The current challenges museums face are spelled out in detail: as the world evolves, the context in which the 1960 recommendation on museums (and museum accessibility) was drafted is no longer relevant to the current reality. Globalization has enabled enhanced access to museums, and has advanced their potential in terms of attendance and use of services; however, it also induces structural homogenization, even in museums' appearance and their activities, to the detriment of a diversity of approaches. Museums have also become economic actors (notably through their contribution in the tourism sector) that improve the well-being of local populations and development of the region in which they are located. In this view, many museums have accordingly increased their income-generating activities, but this tendency may sometimes be pursued to the detriment of their principal functions, in particular the preservation of heritage and research.

The social role of museums, more directly related to the local context, constitutes the second major challenge in the current context. The recommendation's text recalls the importance of the Santiago de Chile Declaration, issued in 1972, a fundamental document in Latin American countries that defines the museum as a tool for social development, fostering integration and social cohesion. The concepts of public space, accessibility, nurturing of citizenship and promotion of human rights are also highlighted. Finally, the role of information and communications technologies is also presented as a major challenge, for the new opportunities they offer in the preservation, study and dissemination of heritage and knowledge.

The policies recommended in the text are broadly divided in general and functional terms. Regarding general policy, museums are called upon to utilize existing international instruments, especially the conventions concerning illicit trafficking and cultural diversity. The preservation of museum diversity is thus a major issue: it is important to respect the different conceptions of the nature of museums throughout the world to ensure the diversity resulting from their activities. Concerning functional policies, the text first emphasizes conservation, in particular of collections that by their nature would not be kept in museums.

The question of (professionally produced) collection catalogues and inventories is particularly emphasized, as it lies at the very heart of the function of museums. Explicit reference is made to the *ICOM Code of Ethics for Museums* in terms of the enhancement of good practice and related functions of museums. The topic of museum funding is also broached, along with that of staff. Member States are encouraged to ensure the adequate financing of the institutions that are under their auspices, and to proceed likewise to the hiring of qualified personnel with adequate expertise and training. The development of digital technologies is also encouraged, although mention is made that this can also hinder museums and audiences who do not have access to such tools. Member States are required to encourage access to these technologies.

More broadly, issues related to accessibility (addressed in the 1960 UNESCO recommendation) are again highlighted. Member States are called upon to integrate these principles into their overall cultural policy. Cooperation between museum professionals within the museum sector (affirming professional associations operating on a regional, national or international level, such as ICOM) is also keenly encouraged, alongside cooperation between Member States.

In overview, the text adopted by the UNESCO General Conference on 17 November 2015 is a document whose main themes are familiar to the dedicated museum professional. However, on a global level, the framework the recommendation proposes is unprecedented, insofar as it specifies for all 195 Member States, and their political or administrative representatives, the function of museums and their role in society. Museums, in the past associated with an elite and neglected in policy terms, have become increasingly popular – to the point that they now are a truly attractive instrument that has aroused considerable investment of public finances (including major 'Bilbao type' projects throughout the world).

Behind such investments, however, lies a superficial vision of the museum, seen as an essentially touristic infrastructure or, by contrast, as a means for social entertainment. Meanwhile this type of venture has often been based on a trivializing view of the museum, conceived primarily as a kind of tourist infrastructure support or, conversely, as a social animation tool, sometimes to the detriment of the essential functions that determine the museum's very nature: the preservation of heritage (tangible or intangible), the conduct of research, and the dissemination of knowledge in various forms for public benefit.

It is in this context that concepts such as the importance of an inventory or catalogue – seemingly obvious yet very unevenly applied across the sector – need to be highlighted, along with questions of funding and grants (including those from public authorities) for museums' basic welfare. Even if a museum can contribute indirectly to regional development, this does not mean it is to be viewed as a profitable investment in terms of financing. It should also be noted that the definition of the museums used in the recommendation states its non-profit nature.

Given the international scope and impact of this UNESCO document, it is hoped that the role museums play within society will now be more widely promoted. Although this text is primarily a legal instrument, not suited to responding to the daily experience or particular concerns of tens of thousands of museum professionals around the world, nevertheless each undertaking by these professionals is likely to be supported and reinforced by most elements of the framework provided in this recommendation. Moreover, these elements and the recommendation will now be those jointly launched by UNESCO and ICOM throughout the museum world, emphasizing museums' roles in the service of society as a whole and for its advancement.

Acknowledgements

I am grateful to France Desmarais for her careful proofreading and comments on this article in its original French version.

Notes

1 In the words (January 1926) of Henri Focillon, a Sorbonne professor who was one of the main instigators of the creation of the International Museums Office in 1926 (and the associated specialized international periodical, *Mouseion*, which became *Museum International*, now published by ICOM).
2 The notion of world heritage is older (see Desvallées, Mairesse and Deloche 2011).
3 The texts related to this instrument are available on the UNESCO website. The recommendation is at: www.unesco.org/new/fileadmin/MULTIMEDIA/HQ/CLT/images/FINAL_RECOMMENDATION_ENG_website_03.pdf (accessed 16 December 2015).
4 The classification of meetings within UNESCO follows a division into eight categories. Category II meetings bear a representative character, that is, participants represent their government. An intergovernmental character differs from international conferences (which belong to Category I).
5 The full text of the *ICOM Code of Ethics for Museums* is provided as *Appendix I* to the present publication. It is also available online for download (with links to translations in French, Spanish, and other languages) at: http://icom. museum/professional-standards/code-of-ethics/.

References

Frey, B., 1998. 'Superstar museums: an economic analysis'. *Journal of Cultural Economics*, 22: 113–25.
Desvallées, A., Mairesse, F. and Deloche, B. (eds) 2011. 'Patrimoine'. *Dictionnaire encyclopédique de muséologie*. Paris: Armand Colin, pp. 421–52.
Mouseion, 1927. 'L'œuvre de coopération intellectuelle et l'Office international des musées'. *Mouseion*, 1: 3–10.

11

PROTECTING CULTURAL HERITAGE AT RISK

An international public service mission for ICOM

France Desmarais

The protection of cultural heritage was included in the founding mission statement of the International Council of Museums (ICOM), an organization to bring together museums and museum professionals in the post-World War II world. Seven decades later, the protection of heritage in emergency situations, and the fight against illicit traffic in cultural goods, is central to the work of ICOM. The following paper will illustrate how a dynamic programme of activities, including the development of innovative tools based on clear ethical guidelines, has ensured ICOM's role as a major international player in the protection of cultural heritage. This is a much-needed role and commitment to action by ICOM, in a period where the world is witnessing the most severe upsurge in attacks on cultural property through armed conflict since ICOM was formed in 1946.

ICOM and the protection of cultural heritage

ICOM was created in the post-World War II era, thanks to the will of a handful of men and women who, by coming together to represent the museum world and promote international cooperation through their professional networks, were placing the role and responsibilities of museum professionals and institutions at the heart of a new organization. As the voice of the international museum community that has placed the protection of the world's cultural heritage in its mission statement since the 1940s, ICOM has been a sustained advocate of the importance not only of interpreting but also of safeguarding cultural heritage, and has actively been working with its members and networks in favour of the advancement of practices in the field of museums.

In 2015, a year before its 70th anniversary, ICOM was tasked with drafting the text for a new UNESCO initiative focused on museums: a *Recommendation on the Promotion and Protection of Museums and Collections, their Diversity and their Role in*

Society adopted by UNESCO in November 2015 (Mairesse, 2016). It had been fifty-five years since the last UNESCO normative instrument specifically addressed museum issues (in 1960). ICOM remains a close partner of UNESCO in actions concerning the promotion and protection of cultural heritage, and holds a consultative status to UNESCO in advancing the important measures for world heritage protection covered by UNESCO's conventions in these areas.

From the *ICOM Code of Ethics for Museums*,[1] now referred to as the international base-standard code for museum professionals worldwide, to the well-known *Red Lists of Cultural Objects at Risk* – directly associated with helping law enforcement agencies recognize and seize important items of cultural heritage in many countries, including quantities of antiquities in recent years – the aim of many of ICOM's programmes has been to develop innovative practical tools designed to help protect cultural property. This article will illustrate the development of ICOM's programmes over many decades in fields relating to the protection of cultural heritage in general, and in countering illegal trade in particular (since the UNESCO Convention of 1970).

ICOM's work on cultural property protection (CPP) has maintained a progressive momentum of development in many forms: from setting standards and guidelines for the industry to editing practical tools used by law enforcement agencies around the world. More than an internal task for ICOM's members or member museums alone, ICOM's mission to protect cultural heritage has caused it to link up with other agencies in a global effort after ICOM was recognized by the Economic and Social Council of the United Nations (ECOSOC) as the NGO expert to support efforts against the illicit traffic in cultural goods. The expert group now pursuing this responsibility connects ICOM with five international/intergovernmental organizations: UNESCO, UNIDROIT, and the United Nations Office on Drugs and Crime (UNODC), for their respective legal instruments on the subject; and INTERPOL and the World Customs Organization (WCO), representing international law enforcement agencies. In this group ICOM provides its resources as the scientific expert on movable cultural goods. ICOM had for years been active in trying to advance collaborative measures for effectively curbing art and antiquities theft and illegal trade in cultural heritage; however, its recent inclusion within such a significant consortium of influential agencies has raised the effects of ICOM's work to a new level and to a broader extent of impact in the twenty-first century.

Innovative developments in countering theft and illegal trade in heritage

Along with theoretical proposals and other normative instruments, practical measures for heritage protection were developed over the decades. In collaboration with INTERPOL, the magazine *ICOM News* featured stolen works of art, in the spirit of 'Most Wanted' posters. Such advertisements, disseminated worldwide, paved the way for significant restitutions throughout the 1980s and early 1990s. Inspired by some success stories, ICOM developed a series of tailored publications, each focused on a specific state or region, titled *100 Missing Objects*. The series was designed to spread information on objects declared stolen and reported to police. The first issue, published in 1993, concerned the severe ravaging of archaeological heritage at Angkor, and was titled *Looting in Cambodia*. Africa was the focus of a similar *Missing Objects* publication on looting in 1994; then *100 Missing Objects* publications covering Latin America and Europe followed.

Although such publications featuring stolen objects were successful in raising awareness, as well as in leading to actual restitutions, it became clear some years later that the use of electronic media and the Internet opened new and more effective channels of public awareness, since print publications could quickly become out-of-date as new information emerged rapidly. This was especially heightened by the development of the INTERPOL database of Stolen Works of Art, which became available to all online.

In 2000, taking into consideration changing circumstances and needs, ICOM created a new practical tool called a *Red List*. The first *Red List* published concerned a continent most affected by decades of intense looting: the *Red List of African Archaeological Objects* presented types of objects most at risk of being looted, imported and sold illegally. This was an instrument that, for various reasons, better responded to its aim of protecting movable cultural heritage – mainly because the majority of objects that are illicitly transferred from their countries of origin and quickly distributed for trade or sale on the international art market have not been officially reported as stolen to police, so they would not readily be featured in a publication like *100 Missing Objects*. Designed to be complementary to the stolen objects included in the INTERPOL database, the objects depicted in an ICOM *Red List* illustrate – thanks to images of artefacts held in museums or public collections – categories of cultural goods that meet three criteria: (i) being protected by national and international legislation; (ii) originating from a particular region, site or place of conservation that has suffered looting; and (iii) meeting a demand in the art market or adjacent markets where cultural heritage objects move illicitly and involve huge financial dealings.

Therefore fifteen years later, and fifteen *Red Lists of Cultural Objects at Risk* after 2000, the series has become – thanks to the support of partners such as the Swiss Confederation, the United States of America, Germany and many others – ICOM's prime tool in collaborative international effort for the protection of movable cultural goods and rare items of natural heritage (such as prized fossils and related materials).

The central role of museums

The international news may seem grim concerning continued massive looting of cultural objects, but there are also positive counter-efforts that achieve some success. The most encouraging example recently concerns, surprisingly enough, the cultural heritage of Afghanistan. The world may have an imprinted memory of devastating images of the destruction of the Buddhas of Bamiyan in 2001. However, there is another story to be told concerning the protection of Afghan heritage. It is a story that starts with the looting of a large number of antiquities, from the National Museum of Afghanistan as well as from sites across the country, but reaches a positive conclusion: with the ultimate return of thousands of objects to the National Museum in Kabul.

In response to the Afghan civil war of the 1990s and the years of conflict and instability that followed, ICOM prepared in 2006 a *Red List of Afghanistan Antiquities at Risk*. This was a *Red List* that, over the following years, the UK Border Force was detailed to use as a reference for more effective control of possible points of entry of Afghan cultural property to Britain. As a result of the efforts of law enforcement, using a practical tool such as the ICOM *Red List of Afghanistan Antiquities at Risk* to identify and seize protected objects, and thanks to an effective memorandum of cooperation with the British Museum, two large consignments of illicitly excavated and stolen objects were ultimately returned to Afghanistan – one of these a consignment totalling 3.4 tonnes and containing more than 1,500 items. The relevance of this case lies in the exemplary cooperation between museum institutions and law enforcement agencies, among others. It also demonstrates how the leadership of one of the world's most important museum institutions (the British Museum) has had a positive effect on the protection of cultural property further afield. When museums realize their potential – and power – as 'independent and confidential centers of expertise on the probable origin of trafficked antiquities', they can have a real and direct impact on hindering illicit trade in cultural objects (Simpson, 2015, p. 181; see also Peters, 2009).

Another example of how museums exercise effective leadership can be found in Berlin, where the Museum of the Ancient Near East (the Pergamon Museum) is developing and leading ground-breaking projects in the protection of cultural goods, including an extensive provenance research initiative (in which ICOM is a supporting partner) and an intervening 'no acquisition' policy until the Museum's strategic objective is accomplished (Hilgert, 2016). The museum is also involved in projects that not only pertain to its mission but that Pergamon contribute to establishing its leadership in issues concerning the protection of heritage at risk. For example, ILLICID is an ambitious transdisciplinary endeavour that aims to map and understand traffic in antiquities in Germany, and the creation of a 3D Digitization Centre for the study and preservation of archaeological material (Hilgert, 2016).

We know museums are, among other things, powerful tools for education, social inclusion and awareness-raising in their communities. They can also be, outside the walls of their institutions, strong advocates *for* and actors *in* the protection and preservation of the world's cultural heritage, by contributing to initiatives that put them at the centre of skills-building capacities and the sharing of knowledge and expertise. This is, for example, what our colleagues do at the Smithsonian Institution. Active in supporting the protection of cultural heritage in emergency within its country – for example, after Hurricane Katrina in 2005 – the Smithsonian Institution began supporting the preservation of cultural heritage abroad after such disasters. The work of the Smithsonian in Haiti, for example, is a strong case study for the field (Kurin 2011). The Under Secretary for History, Art, and Culture of the Smithsonian, Richard Kurin, leading the institution's desire to contribute to helping countries in emergency, recently created a Cultural Heritage Preservation Center whose efforts are managed by Corine Wegener, who is also the Chair of ICOM's Disaster Relief Task Force for Museums (DRTF).

Protecting heritage in emergencies or after disasters

Faced with the large number of museums destroyed in the wake of the 2004 Tsunami and the outpouring of proposals for support from museum institutions worldwide, ICOM decided to create a Disaster Relief Task Force for Museums (DRTF). The DRTF is a technical committee of ICOM dedicated to emergency response for museums, gathering museum-related professionals from different parts of the world that stand ready to provide advice and assistance to international colleagues and their institutions upon request. With the help of the Programmes Department in the ICOM Secretariat, DRTF monitors emergency situations to assess damage to cultural heritage in order to quickly evaluate the most pressing needs of museums and other heritage sites and places of conservation. Since its creation in 2005, DRTF has monitored a large number of different types of emergencies. Keeping in mind that this body was created after a natural disaster, and that since 2011 it has been mainly monitoring armed conflicts, this implies a drastic change in the way the Task Force now needs to operate, including conducting a review of ICOM's monitoring protocols and follow-up methods.

The Disaster Relief Task Force for Museums also contributes to ICOM's efforts as part of the Blue Shield. Following World War II, UNESCO adopted the third Hague Convention (1954), which created rules to protect cultural goods during armed conflicts. This Convention was the first international treaty aimed at protecting cultural heritage in the context of war, and highlighted the concept of 'common heritage'. The Blue Shield is the symbol used to identify cultural sites protected by this Convention. It is also the name of the International Committee of the Blue Shield (ICBS) that works, under the principle of subsidiarity, to protect world cultural heritage threatened by natural and human-made disasters. Created in 1996, ICBS brings together the knowledge, experience and international networks of the following four major international non-governmental organizations (NGOs) dealing with cultural heritage: ICA (International Council on Archives), ICOM (International Council of Museums), IFLA (International Federation of Library Associations and Institutions) and ICOMOS (International Council on Monuments and Sites).

ICBS works for the protection of the world cultural heritage by coordinating preparations to meet and respond to emergency situations, as well as post-crisis support. It promotes strong standards of protective action through risk management training and awareness-raising campaigns for the military, professionals and the general public. The now-unrivalled body of expertise of ICBS in emergency response allows the organization to collect and share information on threats to cultural property worldwide, thus helping international players to take appropriate measures in case of armed conflict or disaster. ICBS intervenes as an advisor and cooperates with other bodies including UNESCO, ICCROM and the International Committee of the Red Cross (ICRC). In emergency situations, ICBS encourages the safeguarding and restoration of cultural property and the protection of threatened goods; it also helps the professionals from affected countries to recover from disasters. ICBS is recognized in the Second Protocol to the Hague Convention (1999), and as an advisory international organization to the intergovernmental Committee for the Protection of Cultural Property in the Event of Armed Conflict.

Return and restitution

Among its international public service missions, ICOM also acts in the domain of cultural diplomacy in the area of return and restitution requests involving cultural property. Offering practical solutions and ethical guidelines to prevent artefacts from transiting illegally is crucial to protecting cultural heritage. Theft and looting can meanwhile lead to restitution requests from the places of conservation of origin of such objects. When the demand for repatriation of cultural objects grew over the years, and the legal framework proved unsatisfactory to countries requesting the return of some elements of their cultural heritage, the support of ICOM has been vital.

It is only through dialogue, discussion and the establishment of not only self-regulation but also trust-based relations that the international museum community has started moving forward on the very sensitive question of returns and restitutions of cultural goods, and can continue to develop innovative measures to settle disputes.

As illicit traffic cases of today will be the return and restitution requests of tomorrow, it is hard to completely dissociate the two – one being at the source of the other. Furthermore, because the international legal framework covering these two topics is intrinsically linked, this means that ICOM is sometimes called upon to intervene and facilitate mediation requests (Phelan, 2016). This was the context in which ICOM facilitated the return of a Makonde mask to the Republic of Tanzania in 2010, after the official negotiations had proved irresolvable for decades between Tanzania and the Swiss museum that possessed the object. The conflict was finally resolved when the two parties decided to enter into discussions under the mediation of ICOM. In such cases, great trust is placed in ICOM in particular, and in museum institutions in general. That is why professional, ethical and confidential behaviour is of utmost importance. Such cases are also proof that dialogue and case-by-case treatment of contentious issues is crucial to solving the difficult questions of the past. We cannot rewrite history nor erase past mistakes or injustices, but we can aim to make amends by acting ethically in the present and for the future.

Fostering cooperation, encouraging research

In 2011, mainly born of the dire need to obtain more information on the whereabouts of stolen objects and more reliable facts and figures on illicit traffic in art and heritage, in order to continue honouring ICOM's role and responsibility in fighting illicit traffic in cultural goods, it became clear that a new approach to ICOM's work in this area might be necessary. It is surprising that while illicit traffic in cultural objects has been recognized as a serious threat for decades, no organization has actually gathered official global statistics to illustrate the extent of the problem over this long period. Many figures are brought forward by different expert organizations to quantify the trade, in conjectured quantities or in financial worth. Some of those figures are astronomical; yet, none can be confirmed or repudiated by official empirical data. While the INTERPOL Expert Group on Stolen Cultural Property concluded in June 2015 that data gathering and systematic research are of high relevance for combatting the illicit traffic in cultural items, it remains impossible to precisely rank illicit traffic in cultural objects in order to measure it against other types of transnational crimes. This is one of the reasons why ICOM decided that it needed to create an International Observatory on Illicit Traffic in Cultural Goods, which was made possible in December 2012, thanks to the financial support of the European Commission.

Although some improvement has been observed in the collection and analysis of the data related to theft and seizures, it is unfortunately still impossible to answer questions regarding the number of objects that disappear or are sold illegally each year. In the big-data era, at a time when massive looting has spread to large areas of the world and both political leaders and the general public seem more than ever concerned about the fate of cultural heritage illicitly trafficked or in danger, it seems paradoxical that it remains impossible to quantify the extent of these activities or their effects. The reality is that, despite this palpable increase in global awareness concerning the importance of protecting cultural objects, the actual means to support their protection are somewhat lagging behind. Nevertheless, if ICOM, as a long-standing actor in the global fight against illicit traffic, is committed to continuing to develop useful tools and propose appropriate response mechanisms to effectively counter the illegal trade, it needs to know and understand the phenomenon as it now exists. Identifying the trade routes employed, the agents involved and the types of objects targeted, would yield necessary data sets and information to comprehend the significance of the illegal art and antiquities market. This can only be tackled through transdisciplinary research initiatives, such as that initiated though ICOM's Observatory project, as relevant organizations are encouraged to do under the 1970 UNESCO Convention – and indeed as Article 17 of the Convention mentions the potential of relevant organizations to conduct studies on matters relating to the illicit movement of cultural property. Looting and illicit traffic represent one of the primary global challenges for which a research and data-gathering body such as ICOM's International Observatory on Illicit Traffic in Cultural Goods is urgently needed.

What is clear, meanwhile, is that museums are particularly concerned about theft in art and heritage: as themselves primary places of conservation and consolidation from which objects can be stolen; but also as collecting institutions that could, unwittingly, end up being exposed to buying looted cultural property, of which the provenance is unclear or falsified. Indeed, objects are not only stolen from museums; they can also land, with the help of sometimes ill-informed accomplices, in the hands of private collectors. Later, through a donation, for example, they might find themselves again – and illicitly – transferred to museums. It is specifically because stolen art and antiquities risk falling into museum collections that it is the duty of the world museum community to cooperate and take determined measures to counter illicit trafficking in art and heritage. The inaugural gesture for this commitment is to apply strict ethical practice concerning the provenance of acquisitions. But it does not suffice. Proactive and policy-focused measures against illicit or illegal acquisition must be supported by strong national legislative programmes.

As a transdisciplinary cooperative professional platform, ICOM's Observatory project aims to encourage States to implement strict laws to curb theft and illicit traffic, while generating knowledge and federating expertise and resources in this cause. It was important that a publication should be added to the outcomes of the Observatory, in order to take stock of where things stand in matters concerning the protection of the world's heritage. Published in December 2015, the volume *Countering Illicit Traffic in Cultural Goods: The Global Challenge of Protecting the World's Heritage*[7] concluded the initial phase of ICOM's International Observatory project. Among the other tangible results of the Observatory is a dedicated website that now includes a searchable databank of over 6,000 diverse resources on the subject (including legislation, guidelines, articles, videos, etc.); and an official glossary of relevant terms, good practices relating to cultural property protection, and specific pages for each country detailing national initiatives in fighting illicit traffic in cultural goods.

After being actively involved in the fight against illicit traffic in cultural goods for decades, the Observatory project has enabled ICOM to create an effective body that could complete its existing or previous practical tools, such as the *Red Lists of Cultural Objects at Risk*, and further contribute to raising awareness and bringing forward solutions in favour of the protection of the world's heritage.

The necessity of international cooperation

ICOM's concern with promoting and protecting the tangible and intangible heritage of the world has taken many shapes and forms over the years, but one thing has always been at the centre of its action: ethical behaviour and practice. This is because protecting our common history and shared memory is not only the right thing to do, it is also the ethical thing to do. Placing ethical practice at the core of our work as museum professionals not only shines positively on the institutions we represent but also benefits the communities we work *with* and *for*. Museums have definitely improved the ethics of their practices in acquisitions, not limiting their action to the legal framework that prevails in their country, as recommended in the *ICOM Code of Ethics for Museums* (ICOM 2004). The example mentioned above concerning the positive role of the British Museum and the return of over 1,500 objects to Afghanistan suggests how this one case, around one *Red List*, could be multiplied infinitely. *Red Lists* that concern more than twenty-five countries have now been published.[2] What is needed, however, is the political will to make such success stories happen elsewhere around the world.

We also have to turn to the art and antiquities market, and insist that it adopts such strict deontological guidelines. This is a market that is still largely unregulated (Adam 2015). Protecting cultural heritage is a shared responsibility. This is why it is also important that collectors are more demanding in terms of object provenance when buying.

Alongside its principal ethical concerns, it is striking to see, looking back, how ICOM's programmes towards the protection of movable and immovable, tangible and intangible, cultural and natural heritage have been developed with three other key objectives in mind: being *innovative*, *committed* and *efficient*.

While the world is suffering violent conflicts in regions that also happen to be the cradles of civilization, and where a wealth of irreplaceable cultural riches and knowledge are at high risk of destruction and disappearance, the work of an organization that came to life in the aftermath of the last major period of sustained international armed conflict, and whose mandate is to promote and protect cultural heritage, is today more necessary than ever.

It is a great honour to pursue the fulfilment of ICOM's public service missions through the development of its programmes, ensuring that its work is complementary to that of museums everywhere. It is also a great responsibility towards the transmission of the world's heritage to future generations. ICOM's work and actions have come a long way over seven decades since its founding, and it remains an important duty to ensure that its manifold programmes and interlinked networks worldwide continue to travel a long distance, for a very long time.

Notes

1 The full text of the *ICOM Code of Ethics for Museums* is provided as Appendix I in the present publication. It is also available online for download from the ICOM website (with links to translations in French, Spanish, and many other languages). The English version is accessible at: http://icom.museum/professional-standards/code-of-ethics.

2 For a list of all Red Lists published by December 2015, see: http://icom.museum/programmes/fighting-illicit-traffic/red-list.

References

Adam, Georgina, 2015. 'Guidelines to regulate market are an "impossible dream": Authors think the trade is more concerned about the risk of losing sales than risks to its reputation'. *The Art Newspaper*, 1 March 2015, at: http://theartnewspaper.com/news/art-market/16382/ (accessed 26 November 2015).

Desmarais, France and Haldimann, Marc-André, 2014. 'Bids on the rise, objects on the go: Are objects commodities like any other?'. *ICOM News*, Vol. 67 (September): 16–17, at: http://archives.icom.museum/icomnews2014-3_eng/index.html#/16-17 (accessed 26 November 2015).

Franz, Michael, 2016. 'Advice and support in the recovery of lost art: The German Lost Art Foundation (Deutsches Zentrum Kulturgutverluste)'. In: Bernice L. Murphy, ed., *Museums, Ethics and Cultural Heritage*. London: Routledge, Chapter 13.

Hilgert, Markus, 2016. '"Definitely Stolen?": Why There Is No Alternative to Provenance Research in Archaeological Museums'. In: Bernice L. Murphy, ed., *Museums, Ethics and Cultural Heritage*. London: Routledge, Chapter 20.

ICOM, 2004. *Code of Ethics for Museums*. Paris: ICOM. Available at: http://icom.museum/fileadmin/user_upload/pdf/Codes/code_ethics2013_eng.pdf [accessed 26 April 2016].

Kurin, Richard, 2011. *Saving Haiti's Heritage: Cultural Recovery after the Earthquake*. Washington, DC: Smithsonian Institution.

Mairesse, François, 2016. 'The UNESCO Recommendation on the Protection and Promotion of Museums and Collections, their Diversity and their Role in Society'. In: Bernice L. Murphy, ed., *Museums, Ethics and Cultural Heritage*. London: Routledge, Chapter 10.

Milosch, Jane, 2016. 'Advocating for international collaborations: World War-era provenance research in museums'. In: Bernice L. Murphy, ed., *Museums, Ethics and Cultural Heritage*. London: Routledge, Chapter 19.

Peters, Gretchen, 2009. 'More Than 1,500 Stolen Afghan Artifacts Return to Kabul'. National Geographic, 6 March 2009. Available at: http://news.nationalgeographic.com/news/2009/03/090306-afghanistan-artifacts-returned-missions.html [last accessed 26 April 2016].

Phelan, Marilyn, 2016. 'Stolen and Illegally Exported Artefacts in Collections: Key issues for Museums Within a Legal Framework'. In: Bernice L. Murphy ed., *Museums, Ethics and Cultural Heritage*. London: Routledge, Chapter 12.

Staaliche Museen zu Berlin. [Online]. 'The ILLICID national research project investigates the illegal trade in cultural artefacts in Germany'. Available at: http://www.smb.museum/en/whats-new/detail/nationales-forschungsprojekt-illicid-will-illegalen-handel-mit-kulturgut-in-deutschland-untersuchen.html [accessed 26 April 2016].

UNESCO, 1972. *Report on ICOM Activities for the Suppression of Illicit Traffic in Antiquities*, at: http://unesdoc.unesco.org/images/0000/000018/001876eb.pdf (accessed 26 November 2015).

12

STOLEN AND ILLEGALLY EXPORTED ARTEFACTS IN COLLECTIONS

Key issues for museums within a legal framework

Marilyn Phelan

There exists a multi-billion-dollar industry in the illicit trading in stolen and illegally exported cultural objects, and most of these cultural treasures are intertwined with cultures as well as the sovereignty of exploited countries and tribal nations. As the persisting international demand for cultural treasures reinforces their smuggling from art-rich countries and Indigenous communities, corresponding demands for the return/restitution of these smuggled cultural objects constantly increase in intensity. Following countries and cultures demanding the return of valuable cultural treasures confiscated by continuing thefts – especially during military conflicts and from colonization – litigation, mediation, and settlement agreements relating to these cultural works continue to be at the core of initiatives to regain or repair sovereignty of vulnerable source countries as well as tribal nations.

Requests and lawsuits brought by countries for the return of stolen and/or illegally exported cultural property are difficult to resolve because of conflicting and often confusing laws and policies. This essay demonstrates that while laws internationally are inadequate to resolve ownership issues, those concerned nonetheless must consider international legal principles as they attempt to resolve return/restitution questions often involving multiple countries with differing laws. This essay posits that as market countries, museums, and other entities acknowledge and respect the cultural heritage of claimant countries as well as the tenets of other cultures, and therein recognize that the demands of a victim nation or a tribal culture for the repatriation of its stolen cultural treasures are linked to the core beliefs of that culture and the sovereignty of the source country, then nations, museums, and other entities can work together to prevent the ruinous destruction of the world's antiquities.[1] Indeed repatriation can bring a halt to the illicit trade in art, antiquities, and other cultural property, with the consequential protection of cultural heritage from its otherwise possible obliteration in this twenty-first century.[2]

Some museums have artefacts in their collections that have questionable provenances. These artefacts may have been stolen or illegally exported from their
country of origin. With stolen art today inundating the art market, many museum
officials have encountered claims of theft victims to works in their collections, and
may have discovered that the museum has defective title to one or more of its valuable pieces. Museum directors must be familiar with laws relating to title to artworks and historical treasures in order to respond correctly, both legally and
ethically, to possible demands from individuals and/or countries for the return of
objects in museum collections that have questionable provenances or that lack
documentation.

Issues relating to a museum's lack of clear title to some artefacts in the collection
are often tied to a concern to protect the cultural heritage on an international scale
and, in so doing, to halt the illicit international trade in cultural property. Cultural
nationalism embraces the theory that cultural property belongs in the first instance
to the country of its origin. As the general public becomes more aware of cultural
property issues and acknowledges that the cultural heritage of each country is bound
up with, and includes, the cultural treasures of all nations, a concern for the preservation of international treasures evolves. The theory maintains that a society learns
of itself by studying its artistic treasures and that a nation's artistic treasures can be
better investigated and understood in their original setting; thus, the principle
demands the protection of international sites and artefacts.

The *ICOM Code of Ethics for Museums* (2004)[3] states that when a country of
origin seeks the restitution of an object that can be demonstrated to have been
exported or otherwise transferred in violation of the principles of international and
national conventions for heritage protection, and can be shown to be part of the
cultural heritage of another country or people, officials of the museum concerned
should, if legally free to do so, take prompt and responsible steps to cooperate in the
return of the object (see ICOM 2004). The American Alliance of Museums (AAM)
Board of Directors has recognized the importance of protecting international cultural sites and artefacts, and has adopted principles relating to museum collections
to stem the international trade in art and antiquities.[4] The AAM Standards Regarding
Archeological Material and Ancient Art, published in July 2008, set out criteria
relating to archaeological material and ancient art to guide operations of museums
that own or acquire archaeological material and ancient art originating outside the
United States. The AAM recommends that museums require documentation that
an object was out of its probable country of modern discovery by 17 November,
1970, the date on which the 1970 UNESCO *Convention on the Means of Prohibiting
and Preventing the Illicit Import, Export and Transfer of Ownership of Cultural Property*
was adopted by UNESCO (UNESCO 1970 [1972]). For objects exported from
their country of modern discovery after 17 November, 1970, the AAM recommends that museums require documentation that the objects have been, or will be,
both legally exported from their country of modern discovery and legally imported
into the United States.

The special status of cultural property

The 1970 UNESCO Convention and related UNIDROIT and other UNESCO Conventions for the international protection of heritage are covered in detail in Chapter 9 of this publication (Rössler and Hayashi 2016). An additional discussion of the special status of cultural property from a legal perspective, and drawing on other legal covenants, is merited here. As the general public becomes aware and acknowledges that the cultural heritage of each country and each tribal nation is bound with, and includes, its cultural artefacts, a concern for the preservation of international treasures evolves (Merryman 2009: 83). Still, cultural nationalism embraces the theory that all cultural objects belong primarily to or should remain in the country of origin or with the affiliated tribe. The cultural nationalism theory favours the idea that a society learns of itself by studying its cultural treasures and that a nation's cultural objects can be better investigated and understood in their original setting. The principle clearly demands a country's protection of its cultural treasures, but also ties the ownership and possession of these treasures to a nation's right, as a sovereign people, to have other countries respect its cultural heritage laws.[5]

Both the International Covenant on Civil and Political Rights (999 U.N.T.S. 171) and the International Covenant on Economic, Social and Cultural Rights (999 U.N.T.S. 3) provide that all peoples have the right of self-determination and that, by virtue of that right, they freely determine their political status and freely pursue their economic, social, and cultural development.[6] One expert on tribal sovereignty concluded that the concepts of government and culture are inseparable and that sovereignty is, in effect, cultural continuance.[7]

Cultural property, which includes tribal artefacts, has been categorized as a 'special category of property', which should be subject to special property laws. As one scholar earlier suggested (Roucounas 1983: 136), cultural property might be included among the natural resources of a nation over which permanent sovereignty is claimed. He noted that the construction of national registers, the registration of objects of special value, the preparation and publication of lists of stolen property, and the computerization of public property and privately owned cultural objects are important tasks which must devolve upon public authorities (ibid.: 140).

Legislation in some countries demonstrates the importance and special status of art treasures and other cultural property to their countries of origin. Some countries' legislation includes acts that limit the rights of private owners of cultural property. The following are a few selected examples of special legislation enacted in some countries to protect the country's culture and sovereignty.

1. Whenever ownership of a privately owned designated site in the Republic of China is to be transferred (except through inheritance), the government must be notified so that it can exercise its rights to purchase the site (Campbell 1998). An individual who transfers privately owned antiques without notifying

the Ministry of Education is subject to substantial fines as well as imprisonment (ibid.).

2. In Egypt, Article 6 of the Antiquities Protection Law (or Law 117) provides that ownership of cultural property is not absolute. The act states that all antiquities, with the exception of religious endowments (*waqfs*), are deemed to be public property.[8]3. The Act with Respect to Antiquities in Greece states that all antiquities belong to the State. Individuals in Greece cannot acquire ownership of antiquities (see Mouliou 1998).

4. The trade in antiquities became illegal in Italy in 1939 with the enactment of the Law for the Protection of Works of Artistic and Historic Interests (or Law no. 1089/39). Under this law, all archaeological objects belong to the State unless they were in private ownership prior to 1902. Furthermore, only the State (or a private citizen by special permit) can conduct excavations. The law in Italy grants the Minster for National Education a right of preemption for objects of artistic and historic interest. Italian law requires private persons who own objects declared to be of exceptional interest to have all transfers of ownership reported to the Minister for National Education (Schairer 1998).

5. The Federal Act on Monuments and Archaeological, Artistic and Historic Zones in Mexico provides that historic and artistic monuments in private ownership are subject to export control.[9] These objects may be exported temporarily or permanently only with a permit granted by the government. Archaeological monuments, both movable and immovable, are the inalienable property of Mexico, and rights may not be acquired over them by possession.[10]

6. In 1926, the Republic of Turkey declared in force and effect a 1906 Decree that all antiquities found in or on lands in Turkey were owned by the Republic. Article 697 of the Turkish Civil Code, adopted by the Republic in 1926, declares that antiquities found on Turkish land are property of the Republic (Ozel and Karadayi 1998).

Return/restitution of stolen and illegally exported artefacts

In common law countries, the judicial remedies for the return/restitution of stolen cultural property are based on the common law principle, the English *nemo dat* rule,[11] which provides that one who purchases property from a thief, no matter how innocently, acquires no title in the property. Title remains with the true owner. The common law countries are those whose laws are based on the English common law and include Australia, Canada (except Quebec), New Zealand, England, Wales, Ireland, India (except Goa), Pakistan, South Africa, Hong Kong, and the United States (except Louisiana).

In most civil law States, a purchaser of stolen property can obtain good title after a limitations period. Countries whose legal systems are based on civil law generally permit a legal owner to recover stolen property from an innocent purchaser for a specified period of years after the theft. After that period of time, the purchaser has good title to the property.[12] As set out in Article 1153 of the Italian Civil Code, the person or entity who purchased stolen property must have been a 'good faith' or 'innocent' purchaser for the limitations period to begin to run. However, Swiss law presumed a purchaser acts in good faith; a victim seeking to reclaim stolen property had the burden of establishing the purchaser did not act in good faith, as stated in Article 934 of the Swiss Civil Code.

The taking of property by a foreign government may in some cases be valid, in which case an original owner will not have a claim for return of the property. Differing principles apply to the taking of property during war. 'Booty' is 'property necessary and indispensable for the conduct of war', such as food, means of transportation, and means of communication; its taking is lawful. 'Pillage' or 'plunder' is the taking of private property not necessary for the immediate prosecution of the war effort. Taking under these circumstances is illegal, and the original owner's title is not extinguished.

ICOM-WIPO Mediation Programme to settle disputes

Because of the difficulty of applying conflicting and often ill-defined laws to resolve cultural property disputes, alternative dispute resolution may be the most effective means of resolving conflicts regarding ownership and possession of cultural property. Submitting complicated issues related to ownership, possession, and repatriation of stolen and/or illegally exported cultural property to arbitration or mediation will prevent one party from becoming subject to another party's national court system, which may be unfamiliar, slow, and expensive.

In addressing the issues related to ownership of valuable cultural property, ICOM established an alternative dispute resolution mechanism in cooperation with the World Intellectual Property Organization (WIPO), a United Nations agency, to provide a more effective system for museums to resolve ownership questions relating to collections with gaps in provenance. ICOM had issued a document in 2007 that cited its policy of many years to 'encourage the negotiated resolution of disputes regarding the ownership of objects in museum collections that allegedly were stolen or illegally exported from the country of origin', and articulated its position that there should be 'the early settlement of such disputes through voluntary settlement procedures rather than through lengthy and expensive litigation or through political decisions'.[13] The further development of ICOM's initiative was advanced when ICOM later joined forces with WIPO.

Although today an agency of the United Nations, WIPO is a product of the 1883 Paris Convention for the Protection of Industrial Property and the 1886 Berne Convention for the Protection of Literary and Artistic Works. A need for the international protection of intellectual property became evident as early as 1883, when the predecessor of WIPO came into existence as a means to address that need. WIPO became a specialized agency of the United Nations in 1974, with the mandate to administer intellectual property matters recognized by Member States of the UN. It entered into a cooperation agreement with the World Trade Organization (WTO) in 1996 and, thus, expanded its role in the management of globalized trade.

A fundamental part of WIPO's activities has been to promote the protection of intellectual property. It currently administers several treaties that establish internationally agreed rights and standards for their protection. While the Paris and Berne Conventions remain the 'cornerstones of WIPO's treaty system', subsequent treaties have expanded the protection they offer. One example is the 1996 WIPO Copyright Treaty, which contains basic rules updating the international protection of copyright and related rights to the Internet age. WIPO had been attempting to simplify and harmonize procedures for obtaining and maintaining trademarks and patents in countries through the Trademark Law Treaty of 1994 and the Patent Law Treaty of 2000. Through its treaties, WIPO has provided services to simplify and reduce the cost of making individual applications or filings in all the countries in which protection for a given intellectual property right is sought.

The ICOM-WIPO Mediation Programme – a joint initiative of both organizations launched in 2011 – provides a feasible and appealing means to settle ownership questions without recourse to the often protracted and costly measures entailed in legal action. Meanwhile, the Mediation Programme provides a corresponding avenue for the increased protection of cultural property.[14] A mediator serves as a non-coercive neutral facilitator. The focus of the programme is to avoid the shortcomings of litigation by assisting parties to reach an agreement through direct communication and increased understanding.

WIPO has a renowned Arbitration and Mediation Center that provides mediation expertise and facilities to combine with ICOM's art and cultural heritage expertise. Mediation is provided through a procedure adapted to the settlement of art and cultural heritage disputes or assistance in negotiations in the art and cultural heritage field, including restitution and authenticity issues. The mediation process is a voluntary procedure in which the parties have primary responsibility for resolving their disputes or reaching an agreement after negotiations.

As Patrick Boylan, an ICOM expert on the means to protect cultural property and the first Chair of the Legal Affairs Committee for the International Council of Museums, stated:

> Much is at stake: the public's access to art in the present, respect and consideration for the individual and/or community whose past is embedded in the work of art, and the museum's ability to perform its service to society of protecting heritage for future generations.[15]

Indeed the effective utilization of a mediation process may be the only adequate method to resolve ownership controversies, and also may be vital to the long-term preservation of the cultural heritage of humanity.

Notes

1 In an article titled 'Understanding tribal sovereignty: Definitions, conceptualizations, and interpretations', Amanda J. Cobb referred to a comment by Clara Sue Kidwell and Alan Velie that '[a]lthough sovereignty is generally considered a political issue, it is also deeply embedded in culture, that is the association between sovereignty and cultural integrity'. (Discussion by Clara Sue Kidwell and Alan Velie [2005] in *Native American Studies*. Lincoln, NE: University of Nebraska Press, 2005 p. 75).

2 A *New York Times* article quoted Corine Wegener, the Cultural Heritage Preservation Officer at the Smithsonian Institution, who helps preserve ancient works at risk in war zones, observing that 'the best we can do as cultural heritage professionals is to remind everyone that cultural heritage belongs to us all' (Rhodan 2015).

3 The full text of the *ICOM Code of Ethics for Museums* is provided as *Appendix I* in the present publication. It is also available online for download from the ICOM website (with links to translations in French, Spanish, and many other languages). The English version is accessible at: http://icom.museum/professional-standards/code-of-ethics.

4 The original name of the AAM was American Association of Museums. This was its name in 2008 when the document was drafted. The name was changed to American Alliance of Museums in 2012.

5 Neil Brodie, a cultural heritage resource director, stated that: 'The real question is sovereignty, not ownership, the right of a country to have its heritage laws respected by other countries' at Stanford University's Multidisciplinary Teaching & Research, in 'Buying, Selling, Owning the Past'. On the same subject, it is well worth mentioning Daniel Contreras's statement: 'The value of antiquities is the story of their culture and their use, and when they're treated only as objects, they lose that.'

6 International Covenant on Civil and Political Rights, Part II, Article 3. International Covenant on Civil and Political Rights, Part I, Article 1.

7 Clara Sue Kidwell and Alan Velie observed that: '[a]lthough sovereignty is generally considered a political issue, it is also deeply embedded in culture, that is the association between sovereignty and cultural integrity' (quoted in Cobb 2005: 83).

8 The Egyptian government declared ownership in 1983 of all its archaeological artefacts pursuant to Article 6 of its Antiquities' Protection Law. Discussion in *United States v. Antique Platter of Gold*, 184 F.3d 131 (2nd Cir. 1999), *cert. den.*, 120 S. Ct. 978 (2000).

9 See Law of Archaeological Monuments, 1897, Article 1; Law on Protection and Conservation of Monuments and Natural Beauty, 1930, Article 1; Law for Protection and Preservation of Archaeological Historic Monuments, 1934, Article 1; Federal Law Concerning Cultural Patrimony of the Nation, 1970, Article 52; and Federal Law on Archaeological Artistic and Historic Monuments and Zones, 1972, Articles 27, 55 and 96.

10 Ibid.

11 *Nemo dat non habe* (He who has not cannot give).

12 See Italian Civil Code, Article 1153; Spanish Civil Code, Article 464; Swiss Civil Code, Article 934; and Sweden Personal Property (Bona Fide) Acquisitions Act (1986: 796).

13 Document: LegComm 2007 – *Guidance Notes on ICOM Mediation Process*, ICOM News, No1/2006. The document provided guidance notes on the ICOM mediation process and referred to ICOM's Panel of international mediators who could be nominated 'to consider issues relating to the return/restitution of cultural property in museum collections that was stolen, illegally exported, illegally confiscated, or otherwise wrongfully expropriated'. Document, p. 1.

14 See discussion at: www.icom.museums.

15 See LegComm 2007 – *Guidance Notes on ICOM Mediation Process*.

References

Campbell, Mei Wan, 1998. 'Laws in the Republic of China protecting its cultural and intellectual properties', in M. Phelan, G. Edson and K. Mayfield, (eds.), *The Law of Cultural Property and Natural Heritage*. Evanston, IL: Kalos Kapp Press, Chapter 10.

Cobb, Amanda J., 2005. 'Understanding tribal sovereignty: Definitions, conceptualizations, and interpretations'. *American Studies*, 46 (3/4) (Fall-Winter 2005): 83–135.

ICOM, 2004. *ICOM Code of Ethics for Museums*. Paris: International Council of Museums. Available online for download at: http://icom.museum/professional-standards/code-of-ethics. See also Note 3, concerning available ICOM translations of the Code.

Merryman, J., 2009. *Thinking about the Elgin Marbles*. Amsterdam: Kluwer Law International.

Mouliou, M., 1998. 'The protection of archaeological heritage of Greece', in M. Phelan, G. Edson and K. Mayfield, (eds.), *The Law of Cultural Property and Natural Heritage*. Evanston, IL: Kalos Kapp Press, pp. 13–57.

Ozel, Sible and Karadayi, Ayhan, 1998. 'Laws regarding the protection of the cultural heritage of Turkey', in M. Phelan, G. Edson and K. Mayfield (eds), *The Law of Cultural Property and Natural Heritage*. Evanston, IL: Kalos Kapp Press, Chapter 20.

Rhodan, Maya, 2015. 'Global art community condemns ISIS destruction of artifacts at Mosul Museum'. *New York Times*, 27 February 2015, at: www.time.com/3725026/isis-destruction-mosul-museum-artifacts.

Rössler Mechtild, and Hayashi Nao, 2016. 'UNESCO's actions and international standards concerning museums', in Bernice L. Murphy (ed.), *Museums, Ethics and Cultural Heritage*. London: Routledge, Chapter 9.

Roucounas, E., 1983. *Proceedings of the Thirteenth Colloquy on European Law. International Protection of Cultural Property*. Athens: University of Athens.

Schairer, Suzanne, 1998. 'A synopsis of the Italian laws protecting cultural property', in M. Phelan, G. Edson and K. Mayfield, (eds.), *The Law of Cultural Property and Natural Heritage*. Evanston, IL: Kalos Kapp Press, Chapter 14.

UNESCO, 1970 [1972]. *Convention on the Means of Prohibiting and Preventing the Illicit Import, Export and Transfer of Ownership of Cultural Property*.

13

ADVICE AND SUPPORT IN THE RECOVERY OF LOST ART

The German Lost Art Foundation (Deutsches Zentrum Kulturgutverluste)

Michael M. Franz

The Schwabing Art Trove

In November 2013, the so-called Schwabing Art Trove (Schwabinger Kunstfund), which is considered to be one of the largest discoveries of lost art in private possession since the Second World War, was announced to the world as being found in the possession of a Mr Cornelius Gurlitt, an elderly reclusive man living in Munich's Schwabing district. This discovery raised attention worldwide and it became a subject of intensive discussion by museums, art experts, politicians, journalists and others.

A few months earlier, in spring 2012, in Mr Gurlitt's apartment, a large private art collection, including works of Liebermann, Toulouse-Lautrec, Klinger, Renoir, Dix, Beckmann, Picasso, Cezanne, Corot and other distinguished artists, had been seized by local authorities. It soon became clear that the provenance of numerous of these objects needed to be investigated very thoroughly, since the father of Cornelius Gurlitt, Hildebrand Gurlitt, had worked as an art dealer between 1933 and 1945, the critical period of extensive spoliation of cultural property from Jewish owners during the holocaust.

During subsequent efforts by German authorities to provide transparent investigation of the contents of this art 'trove', nationally and internationally, details of some 500 of these objects have been placed on the search-website www.lostart.de. In addition, the German government and the State of Bavaria established an international task force to help clarify the provenance of the artworks found in the possession of Gurlitt – who in fact died after the confiscation events, bequeathing his art collection to an art museum in Switzerland (which since has affirmed its institutional support to the investigation of the status of the artworks, and signalled its commitment to return works to descendants of former owners wherever provenance research yields evidence of spoliation).

The Stiftung Deutsches Zentrum Kulturgutverluste, in Magdeburg

As one main consequence of the investigations of the Schwabing Art Trove, and supporting the aim to combine all German efforts in the field of the documentation and research of looted art, as well as creating a central point for contacts, the German government (represented by the federal Commissioner for Culture and the Media), all sixteen German federal states (the *Länder*) and municipalities (*kommunale Spitzenverbände*) decided in 2014 to establish a new institution in Germany to coordinate and facilitate all such activities. These common efforts are all the more important and impressive because the legal as well as political responsibility for cultural affairs in Germany is divided between the federal government, the federal states – which maintain their so-called 'cultural sovereignty' (*Kulturhoheit*) in cultural affairs – and the municipalities.

On January 1, 2015 the German Lost Art Foundation (Deutsches Zentrum Kulturgutverluste, or Centre) took up its work. The Centre is an institution organized as a foundation with legal capacity under civil law, and is located in the city of Magdeburg, the capital of Saxony-Anhalt, in which its predecessor Koordinierungsstelle Magdeburg (Magdeburg Coordinating Office), founded in 1994 in Bremen, had carried out its work in Magdeburg since 1998. In 2000, the Office established the website www.lostart.de, which has continued to provide an important information source and lead to contacts with the Office – now Centre.

The purpose of the Centre[1] is to support art and culture, science and research focused on lost cultural assets, and in addition to foster international exchange, tolerance, and facilitate understanding between peoples. The Centre is both the national and international point of contact in Germany for questions pertaining to the implementation of two key declarations: the Principles of the Washington Conference with Respect to Nazi-Confiscated Art[2] (the so-called Washington Principles) of 1998; and Germany's Common Statement by the Federal Government, the Länder and the National Associations of Local Authorities regarding the tracing and return of Nazi-Looted Art, especially concerning Jewish property (the so-called Gemeinsame Erklärung[3]) of 1999.

The Washington Principles were the result of an international conference on Holocaust-Era Assets hosted in Washington, DC in December 1998. With the aim of developing a consensus on principles designed to assist in resolving issues relating to Nazi-confiscated art, eleven principles had been formulated and were adopted by the Washington Conference. These principles are non-binding legally and cover topics such as transparency ('VI. Efforts should be made to establish a central registry of such information'), as well as the objective of 'fair and just solutions'. For example, the eighth principle states:

> VIII. If the pre-War owners of art that is found to have been confiscated by the Nazis and not subsequently restituted, or their heirs, can be identified, steps should be taken expeditiously to achieve a just and fair solution, recognizing this may vary according to the facts and circumstances surrounding a specific case.

One year later, in 1999, the Common Statement reinforced the Washington Principles in adopting them for Germany, having special regard to the above-mentioned topics of transparency and fair and just solutions, as reflected in the following excerpts from the German statement:

> Irrespective of such material compensation, the Federal Republic of Germany declared its readiness at the Washington Conference on Holocaust-Era Assets on 3 December 1998 [...] and [will], if necessary, take the necessary steps in order to find an equitable and fair solution [...]
>
> Furthermore, the Federal Government, the Länder [states] and the national associations of local authorities resolve in accordance with the principles of the Washington Conference to provide a website on the Internet with information on the following: 1. What the institutions involved can do for publicising art of unclear origin [...]. 2. A search list [...]. 3. Information on the transfer abroad of Nazi-confiscated art [...]. 4. Establishing a virtual information platform [...].

Such commitments, bringing together all levels of government in Germany, shape the Centre's activities in Magdeburg today. The main focus of the Centre's activity is to advise and support cultural and scientific institutions in Germany, in particular on the handling of cultural assets that were looted in connection with persecution measures during the National Socialist period (involving so-called *NS-Raubkunst* or 'Nazi-looted art') or were displaced or lost as a consequence of the Second World War (so-called *Beutekunst* or trophy art). In cases of Nazi-looted cultural assets, the Centre supports 'a just and fair solution' – a key term in the Washington Principles as well as in the Common Statement.

The Centre carries out these objectives today as it brings together the tasks of the former Magdeburg Coordinating Office and connects with tasks of the former Office for Provenance Research (Arbeitsstelle für Provenienzforschung) located in Berlin – which from 2008 to 2014 has financially supported public institutions in their task of provenance research concerning looted art. In consequence, the knowledge and experience of documentation – especially via www.lostart.de which includes searched and found reports from Germany and abroad – as well as research, advice, mediation, conference management and publication know-how of more than twenty years is brought together at the Centre. Thereby, all this cumulated knowledge of lessons learned over more than two decades is of great value for the future programmes involving the Centre's cooperation with museums, libraries and other organizations nationally and internationally.

In particular, the purpose of the Centre is realized both directly and indirectly through the initiation, accompaniment, strengthening and support of provenance research by public institutions at national, state and municipal levels in Germany, above all within the context of claim-related project funding. Accordingly, the Centre provided grants in May 2015 worth €1,150,000 for seventeen provenance research projects, and among these, for the first time, to: the Wilhelm-Hack-Museum in

Ludwigshafen, the State Museum (Landesmuseum) Mainz, the Museum Abteiberg in Mönchengladbach and the City Gallery (Städtische Galerie) of Karlsruhe.

Further tasks of the Centre include advising public institutions in Germany on questions related to achieving the above-mentioned 'just and fair solutions', when considering cases involving possible restitutions and financial compensation. Furthermore, as one main consequence of the Schwabing Art Trove case, the Centre offers support to privately funded institutions and private persons in their own searches for looted art, and questions regarding a just and fair solution – as long as the parties follow the Washington Principles and the Common Statement, and there is an evident public interest in supporting the individual case. The Centre also intends to advance the theme of provenance research via professorships in at least three universities that will incorporate this topic as part of their historical and art historical teaching and research. In consolidating these additional tasks, responsibility for the content of the work of the Centre and its promotion of provenance research lies with Prof. Uwe M. Schneede, who has been appointed as the Centre's Honorary Chairman.

The principal governing organs of the Centre are the Foundation Board (*Stiftungsrat*) – headed by Minister of State in the Federal Chancellery and Federal Government Commissioner for Culture and the Media – and the Board of Directors (*Vorstand*). A Board of Trustees (*Kuratorium*) is formed as an advisory committee. This board comprises between nine and eleven recognized experts, including international specialists. The quality of scholarly and institutional resources is reflected in current expert appointees to the Board – drawn, for example, from the Dutch restitution committee, the University of Hamburg, the State Library Centre (Landesbibliothekszentrum) Rheinland-Pfalz, the French Comité d´histoire auprès de la CIVS, the Provenance Research Working Group (Arbeitskreis Provenienzforschung); the German Museums Association (Deutscher Museumsbund); the Claims Conference Deutschland; and the Cultural Foundation of the Federal States (Kulturstiftung der Länder).

In its first year the newly organized Centre, in addition to its own established activities, added several new initiatives of cooperation. For example, it entered the new field of dispossession of cultural objects that occurred under Soviet occupation and in the former GDR. And as its founding year drew to a close, the Centre organized its first international conference, *New Perspectives on Provenance Research in Germany*, which was hosted at the Jewish Museum in Berlin in November 2015.[4]

Ethics: the Advisory Commission on the return of cultural property

The Centre also supports the independent Advisory Commission on the return of cultural property seized as a result of Nazi persecution, especially Jewish property, by assuming the organizational tasks of the Commission. The Advisory Commission was set up following an agreement in 2003 between the German government, the sixteen German federal states and the municipalities.

The Commission can be appealed to in cases of disputes regarding the return of cultural objects taken from their owners, especially persecuted former Jewish citizens, and which currently are located in museums, libraries, archives or other public institutions in Germany. If both parties agree, the Advisory Commission serves as a mediator between representatives of the collections and the former owners of the objects or their heirs. It can suggest options with the aim of settling disputes on these matters. The legally non-binding recommendations of the Commission are published and documented by the Centre on the Commission's behalf.

Among those who have agreed to serve in an honorary capacity on the Advisory Commission have been academic representatives of law, art history and philosophy, and distinguished judges and political figures, including, for example, the former head of the German Federal Constitutional Court, Prof. Jutta Limbach (chair), the former head of the German Bundestag, Prof. Rita Süssmuth, and the former German President, Dr Richard von Weizsäcker, who was a member of the Commission from its beginnings in 2003 until his death in January 2015. The service of such figures demonstrates the high importance attached to the Commission and the level of commitment to ensuring a strong character of moral purpose upholds its recommendations.

The Centre, as the administrative office for the Advisory Commission, has the task of preparation, implementation and follow-up for the meetings of the Commission; it also serves as facilitating contact for individuals and institutions who wish to appeal to the Commission.

In the coordination of such appeals, by the end of 2014, the Commission had made many recommendations involving restitution, as well as suggesting possible compromises in disputes and proposals for compensation. One of the recent and most complex tasks for the Commission was the case involving the Guelph Treasure (*Welfenschatz*), which has vividly illustrated how difficult and complex cultural property disputes can be, while in such cases, the material covered can also serve to provide a very useful case study for further application afterwards.

Historical background of the Guelph Treasure

According to the Commission's findings, the case of the Guelph Treasure can be briefly summarized, with first a sketch of the historical background[5] as follows:

> The Guelph Treasure is a collection of late medieval works. [...] In October 1929, shortly before the outbreak of the world economic crisis, Jewish art dealers from Frankfurt/Main acquired the collection consisting of 82 individual items at a price of 7.5 million Reich marks. [...] In the years that followed, the art dealers tried in vain to sell the whole collection in Germany and in the USA. [...] In 1930/31, they succeeded in selling only 40 individual items, primarily in the USA, for a total price of approximately 2.7 million Reich marks. The remaining 42 pieces were put into storage in Amsterdam after the collection had been exhibited in the USA. [...] In June

1935, a purchase sum of 4.25 million Reich marks was agreed. [...] In July 1935, the purchase price was paid less a provision of 100,000 Reich marks. The 42 pieces in the collection were brought to Berlin. After 1945, the Guelph Treasure was seized by the occupation authorities and later handed over in trust, first to the State of Hessen and then to the State of Lower Saxony. In 1963, the collection was taken over by the Prussian Cultural Heritage Foundation (*Stiftung Preußischer Kulturbesitz*) and has been exhibited at the *Kunstgewerbemuseum* (Arts and Crafts Museum) in Berlin ever since.

The case of the applicants

According to the Commission, the position of the applicants is as follows:

> In 2008, the heirs to the art dealers demanded that the 42 Guelph Treasure pieces be returned by the Prussian Cultural Heritage Foundation. The claimants are of the view that the sale in 1935 was a case of confiscation due to persecution. They maintain that in 1934 and 1935, the Dresdner Bank and the Prussian state government deliberately exploited the difficult economic situation the Jewish art dealers found themselves in and exerted pressure on them. [...] According to expert estimates, a purchase price of at least 6 to 7 million Reich marks for the 42 individual items would have been appropriate in 1935.

The position of the appellee

The position of the appellee can be summarized as follows:

> The Prussian Cultural Heritage Foundation refused to return the Guelph Treasure. First of all, it referred to the fact that it has not been clarified whether the four art dealers alone or also other participants in the sale were the co-owners of the Guelph Treasure. [...] The sale in 1935, the Prussian Cultural Heritage Foundation maintains, was not a compulsory sale due to persecution. The art dealers had been attempting to sell the collection since 1929 and did not enter into the contract in 1935 under political pressure. The purchase price of 4.25 million Reich marks reflected the market value at that time and was therefore appropriate [...]. If one compared the entire proceeds from the sale of the 40 individual items in 1930/1931 and the 42 individual items in 1935 to the purchase price in 1929, the Jewish art dealers and their business partners made a loss in the amount of c.10% [...].

The recommendation of the Commission

Following the two parties' inability to come to an agreement in their dispute on the Guelph Treasure, they agreed to call upon the Advisory Commission in 2012. Following is the summary of the Commission's recommendation:

Although the commission is aware of the difficult fate of the art dealers and of their persecution during the Nazi period, there is no indication in the case under consideration by the Advisory Commission that points to the art dealers and their business partners having been pressured during negotiations, for instance by Göring [...]. In the end, both sides agreed on a purchase price that was below the 1929 purchase price, but which reflected the situation of the art market after the world economic crisis [...]. Moreover, there is no evidence to suggest that the art dealers and their business partners were not free to dispose of the proceeds. In its meeting in March 2014, the Commission stated, in accordance with its findings on the course of the purchase negotiations, its opinion that the sale of the Guelph Treasure was not a compulsory sale due to persecution. It therefore could not recommend the return of the Guelph Treasure.

Almost a year after the recommendation, in February 2015, the heirs to the art dealers filed a claim on the restitution of the Guelph Treasure in the United States, which is still pending.

The checklist on ethics of cultural property ownership

Another example of productive partnerships in promoting proactive awareness of ethical matters concerning cultural property ownership has been the cooperation between the former Koordinierungsstelle Magdeburg, whose tasks are now continued by the Centre, and the International Council of Museums (ICOM) and the ICOM Ethics Committee. This was achieved notably in the 2011 creation of a jointly form Checklist on Ethics of Cultural Property Ownership, especially concerning museum collections.[6]

The need for such a concise, readily usable checklist became clear as questions concerning ethics in the museums world have steadily grown in importance nationally and internationally in recent decades. Worldwide interest has sharpened around topics related to the impact of colonization on subject peoples and collections built through the expansion of empires historically; of repatriation claims by Indigenous peoples; of cases of looted art as well as trophy art; and of the increasing depredations to the cultural and natural heritage caused by illicit trafficking.

To help overcome the complexity of the field of ethical questions affecting the work of museums today, the Cultural Property Checklist sets out, in a clear format, the eight organizing principles of the ICOM Code of Ethics.[7] It thereby provides a basic orientation and support in identifying issues relating to these complex topics. The Checklist also offers a list of contacts for gaining further advice on particular questions, since museum colleagues or general inquirers may need specialized assistance concerning cultural property items, or have particular questions on which informed advice and assistance could be beneficial.

The future for the German Lost Art Foundation

To sum up, more than seventy years after the end of the second World War and the National Socialist period, complex and difficult cases of contested cultural property ownership, such as that involving the Guelph Treasure, demonstrate vividly the continuing challenges and complexity of the topic of looted art. Against this background, the new Deutsches Zentrum Kulturgutverluste in Magdeburg, building on the work of its predecessor, the Coordinating Office for Lost Art, over more than two decades, will continue its tasks relating to contested property cases such as the Schwabing Art Trove, and maintain its mission of offering assistance, both on a national and international level, to those who need support in such disputes or other questions concerning cultural property ownership in forthcoming years.

Notes

1 The following information on the Centre is based primarily on its Rules (*Stiftungssatzung*), at: www.kulturgutverluste.de/de/ueber-uns/stiftungssatzung (accessed 16 December 2015).

2 The Washington Principles, at: www.lostart.de/Webs/EN/Koordinierungsstelle/ WashingtonerPrinzipien.html (accessed 16 December 2015). The document is also accessible, along with other relevant documents, at: http://www.lootedartcommission. com/Washington-principles.

3 For the *Gemeinsame Erklärung* (Common Statement), at: www.lostart.de/Webs/DE/ Koordinierungsstelle/GemeinsameErklaerung.html (accessed 16 December 2015).

4 Organized in cooperation with the Cultural Foundation of the Federal States (*Kulturstiftung der Länder*) and the Brandenburger Tor Foundation (*Stiftung Brandenburger Tor*), the conference was opened by Prof. Monika Grütters, introducing experts who presented an overview of current provenance research and issues of restitution with respect to looted art.

5 The provided text on lit. a–d is based on the English working translation of the original German wording of the respective recommendation, at: www.lostart.de/Content/06_ Kommission/14–03–20-Empfehlung%20der%20Beratenden%20Kommission%20 zum%20Fall%20Welfenschatz.pdf?__blob=publicationFile (accessed 16 December 2015).

6 The checklist can be found at: www.lostart.de/Content/09_Service/DE/Downloads/ Checkliste-Museumsethik.pdf?__blob=publicationFile (accessed 16 December 2015). It is also accessible for download from the ICOM website at http://icom.museum/ professional-standards/code-of-ethics/checklist-on-ethics/ (accessed 16 December 2015).

7 The full text of the *ICOM Code of Ethics for Museums* is provided as *Appendix I* in the present publication. It is also available online for download from the ICOM website (with links to translations in French, Spanish, and some 30 other languages). The English version is accessible at: http://icom.museum/professional-standards/code-of-ethics (accessed 15 January 2016).

PART IV

Heritage care and ethics through the lens of multiple cultures and regions

14

UNCHANGING ETHICS IN A CHANGING WORLD

Gary Edson

Ethics and practice

People often claim that ethics have changed because we are in the fast-paced world of the twenty-first century. They say things are different now: 'Today's world has placed a premium on material development, sacrificing many moral [ethical] and spiritual values on the altar of material progress' (Bennani 2004: 3). Ethical considerations are too often ranked second to practical concerns, or even completely disregarded. Following this notion, many institutions of traditional trust are no longer viewed as trustworthy – thus the call for greater attention to ethical practices. Ethical principles provide the foundations of a proper social, cultural and professional existence.

Ethics do not change. People, situations, expectations and interpretations may change; but ethics persist as an enduring framework for conduct. Ethical principles may be ignored, misused or manipulated, but they are consistent: their call to good conduct is always robust. Proper care of a collection (consistent with the principle of 'the good') continues to call for proper care of a collection – for whom, or how the care is defined may change, but the in-theory ethical duty remains. Dealing in cultural material by a museum professional is always wrong, no matter how that act may be justified. Situations and circumstances do not make an unethical act ethical, no matter how often that act is repeated or how it may be rationalized. This reality is not about the law that may govern a land; it is about the ethical principles that guide the museum profession. Advocating exceptions to ethical ideals does not constitute an acceptable change to a framework based on principles.

Ethics is about who we are as persons and professionals. Endorsing an ethical attitude is in the interest of every museum professional and every person working in or with a museum. The world is neither ethical nor unethical; only people or actions may be unethical. Therefore, museum ethics considers the theoretical and practical elements of the philosophy of conduct in relation to critical contemporary issues. This consideration includes the procurement of artefacts, the rights of Indigenous people, repatriation, the politics of display, the conservation of objects, human rights and the role of education, as well as the day-to-day management of a museum. All persons active in museum matters – whether as custodians, curators, trustees or in other roles – have an ethical obligation to the museum profession and the public.

The development of museums in many parts of the world has escalated in recent years for a variety of political, financial and cultural reasons. Political and financial motives have often exceeded the ideals of cultural preservation. The goal of tourism to attract travellers with money to spend is often a primary influence on museum construction at the national level. Museums may be built as civic attractions while lacking adequate personnel, or even, in some cases, viable collections. A corresponding problem is the lack of provision for continuing support after opening. Once a new building is constructed, political attention moves on to another location or another activity: 'The government is still in the process of developing a system for supporting established museums.'[1] Asian museums are often directed to follow the 'American style' of seeking donor support to offset reduced governmental funding, yet such skills are often culturally specific and take years to develop in new social contexts.

To paraphrase the famous opening lines of Charles Dickens' *A Tale of Two Cities*: This may be 'the best of times, and the worst of times' for museums. It is a time of growth, a time of challenge; it is an epoch of both commitment and frustration; it is a time of hope, and a time of despair. No one can deny the increasing number and importance of museums in the present world. China, for example, opened 451 new museums in 2013, pushing the country's total to 4,000; meanwhile Chinese museums are said to attract 160 million visitors annually. China's goal is to have one museum for every 250,000 people (Gaskin 2014). While the construction plans are laudable, many existing museums lack professionally trained personnel, a sustainable museological plan or infrastructure, or viable collections.

Across the South China Sea, the government of Taiwan has recently promulgated a Museum Law (in July 2015) that includes a definition of a museum. The definition is based, at least in part, on the ICOM definition. Taiwanese museums are not permitted independent organization or membership in ICOM as a separate nation state according to the UN Charter, because Taiwan falls under the mandate of China. Nevertheless, Taiwan has a strong community of museum professionals and a growing number of museums.

The first Taiwanese museum was opened in 1908, and there are reportedly more than 400 museums currently operating on the island. Some of the museums are called 'mosquito' museums, perhaps because the insects are the main visitors (a building but no personnel, no collections and few activities). Personnel issues are a concern in most Taiwanese museums, along with low salaries and inexperienced leadership.

Although there are low numbers of visitors in some Asian museums, other locations have an exceptionally high number of visitors. The National Palace Museum in Beijing, for example, has set a limit on how many people may enter the museum each day to avoid impossible overcrowding; similarly, the National Palace Museum in Taipei, Taiwan, is also struggling with an overflow of daily visitors. However, a branch of the National Palace Museum in Taipei is scheduled to open in the southern part of the island (Chiayi District) by the end of 2015. The new facility should help to alleviate the crowded conditions facing visitors in Taipei.

Are these comments about Chinese and Taiwanese museums meant to be criticisms? Yes and no. The availability of properly trained personnel is an ethical issue, as is adequate budgetary support and an appropriate museological infrastructure. Both Taiwan and China have university programmes and museum associations committed to prepare a future generation of museum professionals, but the training and mentoring processes are slow. The students being taught today will be better prepared and more knowledgeable about museums and heritage issues than their predecessors. Nevertheless, the resources to support their professional development are often precarious. Funding will continue to be a concern until governments acknowledge cultural preservation as a social responsibility. These concerns raise ethical issues that will influence the future of museums.

Governments in many locations (including Asia) are promoting cultural tourism, and in that process, museum ethics is often circumvented in the name of expediency. The number of 'public' museums in most parts of Asia still outnumbers the 'private' ones, and as public institutions, they depend on government endorsement and financial support. Museum directors are often political appointees with minimal knowledge of museological practices. Curators may be qualified in their discipline area by academic standards, but with minimal experience in a museum. Certainly there are exceptions to this general statement, but outside the larger, more established museums, professional expertise is not well represented. This lack of competency raises issues of ethical concern.

The 2014 (21st) edition of the *Museums of the World* directory, published by De Gruyter in Berlin, identifies more than 55,000 museums in 202 countries (De Gruyter 2014). The conditions influencing museum growth in China, Taiwan and other East Asian countries are not unique. Similar situations are found in other countries. Museums in Central and South America, Africa and the Middle East have faced many of the same challenges as those outlined for some countries in Asia. Museological training is a problem in many locations, as is collections care, audience development, general professionalism and funding. The order and severity of these problems differ from location to location, but all have an influence on the practices within museums; consequently, they directly influence ethical considerations.

These comments are not to suggest there is a perfect balance of museums, personnel and resources in North America, Western Europe, Australia or any other place. Funding of cultural activities, including museums, is under threat in most locations. The temptation to unethical practice becomes greater as the challenges for museums increase. Financial demands have in some cases caused museums to deaccession and sell important pieces from their collections. The cost of collections maintenance has increased, causing some museums to cull and even to destroy important natural history collections. Public demands have increased the need for exceptional exhibitions, which cause available funding to be directed toward high-profile events and away from research and collections care. Exhibition information is often exaggerated (freely editorialized) to increase public interest at the expense of truth. Concessions are made to gain corporate funding, to placate potential donors or solicit political support. All of these practices raise ethical concerns that challenge the professional standards of the museum community.

Any potentially compromising activities can be rationalized as benefiting the museum, serving the public or fulfilling a stated objective. Nevertheless, each situation may also lead beyond the boundaries of responsible museum practice; each may infringe ethical principles, and in some situations even conflict with national or international laws or conventions.

Ethics for museums

The authority of the *ICOM Code of Ethics for Museums*[2] cannot be over-estimated. It has been and continues to be the most influential standards document produced by any organization for the international museums community. The second most-referenced statement internationally is ICOM's definition of a museum. Scores of museums around the world have used these two ICOM documents to establish creditability, fortify their existence, acquire funding, and confirm visitor and donor confidence. Museum personnel have gained personal and professional pride by having these documents as underscoring their life commitment. There can be no claim to professionalism without ethics.

Because of their importance to museums and museum personnel, the *ICOM Code of Ethics for Museums* and the definition of a museum have been translated into numerous languages in addition to the three official languages of ICOM (English, French and Spanish). Although no translation is considered 'official' unless endorsed by at least one national committee in a country in which the language is spoken, there is no viable way to review every translated document to determine its accuracy. The objective here is not to challenge any translation but to maintain consistency in the intention and meaning of a final document in a new language version. For example: the word 'ethics' may be variously translated in different languages, just as it may be interpreted differently by French-, English- or Spanish-speaking individuals.

English language dictionaries frequently define the word 'ethics' as morals, moral principles, or moral values of right and wrong behaviour. Such definitions have resulted in a misunderstanding that often causes an incorrect translation of the intention and substance of professional ethics: '[M]ost people confuse ethics with behaving in accordance with social conventions, religious beliefs, and the law, and don't treat ethics as a stand-alone concept' (Paul and Elder 2006). Morals are of special value as social principles; however, they do not properly address the ethical standards of a profession.

Social ethics (morals) serve the public. They are maintained for social harmony – the idea of people living together in a harmonious relationship. Morality as commonly identified with moral philosophy is an informal system of socially regulated behaviour that can be anticipated from all rational persons. Morals are accepted as passed downward from a higher authority that is omnipotent but ill defined. Professional ethics, in contrast, are formulated within a particular profession, giving special attention to the needs and responsibilities of members who share that profession.

Museum (professional) ethics identifies a type of applied ethics – focused upon standards determining conduct in particular situations. Social ethics and professional ethics may overlap when considered in broad terms. Each advocates honesty, respect and proper conduct. Both types of ethics directly and indirectly promote the ideal of 'good' as providing a framework for interacting with other persons. Social ethics (morals) are general in nature, intended to make individuals tolerable and acceptable within their resident societies. All people, in their social training, are subject to an identifiable moral (social) code to which they are expected to respond. In contrast, professional ethics – such as that promulgated by ICOM – is for museum personnel (staff, and volunteers including board members), and is not inclusive of other persons.

The museum approach to ethics is identified as 'deontological ethics', and is based on the notion of duty (or '*deon*' in Greek). Deontological ethics allows qualifying measures to determine acceptable working principles. Every museum person must give order to the interests, roles and ethical principles that influence their professional life. The museum profession identifies a code of ethics as defining those principles. When museum personnel act out of respect for the principles identified by a museum's code of conduct, they are responding to the duty to act in an ethical way.

Ethics is not an abstract concept although some aspects of ethical thinking have a theoretical foundation. Ethics relates to the daily activities of every museum professional. It defines the principles that underlie practice, so that members of the museum profession can better understand and perform their activities with an ethical awareness. Museum ethics considers the theoretical and practical elements of the philosophy of conduct in relation to critical contemporary issues impacting upon museums (Edson 2009). A code of ethics gives order to various concerns (and related practices) inherent in museum activities, assisting all practitioners to gain an understanding of ethical questions and outcomes. Without a code of ethics, museum personnel may gain a familiarity with certain ethical practices through casual experience, but still lack a systematic approach to making ethical decisions.

Intellectual vision extends to circumstances beyond practical experience, whereby people increase their capacity to theorize whether a situation is right or wrong. The worth of an action is not only derived from the purposes it seeks to achieve, but also from its being in accordance with a governing policy that respects a code of ethics. Contemporary ethics reflects contemporary society in that certain ideals and practices may change to conform to evolving conditions shaping the museum profession. However, it must be reiterated that the principles of ethics do not change. They may be applied differently or expanded to include previously unattended issues, but the principles remain consistent. People may ignore ethics or seek situational solutions, but such manipulations do not alter the enduring principles. An unethical decision is an unethical decision, no matter how it may be explained or justified.

Museum ethics is a component of professional life that has the function of promoting values common to the members of the profession (Singer 1993: 323). Museum ethics advocates a way of thinking about guiding principles and practices for resolving various professional situations that raise questions about 'right conduct'. Pursuing an ethical approach to professional practices requires museum personnel to develop objective reasons to guide group actions, including decision-making. Objective reasons for an ethical position should indicate that a chosen solution is truer to principles than alternative possibilities. An ethical position should also be supported by clarifying facts (truth) and definable values.

Logic and reason are key intellectual activities that influence thinking and, ultimately, decision-making. Logic is a cause-and-effect process – leading to a reaction or outcome. A common cause (or condition) will regularly produce a common effect (or dilemma) that is often resolved by a common solution. Laws are formulated on the basis of logic; whereas, ethics frames action based on reason. When a museum professional employs reason, along with caring and awareness, she or he can choose to respond to higher motives (ethics) than those dictated by pure logic. Ethical principles cannot be so explicit as to deal with every issue that may be encountered within the life of a museum; therefore, the museum professional must assume the responsibility of responding to each situation in a reasoned manner based on ethical principles (an ethical disposition).

A code of ethics may be considered as providing principles of reason to guide action. Each principle frames positive actions, contra to negative or unacceptable conduct. In practice, ethical principles can be viewed as addressing an outcome (intention), or a pending consequence that may require consideration of established principles. There should be a sound reason underlying each museum activity and the resulting outcome of an action should reflect that reasoning. Professional ethics for museums is based on reasoning emanating from within the profession itself.

The correctness of ethical thinking ('the good') can be linked to well-chosen actions. It may be assumed that museum personnel would know right from wrong by intellectual disposition. However, some propositions may arise that are so logically desirable, and some consequences (outcomes) seem so impossible not to desire, that a rational person feels compelled to give his or her approval, regardless of the unethical implications. Truth and reason must be active in ethical thinking. Clear, rational and critical thinking are essential to guide good decision-making.

Translation, transmission and transformation

No book, code, manuscript, lecture or doctrine can make a person ethical. An individual must determine for himself or herself how to act in an ethical way. Ethics is about respect, and perhaps most of all, it is about attitude, and each individual must embrace the idea of 'doing the right thing'. However, thinking and doing are two separate processes. It is not sufficient to say the words and to repeat the phrases of a code of ethics. The essence of ethical practice must be integrated into all the activities of museums and into the attitudes and thinking of all museum personnel. Knowledge of ethical principles guides the enlightened mind to ethical practice, including clarifying what is acceptable practice and what is not.

The adaptation of a code of ethics (ethical principles) for practical museum use requires certain steps that can be defined as a process of translation, transmission and transformation. A method for incorporating a code of ethics into an institutional culture and philosophy is necessary, regardless of the language or location of a practitioner or museum, or whether the code is generated internally or externally. The transmission of ethical principles must be accomplished in a practical and 'user friendly' manner that translates ideas and practices into terms that relate to the host museum and its personnel.

The concept of translation often means more than conversion from one language to another – as in the case of English or French to Chinese, Arabic or Turkic. The translation of a code of ethics into a language of local speech and professional practice that is acceptable by a particular museum or group of museums is of major importance. Words are often viewed as the enemy of understanding – creating a semantic quagmire. In this case, it is imperative that each member of the museum staff understands the code of ethics to be observed and the reasons for each of its principles.

Once understanding is achieved, transmission is possible. The ideals of ethics can be transmitted to all persons involved in museum practice, and once translation and transmission have been accomplished, museum personnel should be transformed in their ethical awareness. This concept of professionalism does not assume that simply because a person claims ethical endorsement, a full transformation into best-practice professional performance has occurred. Persons must also acquire the required skills and training to fulfil the full scope of their museological duties.

Although the ideal norms of the museum profession may be made apparent by the transmission of a code of ethics, it is naive to assume that the mere presence of a code represents an intact and comprehensive acceptance of defined ethical practices. The translation of a code into values of the host culture and social context is inevitable, and that process may modify a code's principles, shifting their concepts and relevance away from the original purpose. Therefore, a code should be stated in terms that can be applied according to the requirements of the host museum, rather than defining key principles in language that is ideologically constrictive in notion, application or expectation.

Museum professionalism

The museum profession and museums that exist today are products of human activities that have achieved a level of reality in both presence and purpose, and persons active in the profession share a particular mission that often has a compelling power for all participants. Collective attitudes and beliefs concerning the museum profession and relations among its members provide the basis for museological discernment. These shared attributes are elements that mould the sense of common purpose shaping the profession. Ethics, attitude, beliefs, norms, values and 'best practices' should be an active part of the museum profession's abiding intellectual foundations.

Museums and museum personnel may nevertheless create their own ethical confusion through disregard of ethical principles. 'Ethics carries with it the idea of something bigger than the individual' (Singer 1993: 10). This concept of ethics as it relates to the museum profession conveys a message that is supported and reinforced by the museum community. A shared approach to valuing 'the good' in daily conduct identifies the obligations and defines the rights for everyone making up the profession, and gives the principles a universal standpoint to guide subscribers, regardless of place, language or culture. While the notion of universally defined judgements (decisions) promotes the concept of universal ethics to guide actions, it also encourages application of consistent principles when considering differences between circumstances (whether involving varied locations, conditions or expertise).

Meanwhile, museum ethics reaches beyond a circumscribed sense of good conduct in purely professional terms: 'A professional is more than a person having skills and knowledge. To become a professional, you must dedicate the use of your skills and knowledge to further human dignity' (Beabout and Wennemann 1994: 27). However, a common problem for all museum personnel when deciding upon 'right' actions may be social acceptance. A situation is often favoured as 'what is', or affirmed 'because that is how we always have done things', instead of determining 'what ought to be'. This tendency often encourages accepting a current or traditional activity as determining the 'correct' way a situation should be addressed. Such attitudes are not unique to any nation or people; however, they often result in a compromise that promotes the continuance of unethical practices. For example, the historical fact that works of art and artefacts were moved unimpeded from country to country (the 'is' factor) is not by itself sufficient evidence for determining to continue that practice (countered by the 'ought' factor). Or, the fact that for many years broken pottery was reassembled with vacant areas filled and in-painted to resemble the original piece (an 'is' factor) has not proved in itself adequate evidence to continue that practice (an 'ought' factor has led to a different judgement on a previous practice long-unquestioned).

A profession such as the museum community is defined by its ethical practices, and it continues to function because ethics is a dynamic concept that reflects the changing values of the social and professional environment. 'The history of ethical ideals indicates that progress has been achieved along with the expansion of the group [profession] to which the [guidelines of acceptable] conduct were applied' (Patterson 1949: 400).

Museum ethics is a system of principles built upon reasoning and experience that defines responsible stewardship of people and collections, and highlights practices to be avoided. Ethics is a means to an end; it is not an end unto itself. Museum personnel are learning that the correct way to do a particular job may no longer be the way they learned or practised in the past. Instinctive or intuitive behaviour favoured previously has often given way to a higher level of judgement in which social roles and expectations are reshaped by the principles of ethical practice defined and endorsed by the museum profession (Edson 2009). Meanwhile exploration of the complexities of museums and museum operations are continuing to advance as the expectations of ethical practice are becoming more inclusive.

However, individuals in many locations often still want museum ethics to define strict 'rules of practice', to provide authority and justification for particular actions or decisions. A problem with a 'rule mentality', however, is that when a person knows the 'rules', he or she might manipulate that system to meet their own objectives. Ethical life cannot be reduced to rules. In addition to ethics, museum personnel must cultivate a caring attitude. Rules alone are not capable of transforming a person's thinking to an attitude of respect or understanding (of caring).

Museum ethical principles guiding correct actions are also central to building the respect and value due to people and institutions: 'Respect is a self-chosen criterion of moral [ethical] decision-making' (Beabout and Wennemann 1994: 25–26). Ethical practice therefore frames all aspects of a museum professional's life, including inter-personal behaviour. It is about how people treat each other every day. Respect as it relates to museum ethics is more than respect in conventional terms. It is more than respect for people or persons (in all aspects including values and beliefs); it includes self-respect, respect of duties, respect of objects, respect for cultural and natural heritage and respect for the profession. Respect is nurtured by an ethical attitude and fulfilling responsibilities.

Professional decisions must be based on deontic judgement of rights and duties as well as a sense of personal responsibility. Ethics fosters honesty, accountability, pursuit of excellence, loyalty, integrity and responsible citizenship. Ethics is about how museum people view their professional reality, and the function of promoting shared values common to the members of the profession regardless of cultural, financial or social disposition (Singer 1993: 323). Ethics is professional validation. It protects, explains and reinforces the proper functions of the museum.

Conclusion

Ethics is intended to bring order to the museum community in a way that promotes commonality of purpose and responsible actions. Museum ethics has evolved to make museums more responsive to social, cultural and professional needs, and to give greater clarity to acceptable practices. Ethics, in earlier times, were not as refined and detailed as today, leading some persons to believe that ethics have changed. This is not the case. The application, interpretation or implications may change but the ethical principles remain unaltered.

Ethics as a universal concept brings together various parts of an expanding and increasingly complex museum community around the central principle of service to humanity. Museum ethics is derived from fact, experience, values and beliefs, as well as an element of positive belief in social good as a humanitarian reference (caring). The ICOM *Code of Ethics for Museums* is founded on the belief in service. Belief may define a general logic of practice for museums, although some nation states have reinforcing rules, laws or conventions to identify and guide the special nature of museums' conduct; nevertheless, social service is a passion generated by belief in a common good.

Museological obligation has little meaning unless each member of the museum profession accepts, articulates and promotes the ethics underpinning practices of the profession. It is only when museums succeed in nourishing, preserving and projecting the common heritage of humanity, and equipping people as individuals to meet the challenges of their existence, that a claim to the unique nature of museums as institutions 'in the service of society and of its development' can be validated (ICOM 1996: 3).[3]

Notes

1 Li Xu. Quoted by Sam Gaskin, for CNN 2014, 'China's aggressive museum growth brings architectural wonders', at: http://edition.cnn.com/2014/04/29/world/asia/china-museums (accessed 19 September 2015).
2 The full text of the *ICOM Code of Ethics for Museums* is provided as *Appendix I* in the present publication. It is also available online for download from the ICOM website (with links to translations in French, Spanish, and many other languages). The English version is accessible at: http://icom.museum/professional-standards/code-of-ethics.
3 This phrase has been constant in ICOM's 'Museum' definition since 1974. See International Council of Museums, 'Definitions', in *ICOM Statutes*. Paris: International Council of Museums, 1996, p. 3.

References

Beabout, G.R. and Wennemann, D.J., 1994. *Applied Professional Ethics: A Developmental Approach for Use with Case Studies.* Lanham, MD and London: University Press of America.
Bennani, A., 2004. 'Introduction', in Jérôme Bindé, (ed.), *The Future of Values: 21st Century Talks.* Paris: UNESCO Publishing and Berghahn Books.
De Gruyter, W., 2011. *Museums of the World.* Berlin: Walter De Gruyter.
Edson, G., 2009. 'Practical ethics and the contemporary museum'. *Museology Quarterly*, 23 (1): 5–24.
Gaskin, S., 2014. 'China's aggressive museum growth brings architectural wonders'. *CNN*, 30 April 2014, at: http://edition.cnn.com/2014/04/29/world/asia/china-museums (accessed 4 September 2015).
ICOM, 1996. 'Definitions'. *ICOM Statutes.* Paris: International Council of Museums.
Patterson, C.H., 1949. *Moral Standards: An Introduction to Ethics.* New York: The Ronald Press Company.
Paul, R. and Elder, L., 2006. *The Miniature Guide to Understanding the Foundations of Ethical Reasoning.* Tomales, CA: Foundation for Critical Thinking Free Press.
Singer, P., 1993 [1994]. *Practical Ethics.* Cambridge: Cambridge University Press.

15

REMODELLING SHARED HERITAGE AND COLLECTIONS ACCESS

The Museum Island constellation and Humboldt Forum project in Berlin

Hermann Parzinger

The Prussian Cultural Heritage Foundation (Stiftung Preußischer Kulturbesitz, or SPK) is by far the largest cultural institution in Germany and one of the largest of its kind in the world. It emerged from the cultural institutions of the former State of Prussia, which was dissolved after the end of the Second World War. The Prussian Cultural Heritage Foundation is the only cultural institution in Germany that is maintained by both the Federal Government and all sixteen states, which is due to the Foundation's particular national importance.

SPK today oversees the sixteen State Museums of Berlin with their outstanding collections covering art and cultural development from antiquity to the present day. In addition, the State Library of Berlin, with its two buildings at Unter den Linden and at Potsdamer Straße, is part of the Foundation, too. Comprising more than eleven million volumes, it is one of the largest academic encyclopaedic libraries in Germany. The Secret State Archive of Prussia is considered the third institution of the Prussian Cultural Heritage Foundation, where thirty-eight kilometres of files and documents on Prussian and German history are kept and made accessible for research. The Ibero-American Institute is one of the most important research institutions of its kind outside the Latin American world and has one of the most comprehensive libraries. The State Institute of Music Research, with its Museum of Musical Instruments, is the fifth institution of the Prussian Cultural Heritage Foundation. Hence, it can be said that the Prussian Cultural Heritage Foundation comprises all branches of cultural tradition and heritage, ranging from art and material culture to literature, documents and music. This can be regarded as the uniqueness of SPK, because in many other countries, national museums, national libraries and national archives are separate institutions independent from each other, whereas in Berlin they find themselves under one umbrella due to their Prussian origin.

One of the most prominent tasks of the Prussian Cultural Heritage Foundation is the development of the historical centre of Berlin. This comprehensive task is divided into restoration measures, that is, reconstruction or rebuilding, and the addition of new building units in order to optimize access to the cultural heritage kept in these institutions, both for research and for the culturally interested public.

The place of origin of the Berlin Museums is the Museum Island (*Museumsinsel*), which spreads out into the plain of the Spree Island like an acropolis of knowledge and art (Figure 15.1). The development of the Museum Island began with the so-called Old Museum (*Altes Museum*) built by Karl Friedrich Schinkel, which was opened in 1830. The head of the museum commission was Wilhelm von Humboldt, who insisted that the works of art – both sculptures from antiquity and paintings and drawings of Old Masters – had to be exhibited without any chronological, cultural or other contextualization. A few years later the Prussian King Friedrich Wilhelm IV came to envision the Museum Island as a complex of several separate museum buildings which, as a whole, had been designated since then as an open space for arts and sciences (*Freistätte für Kunst und Wissenschaft*). While other large encyclopaedic museums in the world attempt to accommodate the legacies of different epochs and cultural regions in separate wings and storeys of one and the same building (as in the Louvre, the British Museum and New York's Metropolitan Museum of Art), the Museum Island was based on a different concept from the very beginning. Importance was attached to giving each cultural region and each art genre a building of its own, with every building also representing a particular stage of museum history in the nearly 200 years of the Museum Island's existence.

During the Second World War, all buildings of the Museum Island were damaged. However, it was possible to modernize and restore most of them, except the so-called New Museum (*Neues Museum*) from Friedrich August Stüler. Nevertheless, the realization of the so-called Master Plan Museum Island began in the late 1990s (Figure 15.1). It involves the complete overhaul of all buildings, the first-time restoration of the New Museum and the addition of new buildings where necessary, such as the James Simon Gallery as the new entrance building for the Museum Island complex.

The first building of the Museum Island to be restored was the Old National Gallery (Figure 15.2), which was reopened in 2001 in its former Wilhelminian splendour and has since been regarded as an outstanding museum for nineteenth-century painting and sculpture. The second building to be restored was the Bode Museum. Completed in 2006, it is a marvellous neo-Renaissance building that, just like the Old National Gallery, re-emerged in its old splendour. Today, it comprises the collections of the Museum of Byzantine Art and of the Sculpture Collection, and thus gives an excellent overview on the history of sculpture from late antiquity to the eighteenth century.

In 2009, the New Museum was reopened after its heavy destruction in the Second World War. Prior to its restoration it stood on the Museum Island as a ruin for almost seventy years because it had suffered the worst war damage: more than one-third of its entire structure was completely destroyed. The concept pursued by English architect David Chipperfield in the restoration of the New Museum included the preservation of all structures and interior design that had survived from

FIGURE 15.1 Simulation of Museumsinsel Berlin with the Humboldt Forum in the foreground © SPK / ART+COM / Schloss: eldaco, 2015.

FIGURE 15.2 Museum Island, Berlin, Old National Gallery (Alte Nationalgalerie) in the colonnaded courtyard © SPK / Pierre Adenis.

the time of Stüler, as well as the addition of new architectural elements that blend in harmoniously with the historical structures while at the same time clearly contrasting with them (Figure 15.3). The result was a new masterpiece of museum architecture.

The restoration of the New Museum resembled a large research project. Each surviving wall of the individual rooms was carefully documented. A team consisting of architects, building historians, archaeologists, conservators and other specialists then developed suitable concepts for the restoration of each room. The rooms of the New Museum reflect museum history. This becomes particularly apparent in the so-called Mythological Hall. The opulent decoration of the ceiling and walls, dating from the middle of the nineteenth century, was meant to orient visitors atmospherically for the Egyptian antiquities. In the 1930s, however, this rich design was gradually reduced; there was a first move towards a more pedagogical approach, and the hall was supplied with geographical maps and chronological schemata of the historical and cultural development of Egypt. Today, it is still possible to discover these layers of superimposed concepts of museum presentation in several halls of the refurbished museum.

Of particular importance is the so-called Egyptian Courtyard, the north inner courtyards which was completely destroyed. Following David Chipperfield's concept, the level of the inner courtyard was lifted from the ground floor to the first floor, and the portraits of the royal family of Amarna are exhibited there – of Akhenaton, Nefertiti and their daughters. The interplay with the daytime sunlight and the night-time artificial spotlight shining through the glass roof is allusive of the

FIGURE 15.3 View toward the great staircase of the renovated Neues Museum (New Museum) on the Museum Island, Berlin © bpk / Ute Zscharnt.

Amarna period, a short-lived stage of ancient Egyptian history, during which poly-theism was abolished in favour of the exclusive worship of the sun god Amun.

The James Simon Gallery – the new centralized entrance building of the Museum Island – is currently under construction. Offering central guidance for visitors and featuring other infrastructure such as cloakrooms, museum shops and gastronomy (Figure 15.4), it has all the practical, functional amenities needed in a modern museum complex that attracts several million visitors every year, with this number increasing. All historical buildings on the Museum Island go back to the nineteenth and early twentieth centuries. These original plans did not – and could not – take into account the needs of modern museum tourism. In that respect, the James Simon Gallery is an important addition to the Museum Island. It can be considered as the contemporary continuation of building activities at this UNESCO World Heritage site, taking the Museum Island into the twenty-first century. Seizing Stüler's motif of the colonnades that surround the New Museum and the Old National Gallery to the east and south, David Chipperfield extends these – trans-lated into a modern design – leading to the west where they merge into the James Simon Gallery through a large flight of stairs. In addition, the semi-basement of the James Simon Gallery will have space for special exhibitions. Such space is crucially important, because the museums of the Museum Island are completely 'filled' with presentations of their collections and do not offer much space for temporary exhi-bitions; these possibilities will be provided in the James Simon Gallery.

FIGURE 15.4 Museum Island Berlin: the restaurant at the future entrance of the James Simon Gallery building © SPK / ART+COM, 2015.

The restoration of the Pergamon Museum began in January 2013. It will take at least thirteen years. The building cannot be completely closed for any longer period of time, and the restoration will be carried out step by step, proceeding from one wing to the next. Besides the restoration of the individual halls, the fourth wing at the Kupfergraben will be built as was already planned at the beginning of the twentieth century (Figure 15.5). However, that wing will not be constructed in the architectural style originally envisioned, but in a modern form designed by the architect Oswald Matthias Ungers.

Thanks to the fourth wing, visitors will have the opportunity to make a true round tour on the main level of the Pergamon Museum; this has never been possible before. The round tour begins in the fourth wing that features architectural elements and monumental sculptures from pharaonic ancient Egypt, such as the Sahuré temple and the Kalabsha gate. Through an opening that will frame the gate of Tell Halaf, the tour then takes visitors to the south wing of the Pergamon Museum. That wing is entirely dedicated to the presentation of ancient oriental cultures from Mesopotamia, beginning with late Hittite monuments and architectural elements from northern Syria, continuing with the procession road from Babylon, and ending with the Ishtar gate from the same site (Figure 15.6).

From there visitors will enter the east wing, consisting of three halls with architectural elements from the Greek and Roman periods. They begin with the hall crowned by the market gate of Miletus. Next is the middle hall with the altar from

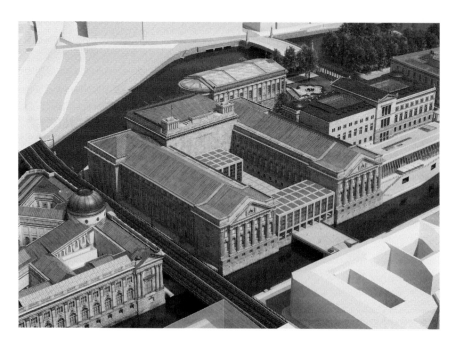

FIGURE 15.5 Museum Island, Berlin: view of the future Pergamon Museum including the fourth wing © SPK / ART+COM, 2015.

FIGURE 15.6 The Ishtar Gate at the Pergamon Museum, Museum Island, Berlin © SPK / Pierre Adenis.

Pergamum and finally the so-called Hellenistic hall in the north-eastern corner. The visitor then moves on to the north wing where the façade of Mshatta, one of the most important architectural monuments from early Islamic times, will be presented in its full length for the first time. The main round trip of the Pergamon Museum will therefore offer a worldwide unique tour through the architectural history of antiquity, beginning with ancient Egypt, continuing with ancient Mesopotamia and then proceeding through the Graeco-Roman world into early Islam. This enables visitors to understand the connections between the various epochs. Besides the architecture, the complete associated material culture will be presented in the adjoining halls and on the first floor. The collection of the Museum of the Ancient Near East will be exhibited in the south wing, and the north wing will present the collections of the Museum of Islamic Art.

Once the Master Plan Museum Island is completed, the so-called Archaeological Promenade will connect four of the five museums on the Museum Island (Figure 15.7). The Promenade will begin at the Old Museum to the south, leading through the New Museum and the Pergamon Museum and ending in the Bode Museum located at the northern tip of the island. Before the Second World War, these museums were connected on the first floors by bridge passages, which have been destroyed due to war damage. There have never been plans to rebuild them. Instead the central courts of the individual museums are being lowered one floor in the course of the restoration, which has already been done in the Bode Museum and the New Museum, and they will be connected by subterranean galleries. In a way, this Archaeological Promenade can be regarded as the sixth museum on the

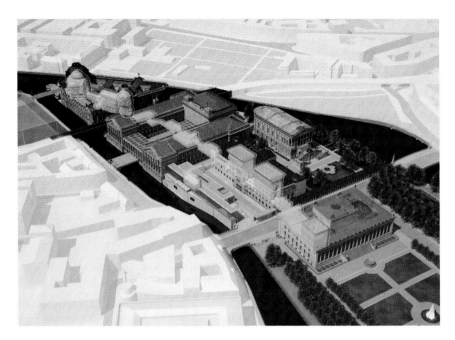

FIGURE 15.7 Museum Island, Berlin: a simulation of the location of the Archaeological Promenade, which will in the future connect five of the six buildings © SPK / ART+COM, 2015.

Island because it is not merely devised as a suite of connecting corridors but also as an extended series of exhibition rooms for interdisciplinary presentations. The Archaeological Promenade may be characterized as a cross-total of those collections that are shown separated into cultural regions, epochs and art genres within the individual museums of the island. The Archaeological Promenade will address multi-focus topics that have occupied the human mind independently of time and cultural region, be it the question of life after death or issues of beauty and other topics.

On the other side of the Kupfergraben, opposite the Bode Museum, the so-called Archaeological Centre has emerged. It is actually located in renovated land-marked barracks dating from the end of the nineteenth century, to which an L-shaped modern functional building has been added. This centre accommodates all those scientific activities that have been outsourced from the buildings on the Museum Island, so that the museums can be exclusively used for the presentation of their collections. At the Archaeological Centre there is a concentration of specialized libraries, research archives, study collections and restoration laboratories as well as the workrooms and offices of the scientists.

The area south of the Archaeological Centre can be characterized as the natural spatial extension of the Museum Island, and there is still vacant space of a size approximating that of the Bode Museum. There are plans for the future use of this space for another large gallery building at a later stage. That new building is intended to complement the Bode Museum and to present painting and sculpture dating from medieval times to the eighteenth century. Being a site where cultural and artistic developments from antiquity to the nineteenth century are exhibited, the Museum Island will only be truly complete with this building, because it will remain unfinished without the paintings, the most important key medium of art both in medieval times and the modern age. Currently, the Sculpture Collection is accommodated exclusively in the Bode Museum, while the painting gallery of Old Masters is several kilometres away in another building near Potsdamer Platz. It is the goal of the Museum Island Master Plan to return these collections to their historical place, the Museum Island. Traditionally, Berlin is one of the few places in the world where from the very beginning paintings and sculptures have been collected in almost equal quantity and quality. By juxtaposing paintings and sculptures dating from the Renaissance to the Baroque, the various art genres – complemented by prints and drawings – can be brought into a wonderful dialogue that transcends the purely sector-related presentation of art. As a result, the various stages of time become graspable as epochs not only of art history, but also of broader cultural history.

The Museum Island was the great vision of the nineteenth century, showing the artistic and cultural development of Europe together with its roots in the ancient civilizations of the 'Near East'. The various museums offer the visitor a comprehensive overview and understanding of these cultures and historical processes by outstanding collections brought together in the eighteenth and especially in the nineteenth and early-twentieth centuries. It was the time when European art from the antiquity to the nineteenth century was collected, whereas the archaeological collections originated to a great extent from scientific excavations undertaken in the former Ottoman Empire and in Egypt. At that time in many of these countries there existed the law of 'partage' of archaeological finds. This meant that a foreign archaeological expedition which financed an excavation had the right to keep half of the finds. The Ottoman Empire had additional agreements with the German Empire and many antiquities arrived in Berlin as gifts to the Kaiser.

For us today, it is crucially important that the collections which we are holding in our museums reached these museums legally following the legal regulations of the time. Nevertheless, we feel obliged to have the closest possible cooperation with the countries of origin, to preserve in the best sense of the word, a 'shared heritage'. In Jordan, for several years SPK organized a research project on the site of Mshatta, near Amman, in order to investigate the building history of this Omayyad palace, whose decorated façade has been shown in the Museum of Islamic Art in Berlin since the beginning of the nineteenth century. The research at Mshatta is combined with extensive restoration work and planning of measures for site management in order to prepare the site for visitors. After its renovation, the Museum of the Ancient Near East in the south wing of the Pergamon Museum will exhibit the famous sculptures from Tell Halaf in northern Syria. Since its opening in 1930, the Pergamon Museum has been exhibiting antiquities from Iraq, of which the reconstructed Ishtar Gate from Babylon rates among the most prestigious. Museum staff have always maintained close relations with these countries: in Tell Halaf there was a large excavation ongoing until the beginning of the civil war, and in recent years the Foundation has been supporting the authorities in the preservation of the cultural heritage of these countries in their difficult fight against illicit trafficking of antiquities and the destruction of ancient sites. In Minya, in middle Egypt, we are advising the Egyptian Service of Antiquities in the preparation of an Amarna Museum, utilizing the recent finds from that site, which are so closely related to Nefertiti. There are many ways in which Western museums can cooperate with the countries of origin of these antiquities, including the exchange of specialists, curators and restorers, organizing training programmes and common research projects.

The UNESCO World Heritage site of the Museum Island is still far from being completed. Only about half of the Master Plan Museum Island has been accomplished to date. It is a large project whose goal is not only the restoration of this splendid site, but also the further development of the Museum Island into the future (see Figure 15.1). This includes the project of rebuilding the Berlin Palace, the future home of the Humboldt Forum south of the Old Museum, which was blown up by the communist regime in the GDR in 1950–51.

There has always been a close relation between the Palace and the Museum Island, because all the museum collections that were later exhibited in the buildings of the Museum Island had their origins at the Prussian Palace. Both Friedrich Wilhelm IV and Stüler, who was his master plan architect at the time, drew sketches that envisioned an architectural connection linking the Palace and the Museum Island. This vision, which in the middle of the nineteenth century was no more than an indicated idea, has now had the chance to become a reality in the early twenty-first century (see Figure 15.1).

The institution that will move into the partly rebuilt Berlin Palace is the so-called Humboldt Forum, named after brothers Alexander and Wilhelm von Humboldt. It will be a place where the collections of the so-called non-European cultures are presented. There is a particular association between these cultures and Alexander von Humboldt, the 'second Columbus', the scientific discoverer of South America. At the same time, the institution was named after Wilhelm von Humboldt. This is due to the fact that he was a linguist who did thorough research on non-European languages, particularly from South East Asia and the Pacific region.

In 2002, the German Bundestag decided to tear down the Palace of the Republic, built by the former GDR in the 1970s, and to replace it with a rebuilding of the Berlin Palace. However, this will not be a complete reconstruction. Only the southern, western and northern façades of the exterior, and three façades of the so-called Schlüter Courtyard, will receive their original Baroque look. All other parts will be designed in a modern style, geared to the specific requirements of the Humboldt Forum.

The project of reconstructing the Berlin Palace (*Berliner Schloss*) (Figure 15.8) from the beginning was to some degree controversial. The main argument in its favour was the consideration that rebuilding the Palace would close a gap in the historical urban planning of Berlin's old centre. That way, a historical ensemble would be reconstructed in its original context, and thus become comprehensible as a whole.

FIGURE 15.8 Construction site of the Berliner Schloss (Humboldt Forum) with the Museumsinsel (Museum Island), Berlin, in the background © Stiftung Berliner Schloss – Humboldtforum / Stephan Falk.

If one looks at aerial photographs dating from the time before the destruction of the Palace, it becomes very apparent that the big street axes that transect the centre of Berlin are virtually oriented towards the corners of the Palace building. This means that the structure of the Palace has a clearly formative character in the centre of Berlin. Actually, that centre was laid out from the Palace and not vice versa, because the Brandenburg Gate, as well as Schinkel's Old Museum with its colonnade façade, had been planned from and in context with the Palace.

The Berlin Palace was damaged in the course of the Second World War. However, immediately after the war it was again used as a museum, and various academic institutions had offices in the building. Then the government of the GDR gave orders to blow up and completely remove it in 1950–51 – an ideologically motivated action, as the Palace was considered to be a symbol of militarism and feudalism that ought to be completely erased by a Socialist state. Back then there were unsuccessful protests against this barbaric act of destruction, because the Berlin Palace was one of the most important Baroque buildings of northern Germany.

In a few years' time, the gap in the urban planning of Berlin's centre will be closed, and the historical façade of the Berlin Palace will once again blend in harmoniously with its environment, which is characterized by other historical buildings (see Figures 15.1 and 15.8). As the most ancient core of the city of Berlin is located in the Palace area, the beginning of the reconstruction works was preceded by excavations that took several years. The residence of the Brandenburg Electors stood at this site as early as the fifteenth century. Unfortunately, none of the remains of the older buildings found at the site were documented, neither when the Palace was exploded nor when the Palace of the Republic was built in the 1970s. As a result, all older historical traces were destroyed. However, to the west of that area the basements of parts of the former Palace structure still exist, enclosing the Eosanderhof in the north, west and south. They have been excavated, and parts of them will become integrated into the rebuilt Palace, offering the visitor a so-called 'archaeological window' to the history of the site and the building.

At the same time, the future Humboldt Forum in the reconstructed Berlin Palace will be situated in the centre of a future-oriented topography of art and culture, science and education: to the north the Museum Island, to the west the German Historical Museum, the main building of the Humboldt University, and the State Library Unter den Linden, as well as the main building of the Central and Regional Library of Berlin to the south-east. The Humboldt Forum will be furnished by three institutions. The largest space will be used by the Prussian Cultural Heritage Foundation with the non-European collections of its State Museums starting on the first floor and occupying the whole second and third floors. The remaining part of the first floor will be shared by the City Museum of Berlin with an exhibition space on the history of Berlin's relations with the world. Finally, an exhibition space for the Humboldt University of Berlin to display their collections originating in the Berlin Art Chamber (Kunstkammer) and showing exhibitions on different topics of science and research. The historical legitimacy for conjoining these institutions at this place derives from the former Art Chamber. The Art Chamber at the Palace was the origin of all the museum collections that later moved to the Museum Island (Figure 15.9). Therefore, the Palace was always more than just a residence of the Brandenburg Electors or Prussian Kings; it was also a building housing collections which have been brought together since the late seventeenth century in order to understand the world, its cultures and history, but also its nature.

The so-called non-European collections of SPK's State Museums are kept at the Ethnological Museum and the Museum of Asian Art. These collections are to some extent associated with Germany's colonial history. However, much more important for their emergence and development were Prussian-German scientific expeditions. Georg Forster, for example, accompanied James Cook on his second voyage to the Pacific and laid the foundations of the Pacific collection of the Ethnological Museum. Alexander von Humboldt brought the first objects from Mesoamerica to Berlin. Johann von Hoffmannsegg was one of the collectors who contributed to the abundant collections from the Amazonian cultures, and Hermann Schlagintweit travelled to Mongolia and Tibet. Many others might be mentioned in this context. Hence, it was Prussian scholars and explorers who in the course of the nineteenth century made an essential contribution to the compilation of worldwide unique collections from all continents in Berlin.

The inside dramaturgy of the Humboldt Forum is divided into various spheres. On the ground floor there will be a large events centre. The Humboldt Forum will include spaces for temporary exhibitions, multi-functional rooms,

FIGURE 15.9   Kunstkammer in the Berliner Schloss. Etching (1696) by Samuel Blesendorf © bpk / Kunstbibliothek, SMB / Dietmar Katz.

and auditoriums for music performances, theatre and cinema shows, panel discussions and academic events. All these spaces are intended to generate intense activities that create bridges, so to speak, from the historical collections to present and future issues. In addition, they will provide a vivid experience of the whole diversity of cultural expression. The ground floor will offer practical visitor services and facilities such as museum shops, cafés and restaurants, particularly in its eastern part close to the Schlüterhof.

After entering the building beneath Portal III under the cupola, visitors come into the entrance hall (Figure 15.10). In its immediate surroundings, special exhibition spaces are grouped in the south, and the multi-functional hall and auditorium are in the north. The large entrance hall is intended to aid quick visitor orientation and guidance, and it is from this central entrance area that the various parts of the Humboldt Forum can be accessed and explored. In addition, this central hall can be used for major events, with up to 2,000 seats.

In the south-eastern part of the ground floor is the so-called Museum of the History of the Site. In the area designated as the 'archaeological window', visitors can view the surviving excavated original basements which, in a way, lend legitimacy to the entire rebuilding project. On the ground floor, immediately above the archaeological window, the history of the site is then presented in various rooms, beginning with the building history of the Palace, continuing with the Palace of the Republic, and concluding with the rebuilding of the Palace as the Humboldt Forum. The Schlüterhof in the eastern part of the Palace will not be covered by a roof. In the north, east and south it will regain its former look thanks

FIGURE 15.10 View of the foyer of the future Humboldt Forum © Stiftung Berliner Schloss – Humboldtforum / Franco Stella.

to the reconstruction of the so-called Schlüter façades. It lends itself as a location for open-air major events on specific occasions.

The visit to the exhibitions of the museums starts on the second floor, but the presentation of large objects from the South Pacific, such as boats and meeting houses, in two cubes immediately to the north and south of the reduced Eosanderhof goes down to the first floor. The second and third floors are exclusively reserved for the presentation of the non-European collections, and will invite visitors on a journey around the world, based on the immense collections of the Ethnological Museum and the Museum of Asian Art, both of which are among the most important of their kind in the world. In that process, we attempt to present the collections in a completely new manner, in order to convey to visitors the stories told by the objects and, at the same time, to enable them to understand the structures of past and foreign cultures. As becomes evident from the excellent collection of boats from the Pacific (Figure 15.11), the phenomenon of navigation, for example, is of particular importance in Oceania and needs to be illustrated accordingly in the presentation of these objects.

Almost every ethnographical collection in the world includes masks from Africa. However, the masks are not works of art, even though we perceive them as such today. A modern presentation needs to take this into account, and inform visitors about what these 'works of art' reveal about the structure of the respective culture –

FIGURE 15.11   Display of sailboats from the Santa Cruz Islands, 1960, at the Ethnologisches Museum (Ethnology Museum), Berlin-Dahlem, 2013 © Staatliche Museen zu Berlin, Ethnologisches Museum / Dietrich Graf.

that is, what they contribute to 'descent beliefs', issues of political representation, and so on (Figure 15.12). A king's throne from Cameroon was bestowed as a gift on the German emperor Wilhelm II, who immediately passed it on to what was then the Ethnographical Museum. As an irony of fate, this diplomatic gift will now move to the place for which it was originally destined – the Berlin Palace. Of course, the history of this throne will explain German colonial history in Cameroon.

FIGURE 15.12 Commemorative head of a queen mother, Kingdom of Benin, Nigeria, early sixteenth century © Staatliche Museen zu Berlin, Ethnologisches Museum / Martin Franken.

However, it is important to consider not only the German or European outlook on the world but also the perspective from the opposite direction. From all times when Europeans came into contact with cultures of other continents, there are numerous testimonies reflecting 'the reverse glance', be it in Africa, Asia or America. The Humboldt Forum needs to tell these stories, too. Europe has long ceased to be the centre of the interpretation of the world. In this respect, people's present perspective both on their respective cultures and on the Europeans, needs to be taken into account.

The collection of the Ethnological Museum includes a whole range of objects from Central and West African cultures that were forcibly moved to South and Middle America in the course of the slave trade. Whole ethnic groups were brought to the 'New World', bringing along their own rituals, their own religion and their own artistic concepts. These merged with the autochthonous cultures of Latin America, and in addition absorbed elements of Catholicism and the art of Europe. This amalgam, the result of a fusion of diverse cultural currents, is one of the most fascinating phenomena of the modern age, and can be addressed in many ways by means of the collections of the Ethnological Museum. Another particular focus will be on the collections from Mesoamerica, which are among the largest worldwide outside Mesoamerica. They make it possible to closely trace the development of the Maya and Aztecs who, after all, built – among others – the first megacities in the New World.

The art of Asia is mostly of a religious nature, and this is particularly true for Buddhism. In this respect, the Museum of Asian Art has a well-stocked collection that will be presented in the Humboldt Forum in its whole range. In the case of Asia, too, the presentation of cultural development begins with archaeological finds dating from early times, such as the bronze products of the Shang dynasty in China and works of art from the Gandhara culture.

The Buddhist wall paintings from the caves of the Silk Road are of special importance. Particularly in the Turfan Basin area the Silk Road caves were explored by several German expeditions from Berlin at the beginning of the twentieth century. Wall paintings were brought to Berlin, and it is possible to reconstruct the caves in their original form with the original arrangement of the paintings. Central Asia at that time was indeed one of the earliest 'globalized' regions of the world with traces of religions, languages and arts of different cultures from the West as well as from the East (Figure 15.13). The presentation of Asian arts concludes with paper paintings, folding screens, hanging scrolls and other objects from the eighteenth- and nineteenth-century arts of China, Japan and Korea.

It will be particularly important to intersperse and enliven the exhibition floors at the Humboldt Forum with zones that allow for various activities indicating the respective cultural regions. During the planning process of the Humboldt Forum, there are already considerations about how to deal with the phenomena of contemporaneity. This includes the dialogue with commissioned works by contemporary artists. We have recently practised this using an eighteenth-century Chinese imperial throne as the point of departure (Figure 15.14): various artists created works of art that represent their way of responding to the object (Figure 15.15).

FIGURE 15.13   Design of the exhibition area for Central Asia with the Cave of the
Sword Bearers in the Cupola Hall © Stiftung Preußischer Kulturbesitz,
Ralph Appelbaum Associates/malsyteufel, 2014.

FIGURE 15.14   Screen for the imperial throne, China, c.1670–1700 © bpk / Staatliche
Museen zu Berlin, Museum für Asiatische Kunst / Jürgen Liepe.

FIGURE 15.15   Zhao Zhao's work, 'Waterfall' (2013), was part of the Humboldt Lab project 'Game of Thrones', which dealt with experimental artistic forms for presenting an imperial Chinese throne from the collection of the Museum für Asiatische Kunst. Photo: Jens Ziehe, Courtesy Alexander Ochs Galleries Berlin / Beijing

The distinguished Chinese architect Wang Shu will now design the exhibition hall, which will be dedicated to the presentation of Chinese imperial art of the eighteenth century. This is another valid example of what shared heritage can mean, when an architect from the country of origin designs an entire exhibition space. The various exhibition modules from other continents strongly depend on cooperation with scholars, curators, artists and representatives of Indigenous groups from the countries of origin. These exhibitions must reflect multi-perspectivity; this means that we have to tell the different stories inscribed in these objects, not only our view of them. We are cooperating with an Indigenous university at Tauca in Venezuela, for example, and will create a web-based platform for visitors to the Humboldt Forum in order to get in touch with these people, the information they can provide and the challenges of their present life. We will also work with historians from Tanzania to tell the story of the Maji-Maji insurrection against German colonial power in the early twentieth century, which can be illustrated by a few objects from the Ethnological Museum. Many other examples could be mentioned, but it will be characteristic for the Humboldt Forum that we tell the story of the world through the enlightening objects of our collections, together with the perspectives of the cultures of origin. This means not only giving the cultures and countries of origin a voice in the Humboldt Forum, but also developing co-productions together and showing the results. This is our understanding of shared heritage, and this is the challenge for the Humboldt Forum as a place for reciprocal dialogue between cultures.

The Humboldt Forum is intended to be not only a museum, but also a place of manifold encounters with the arts and cultures of the world. There will be a focus on special programmes for children and adolescents, with the goal of introducing them to other cultures of the world. Particularly in a city like Berlin, which is becoming increasingly multicultural and multi-ethnic, it is of crucial importance to give people from other cultural spheres a 'cultural home' and the opportunity to share things from their regions of origin with them. That way, they will hopefully establish ties with the Humboldt Forum as a site of their cultures and histories.

When the Humboldt Forum opens its gates in 2019, a big vision of the twenty-first century will become reality – a vision that goes back to preliminary considerations in the middle of the nineteenth century. As a site of the art and culture of Europe and their roots in the 'Near East', the Museum Island was the great idea of the nineteenth century. The Humboldt Forum, featuring the arts and cultures of Africa, Asia, Australia, Oceania and the Americas and connecting them with Europe, is our vision in the early twenty-first century. Jointly Museum Island and the Humboldt Forum will be an outstanding unit where the presentation of the cultures of the world (see Figures 15.1 and 15.8) and of their narratives will not only tell fascinating stories about mankind, but will also reflect a new spirit of worldwide cooperation in the best sense of shared heritage.

References

Eissenhauer, M., Bähr, A. and Rochau-Shalem, E. (eds.), 2012. *Museumsinsel Berlin*. Munich: Hirmer.

Flierl, T. and Parzinger, H. (eds.), 2009. *Humboldt-Forum Berlin. Das Projekt*. Berlin: Theater der Zeit.

Heizmann, K. and Parzinger, H., 2011. 'Workshop des International Advisory Board zur Neupräsentation der Sammlungen des Ethnologischen Museums und des Museums für Asiatische Kunst im Humboldt-Forum'. *Jahrbuch Preußischer Kulturbesitz* 47: 293–317.

Parzinger, H., 2009. 'Eine steinreiche Zeit', in *Kleider machen Leute – Bauten machen Staat. Nationale Selbstdarstellung im öffentlichen Raum. Festschrift für Florian Mausbach*. Berlin: Bundesamt für Bauwesen und Raumordnung, pp. 44–47.

Parzinger, H., 2010a. 'Das Humboldt-Forum nimmt Form an', in J. Haspel (ed.), *Welterbe weiterbauen – St Petersburg und Berlin-Potsdam. ICOMOS – Hefte des Deutschen Nationalkomitees* 49. Berlin: ICOMOS Deutschland, pp. 98–104.

Parzinger, H., 2010b. 'Humboldtforum – Das Schloss zur Welt. Aufgabe und Bedeutung des wichtigsten Kulturprojekts in Deutschland am Anfang des 21. Jahrhunderts'. Berliner Extrablatt. *Mitteilungsblatt des Fördervereins Berliner Schloss e.V. 5, Oktober 2010*. Berlin: Förderverein Berliner Schloss e.V., pp. 6–12.

Parzinger, H., 2010c. 'Schlossdebatten. Nutzungskonzepte und ihre Folgen zwischen Geschichtsbezogenheit und Zukunftsvision'. *Jahrbuch Preußischer Kulturbesitz* 45, pp. 409–34.

Parzinger, H., 2011a. *Das Humboldt-Forum. 'Soviel Welt mit sich verbinden als möglich'. Aufgabe und Bedeutung des wichtigsten Kulturprojekts in Deutschland zu Beginn des 21. Jahrhunderts.* Berlin: Stiftung Berliner Schloss-Humboldtforum.

Parzinger, H., 2011b. 'Arkadien in Berlin-Mitte'. *Jahrbuch Preußischer Kulturbesitz* 46: 53–60.

Parzinger, H., 2011c. 'Das Humboldt-Forum. Aufgabe und Bedeutung'. *Jahrbuch Preußischer Kulturbesitz* 46: 216–44.

Parzinger, H., 2011d. 'Die Kraft der Kunst und die Macht der Reflexion: eine Geschichte vom Widerstreit zum Wechselspiel'. *Berlin-Brandenburgischen Akademie der Wissenschaften (vormals Preußische Akademie der Wissenschaften). Jahrbuch 2010* (2011): 200–13.

Parzinger, H., 2011e. 'Die Kultur in der Mitte Berlins', in *Berliner Wirtschaftsgespräche e. V. Themenbroschüre Berlin im Aufwind.* Berlin: Berliner Wirtschaftsgespräche e.V., pp. 93–94.

Parzinger, H., 2011f. 'Museumsinsel Berlin – UNESCO-Welterbe auf dem Weg zu neuem Glanz', in *Wirtschaftsstandort Berlin-Brandenburg, Chancen und Perspektiven einer Region.* Berlin: Berliner Wirtschaftsgespräche e.V., pp. 142–47.

Parzinger, H., 2011g. 'The Museum Island Master Plan'. *UNESCO Today. A Magazine of the German Commission for UNESCO* 3. Paris: UNESCO Publishing, pp. 48–49.

Parzinger, H., 2011h. 'Von der Kultur her gedacht. Die historische Mitte Berlins als Ort der Weltkulturen', in *Die Museumsinsel. Generalinstandsetzung eines Welterbes. Architektur & Bauphysik* 14 (2011): 6–9.

Parzinger, H., 2012a. 'Das Humboldt-Forum – Zum Stand der Konzeptentwicklung bis 2013'. *Jahrbuch Preußischer Kulturbesitz* 48 (2014): 470–77.

Parzinger, H., 2012b. 'Die Mitte Berlins von der Kultur her neu denken – das Humboldt-Forum im Berliner Schloss', in M. Eissenhauer, A. Bähr and E. Rochau-Shalem (eds), *Berlin: Museumsinsel Berlin.* Munich: Hirmer, pp. 392–403.

Parzinger, H., 2012c. 'Sammlungen und die Dynamik des Denkens', in C. Behrmann, S. Trinks and M. Bruhn (eds), *Intuition und Institution: Kursbuch Horst Bredekamp.* Berlin: de Gruyter, pp. 19–40.

Parzinger, H., 2013. 'Die Stiftung Preußischer Kulturbesitz und die UNESCO-Welterbestätte Museumsinsel Berlin'. *UNESCO-Welterbe in Deutschland und Mitteleuropa. Bilanz und Perspektiven. ICOMOS Hefte des Deutschen Nationalkomitees* 57. Berlin: ICOMOS Deutschland, pp. 69–76.

Parzinger, H., 2014a. Berlin braucht einen solchen Ort. Rede zur Grundsteinlegung für das Humboldt-Forum. *Jahrbuch Preußischer Kulturbesitz* 49 (2013): 384–89.

Parzinger, H., 2014b. 'Berlin wird wieder Zentrum der altertumswissenschaftlichen und archäologischen Forschung: Eröffnung des Archäologischen Zentrums der Staatlichen Museen zu Berlin'. *Jahrbuch Preußischer Kulturbesitz* 48 (2012): 62–65.

Parzinger, H., 2014c. 'Das Entrée zur Museumsinsel. Grundsteinlegung für die James-Simon-Galerie'. *Jahrbuch Preußischer Kulturbesitz* 49 (2013): 102–06.

Parzinger, H., 2014d. 'Veränderung der Berliner Museumslandschaft'. *Das Neue Berlin – 25 Jahre nach dem Fall der Mauer. Berliner Wirtschaftsgespräche e.V. Themenbroschüre 2014.* Berlin: Berliner Wirtschaftsgespräche e.V., pp. 107–08.

16

A MUSEUM TRIANGLE

Ethics, standards of care and the pleasure of perception

Dorota Folga-Januszewska

It is almost 2,500 years since the earliest debates emerged on the phenomena that would later shape the long life of the museum as an educational institution, a place of heritage commemoration, and a platform for public discussion and culture-based therapy. Another topic of debate was to what extent ethics is a product of advanced human civilization or a genetically encoded arrangement of social relations?[1] Two decades ago these questions were joined by a new one: What makes the physical and social space of the museum so special as to elicit such high attendance? The remarkable queues forming outside these often unprofitable, knowledge- and cognition-oriented places are among the most interesting psychological, social and perceptual phenomena about museums.

The following are three seemingly disparate features of museums that shape the essence, or even *are* the essence, of a museum:

1. Operations that are regulated by the principles of ethics;
2. Heritage resources that must be taken care of according to established standards and best knowledge;
3. A place in time and space, so shaped that tangible and intangible wealth inter-twine to form a deep sensory and mental experience: where perception is the goal and, at the same time, the pleasure of existence.[2]

The standardization of these three features makes the museum a supra-local entity, and a global phenomenon whereby that which is immediate and sensory must interconnect with that which is regulated by external factors and a measure of objectively determined agreement. It is a worthwhile endeavour to think about these three features, and the borders that can divide as well as connect them.

Ethics

The experience of the last two decades clearly demonstrates that codes of ethics, in particular the *ICOM Code of Ethics for Museums*, have international scope and impact. In the world of museums, the principles included in the ICOM Code[3] play the role of providing a model for the thought and work of a museum, as well as philosophical issues underlying its sense of 'mission' and key purposes. The *ICOM Code of Ethics for Museums*, adopted in 1986 at the ICOM General Conference in Buenos Aires, was later amended in a two-stage process in 2001 and 2004 – providing the Code of today. In 2013, ICOM adopted a further (and supporting) collection of principles and guidelines, this time aimed at museum personnel devoted to the study and storage of evidence of life: the *ICOM Code of Ethics for Natural History Museums* (ICOM 2013), developed by ICOM's International Committee for Natural History Museums (NATHIST).

Much has been written about the ICOM Code of Ethics. However, one should remember that its roots, just like the roots of the *musaeum* (Folga-Januszewska 2015), stretch back to the Graeco-Roman world and indirectly stem from Aristotle's *Nicomachean Ethics*, combining the tradition of Aristotle's works with the history of the creation of one of the first natural history museums in Athens in the fourth century BCE (see Phillips Simpson 1997; Besterman 2011). Throughout museums' history, the need to moderate the overriding principles of morality and integrity were recognized. This is not surprising, given that during the earliest centuries of their development museums were located in temples, and theft of an object from a venerated treasury was considered sacrilege (Pomian 1987). Whether they were the *pinacothecas* (painted wooden objects) associated with Greek temples of the fourth or third centuries BCE; treasuries concealing calligraphy scrolls that ranked among the prized accessories of Chinese Emperors' palaces; Japanese Buddhist temples, such as *Tōshōdai-ji* (唐招堤寺) from the eight century; or Islamic *waqf* (وقف): all of these collections, however differently disposed and located, were under a special kind of protection, where not only tangible wealth, but also associated intangible traditions, such as the treatment of cult objects and respect for human remains, imposed norms of care whose essence could not always be recorded in formal regulations at the local level.

Museum 'personnel' in these disparate contexts were held in the same esteem as doctors, priests and judges. They were respected by communities, and this respect obliged them to formulate rules of care and treatment of sacred objects that changed over time and according to different cultures, but were governed by an important common imperative: the welfare of a collection and its commemoration, which required protection from intentional or unintentional acts causing any harm. In this brief historical sketch, the development of carefully delineated codes of conduct in the care and housing of special objects of heritage can be seen to have a long tradition in many different cultural and social settings.

The first modern code of museum ethics was published in 1925 by the American Association of Museums, founded in 1906, to disseminate the principles and standards of conduct appropriate for modern museum institutions (Lovin 1994; AAM online). From that time, until the first comprehensive ICOM Code was adopted in 1986, the implementation of museum ethics principles in such institutions worldwide was more or less left to local discretion, or various national codes to determine. However, in practice, a sense of regulated museum conduct according to ethical ideals was generally omnipresent in museums on all continents. Globally destructive wars and armed conflict on a huge scale in the twentieth century brought to fresh attention the need to employ ethical norms – in particular when it came to collections that were appropriated by force through armed conflict or acquired in breach of international agreements or treaties. Whatever could not be enforced politically became deferred to a generalized professional 'principle of moral conduct' of museum workers themselves. For example, in the 1990s, after negotiations on collections appropriated during the Second World War deteriorated, Europe evidenced grass-roots initiatives by ICOM members themselves, who proposed to study *avant la lettre* the provenance of numerous 'orphan works' housed in European museums. As time went by, this project became an administrative obligation in many states, where systematic provenance research was introduced, and this stimulated the production of new catalogues, including indication of works of unknown origin.

In 2005, museum ethics principles received greater attention following the integration of the ICOM Code of Ethics, at the European Council's initiative, into the recommendations for museums that undertake international exhibition exchanges between EU member-states (see European Council 2005). The supra-local norms included in the ICOM Code thereby increasingly became model procedures to follow in many difficult situations, particularly when international conventions were not ratified by particular countries or there was a need to administer collections that contained pieces belonging to the sphere of spirituality (human remains, grave goods, or objects of cult and religion).

When speaking of the principles of ethics in museums, one cannot forget two other regulative instruments, including the 'Washington Principles' – rules developed during the 1998 Washington Conference on Nazi-confiscated art – and the so-called Terezín Declaration of 2009, a 'non-binding agreement whose signatories agree to take steps to implement national programmes addressing the issue of looted property according to best-practice principles for restitution and compensation' (Matassa 2011). The United Kingdom was the first country to adopt both these recommendations even as it regulated other problems, whose solution was considered to be the area of so-called pro-ethics, as illustrated in, for instance, *Combating Illicit Trade: Guidelines for Museums, Libraries and Archives* (2005) or the *Data Protection Code of Practice* (2007) and Matassa (2011). In recent years, museums in many countries were confronted with 'culture wars' – a result of post-colonial movements and government-backed support for religion in many states (Dubin 2006). In these sometimes extreme situations, the supra-local principles of ethics turned out to be much more effective as a standards framework for museum administrators rather than local laws.

At the core of the *ICOM Code of Ethics for Museums* is the assumption that the mission of public museums is the care, interpretation and preservation of tangible and intangible cultural heritage entrusted to them by society. This assumes that museum collections are public property, and that the curators employed in museums fulfil the role of caretakers who represent a given community. This interpretation of the museum's function is the source of obligations placed on museum workers to place public interest above individual interests. And, as a result, there is pressure to adjust administrative, civil and criminal laws to uphold the principles that initially functioned merely as ethical norms. We may therefore conclude that the generally positive attitude of legislative bodies to the principles of museum ethics is a measure of their democratic nature, and disfavours anti-social attitudes.

Procedures and standards of care

Another set of rules referred to as standards or museum procedures plays a different role in museums. Unlike the principles guiding good conduct, as set out in the ICOM Code, standards lay down the procedures to follow in museums, in a detailed, sometimes meticulous, manner. The precise nature of such standards is both an asset and a disadvantage: an asset because the standards regulate complex activities that require a lot of attention and determine the safety of exhibits and people, almost leading museum workers by the hand; and a disadvantage because that which is overly detailed quickly becomes obsolete, especially when it comes to advances in technology. Thus these standards may often prove to be short-lived. Safety norms and security systems protecting against theft of information, for instance, have to be updated on a regular basis. Nonetheless, today it is hard to imagine a large, multi-functional museum facility whose administrative staff fail to produce new regulations on an ongoing basis. Some might include specific documents, such as contracts for museum exhibit loans, which are similar in the majority of EU member states; or detailed regulations such as instructions for cleaning atypical objects (Folga-Januszewska 2008). In their everyday work, contemporary museum organizations such as NEMO (Network of European Museum Organisations), or ICOM's many International Committees for specialized disciplines, provide model contracts, digitization or restoration standards.

Today, the widespread presence of operational standards includes nearly all areas of museum life. The conduct of various EU commissions or working groups often requires excessive standardization of procedures, which is now considered to be a threat to the diversity of cultures. In fact, only artistic actions or situations where uniqueness is valued in its own right are exceptions maintained that confirm the general rules. Museums, which for the most part are cultural or educational institutions, approach the standardization process in a specific way. Presently, thanks to the work of specialized committees on standard requirements, and reports on their implementation, nearly all museums' operations have strictly defined procedures (Pettersson *et al.* 2010). Yet their diversity, number of details, or differences arising through the particular area of application do not alter the common goal of their formulation: which is standardization.

Many authors who study the common-standards process in museums emphasize that the introduction of standardization improves the safety of collections and people, reduces conflict or uncertainty of purpose, and increases the effectiveness of supervision and management of the institutions (Lord and Lord 1997). Thus, the nature of such actions is not only pragmatic but also psychological and social: it increases the transparency of the relationship between museum personnel and the outside world. Although artists' and humanists' reluctance to apply detailed regulations and procedures is widely known, the fundamental role of standards – that is, the development of a common language to describe museum activities – is maintained.

Furthermore, it is assumed that standardization should include rules that *must* be followed – since this is an essential prerequisite for a given institution to be considered a museum – as well as providing procedures that define the high quality of an institution's services and activity in the external world beyond its walls. One can conclude that the standardization of rules of care of collections, and procedures for contact with the public, serve not only to regulate internal activity, but become specific criteria of evaluation for auditors and controlling bodies. It is much easier for officials who supervise museums to scrutinize internal processes based on requirements adopted and described in the standard procedures – in this situation, opinions formed about an institution's performance will be closer to a common truth than would be the case if judgements were formed on the basis of unclear or imprecise translations of mission or purposes. However, it should be emphasized that all procedures must nevertheless be consistent with both the adopted museum mission and applicable laws of a given country.

The methodology of standardization should always be a product of the adoption of rules of cooperation between museums, including international cooperation, local traditions and respect for cultural identity. Yet of course, the whole process is not without difficulties; the management of a museum requires finding a happy medium between long-developed cultural traditions and the strict safety requirements developed under more contingent circumstances of the present. And cultural differences remain significant: it is no surprise to find that the rules governing access to collections in Japan are very different from those applicable in Europe or in African countries.

Thus, the second general feature of museums – the protection of collections – is largely conditioned by the level and quality of standards, but in small part also by a society's awareness of its own culture, which also provides crucial indicators of varying levels of education, both within the home and in formal education, for which standards are established by social and political organizations (both at national and local government levels).

The pleasure of perception

During the process of regulation of norms and standardized practices, we sometimes forget about the third feature of operations that determines the success of museums: the way they display their collections according to factors of the physiology and psychology of perception, and taking into account another important phenomenon, the experience of pleasure. The organization of exhibitions, displays and museum architecture design have a long history that, just like ethical norms and the notion of *musaeum*, extends back over 2,000 years. Today, this area or field of study may be called neuro-museum practices or neuromuseology.

The 1990s and first decade of the twenty-first century were characterized by an intensive development of all branches of cognitive neuroscience, a field of study covered through linking disciplines across faculties of medicine, neurobiology, philosophy, sociology and even economics. Cognitive neuroscience was then largely apprehended in the museum field through issues involving architecture, design, interior design (including museum interiors) and, finally, art. After 2002, the fundamentals of neuroaesthetics became an obligatory subject in many art schools, but also in business schools (through attention to neuro-marketing), and in the training of emergency-response teams. For art historians, the sign of changing times was the 2007 publication of John Onians's *Neuroarthistory* – an analysis of source texts from ancient history to present times, dedicated to the atypical or even impossible phenomena in the 'real' world, and especially the response of the human brain to aesthetic experience, or works of art. Other art historians, such as Norman Bryson or Warren Neidich (2003), had also demonstrated strong intuitions as to the role of art and culture creators in the evolution of the brain. It was noticeable in discussions and texts at the end of the twentieth century and shortly after 2000 that art history methodologists and theorists increasingly observed that two different ways of interpreting art were converging: one of a semiotic nature; the other based on the analysis of form and the psychological and physiological effects of aesthetic phenomena on human mechanisms of visual cognition. These two tendencies were merging in interdisciplinary studies of which the starting point is the neural foundation of consciousness (Koch 2004).

The history of such studies, conducted independently in many dispersed centres around the world, is complex (Zeki 1999), and to comprehend the methodologies involved requires cross-linked knowledge from various fields of study. However, one effect of great interest is that studies in cognitive neuroscience were gradually migrating from laboratories, hospitals and university institutes to museums (see Francuz 2013 and 2014). It turned out to be observable (as often occurs coincidentally in the history of science) that the so-called 'museum situation' or the 'museum space context' changes and reorganizes the kind of perception our brain employs in such an environment into positively apprehended but 'non-specific' experience. To simplify the matter, one may say that an object in its original environment is perceived in a completely different way when it is relocated and becomes part of a museum exhibit. In the 1970s, this phenomenon had already been described in the expanding field of semiology by Krzysztof Pomian, in his theory of *semiophores* (Pomian 1987). From a different aspect, the study of the development of 'conceptual art' in the twentieth century would pursue a parallel journey back to the bicycle wheel, urinal, or similar standardized objects selected from ordinary life by Marcel Duchamp – and *transformed* when relocated in a museum.

An exposition of the simplest mechanisms of this phenomenon, which is also called the 'museum syndrome', would take up an entire publication. It is a subject of numerous works associated with the so-called 'visual brain' published since the second half of the 1990s (Milner and Goodale 2006). For many of us – museum practitioners and theorists – this is significant for practical reasons. The discovery of the phenomenon can be compared to the influence exerted by psychoanalysis at the beginning of the 1920s on the shape of psychology and psychiatry, or of the invention of photography on the way our civilization is documented. It turns out that the process of brain evolution, which conditions our individual and group activity, has found itself, as neurobiologists say, a *specific enclave* for intensified activity – in museums.

Human beings first lived in the natural world and had to adapt; they then developed a 'second nature' and designed cities. To function in this new, urbanized environment they developed new skills, new perceptions and reflexes, new communication methods; and different rules of life, more varied standards and rules of coexistence.

From the perspective of contemporary advances in cognitive neuroscience, the next form of our civilization to evolve intensively will be museums. This is of utmost interest to museum practitioners, as in their tangible and intangible, practical and spiritual dimensions, museums encompass all areas of human activity, cumulated knowledge, and all fields of continuing study. Art, nature, science and technology museums today are all undergoing self-transformations as they provide their collections with 'new contexts', incorporating dedicated spaces for displays, specialized narratives of interpretation, and diversified communication codes. Organized according to their own rules and governed by laws beyond the conditions of everyday reality, museum interiors will stimulate our development 'in very different ways'. The ability to move around this imaginary, and at the same time real, museum time and space is already becoming an increasingly common element of cultural education; and it intertwines in new ways with the most important continuing objective of the museum – the accomplishment of its public mission of engagement of human minds and sensibilities.

In the longer overview: the foundation processes of museums changed significantly after the second half of the eighteenth century. The essence of the change was the rendition into the public domain of former private collections: providing a transformative access of cultural heritage and scientific knowledge to the so-called general public, making museums places of common education, and over the last decades of the twentieth century, places of therapy and intensified social interaction on the part of visitors. The process continues to progress towards the formation of different areas of cognitive and sense perception being heightened in museums. From the present vantage point, it was and it still is an interesting process of evolution of a new phenomenon of 'theatres of the world' where, as Umberto Eco pointed out, there is now a vertigo of lists jostling our consciousness,[4] but their aim is to heighten cultural awareness. This is particularly important for the social practice of museums, as highlighted by the 'new museology'.

One should remember that a museum (as has always been the case in history) is an institution where emotions evoked by sensory perception immediately overlap with interpretation of significance and with the sense of identity. One cannot forget that museums, as 'temples of perception', were first organized as sites that were on the one hand strictly semiotic (language classification, records, marks, codes, descriptions, standardization); while on the other hand, they were characterized by unique form and matter shaped by their particular character (and not least, the cult of the original). It was in museums, from the very beginning of their existence – from the *Mouseion* of Athens and Alexandria, through Greek *pinacothecas*, medieval treasuries, Renaissance collections and cabinets of curiosities of the sixteenth, seventeenth and eighteenth centuries – that the publicly displayed galleries *collided*, at all times, in their difference from everyday practice. There were dissonances created in those pervasive devices of *ekphrasis* – or the word descriptions that accompanied visual images since antiquity (and the implication that every object has its own imaginary image), creating multiple tensions with the fully sensory presence of art works, or with museum exhibits as objects of very specific tangibility. Anyone who has ever worked in a museum will know that the first work (s)he memorably performed at this entrusted facility involved the 'artificial' separation of the 'meaning' (content) of a described object from the tangible features of its being that must be objectified. The first expert contact with the object invariably occurred in the evaluation of its physical existence – thus a sculpture of the *Pensive Christ* first had to be apprehended as a piece of polychrome lime-wood of specific dimensions – 'forcing' the object to refer back to its quotidian, material origins. Meanwhile to all sensory experience, it was an iconographic, cultural, contextual and semantic being.

Every day museums witness in practice what some art historians consider to be impossible: context-free perception of an object, and its removal from an original setting. A work of art, yet surely also every element of a museum collection, becomes – for that moment – a context-free object; and only after tangible and sensory identification does it shift back to acquire other identifying factors such as significance, influences, meaning. During this process, in an unavoidable way, a museum exhibit momentarily loses its former affiliation to an anterior whole. It becomes an atom in a new compound – a part of a structure known as a collection. Building collections in museums is like *building new realities, new connections, new references*. This is *at the heart of neural museology's methodology*: it examines the way our brain adapts to the behaviour and interpretation of elements functioning in a new system, abstracted from reality. The phenomenon has attracted the interest of writers for centuries. As observers, they perceived in museums unusual worlds – for some fascinating, for others deterring – as a result of the experience of objects singled out from the order of everyday life. Such experiences have been described variously by Max Frisch, Thomas Mann, Gustave Flaubert, Vladimir Nabokov, Tadeusz Różewicz or the Polish Nobel Prize winning author, Wisława Szymborska (Stölzl 1997; Szymborska 1981: 36).[5]

In the second half of the twentieth century, a new enquiry into art, culture and science studies began to take shape, although it was generally ignored for a long time. The methodology of this knowledge was based on the analysis of the effects of museum exhibits in new and identifiably artificial contexts. In 1999, in *Contemporary Cultures of Display*, Emma Barker reflected on Malraux's *Musée Imaginaire* (Museum Without Walls):

> For Malraux, the museum without walls is the latest stage in a process of the 'metamorphosis' begun by the museum proper. It is the museum, he argues, that transforms an object (such as a fourteenth-century altarpiece) into a work of art by allowing it to be appreciated for its formal qualities alone without regard to the setting for which it was made or the function it once fulfilled.
>
> *(Barker 1999: 9)*

But that which Malraux considered in the 1960s as 'the latest stage' of the museum has now become a starting point for a new contemporary museology (in neural museology). Somewhat ironically, the more the humanities, and art history and theory in particular, suffer from the crisis of method, the more museums continue to flourish with new activities, exhibitions and projects whose dimension is not only scientific, cultural or artistic, but also psychological and social.

For museum theorists (especially museologists), this is a sign that the philosophy of the institution of the museum is providing the decisive direction that shapes and organizes the institution in new ways today; that the *exhibition* is the finale of a long, conscious process of collecting, selecting and displaying; and that the creation of a *collection* proper – building the paths of awareness and interpretation – provides the materials and organizing activities of museums' continuing process of comprehending the world. And more importantly, during these processes we (as the social subjects of the museum) experience crucial changes in perception, in an evolution of awareness and accumulation of multiple mechanisms of seeing, interpreting and understanding. Thus, in museums we practise the interconnection and combination of two crucial areas of human cognition, incorporating the dimensions of both spiritual and sensory experiences.

At this stage, a final question arises and points back to the domain of ethics: How should this new and heightened awareness of the conditions shaping museum time and space be linked with the notion of ethics and the rules of heritage protection? This arouses an encounter bound to be full of controversy: a meeting between the ungovernable and 'crazy' world of art and design (and at the same time its most inspiring features), and the 'safe' world of a museum, shored up by its rules, its political and social strictures, and its action methods and procedures regulating its behaviour around standardization. It is time to acknowledge that the institutions where we work are actually offering innovative opportunities for development: becoming new scientific and social centres of experiencing development, emotions, education and awareness in the post-digital era, where, after decades of fascination with multimedia and technology, the value of the senses and the conditions of real space are appreciated anew.

This is why the triangle of ethics-standards-pleasure of perception is slowly assuming the shape of a circle, where there is neither beginning nor end, only a beautiful shape functioning perfectly.

Notes

1 See, for instance, the theses of Lori Gruen, *Ethics and Animals*, Cambridge Applied Ethics. Cambridge: Cambridge University Press, 2011. In particular, the chapters titled 'Analyzing human exceptionalism' and 'Who is ethically considerable?', pp. 4–30.
2 Perception is understood here as rational observation – as when the role of sense-perception correlates with objectively apprehended knowledge.
3 The full text of the *ICOM Code of Ethics for Museums* is provided as *Appendix I* in the present publication. It is also available online for download from the ICOM website (with links to translations in French, Spanish, and many other languages). The English version is accessible at: http://icom.museum/professional-standards/code-of-ethics.
4 Exhibition: *Mille e tre*, opened on 7 November 2009 at the Louvre Museum, and Umberto Eco reflections in *La vertigine della lista*.
5 In the poet W. Szymborska's (the 1991 Nobel Laureate) words:

> 'Museum'
> There have been plates but not appetite.
> Wedding rings but no love returned
> For at least three hundred years,
> There is a fan – where are the rosy cheeks?
> There are swords – where is the anger?
> Nor does the lute twang at dusk.
> For want of eternity the thousand
> Old things have been assembled [...].

References

Ambrose, T. and Paine, C., 2006. *Museum Basics. Second Edition, The Heritage: Care – Preservation – Management*. London: Routledge.

American Association of Museums, 1925. New York: American Association of Museums.

Barker, E., 1999. 'Introduction', in E. Barker (ed.), *Contemporary Cultures of Display*. New Haven, CT: Yale University Press; London: The Open University.

Besterman, T., 2011. 'Museum ethics', in Sharon Macdonald (ed.), *A Companion to Museum Studies*. Oxford: Blackwell, pp. 431–41.

Cooper, D.E. (ed.), 1997. *Ethics: The Classic Readings*. Oxford: Oxford University Press.

Data Protection: Code of Practice, 2002 [2004], at: www.open.ac.uk/university-documents/data-protection-code.html (accessed 18 December 2015).

Dubin, S.C., 2006. 'Incivilities in civil(-ized) places: "Culture wars" in comparative perspective', in Sharon MacDonald (ed.), *A Companion to Museum Studies*. Oxford: Blackwell, pp. 477–93.

European Council, 2005. *Lending to Europe: Recommendations on Collection Mobility for European Museums*. [Council Resolution 13839/04], compiled by R. De Leeuw, C. Acidini, K. Berg, D. Folga-Januszewska, *et al.*

Folga-Januszewska, D., 2008. 'Umowa wypożyczenia rekomendowana przez NEMO', '*Muzealnictwo*', Vol. 49: 42–67.

Folga-Januszewska, D., 2015. Folga-Januszewska, D., 2015, *Muzeum. Fenomeny i problemy*, Universitas; Cracow.

Francuz, P., 2013. Jak ludzie oglądają obrazy? Perspektywa nauki poznawczej', in D. Folga-Januszewska and E. Grygiel (eds), *Edukacja w muzeum rzeczywistym i wirtualnym*, Universitas; Cracow.

Francuz, P., 2014. *Imagia. W kierunku neurokognitywnej teorii obrazu*. Lublin: Wydawnictwo Kul.

ICOM, 2013. *ICOM Code of Ethics for Natural History Museums*. Paris: ICOM, at: http://icom.museum/uploads/media/nathcode_ethics_en.pdf (accessed 16 December 2014).

Koch, Christoph, 2004. *The Quest for Consciousness: A Neurobiological Approach*. New York: Roberts and Company Publishers.

Lord, B. and Lord, G.D., 1997. *The Manual of Museum Management*. Walnut Creek, CA: AltaMira Press.

Lovin, R.W., 1994. 'What is ethics?', *American Association Museum Forum: Occasional Papers and Readings on Museum Issues and Standards*. Washington, DC: American Association.

Matassa, F., 2011. *Museum Collections Management: A Handbook*. London: Facet, pp. 31–42.

Milner, A.D. and Goodale, M.A., 2006. *The Visual Brain in Action*. Oxford: Oxford Univeristy Press.

Neidich, W., 2003. *Blow-Up: Photography, Cinema and the Brain*. New York: D.A.P.

Onians, J. 2007, *Neuroarthistory: From Aristotle and Pliny to Baxandall and Zeki*. New Haven, CT: Yale University Press.

Pettersson, S., Hagedorn-Saupe, M., Jyrkkiö, T. and Weij, A. (eds), 2010. *Encouraging Collection Mobility: A Way Forward for Museums in Europe*. Helsinki: Finnish National Gallery.

Phillips Simpson, Peter L., 1997. *The Politics of Aristotle, by Aristotle*. Chapel Hill, NC: University of North Carolina Press.

Pomian, K., 1987. *Collectionneurs, amateurs et curieux Paris, Venice: XVIe–XVIIIe siècle*. Paris: Gallimard.

Stölzl, C., 1997. *Menschen im Museum. Eine Sammlung von Geschichten und Bildern*. Berlin: Deutsches Historiche Museum.

Szymborska, W., 1981. *Sounds, Feelings, Thoughts: Seventy Poems by Wisława Szymborska*. Translated and introduced by Magnus J. Krynski and Robert A. Maguire. Princeton, NJ: Princeton University Press, p. 36.

UK Department of Culture, Media and Sport, 2003. *The Report of the Working Group on Human Remains*, at: www.sc.ehu.es/scrwwwsr/Medicina-Legal/_private/Human%20remains%20report%20MUSEUM.pdf (accessed 18 December 2015).

UK Department of Culture, Media and Sport, 2005. *Combating Illicit Trade: Due Diligence Guidelines for Museums, Libraries and Archives on Collecting and Borrowing Cultural Material*, at: http://webarchive.nationalarchives.gov.uk/+/http:/www.culture.gov.uk/reference_library/publications/3697.aspx (accessed 18 December 2015).

Zeki, S., 1993. *A Vision of the Brain*. London: Wiley-Blackwell.

Zeki, S., 1999. *Inner Vision: An Exploration of Art and the Brain*. Oxford: Oxford University Press.

17

THE CHINESE MUSEUM

Transformation and change through ethics construction

An Laishun

In order to define and guide the basic values, working principles and behaviour of museum institutions and individual museum professionals, ethical guiding principles have been developed to ensure the professionalization of the museum in China. Professional ethics standards in the museum field are universal, regardless of the museum's location, how it is managed or its specific disciplines. However, the specific political and economic environments, cultures and traditions, law systems and governance structures in different countries require that the establishment of professional ethical standards be a process of continuous development and maturity. The *ICOM Code of Ethics for Museums* (ICOM-CEM) in China, and its promotion, dissemination and utilization, has brought about profound and positive transformation for museums in China. Indeed, to a large extent, this basic principle of professional ethics encourages change in or transformation of Chinese museums, largely due to the increasing internationalization of Chinese society, and reflection on and reassertion of museums and their practitioners' unique identities. Nevertheless, many problems and challenges remain.

Since the beginning of the twenty-first century, Chinese museums have seen an unprecedented period of rapid development, with remarkable growth in numbers. Compared with only 2,970 museums registered in China in 2008, there were 4,500 in 2014, with 1,540, established within six years. This represents an average of 256 museums created each year. Together, these museums collect approximately 35.05 million movable cultural relics and organize and hold 22,000 exhibitions, attracting about 600 million visitors on average each year. The number of visitors reached 718 million in 2014.[1]

The diversification of founders and governing bodies of Chinese museums in recent years has been a cause for concern. Although few privately run museums existed twenty years ago, the annual registration inspection conducted by the State Administration of Cultural Heritage (SACH) in 2013 showed that 164 new private

TABLE 17.1 Statistics of Registered Chinese Museums 2008–2014. Data compiled and summarized by An Laishun, according to the relevant statistics of the State Administration of Cultural Heritage.

Year/Type of museum	2008	2009	2010	2011	2012	2013	2014
Number of national registered museums	2,970	3,020	3,252	3,589	3,866	4,165	4,510
State-owned	2,651	2,692	2,819	3,054	3,219	3,354	3,528
Heritage sector-owned	2,161	2,193	2,330	2,473	2,560	2,693	2,798
Non-heritage sector-owned	490	499	489	581	659	661	730
Non-state-owned	319	328	433	535	647	811	982

museums were created in 2013, representing an increase of 19.5 per cent in 2013, over 2012, in the total number of museums. This growth continued in 2014, with 171 new privately run museums created, accounting for 21.8 per cent of the total number of registered museums in China. At the same time, the number of museums run by institutions outside the culture and heritage systems also surged.

In the context of the new museum landscape, the construction of professional ethics for Chinese museums involves similar issues to those facing museums world-wide. These include the professional ethics of preserving cultural and natural heritage, the relationship with different communities and cultural groups, as well as illicit traffic in cultural heritage. However, Chinese museums must also consider the specific political, legislative and administrative environment in China. Further, they must contemplate how to promote and provide training on professional ethics standards for newcomers, to enable them to establish professional ethics systems in their individual practice while strengthening the overall ethical value of a museum as a whole.

From general rules to a system of professional ethics

In the past decades, the establishment of professional ethics standards for Chinese museums evolved from general working rules for museums outlined by Chinese governments into the construction of a relatively complete museums value system. Before the 1980s, Chinese museums did not have a complete set of professional ethical standards. For historical reasons, China's public museums mostly belonged to so-called public institutions – that is, 'social service organizations run by national authorities through the use of state-owned assets were mainly engaged in the activities of education, science and technology, culture and health, etc. for the purpose of public benefit'.[2] Meanwhile, privately run museums emerged only a dozen years ago. As for public museums as public institutions, professional ethics were often confused with political requirements and working discipline, which were sometimes used to replace professional ethics. For example, the Publicity Department of the CPC Central Committee agreed on 28 April 1981 that the Code of Conduct for Cultural Relics Staff, formulated and issued by the State Administration of Cultural Heritage, included ten provisions, such as the following:

[…] devoting oneself wholeheartedly to the work, strictly implementing post-responsibility, and striving to fulfill the assigned task; caring for heritage to ensure its safety just as the soldiers do with their weapons; forbidding embezzlement and defalcation of public heritage; forbidding national heritage to be given as a gift to any individual [including superiors]; prohibiting the purchase of cultural relics sold by civilians for themselves or relatives; insisting that cultural relics for sale approved by superiors can only be sold to relic stores and not to individuals in any form; prohibiting the resale of cultural relics for enrichment; prohibiting the lending of national collected relics to any individual […].

Although some regulations inspired by the *Code of Ethics for Museums* (CEM) in China were issued by the Chinese government between 1980 and 1990, they do not constitute a real code of conduct, but rather general rules with simpler content. However, this situation started to change from the middle of 1980, and continues to vary today from earlier official standards frameworks – as described earlier.

In 1986, soon after reform in China and its opening up to the outside world, a delegation of the Chinese National Committee of ICOM (ICOM China) attended the fifteenth ICOM General Conference, held in Buenos Aires, Argentina. One of the major outcomes achieved by that delegation was the first edition of ICOM-CEM for the Chinese museum community, which was viewed as an international standard. Within the next year, ICOM China translated ICOM-CEM into Chinese and published it in the Chinese museums magazine in 1987, which prompted study and discussion among policy makers and administrators of nationwide museums, and among museum professionals, leading to its acceptance. ICOM-CEM was then used in college and university programmes, in official government documents, vocational training courses and teaching materials. Today, ICOM-CEM is included in the curriculum of specialized courses in cultural heritage and museology in nearly twenty universities and colleges in China.

Meanwhile, most government-led, in-service training workshops for museum directors and curators include specialized lectures on ICOM-CEM. ICOM-CEM is also an important component of the Chinese Museums Association (CMA) and ICOM China, which hold training classes for new members and for education and conservation museums staff on an annual basis. Many experienced international experts have also presented and promoted ICOM-CEM on different occasions – for instance, at museum directors' forums and senior management seminars. Bernice Murphy, former Chair of the ICOM Ethics Committee, and Dr Martin Schärer, current Chair, have done much to promote and explain ICOM-CEM among the Chinese museum and heritage communities. These efforts from all sides have brought about concrete results. Today, ICOM-CEM is one of the most important guidance documents in the museum field both at governmental and non-governmental levels.

In December 2015, the major principles of ICOM-CEM were relatively comprehensive, as explained in the Museum Management Approach promulgated by the Ministry of Culture of China. In July 2012, CMA and the Chinese Society of Cultural Relics jointly published/revised the Code of Ethics for Chinese Relics and Museum Workers, which reiterated the major principles of ICOM-CEM and emphasized:

> [the] principle of devotion to society and serving the people as the tenet to fight against illegal traffic in cultural relics; prohibit the collection of and trading in relics; prohibit the illegal occupation of relics and documents; and forbid any personal gain from the relics based on the vocation of the museum.

Following several symposiums and questionnaire surveys conducted over two years from 2012 to 2014 by CMA among its 7,980 institutional and individual members, CMA released an official version of the Code of Ethics for Chinese Relics and Museum Workers based on ICOM-CEM, which had significant influence on the museums of China. This illustrates that we are now going beyond the limitations of working regulations initiated by governments and are striving to establish relatively complete and systematic museum professional standards in the construction of the Chinese CEM.

Further compatibility of CEM with museum regulations

The latest development in the construction of ICOM-CEM was to realize the maximum compatibility between the basic frame, based on internationally accepted professional, ethics standards and current museums laws. As the most influential value system of the museum profession, ICOM-CEM operates with some variations in different countries. It is sometimes viewed as being part of relevant local legislation, making the development of specific legislation unnecessary. Meanwhile in China, ICOM-CEM is embedded in the existing legal regulations for museums where possible, with the most typical example being the Museum Regulations implemented by the State Council of the People's Republic of China (PRC) in March 2015.[3]

In this latest legal museum document, the eight principles of ICOM-CEM, specific to the Chinese national environment, have been explained and interpreted. For instance, the Museum Regulations emphasize that:

- the organizers (governing bodies) of museum institutions will be responsible for the human, material and economic resources needed by cultural and natural heritage;
- museum collections will receive legal protection and belong to the legal entity of the museum with no infringement from any individual or institution, including governing bodies contributing funds;
- the specific requirements and standards for a number of specialized fields such as collection, registration, scientific preservation of the collections, especially relics, clearly require that the museum institutions: i) strengthen the protection

of and research on collections, ii) promote resource-sharing among museums themselves and with other social organizations, iii) revitalize the stock resources to improve the utilization efficiency, and iv) publish the registered and recorded collections for the public;

* museums are prohibited from receiving unidentified or illicit collections, which is not only illegal, but is also the baseline of CEM;
* all museums should protect their public welfare property from all violations and cannot engage in any commercial activity involving its collections and so on.

Of particular note is the elaboration of a special chapter in the Museum Regulations devoted to regulating how the museum serves society. This accounts for more than 25 per cent of the contents, and contains clear and specific requirements. In addition to the CEM requirements, the Museum Regulations, as the highest level of administrative regulation, require that the educational administrative authority under the State Council and the Department of National Cultural Heritage assume the responsibility of formulating policies on the museum's role in serving society. It also requires that educational administrative authorities within local governments ensure that museums are integrated into the school curricula and used to help students develop social and practical activities. It should be mentioned that one of the characteristics of the construction and development of CEM is to ensure its maximum compatibility with the current museum laws in China. Although we do not believe that the law of a nation can replace a professional code of ethics, we should highlight their compatibility as an ideal. So in this sense, the promulgation and implementation of Museum Regulations is one of China's greatest achievements in promoting the construction of CEM in the past ten years.

A positive role in disseminating ICOM-CEM

In recent years, Chinese museums, together with the international community, have played a positive role in facilitating the promotion of and training in ICOM-CEM standards, and have played an active role in its construction. Some examples of this cooperation are as follows.

In October 2010, the 22nd ICOM General Conference – the largest conference held by ICOM to date, with more than 3,400 delegates – was held in Shanghai. During the conference, Bernice Murphy, then Chair of the ICOM Ethics Committee, who also led a working group including representatives from the host country and Europe, Africa and Latin America, proposed a draft resolution titled Shanghai Declaration on Museums for Harmonious Social Development, which was passed as Resolution No. 1 at the 25th ICOM General Assembly.[4] The resolution reconfirmed ICOM-CEM as an affirmation of the enlarged ethical responsibilities of museums, as set out in the eight broad principles in ICOM-CEM (2004), including the following statements:

- Principle 1. Museums preserve, interpret and promote the natural and cultural inheritance of humanity.
- Principle 4. Museums provide opportunities for the appreciation, understanding and management of natural and cultural heritage.
- Principle 5. Museums hold resources that provide opportunities for other public services and benefits.
- Principle 6. Museums work in close collaboration with the communities from which their collections originate as well as those they serve.

After three years of elaborate preparation, the ICOM International Training Centre for Museum Studies (ICOM-ITC), which was jointly established by ICOM, ICOM China and the Palace Museum, opened its doors in Beijing in July 2013. The Centre aims to provide opportunities for capacity building for international museum professionals, especially for those from emerging countries. ICOM-ITC has held six training workshops in the past two and a half years, benefiting 180 and mid-career museum professionals from more than seventy countries. The preparation of the sessions for the aforementioned training workshops includes vital discussions and practices in combination with themes of museum management, exhibition development, research and collection preservation.

Another successful example was the China-South Asian Museum Senior Management Personnel Training Workshop held in Beijing in June 2015, which also listed the instruction and discussion of ICOM-CEM as the core course. Through

FIGURE 17.1 Dr Martin Schärer, Chairman of the ICOM Ethics Committee, explaining ICOM-CEM ethics principles to trainees at the ICOM-ITC workshop, Beijing, in November 2013 © ICOM-ITC.

FIGURE 17.2 Bernice Murphy, former Chair of the ICOM Ethics Committee, explaining ICOM-CEM ethics principles at the China–South Asian Museum Senior Management Personnel Training Workshop, Beijing, in June 2015 © ICOM-ITC.

these efforts, Chinese museums are sharing the universal values and guiding principles within codes of conduct in the field of international museums with museum institutions and professionals from other countries, through multiple channels and arenas, while continuing to improve their own ethical standards.

Chinese museums face the same tough challenges during the construction of their own CEM, some of which are universal, while others are more specific to the Chinese environment. For example, there is a lack of clear recognition that 'public benefit' is the core value of museums, and some museum staff consider that their individual daily work reflects the museum's overall value system, and thereby neglect the organizational characteristics of museums, as follows:

- some museums are unaware that, they as 'social trusts' should assume the management of heritage as a social responsibility. The founders and administrators of museums and museum collections have not set clear legal limits for the ownership of museum assets;
- some museums even collect unidentified or illicit cultural heritage, while others do not have sufficiently high conservation standards for collections and lack adequate protection conditions. They therefore unintentionally hamper sharing with the public and other organizations;

- some museums are highly engaged during the construction phase, but lack the human resources with high-level professional qualities, skills and management ability following the museum's establishment and inauguration; they are therefore unable to guarantee their daily operation and social service activities.

(Song Xiaoguang 2014)

With the increasingly diverse profile of museum administrators today, museums run by non-heritage-related public bodies also participate in the growth of Chinese museums to a large extent. The privately owned museum is a new type of social organization that has grown rapidly in China in a short space of time. However, it faces setbacks when developing ethical standards, both from within the institution and from external environments. These issues and tendencies are being observed attentively by the museum community and administrators, as China continues to reflect upon the huge growth and diversification of its museum sector over several decades.

The following aspects have become key factors in the construction of ICOM-CEM: first, to emphasize the principle of service to society as the first task of museums, and to strengthen further its public welfare characteristics; second, to focus on professional development as the core framework to guarantee the sector's operational quality and level of achievements and outcomes; third, to expand the complex functions of the museum, to improve its level of services to and integration into society; and fourth, to strive for and achieve equal development between public-owned and private-owned museums in terms of management and operational development.

The establishment and constant improvement of ICOM-CEM has been key to the positive transformation of the entire Chinese museum sector, ensuring that ethical principles are secured as central guidelines and values of Chinese museums' continuing development today.

Notes

1 Statistics provided by the State Administration of Cultural Heritage (SACH).
2 The first and second articles of Provisional Regulations on the Registration and Administration of Public Institutions issued by the State Council of PRC on 25 October 1998, and revised on 27 June 2004.
3 The Museum Regulations adopted at the 78th Executive Meeting of the State Council on 14 January 2015 came into force on 20 March 2015.
4 Shanghai Declaration on Museums for Harmonious Social Development, Resolution No. 1, Shanghai, China, 12 November 2010, the 25th General Assembly of ICOM.

Reference

Xiaoguang, Song, 2014. 'Code of Ethics for Museums is the ideological guarantee for the development of museums'. *Chinese Museums*, Vol. 1. Beijing: Chinese Museums Association.

18

ETHICS, MUSEOLOGY AND PROFESSIONAL TRAINING IN JAPAN

Eiji Mizushima

The need for collaboration among museums in Asia Pacific

The early twenty-first century has seen the advance of collaboration and cooperation between Japanese museums and their counterparts elsewhere in the Asia-Pacific region in a wide range of forms. At the Asian Art Museum Directors' Forum, an event held annually since 2006, museum directors discuss issues that confront museums and art galleries in Asia and deliberate actively on future measures for mutual cooperation. In Ningbo, China, in December 2008, museum representatives from fourteen countries gathered for the International Museum Forum, conducting lively discussions on the theme of 'New tasks and core values for museums in the twenty-first century'. In February 2009, a Round-Table Discussion among Museums in Japan, China and South Korea was realized at Tokyo National Museum, under the sponsorship of the Japan Museum Management Academy. This conference formed part of ongoing deliberations by Japan's Ministry of Education, Culture, Sports, Science and Technology (MEXT) and the Japanese Association of Museums. The gathering was organized partly in response to a statement in February 2008 that 'the Asian museum community strongly desires an international contribution by Japan', when Dr Bae Kidong, the then Chairperson of the Korean Association of Museums, and Chang Inkyung, the former Chairperson of the International Council of Museums Asia-Pacific Alliance (ICOM-ASPAC), were invited to visit Japan for regional museums cooperation and planning.

Expectations of ICOM's networks

ICOM globally includes some 114 National Committees (NCs), 30 International Committees (ICs), and four Regional Alliances, of which ICOM-ASPAC is the largest, both in number of museology personnel within the region, and geographic extent across the world's continental landmasses and interconnecting seas. ICOM-ASPAC includes museums and personnel from North and South Asia, East and Southeast Asia, as well as Pacific Island states with a range of museums and cultural centres. It also incorporates within the huge 'lake' of the Pacific, the countries of Papua-New Guinea, the Solomon Islands, Vanuatu, New Caledonia, Australia and New Zealand, with their very substantial museums, collections and diverse cultural communities. A total of twenty-three National Committees participate in ICOM-ASPAC.

At the 2007 ICOM-ASPAC conference in Shiraz, Iran, the question, 'What does it mean to be a museum in Asia?' was tabled as a crucial subject for colleagues' attention. This was a call to reorient many topical issues from different geographic and cultural coordinates, in contrast with discussions formulated repeatedly from traditional assumptions and viewpoints linking museums and people in Western countries. The Shiraz Declaration, adopted at ICOM-ASPAC 2007, stated that the museums of Asia intended in future to collaborate more closely and strengthen their inter-organizational networks within and across the large Asia-Pacific region. ICOM Japan is one of ICOM's longest-serving National Committees. While ICOM was founded as an international organization in 1946, Japan joined ICOM six years later, in 1952.

In the 1960s and 1970s, Japan cooperated with UNESCO and other organizations on joint initiatives in support of culture and heritage, such as the holding of seminars on museums in the Asia-Pacific region and the development of training courses for museum employees. From the perspective of its international contribution, however, Japan tended to focus strongly on internal concerns of museums within its own national community. This meant that, despite Japan's regular representation in ICOM's annual meetings of its large Advisory Committee in Paris, for a long period Japan did not generally take a proactive stance towards building links with other countries and museum organizations in its close vicinity and surrounding region. Links between Japan and other countries were always occurring at the museum-to-museum level (especially in the area of loans of individual works, and in exhibition exchanges), but there was little activity in the broader channels of network building or inter-professional cooperation at the national association level. This is necessary to facilitate activity within a regional or larger international scope of capacity-building, professional development and leadership.

A substantial change in outlook, however, has occurred in recent years. Japan has adopted a more active approach to building its international networks, especially through ICOM. Perhaps the strongest outcome of this changed planning and initiatives has been demonstrated in Japan's (successful) bid to host the ICOM triennial General Conference and Assembly for the world museums community in 2019, which will take place in Kyoto.

Planning for the ICOM-ASPAC conference in Japan (Tokyo, 2009)

ICOM headquarters was keenly interested in this conference. For people involved with museums in the Asia-Pacific region, the event constituted a vital step towards strengthening ASPAC collaboration, as participants could form connections and comparisons across widely distributed and different national contexts (including great cultural diversity within those boundaries). Participants could engage in first-hand study of very different professional settings in which museums seek to serve their local and national communities, while at the same time addressing the global challenges of heritage care and museum work today. The ICOM-ASPAC Conference in Tokyo took place over three days in late 2009 (7–9 December), involving 150 participants from twenty countries.

The basic theme of the ICOM-ASPAC conference was *Rethinking Museums' Core Values and Regional Heritage*. In view of ICOM's 2008 to 2010 strategic plan, which included an aim of 'support [for] activities to preserve cultural heritage and raise awareness of cultural heritage in society', the theme was timely. It also connected with and reinforced the main theme of the 2008 International Museum Forum in Ningbo, China, which had focused on *Core Values and Social Responsibility of Museums in the 21st Century*, while pointing forward to the theme of the ICOM Triennial General Conference in Shanghai in 2010, *Museums and Social Harmony*.

The session themes for the Tokyo gathering of ICOM-ASPAC delegates were: (i) Regional heritage in the Asia-Pacific region; (ii) Network building for museum information in the Asia-Pacific region; and (3) Human-resources development to establish a code of ethics for museums in the Asia-Pacific region. Planning of the sessions pursued innovative representation of younger personnel. All participants were invited by public appeal through ICOM's National Committees in the region (and backed by many forms of grant support); and there was an additional affirmative aim of including one specialist for each session who was forty years of age or younger (some were much younger, finally). Representatives of all countries were very positive afterwards concerning the value of achieving a cross-section of ages and experience among participants, as a means of ensuring inter-generational building of expertise and leadership capacities across the ASPAC region.

Principal sessions and workshops

Following an opening address by the head of the museums section in UNESCO's Division for Culture, Dr Christian Manhart, keynote addresses were offered on each session theme:

- 'Regional heritage and museums: Creating a museum network in the Asia-Pacific': Prof. Ken'ichiro Hidaka of Tsukuba University provided a rationale and steps for an ASPAC network of museums to be achieved.
- 'Opening museums to the world: Great rivers of information': Dr Martin Gomon of Museum Victoria in Melbourne outlined a rationale for proposed standardization of natural history collection records and metadata, and public use of such data, from the standpoint of natural history museums.
- 'Museum ethics in their dynamic interface with the world': Bernice Murphy, former Chairperson of ICOM's Ethics Committee and National Director of

Museums Australia, presented an overview of key issues in the *ICOM Code of Ethics for Museums* and their daily application in the work of museums.

- Conference work sessions took place over two days, during which fourteen papers were presented (from an original field of 42 proposals, offered by participants from 17 countries and one additional region). Concerning ethics, in particular, the focus of participants was set early in a paper delivered by Hidehiko Sasaki, a former curator of the Tokyo Metropolitan Art Museum, who provided an address on: 'Foundational law, standards and ethics: The status of Japan'. While reporting on the development of museum standards and ethics in Japan, this paper also provided a bridge to a substantial workshop on ethics that occupied the last morning of the conference. The paper also made clear that the subject was highly topical for Japan's museum community, which had not yet drawn up a code of ethics for its national use – although ICOM Japan meanwhile observes the ICOM Code of Ethics[1] as the international base-code reference standard for all aspects of museums' work.

Human-resources development to establish a code of ethics for museums for the ASPAC region

This session (on the final day) was jointly facilitated by Bernice Murphy and the author. The session dealt with establishing a professional code of ethics within a national museum community; comparing associated human-resources training in ethics in different countries; then these two themes were enlarged upon through presentations concerning three different national contexts in Asia – through papers presented by Dr Chih-Ning Hsin of Taiwan, Mr Nguyen Hai Ninh of Vietnam and Dr Yang Jongsung of South Korea.

Dr Hsin outlined professionalism in museum ethics and its relationship with professional identity, providing a reflection on the importance and role of a code of ethics in human-resources development; she also offered an overview of some of the leading-edge museum research now taking place in Taiwan. Mr Hai Ninh presented useful case studies, including of some antagonism that had arisen between museum directors and curators in Vietnam regarding museum education and exhibitions. Dr Yang Jongsung finally provided a report on how the translation of the (revised) *ICOM Code of Ethics for Museums* was approached in South Korea (after its formal adoption at ICOM's General Conference in Seoul in 2004); the Korean overview was full of useful suggestions for Japan concerning its planned drafting of its own Code of Ethics.

The ASPAC region's first ethics-in-action workshop – a model for ethics training in museums

One of the features of the last day of ICOM-ASPAC in Tokyo was an ethics-in-action workshop, related to principles set out in the ICOM Code of Ethics, which was conducted on the final morning before the closing session, and was the first workshop of this kind in the region. With the participation of ICOM President Alissandra Cummins; ICOM Vice-President, W. Richard West; ICOM Director General Julien Anfruns; and former ICOM Secretary General Manus Brinkman (then living and working in Thailand), this was a workshop backed by high-level commitment from ICOM and of exceptional interest to participants.

The workshop was led by Eva Maehre Lauritzen, former Chairperson of ICOM Norway, who has developed a useful action-ethics training model (see Lauritzen 2016) that she implemented first with the Nordic countries, and later elsewhere. At the Tokyo workshop, fifteen fictional scenarios had been prepared, for exploration in small collaborative groups. These were seemingly simple, invented 'tales' involving people working in or for museums, presenting dilemmas around 'the right thing to do'. Working in four groups, colleagues focused on different themes with an ethical dimension, concerning: (i) collections and communication; (ii) facilities and resources; (iii) museums, society and the law; and (iv) museum-specialist activities and conflicts-of-interest. Based on these four themes, the groups discussed each scenario and considerable differences emerged, often according to the participants' countries of origin. The intensely animated debates produced by the workshop, despite limited time and the barriers of language (participants translated for each other in multi-lingual groups, with remarkable reflexivity and collaboration), was testimony that the exercise was very fruitful. It provided easily approached,

FIGURE 18.1 First workshop in the ASPAC region on issues for a museum Code of Ethics (December 2009, Tokyo). Photo: National Museum of Science and Nature (Tokyo, Japan).

everyday scenarios for 'situational learning' among museums people drawn from very different national and cultural contexts. Participants later provided high evaluation scores for the workshop for these reasons.

This was the first-ever workshop in the ASPAC region on issues for a museum Code of Ethics (December 2009, Tokyo).

At the conclusion of the ethics workshop the conference drew to a close, with the final action of adopting a Tokyo Declaration, bringing together an action statement around the three main conference themes. The Tokyo Declaration was endorsed by further calls to strengthen international cooperation and collaboration among museums in the Asia-Pacific region, and a recommendation to move affirmatively on cooperative efforts to advance the digitization of museum resources. Concerning ethics, paragraph 4 of the Tokyo Declaration stated:

> ICOM-ASPAC will promote the *ICOM Code of Ethics for Museums* as an indispensable tool for the training of museum personnel, and for the advancement of the museum sector in each country, and will cooperate in strengthening human resource development programs and training systems in the region.

Effects in Japan (post-ICOM-ASPAC conference)

The 2009 ASPAC conference was followed by several years of concerted debate and research among museum-related people in Japan, culminating in July 2012 with the enactment by the Japanese Association of Museums (ICOM Japan committee secretariat) of two important new instruments to guide museum work: *Principles for Museums* and a *Museum Code of Conduct*. Although these resolutions cannot be described here in detail, their main contents are outlined below.

Principles for museums in Japan

As organizations in the public interest, museums shall act in accordance with the following principles:

1. Museums shall contribute to humanity and society by transmitting, developing, creating and educating the public about heritage knowledge and culture.
2. Museums shall respect the multifaceted value of records/objects and their environments as assets-in-common for humanity.
3. Museums shall provide a human, material and resources-base for the accomplishment of the purposes and missions for which they are established.
4. Museums shall establish policies and targets based on their missions, carry out activities according to those policies and targets, evaluate the results of their efforts, and seek to improve those results.
5. Museums shall form systematic collections, to bequeath these collections to future generations in good condition.

6. Museums earn the trust of society through activities backed by surveys and research.
7. Museums shall create new value through exhibits, education and enlightenment.
8. Museums endeavour to improve their professional capabilities, for the enhancement and development of their activities.
9. Museums shall collaborate and cooperate with related organizations and regions to improve their overall capability.
10. Museums shall understand and respect related laws, regulations and ethics.

Museum code of conduct

1 Contribution

Persons involved in museums shall conduct activities for the transmission, development and creation of learning and culture, mindful of the public benefit brought by their museums and their responsibilities to the future.

2 Respect

Persons involved in museums shall respect the multifaceted value of records/objects, handle records/objects with respect, and conduct activities with consideration of the diverse values and rights of the people connected to records/objects.

3 Establishment of facilities

Persons involved in museums shall strive to achieve a strong base for acquisition of resources, personal conduct and maintenance of facilities, for the purpose of fulfilling the missions of their museums and improving their public benefit. They shall also secure the safety of persons connected to their museums and their museums' collections.

4 Management

Persons involved in museums shall understand the missions, policies and objectives of their museums, make the utmost efforts to fulfil those objectives, and participate in the evaluation and improvement of those efforts. Managers of museums shall deploy management resources to maximum effect to maintain transparency and stable management, to contribute to the advancement of public benefit.

5 Collection and preservation

As they strive to collect and preserve records/objects, persons involved in museums shall be mindful of their duty, entrusted to them by society, to pass on records/objects from the past to the present and future. Persons involved in museums shall form systematic collections using appropriate procedures, in accordance with the policies and plans stipulated by their museums.

6 Surveys and research

Persons involved in museums shall conduct surveys and research based on the policies of their museums, and reflect the results of those surveys and research in their activities, to enhance public trust in their museums. Moreover, persons involved in museums shall actively publish the results of their surveys and research and strive to make academic contributions.

7 Exhibitions, education and enlightenment

Persons involved in museums shall grasp every opportunity to exhibit and use for education and enlightenment the records/objects and information gathered in their museums, and share them with the general public as assets for humanity in common, to promote mutual understanding and create new value.

8 Diligent study

Persons involved in museums shall strive to improve their professional knowledge, capabilities and techniques through education and training, and execute their duties to the best of their ability. Persons involved in museums shall share their knowledge, experience and accumulated skills with related parties, and evaluate each other for the advancement of museum activities.

9 Communication and collaboration

Persons involved in museums shall strive to motivate people and regional communities, engage in dialogue and collaboration with other organizations, and enhance the general capabilities of their museums.

10 Autonomy

Persons involved in museums shall act in accordance with the *Principles for Museums* and *Museum Code of Conduct*. Persons involved in museums understand and comply with related laws, and respect the ICOM Code of Ethics as well as the ethics and standards of related academic fields. When faced with unforeseen circumstances, persons involved in museums will consider the circumstances in a sincere spirit, with reference to their own standards, and work with related parties to achieve solutions.

The roles of both ICOM and Japanese museums in regional and international developments

The author believes that considerable time will be required for all personnel related to museums in Japan to absorb and act upon the approaches outlined above, in the two new instruments to guide museums in future years. The presentation of the ICOM-ASPAC, conference in Tokyo was of great significance from the standpoints of considering the activities of museum personnel as professional, advancing methods of increased inter-regional and international collaboration in the light of shared standards and codes of ethics, and fulfilling the role of codes of conduct also as encouraging a bridge among cultures, for greater inter-cultural cooperation.

While Japan's museum community has now established the *Principles for Museums* and the *Museum Code of Conduct*, strictly speaking these are only general principles at this stage. For the next step, Japan's museums will need to develop more detailed ethical guidelines (including collections of case studies) to advance this professional work as a regular part of museum life and discussions.

As the role of museums in international society changes, Japan is being called upon to exercise greater leadership and contribute internationally. Meanwhile, as globalization advances in society as a whole, it may be no exaggeration to say that museums will find it difficult to survive if they do not grasp international trends and stronger initiatives of public service and public-oriented performance, as outlined above. What is still lacking in Japan (and more broadly, in museums in the Asia-Pacific region) is museum policy that overviews and builds connections with international society as a whole. In a two-way process, Japan must not only learn from international society but also raise awareness in international society of Japan's own achievements and cultural resources.

ICOM's international networks, leadership and initiatives to unite museum-related personnel worldwide, to develop policies and strategies for museums of the future, will continue to be an important influence and stimulus in the Asia-Pacific region in the years ahead.

Note

1 The full text of the *ICOM Code of Ethics for Museums* is provided as *Appendix I* in the present publication. It is also available online for download from the ICOM website (with links to translations in French, Spanish, and many other languages – including Arabic, Chinese, Japanese, and Korean). The English version is accessible at: http://icom. museum/professional-standards/code-of-ethics.

Reference

Lauritzen, Eva Maehre, 2016. 'Ethics in action: Situational scenarios turning the keys to the Code of Ethics', in Bernice L. Murphy, (ed.), *Museum, Ethics and Cultural Heritage*. London: Routledge, Chapter 34.

PART V

Evolving issues: Collaboration, provenance research, deaccessioning, social responsibility and public participation in museums

19

ADVOCATING FOR INTERNATIONAL COLLABORATIONS

World War II-era provenance research in museums

Jane Milosch

In 2009, not long after I had taken on the leadership of the Smithsonian's World War II-era provenance project, I attended a series of town hall meetings hosted by the US Department of State to consider an alternate dispute route for legal proceedings involving World War II-era claims.[1] I will never forget the first meeting, as it was there I first witnessed outright hostility toward museums from claimant attorneys and representatives, who criticized museums essentially for following U.S. legal procedures and standard museum practices. A few years later, I attended an international symposium at which an historian declared that, 'Until all museum directors and curators are in handcuffs', museums would not be returning looted art in their collections. After a lecture on the 'Monuments Men' in Washington, D.C., a colleague overheard a visitor remark: 'You know, most things in museums were looted or stolen.' How is it that art museums – public, educational institutions that preserve cultural treasures – are now cast in a light that makes them appear shady, or even unlawfully detaining collection items in their care?

Educating the public about what we do

Various factors converge to cultivate this distrust of museums. The press fans the flames when its reporting of World War II-era claims is misleading, one-sided and sensationalist. The negative publicity resulting from accusations against any art institution can deeply affect the standing of museums overall.[2] Some books, such as *Chasing Aphrodite: The Hunt for Looted Antiquities at the World's Richest Museum* by Jason Felch and Ralph Frammolino, chronicle gross negligence in antiquities collecting. But, while corruption can occur in any organization, museums have checks in place to prevent this as part of their professional standards, which they are continually updating and improving (AAM 2014).

Recent stories about the systematic looting of antiquities in Iraq, Afghanistan and Syria have raised public awareness that objects taken from these and other countries are today making their way through international art markets, and some museums are advocating 'safe haven' for them.[3] Less known to the public is that many museums advocate and help write the laws that ban the importation of looted antiquities and, in the case of the Smithsonian, even train US Immigration and Customs Enforcement (ICE) agents to identify potentially looted art before it enters the country.[4]

On the other hand, over the last three years, several German museums have mounted exhibitions that highlight their efforts in provenance research.[5] One example of such an exhibition, *The Black Years: Histories of a Collection 1933–1945*, organized by the Stiftung Preußischer Kulturbesitz (SPK)/Berlin State Museums, features works from and curated by the Nationalgalerie which were created between 1933 and 1945, acquired by the collection during this period, or seized by the National Socialist regime; SPK further provides rich contextualization of these works through their ownership and exhibition paths at that particular time in German history (see Staatlich Museen zu Berlin, online). An American example of an exhibition that developed around a museum's provenance research efforts, *This Is No Less Curious: Journeys Through the Collection*, and presented at the Herbert F. Johnson Museum of Art, Cornell University, provides an inside look at the discoveries the curator made while delving into ownership histories of works in the collection (see Johnson Museum, online). An online exhibition-related resource also worth noting is the collation of archival labels and stamps found on the artwork in the Metropolitan Museum of Art's Leonard A. Lauder Cubist Collection. Such exhibitions and resources highlight and contextualize the results of the good and conscientious work that museums are already doing with their provenance research.

Another incident that has escalated public awareness of looted art has been the media reporting on the 2013 discovery of the 'Schwabing Art Trove' (commonly referred to as the 'Gurlitt Trove') in Munich (Schwabinger Kunstfund, online). The often inaccurate reporting on this trove has not remarked on the unique difficulties Gurlitt Task Force researchers face, and the time it takes to carry out the highly specialized research these art works now require (see Hüneke 2015). Such a lack of factual and sound educational reporting, combined with a disproportionate coverage of the lawsuits against museums for restitution of Nazi-era looted art, tends to confuse the broad public and museum stakeholders about the important issues surrounding the probity of museum holdings. Few seem aware of how often museums work constructively and ethically with potential heirs to clarify and amicably resolve questions of ownership (see Clark 2014).

Recent events in the Middle East and in Germany have led many museums to increase provenance research into their collections, and to pursue new ways to bring their research and preservation efforts to the forefront of their work. Museums exist to care for and share their collections with the world. When a museum shares the complexities of the processes and expertise needed to generate provenance research findings, it demonstrates conscientious respect for its public mission. When it further introduces these stories, together with connoisseurship histories, into its public programming, the museum cultivates the public's appreciation for what an art museum can uniquely do – provide opportunities for the public to experience the power of art by engaging with the objects and their histories.

Provenance research and collection stories

Provenance, when associated with a work of art, refers to the history of ownership of that object since its creation. It has a long tradition as a methodology of art history, connected with the development of connoisseurship as an aspect of the history of both art and aesthetics. In the 1980s and 1990s, art historical focus on provenance expanded beyond traditional connoisseurship and socio-cultural histories to include Reception Studies, Exile Studies and the History of Collecting and Taste. More recently, twenty-first-century scholars and curators are interested in transnational art histories and interdisciplinary provenance studies, in order to gain deeper understanding of objects and their ownership paths, and to better comprehend the historical, social and economic context in which those artworks were created and collected and through which they changed hands over time.

Lynn Nicholas, author of *The Rape of Europa: The Fate of Europe's Treasures in the Third Reich and the Second World War* (1995), has noted that provenance research produces narratives that are often 'as fascinating a social and historical document as the work of art itself' (Nicholas 2014). Her big-picture assessment of provenance research's persistent challenges also outlines a vision of the field that takes into consideration the total context of a work of art as it moves through time.

Another reason to make provenance stories more widely known is that few outside our institutions are aware of the vast contributions to World War II-era provenance research that museums have provided in the last fifteen years. Indeed, most of the new databases used by governments, the legal profession, auction houses and the art trade in general are the products of research and data organization produced by art institutions, archives and libraries, such as those I will describe in this essay.

Smithsonian Provenance Research Initiative (SPRI)

In 2009, the Smithsonian expanded its commitment to World War II-era provenance research on works of art, creating an institution-wide project to clarify questions concerning gaps in ownership history, transfer of ownership and unlawful appropriation of objects.[6]

The chief task of the Smithsonian Provenance Research Initiative (SPRI) is to re-anchor the museum in its core missions – stewardship, education and appreciation of all cultures – by enabling the work of World War II-era provenance throughout the Smithsonian.[7] SPRI matches provenance specialists with curators and collection managers; together, to date, we are working with six of the nineteen

Smithsonian museums and archives to build our long-term strategies and priorities for provenance research. Factors we consider in setting research priorities include existing collections, future acquisitions, publications, exhibition preparation, and incoming and outgoing loans. SPRI also trains and assists curatorial staff with this research, since curators today often do not have the time to perform the ongoing collection research that has been central to museum practice in the past.

SPRI shares its research findings as widely as possible to increase public access to collections.[8] At the present time of widespread public disenchantment with public institutions, whether deserved or not, timely performance of provenance research, and also timely publication of results, can help restore confidence in the integrity of museums. It can also engage the public's interest in the art works themselves, through the new stories the research reveals. This can only be of benefit to museums, which rely on the patronage and financial support of the public to carry out their missions.

SPRI considers World War II-era research within its larger historical and geographic contexts, and looks for solutions for the better preservation of art and cultural heritage – both tangible and intangible – for future generations. Over the longer term, SPRI aims to expand beyond the World War II era, to assist with more current provenance issues, and to explore the implications of provenance research for art history and connoisseurship. Given the Smithsonian's mandate for broad service to the arts, SPRI promotes research beyond the Smithsonian's own museums and archives. Through scholarly exchange beyond the USA and Europe – symposia, publications, online resources and training programmes for established and emerging professionals – SPRI fosters partnerships with other institutions (museums, archives, libraries and universities around the world) that speed up the work and often lead to new findings. Currently SPRI is focused on Asian art and decorative arts, which are emerging fields of study in World War II-era collecting.

SPRI projects and new resources

The Freer Gallery of Art and Arthur M. Sackler Gallery

Since the founding of these museums – the Freer in 1928 and the Sackler in 1987, which together are considered to have one of the world's finest collections of the arts of the Far and Near East – both have worked to ensure complete access to their provenance research. Founder Charles Lang Freer grounded his collection in 'connoisseurship tempered by the subsequent disciplines of scholarship'. Freer not only acquired objects, he also collected collateral materials that related to their provenance. The gallery's provenance work brings to the forefront current scholarly interest in Euro-American aspects of the Asian art market before, during and after World War II.

In the wake of an amicably resolved claim against the museum, the Freer|Sackler hired Laurie A. Stein, a widely respected World War II-era provenance research expert, to help develop a systematic, long-term plan of research for the museum, working closely with Freer|Sackler Director Julian Raby, Head of Collections

Elizabeth Duley, and the museum's curators (see Freer Gallery of Art and Arthur M. Sackler Gallery Press Room, 2010). This plan recommended hiring an on-site, museum-based provenance research specialist to work with the collections staff and curators, and for the expert to guide, review and publish the research. The plan led to staff training sessions, and the development of the first online workbook outlining museum methods for Asian art provenance research, 'Guidelines and procedures for World War II provenance issues'.[9] This website portal received 6,000 hits in its first sixteen months of public access. At the Freer|Sackler nearly 400 art works with World War II-era provenance gaps have been researched and are now available on the museum's website, with links to AAM's Nazi-Era Provenance Internet Portal (NEPIP 2014).

Through SPRI, the research of the last five years has resulted in a further new project to develop a web resource that includes biographies of collectors and dealers of Asian art who were active in Europe during the critical period of 1933–45. These biographies of individuals and companies will link to specific objects in the Freer|Sackler collections and to associated archival sources, and includes inventories, sales records, exhibition catalogues and other published materials. The data will assist in establishing ownership transfer by delineating the history of Western collections of Asian art and relationships between people, and will provide insights into the business operations of various dealers and auction houses, thereby assisting in tracking the movement of specific works. I will further discuss this project later in this essay.

In 2013, Freer|Sackler was one of the first seventeen institutions to partner with Google Cultural Institute to promote history, art and culture through the digitization and online exhibition of rarely seen archival materials. The Freer|Sackler's collection of photographic portraits gifted to Alice Roosevelt by Asian heads of state were exhibited as 'Imperial Exposures: Photographic portraits of East Asian rulers', and provided individuals across the globe with access to a small piece of the wealth of information housed in the Freer|Sackler archives.

The Archives of American Art: Digitized Resources, Finding Aids, and Guide

SPRI experts are working with the Smithsonian's Archives of American Art (AAA) to highlight its rich holdings of provenance-related resources and materials. One of the most widely used resources on the history of visual arts and culture in America, the AAA stewards a growing collection of some twenty million letters, photographs, diaries, oral history interviews, sketches, scrapbooks, business records and other documents. While Europe has many essential World War II-era provenance-related resources, AAA collections are some of the most sought-after material in provenance research.

From 2010 to 2014, the Samuel H. Kress Foundation provided major support to digitize collections such as the Jacques Seligmann & Co. records, as well as selected documents from additional collections, and to create online finding aids for collections that are valuable archival resources for World War II-era art provenance research.[10] Funding also provided support for a guide to 'Provenance Research at the Archives of American Art'. This publication has substantially increased the information available to researchers about the contents of these collections.[11]

Through SPRI, we are applying lessons learned at Freer|Sackler and AAA, utilizing these projects as models for other World War II-era provenance projects at Smithsonian museums and archives, including the National Museum of American History, the Cooper-Hewitt National Design Museum, and the Hirshhorn Museum and Sculpture Garden. At the same time, we are developing:

- a network of museum professionals and scholars to expedite and contextualize the research;
- training programmes with established and emerging museum professionals; and
- new technology to better share, interpret and disseminate results.

This does not mean that we can set rigid international standards or policies – quite the opposite. We must continue to respect the historical, cultural and political-legal positions of each country, while establishing ways to share, train and implement technology that will help us achieve the work that needs to be done at each museum, but also networked to avoid 'reinventing the wheel' at every step of the research, or duplication of efforts, as is now so common in the field.

International advocacy

Although most of my twenty-five-year career in museums has been in the curatorial area, it has also involved collections research, publications, technology and management. Over the last seven years as SPRI director, I have been intensively involved in developing and facilitating provenance research projects. This position has afforded me insight into provenance approaches in museums internationally, principally through conversations and work with colleagues both American and European – in Austria, France, the Czech Republic, Poland, Switzerland, the United Kingdom and especially Germany – and more recently in Israel and Australia. SPRI experts have published widely in journals and conference proceedings during this time.[12]

From 2014–2016, I served on the eleven-member international Advisory Group to the 'Schwabing Art Trove' Task Force in Germany, where I saw up close the differences and similarities between the two countries' approaches to provenance research. My invitation to speak at the first Deutsches Zentrum Kulturgutverluste (DZK, German Lost Art Foundation) symposium in December 2014 (in Berlin) was an opportunity to formulate the following recommendations for German museums, but they could be applied more widely.

- Enable specialists to perform provenance research at the highest level in their scholarly fields, in order to uncover histories of ownership through closest factual documentation and contextualized analysis.
- Invest in long-term, systematic research projects – and we need to encourage the creation of permanent positions at museums and archives.

- Increase access to provenance sources utilizing new technology, including digitized documents with finding aids and research results, so that professional researchers can continuously monitor and share updates via the web.
- Train people to do the work, with a range of sub-specializations, that is, inter-disciplinary and transnational.
- Build a network of people who do AND share the work.
- Mentor the upcoming generation of scholars, on-the-job and with museum experts supporting them in various areas: curation, collection and exhibition management, cultural policy, and public education and outreach.
- Inform the public and media of provenance research projects and results of the work through a variety of means, such as exhibitions, public programmes, web portals and other online resources.
- Publish research results online, both in English as well as the institution's language, rendering them more universally accessible.

With transparent, timely sharing of information, we can effectively educate interested parties and the general public about the specialized, time-consuming nature of this work, with its often inconclusive results and ongoing nature. While the greatest focus and challenge of provenance research remains sifting through immense amounts of both paper and digital archival materials, we now see that communication and collaboration are essential to its success.

SPRI is building on the Smithsonian's ongoing provenance efforts, and expanding them to achieve international impact. We are working on three major projects that turn our national efforts into broader international collaborations and exchanges.

Building networks of exchange

Although the aggregation of information facilitated by digital resources is crucial, it does not eliminate the need for human contact. Provenance researchers and museum professionals need opportunities to meet face to face with their colleagues to exchange information and to develop collaborative research projects.

In 2011, SPRI partnered with several institutions to invite US and European colleagues to a two-day seminar in Washington, DC, highlighting the progress of efforts to increase access to materials pertaining to cultural objects looted during World War II.[13] Museum professionals and others interested in provenance learned about new electronic tools, collaborative projects and strategies for research. Experts guided discussions about using new online resources, especially the web portal linking researchers to archival materials from the National Archives and Records Administration (NARA), the German Bundesarchiv and the National Archives of the United Kingdom, among other partners. The seminar demonstrated that coordination is key to avoiding duplication of efforts (NARA 2014).[14]

In 2013, SPRI initiated a publication project, 'Provenance Research in American Institutions', with Juilee Decker, editor of *Collections: A Journal for Museum and Archives Professionals. From the Practical to the Philosophical*, a multidisciplinary journal for all aspects of handling, preserving, researching, interpreting and organizing collections. Twelve essays from nine major US institutions highlight advancements in the field, especially the documentation of original materials and the launching of cross-institutional collaborations.[15]

The first section of the journal is devoted to a discussion of resources and initiatives, and includes an essay that introduces 'The German Sales 1930–1945 Database Project' at the Getty Research Institute (GRI), Los Angeles. This essay outlines a collaboration of thirty-eight contributing institutions working to create an easily searchable, comprehensive online database of World War II-era German art sales records. Also noteworthy, though not mentioned in the journal, is GRI's 2013–14 provenance-related workshop, which builds on the rich digital resources outlined through scholarly exchange: 'Market and might: The business of art in the "Third Reich"'. A selection of scholarly essays that grew out of this exchange is forthcoming. Furthermore, Laurie A. Stein's '"Everyone brings a piece to the puzzle": Conversations with Elaine Rosenberg and reflections on provenance research among The Paul Rosenberg Archives' relates well to the holdings of the Museum of Modern Art, New York (Stein 2014).

Since 2014, SPRI and SPK have been developing a German-American Provenance Research Exchange Program (PREP) to encourage and support experienced and emerging German and American professionals to learn about current research, education and technology related to Nazi-era provenance research in Germany and the USA. This project envisions the creation of a 'transatlantic research *autobahn*' to acquaint provenance professionals in both countries with each other's research methods and priorities, and to collaborate on research projects to illuminate and connect provenance stories on both sides of the Atlantic, in order to form a more complete picture of the chains of provenance torn apart during World War II. The project will be the first to focus on introducing provenance researchers in Germany and the USA to the professional practices and resources, cultural histories and related legal systems of each other's countries. German and American personnel, collections, resources, experiences and expertise will be drawn together for the first time in these closely collaborative endeavours.

During a visit to Australia in July 2015, I presented Smithsonian provenance resources and SPRI initiatives, it became clear during many conversations with Australian colleagues that we need an international museum forum to bring an increasing number of provenance-related activities together within a shared overview. SPRI has since co-organized panels for the 2016 AAM Meeting in Washington, DC, themed 'Power, influence, and responsibility'. Chief executives of the Smithsonian, SPK and the National Gallery of Australia, Canberra, and legal and policy experts from the Metropolitan Museum of Art, New York and the Cultural Property Advisory Committee in the US Department of State will discuss current issues in the overlapping of provenance research and cultural heritage preservation, in a panel titled 'Today's looted art = tomorrow's provenance problem'. We hope ICOM will build on these initiatives, utilizing its further networks through its many National Committees and thirty specialized International Committees to cultivate an expanding exchange of timely information about our respective provenance projects at their annual meetings and international conferences.

Training and education

The Smithsonian runs collaborative research centres and training programmes around the world, and works closely with other national and international archives, museums, universities and libraries, as well as with other branches of the US government, including the Department of State's Office of the Special Envoy for Holocaust Issues and Department of Homeland Security.

SPRI organizes and participates in educational programmes on provenance.[16] For example, the Smithsonian's Museum Conservation Institute organizes training workshops for ICE officers who work to prevent the trafficking of illicit objects. In 2010, after the earthquake in Haiti, we led international efforts to prevent looting and to conserve Haitian cultural heritage sites and artefacts.[17]

Through its Cultural Heritage Preservation Officer, Corine Wegener, the Smithsonian has worked with ICOM and UNESCO to address crises in Syria and Mali, to prevent looting and destruction of their cultural treasures.[18] In this connection, in October 2015 the Smithsonian organized an international three-day symposium, 'Uniting to save world cultures: Investigating the attributes of successful emergency Cultural Heritage Protection Interventions', at the National Museum of American History. Disaster relief experts, government officials, museum professionals and academics who specialize in related studies, from the USA, Nepal, China, Haiti and Syria, discussed key attributes associated with the successful protection of cultural heritage during complex emergencies. These efforts parallel SPRI's provenance efforts to design and facilitate country-specific, culturally sensitive collaborative projects to protect tangible and intangible cultural heritage. Under Secretary Richard Kurin, himself an anthropologist and renowned cultural heritage expert, has made these efforts a priority at the Smithsonian Institution.

Over the last seven years, SPRI has accepted more than twenty interns, as emerging museum professionals who are interested in specializing in provenance research. Fledgling art historians need extensive archival research experience, both acquired by training and put to the test on-the-job, reinforced by ongoing mentoring by established provenance researchers and curatorial experts who know their collections. The confidential nature, complexity and length of time World War II-era provenance research requires means that the discipline cannot be learned during a single internship, or a week-long introductory classroom course; rather, it presupposes hard-earned, advanced knowledge of art and art history, foreign languages, museum and collection expertise, and years of work. Programmes such as SPRI's will help train future scholars, curators and collection managers comprehensively in the rigours of twenty-first-century provenance research.

Glasgow Partnership

Under the leadership of Professor Nick Pearce of the University of Glasgow, and SPRI's first Senior Research Fellow, 2014–15, SPRI and the University of Glasgow are launching a unique Master's programme in Art History: Collecting and Provenance in an International Context at Glasgow, planned to open in 2016 with Kelvin Hall leading the faculty; this programme will offer collections access, linked to research, teaching and learning. Provenance studies set within the context of the history of collecting practices globally has long been a subject of research and teaching in Art History at the University of Glasgow, which will now build on this record by incorporating art law and studies in criminology into the programme.[19]

College Art Association

For the February 2016 College Art Association's Annual Meeting in Washington, D.C., SPRI organized a panel session titled 'Awareness → Professionalization → Career Opportunities? Teaching provenance research in the field of art history', which includes provenance experts, curators and art historians from DePaul University, the University of Glasgow, Free University Berlin's 'Degenerate Art' Research Center, the Metropolitan Museum of Art, and Art Recovery International, LLC. The panel will compare how provenance is taught at universities in the USA and Europe.

Developing new technologies

SPRI's current development of the Freer | Sackler shared Asian art dealer/collector online resource mentioned earlier in this essay will link collection data with archival data through new technology and visualization software, which will then direct visitors back to the specific museum's website to contextualize the findings. This project aims to produce a database that is scalable, with methodology suitable for both non-Asian (e.g. decorative arts) material and for use with other museum collections, and represents a long-term commitment to provenance research in its widest sense. One of the challenges is establishing a new electronic platform for this collaboration between museums and archival institutions nationally and internationally, so as to share crucial information on objects, their movement and ownership.

SPRI has engaged DesignForContext, LLC to help design and develop a provenance research sharing platform for the Freer | Sackler project, which we envision having separate-yet-related scholarly and public components, potentially through the use of OpenLinked Data.[20] We are in contact with several museums, as well as universities and archives, including the University of Maryland's Department of Art History and Archaeology and its Digital Curation and Innovation Center with the Enhanced International Research Portal for Records Related to Nazi-Era Cultural Property Project (IRP2) (formerly known as Looted Holocaust Assets Research Project [L-HARP]. We are particularly interested in investigating how best to search across

World War II-era provenance research-related data in museum collection databases and archival holdings.[21] We are also starting a new collaboration with the Carnegie Museum of Art to develop a vocabulary and ontology for expressing provenance information as linked data. This new collaboration parallels and builds on the Carnegie's ongoing provenance project, 'Art Tracks Provenance Visualization Project'.[22]

Conclusion

My recent experiences on the Gurlitt Task Force and at the first DZK symposium in Berlin started me thinking about silos, as a useful image for the past, present and future of provenance research. Silos store and protect the resource (grain) for future use. Similarly, our 'silos' – our museums, archives, libraries and research centres – protect and maintain the integrity of objects and related information, within a specific context. Provenance resources and research are often 'siloed' within institutions and nations, for powerful reasons – relating to specific legal and cultural heritages, traditions of museum and art historical studies, as well as lack of means to easily share information while protecting its integrity.

When, through human exchange, and now technology, we can *network these silos* together, then the information and resources stored in each can be used to create a richer, more globally extended understanding of human culture. And we can do this while remembering that provenance research is not a matter of one-size-fits-all – we need each unique silo, *not* one huge silo to contain all resources. Working collaboratively, we can piece back together the ownership history of an object in a way that appreciates its unique, individual circumstances and its often long journeys across space and time. Through careful, long-term provenance research, we can gain a broader appreciation of the complexities and the differences of heritage which, paradoxically, unite us all.

Acknowledgements

I would like to thank several of my Smithsonian colleagues, SPRI contractors, interns and volunteers of the last seven years, for their collaborative efforts that have greatly contributed to the ideas, research, projects and new initiatives presented in this essay: Freer Gallery of Art and Arthur M. Sackler Gallery: Julian Raby, Director; Elizabeth Duley, Head of Collections; Jeffrey Smith, Assistant Registrar; David Hogge, Head of Archives; and Alice Tracy, Foundations Officer; Office of the Provost and Under Secretary for Museums and Research: Richard Kurin, Interim Provost and Under Secretary; Corine Wegener, Cultural Heritage Preservation Officer; Elizabeth Kirby, Grant Specialist, Office of the Grand Challenges Consortia; and Michelle Delaney, Director, Grand Challenges Consortia for the Humanities; National Museum of American Art: Bonnie Campbell Lilienfeld, Assistant Director for Curatorial Affairs; Hirshhorn Museum and Sculpture Garden: Valerie Fletcher, Senior Curator for Modern Art; Cooper-Hewitt National Design Museum: Cara McCarty, Curatorial Director; Matilda McQuaid, Deputy Curatorial

Director; and Wendy Rogers, Registrar; Archives of American Art: Kate Haw, Director; Liz Kirwin, Deputy Director; Marisa Bourgoin, Head of Reference; and Barbara Aikens, Head of Collections Processing.

SPRI project consultants (unless otherwise noted currently working on projects): Laurie A. Stein, LLC and SPRI Senior Provenance Advisor (since 2008); Dorota Chudzicka, Provenance Research Associate (2008–13); Patricia Teter, Provenance Advisor (2008–09); Lynn H. Nicholas, Provenance Advisor (since 2013); Nick Pearce, Richmond Chair of Fine Art, University of Glasgow, UK and Senior Research Fellow (2014–15); Samantha Viksnins, Freer/Sackler, SPRI Project Manager; Andrea Hull, SPRI Editing and Grants; Fulvia Zaninelli, Provenance Research Associate; and Neal Johnson and Duane Degler, DesignForContext, LLC. Recent SPRI interns include: Manon Gaudet (2013–14), Maria Tischner (2014), Lauren Clark (2014–15), Stacy Moo (2015), Phoebe Coleman (2015); and Katie Bryan (2015–16); Colleen Carroll (2016). SPRI volunteer: Kate Hughes (2014–15).

I would also to thank the numerous supporters for grants and private gifts to further our research projects and programmes: American Council for Learned Societies, The David Berg Foundation, The Samuel H. Kress Foundation, Norman and Suzanne Cohn, Jim Hayes, Kate Hughes and John Christian.

Notes

1 For an overview of the US Department of State's current summary of the challenges of World War II-era provenance research, see remarks delivered by Douglas Davidson, Special Envoy for Holocaust Issues, Bureau of European and Eurasian Affairs, US Department of State, at The Hague, Netherlands, for the 'International symposium on alternatives to litigation in Nazi-looted art disputes', 27 November 2012, at: www.state.gov/p/eur/rls/rm/2012/201790.htm (accessed December 2015).

2 Art journalist Lee Rosenbaum, in her 16 July 2013, *CultureGrrl* blog piece titled 'Repatriation and restitution: Crimes of omission in *NY Times*' cultural property coverage', chides two *New York Times* reporters for irresponsibly having 'omitted crucial facts bolstering museums' cases for retention of two hot-button objects'.

3 See AAMD's 'Proctocols for Safe Havens for Works of Cultural Significance from Countries in Crisis', at: http://aamd.org/document/aamd-protocols-for-save-havens-for-works-of-cultural-significance-from-countries-in-crisis (accessed 18 December 2015).

4 Since 2009, the Smithsonian's Museum Conservation Institute (MCI) and the Office of International Relations (OIR), with the support of the US Department of State's Cultural Heritage Center (CHC) and the Department of Homeland Security's Homeland Security Investigations (HSI), have organized training workshops for HSI agents. HSI agents investigate crimes involving the illicit importation and distribution of cultural property, art and antiquities. CHC implements US obligations with regard to the 1970 UNESCO Convention. Acting with the Department of Justice and INTERPOL, these agencies slow and prevent the illicit trade of art and antiquities as a means to protect and preserve cultural heritage. The training covers legal aspects, including investigative methods and procedures appropriate for international cultural property cases, as well as Smithsonian specialists' perspectives on identifying, provenancing and assessing authenticity of cultural heritage materials. Smithsonian museum partners provide behind-the-scenes introductions to objects from regions that are at greatest risk of looting and

trafficking, as well as practical skills training in handling, photographing, recording and packing objects.

5 More than fourteen museums participated in an online exhibition *Alfred Flechtheim: Art Dealer of the Avantgarde*, at: http://alfredflechtheim.com/home (accessed 18 December 2015). This website includes more than 300 works of art whose provenance (ownership history) has a connection with Alfred Flechtheim's galleries. Though this is an impressive effort and resource, American museums did not participate for a variety of reasons, mostly because we record our provenance research on our respective websites already, and a data transfer to this site would date the information and potentially cause confusion.

6 Since 2008, the Smithsonian's World War II-era provenance research projects have been supported by Richard Kurin, Under Secretary for History, Art, and Culture. He tasked me to direct the project as part of my role as Senior Program Officer for Art in the Office of the Under Secretary for History, Art, and Culture (OUSHAC). Previously, the Smithsonian's provenance research efforts were based out of the Office of the Under Secretary for Art, and supported by Edwin (Ned) Rifkin, former Under Secretary for Art, and Susan Talbott, former Director of Smithsonian Arts. Talbott recruited Laurie Stein, an art historian and former foundation director, to assess and report on the Freer | Sackler museums' provenance project and to write a comprehensive plan for the museum. That report helped lead to the founding of the Smithsonian Provenance Research Initiative (SPRI) in 2009. From 2009 to 2012, the following served as advisers to the project: Julian Raby, The Dame Jillian Sackler Director of the Arthur M. Sackler Gallery and the Freer Gallery of Art; Martin Sullivan, Director of the National Portrait Gallery (emeritus); and John W. Smith, Director, Archives of American Art (now director of the Museum of Art at the Rhode Island School of Design).

7 Since 1999–2000, the Smithsonian administration has closely followed developments including: the Washington Conference in 1998; the Presidential Advisory Commission on Holocaust Assets in the United States in 2000; the establishment of the AAM (American Association of Museums) Guidelines; and AAMD (American Association of Art Museum Directors) Guidelines concerning museum holdings which may have been unlawfully appropriated during the Nazi era. In the *Smithsonian Institutions/SD 600 Collections Implementation Manual*, Chapter 23, a section titled 'Specific legal and ethical issues, unlawful appropriation of objects during the Nazi era', the Smithsonian committed itself to a pan-institutional approach to provenance-related principles, policies, collecting and acquisition consideration standards, and transparency.

8 Since 2000, the Smithsonian's central administration has financially supported provenance research historians to assist museum curators with their research and, in 2004, launched the 'Smithsonian Institution World War II Provenance' website. Aside from a searchable object database, the site includes resources and additional information on World War II-era provenance issues, documentation, history, laws, policies and research. See: Smithsonian Institution, 2004, 'Provenance in the World War II Era, 1933–1945', at: http://provenance.si.edu (accessed 18 December 2015).

9 See Freer Gallery of Art and the Arthur M. Sackler Gallery (2009). 'Guidelines and procedures for World War II provenance issues', at: www.asia.si.edu/collections/downloads/FSgGuidelinesProcedures.pdf (accessed 18 December 2015). At the Freer and Sackler Galleries, nearly 400 art works with World War II-era provenance gaps have been researched and are available on the museum's website with links to NEPIP. See: Freer Gallery of Art and Arthur M. Sackler Gallery (2014), 'World War II Era Provenance Project', at: www.asia.si.edu/collections/ww2provenance.asp (accessed 18 December 2015).

10 See www.aaa.si.edu/news/archives-receives-kress-foundation-grant. In 2010, the AAA was awarded a grant by the Samuel H. Kress Foundation's Digital Resources programme to digitize the Seligmann & Co. records. Jacques Seligmann & Co. Inc. is counted among the foremost French and American art dealers in antiquities and decorative arts, and was among the first to foster and support the growth of and appreciation for collecting

in the field of contemporary European art. The company's clients included most of the major American and European art collectors of the era, and the art that passed through its galleries often ended up in the collections of prominent American and European museums through the donations of the wealthy benefactors who purchased them from the company. In 2012, a further grant from the Kress Foundation led to the second phase of this project – to preserve, create and arrange online electronic finding aids for their archival collections that are crucial to provenance research for the history of art during World War II.

11 See www.aaa.si.edu/collections/projects/provenance. In 2014, the AAA launched online finding aids for ten archival collections central to World War II-era provenance research that link oral-history interviews and related collections at the Archives, including detailed online finding aids for the historical records of Schaeffer Galleries and World House Galleries, as well as the personal archives of art historians and World War II Monuments Men S. Lane Faison, Walter Horn, Thomas Carr Howe, J.B. Neumann, Perry Townsend Rathborne, James J. Rorimer, George Leslie Stout and Otto Wittman, together with an invaluable guide to the aids written by SPRI Senior Advisor Laurie A Stein.

12 Some of these include 'Arbeitskreis for German–American collaborations', Roundtable Discussion on possible collaborative projects, Munich, 2010; *Wie das Zweite Exil des erste Sprechen bringt: Moskauer Archive und die Künste in Paris, 1933–1945*, International Conference, German Art Historical Institute, Moscow, 2011; *Collecting Art–Dealing Art*, Symposium, Commission for Provenance Research, Vienna, 2011; *Nationalsozialistischer Kunstraub und Restitution heute*, Friedrich Naumann Stiftung, Berlin, 2012; Center for the History of Collecting, The Frick Collection, New York, 2012; *From Plunder to Preservation: The Untold Story of Cultural Heritage, WWII and the Pacific*, The Lawyers Committee for Cultural Heritage Preservation, Washington, DC, 2012; *Sammlungsgeschichte und Provenienzforschung – Erwerbungspolitik im 20. Jahrhundert*, symposium on Asian art collector Eduard von der Heydt, Museum Rietberg, Zurich, 2013; Mečislav Borák (ed.) (2014), *'The West' Versus 'The East' or The United Europe?* Prague: Documentation Centre for Property Transfers of Cultural Assets of World War II Victims; *Looted – Recovered. Cultural Goods – the Case of Poland*, Conference, Krakow, 2014; EHRI International Workshop on Holocaust Art, *An Essential Tool for the Methodology of Constructing a Historical Narrative*, Yad Vashem, Jerusalem, 2015; *New Perspectives on Provenance Research in Germany*, First Conference of the German Centre for Cultural Property Losses, Jewish Museum, Berlin, 2015.

13 For the programme, see https://ww2provenanceseminar.files.wordpress.com/2011/02/ wwii-finalprogram.pdf (accessed 18 December 2015). The seminar was sponsored by the United States National Archives, the Association of Art Museum Directors, the American Association of Museums and the Smithsonian Institution, with additional support provided by The Samuel H. Kress Foundation and James P. Hayes. Remarks by Jim Leach, Chairman, National Endowment for the Humanities, opened the seminar and discussed the reasons we are still dealing with World War II-era provenance questions more than seventy years later; 150 people attended, including thirty-five guest speakers and representatives from sixty museums, thirty-four US states, and ten European countries. See also https:// ww2provenanceseminar.wordpress.com/about-2 (accessed 18 December 2015).

14 The launch of NARA's Research Portal and the coinciding seminar are evidence that research exchange at the transatlantic level is happening. As of yet, however, only large national institutions have the resources and infrastructure available to engage in this type of international collaboration.

15 The special focus issue, 'Provenance Research in American Institutions', in *Collections: A Journal for Museum and Archives Professionals, From the Practical to the Philosophical*, 10 (3). New York: Altamira Press, is currently sold out and not available online, hence some of the information covered in the journal has been incorporated into this essay. For a complete list of authors and essays, see: www.collegeart.org/news/2014/08/28/provenance-research-in-american-institutions.

16 Some of these include programmes for UNESCO, the Association for Research into Crimes Against Art, the International Society of Art Appraisers and the European Shoah Legacy Institute, as well as public lectures at museums and universities.

17 For more on the Smithsonian's Haiti Cultural Recovery Project, see http://haiti. si.edu. Also see Richard Kurin, *Saving Haiti's Heritage: Cultural Recovery after the Earthquake*. Washington, DC: Smithsonian Institution Press, 2012. The project works to rescue, recover, safeguard and help restore Haitian artwork, artefacts, documents, media and architectural features damaged and endangered by the earthquake and its aftermath. The project is organized by the Smithsonian Institution with the Government of Haiti, Ministry of Culture and Communication and the Presidential Commission for Reconstruction, in partnership with the US President's Committee on the Arts and the Humanities.

18 In 2012, the Smithsonian hired Corine Wegener, Cultural Heritage Preservation Specialist. See Lee Binkovits (2012). 'How to save the arts in times of war', *Smithsonian Magazine*, at: www.smithsonianmag.com/arts-culture/smithsonian-institution/qa-how-to-save-the-arts-in-times-of-war.html (accessed December 2015). See also UNESCO (2010), 'UNESCO and the Smithsonian sign a Memorandum of Understanding for cultural and natural heritage', at: http://whc.unesco.org/en/news/663 (accessed 18 December 2015).

19 See www.gla.ac.uk/postgraduate/taught/provenanceandcollecting. SPRI and the University of Glasgow are working to expand the programme to include partnerships with the George Washington University's Museum Studies Program and the Free University of Berlin's Entartete Kunst Forschungsstelle, which developed one of the first universities in Germany to initiate an academic programme in Germany on World War II-era cultural plunder and provenance research. Recently new courses have been added at universities in Munich and Hamburg.

20 See www.designforcontext.com/about-us. We are working with DesignForContext, which has expertise in the design of interactive applications and search user interfaces. The right platform critical for this project, as the Internet, while it shares information with great speed, can also distort and decontextualize it in the process. Some of the challenges in building out this collaboration on an international level are the different collection management software used by museums, the formatting of provenance research data, and legal systems that impact data sharing.

21 See http://dcic.umd.edu/projects. The Looted Holocaust Assets Research Project (L-HARP) is a partnership between the DCIC, the National Archives and the Holocaust Memorial Museum to create a linked database spanning national and international institutions vital for heirs and claimants to lost cultural property, Holocaust/Truth Commissions, international organizations (e.g. World Jewish Congress), historians, lawyers and genealogists.

22 See http://blog.cmoa.org/2014/08/visualizing-the-stories-and-lifespan-of-an-artwork. The Carnegie Museum of Art's 'Art Tracks: Provenance Visualization Project' will engage the public more deeply with works of art by bringing their histories to life. The museum is in the process of developing a technology-based interactive framework that will employ standard art museum cataloging data and best practices to allow users to visually chart the life cycles of art objects over time and across distances. Freer|Sackler is part of a grant application to collaborate with them on this project.

References

Alfred Flechtheim: Art Dealer of the Avantgarde, at: http://alfredflechtheim.com/home (accessed 18 December 2015).

American Alliance of Museums (AAM), 2014. 'Standards regarding the unlawful appropriation of objects during the Nazi Era', at: www.aam-us.org/resources/ethics-standards-and-best-practices/collections-stewardship/objects-during-the-nazi-era (accessed 18 December 2015).

American Alliance of Museums Nazi-Era Provenance Internet Portal (NEPIP), 2014. Online. www.nepip.org.

Anderson, Maxwell L., 2011. 'The crisis in art history: Ten problems, ten solutions'. *Visual Resources*, 27 (4), at: http://dx.doi.org/10.1080/0197362.2011.622238 (accessed 18 December 2015).

Association of Art Museum Directors, (AAMD), 2013. 'Guidelines on the acquisition of archaeological material and ancient art', at: https://aamd.org/standards-and-practices (accessed 18 December 2015).

AAMD. 'Proctocols for safe havens for works of cultural significance from countries in crisis', at: https://aamd.org/document/aamd-protocols-for-save-havens-for-works-of-cultural-significance-from-countries-in-crisis (accessed 18 December 2015).

Binkovits, Lee, 2012. 'How to save the arts in times of war'. *Smithsonian Magazine*, at: www.smithsonianmag.com/arts-culture/smithsonian-institution/qa-how-to-save-the-arts-in-times-of-war.html (accessed December 2015).

Borák, Mečislav, (ed.), 2014. *'The West' Versus 'The East' or The United Europe?* Prague: Documentation Centre for Property Transfers of Cultural Assets of World War II Victims.

Chudzicka, Dorota, 2012. 'The dealer and the museum, C.T. Loo (1880–1957): The Freer Gallery of art, and the American Asian art market in the 1930s and 1940s', in *Kunst Sammeln, Kunst Handel/Beiträge des Internationalen Symposiums Wien*. Vienna: Boehler.

Chudzicka, Dorota, 2014. 'In love at first sight completely, hopelessly and forever with Chinese Art. The Eugene and Agnes Meyer Collection of Chinese Art at the Freer Gallery of Art', in Juilee Decker, (ed.), *Collections: A Journal for Museum and Archives Professionals, From the Practical to the Philosophical*, 10 (3). New York: Altamira Press.

Clark, Stephen W., 2014. 'Nazi-era claims and art museums: The American perspective', in Juilee Decker, (ed.), *Collections: A Journal for Museum and Archives Professionals, From the Practical to the Philosophical*, 10 (3). New York: Altamira Press.

Cuno, James, (ed.), 2009. *Whose Culture? The Promise of Museums and the Debate Over Antiquities*. Princeton, NJ: Princeton University Press.

Die Schwarzen Jahre: Geschichten einer Sammlung 1933–1945, 2015. Berlin: Staatliche Museen zu Berlin.

Feigenbaum, Gail and Reist, Inge (eds), 2013. *Provenance: An Alternate History of Art*. Los Angeles, CA: Getty Research Institute.

Freer Gallery of Art and the Arthur M. Sackler Gallery, 2009. 'Guidelines and procedures for World War II provenance issues', at: www.asia.si.edu/press/past/prProvenance. htm (accessed 18 December 2015).

Freer Gallery of Art and Arthur M. Sackler Gallery Press Room, 2010. 'Freer and Sackler Galleries launch web site for World War II Provenance Project', at: www.asia.si.edu/press/past/prProvenance.htm (accessed 18 December 2015).

Freer Gallery of Art and Arthur M. Sackler Gallery, 2014. 'World War II Era Provenance Project', at: www.asia.si.edu/collections/ww2provenance.asp (accessed 18 December 2015).

Hollevoet-Force, Christel, 2014. 'One painting concealed behind another. Picasso's *La Douleur* (1903) and *Guitar, Gas Jet, and Bottle* (1913', in Juilee Decker (ed.), *Collections: A Journal for Museum and Archives Professionals, From the Practical to the Philosophical*, 10 (3). New York: Altamira Press.

Huemer, Christian, 2014. 'The "German Sales 1930–1945" Database Project' at The Getty Research Institute (GRI).

Hüneke, Andreas, 2015. *Fund Gurlitt – Fall Kunstkritik. Der Nazi-Schatz – Analyse einer Berichterstattung*. Deiningen, Germany: Steinmeier.

Imperial Exposures: Photographic Portraits of East Asian Rulers. Curated by David Hogge, Head of Archives, The Freer Gallery of Art and Arthur M. Sackler Gallery, at: www.google.com/culturalinstitute/exhibit/imperial-exposures/AQqvgyc (accessed 18 December 2015).

Kurin, Richard, 2012. *Saving Haiti's Heritage: Cultural Recovery after the Earthquake*. Washington, DC: Smithsonian Institution Press.

Metropolitan Museum of Art's Leonard A. Lauder Cubist Collection, at: www.metmuseum. org/research/leonard-lauder-research-center/cubist-collection/archival-labels (accessed 18 December 2015).

Milosch, Jane, 2014a. 'Creating a community of international exchange: World War II-era provenance projects at the Smithsonian Institution', in Mečislav Borák, (ed.), *"The West" Versus "The East" or The United Europe?* Prague: Documentation Centre for Property Transfers of Cultural Assets of World War II Victims.

Milosch, Jane, 2014b. 'Provenance! Not the problem (the solution)', in Juilee Decker (ed.), *Collections: A Journal for Museum and Archives Professionals, From the Practical to the Philosophical*, 10 (3). New York: Altamira Press.

National Archives and Records Administration (NARA), 2014. International Research Portal for Records Related to Nazi-Era Cultural Property, at: www.archives.gov/ research/holocaust/international-resources (accessed 18 December 2015).

Nicholas, Lynn, 1995. *The Rape of Europa: The Fate of Europe's Treasures in the Third Reich and the Second World War*. New York: Random House (Vintage Books).

Nicholas, Lynn H., 2014. 'Introduction', in Juilee Decker, (ed.), *Collections: A Journal for Museum and Archives Professionals, From the Practical to the Philosophical*, 10 (3). New York: Altamira Press.

Rosenbaum, Lee, 2013. 'Repatriation and restitution: Crimes of omission in *NY Times*' cultural property coverage'. *CultureGrrl* blog, 16 July 2013.

Smithsonian Institution Cultural Heritage Preservation Projects, at: http://unitetosave.si. edu (accessed 18 December 2015).

Smithsonian Institution, 2004. 'Provenance in the World War II era, 1933–1945', at: http:// provenance.si.edu (accessed 18 December 2015).

Stein, Laurie A., 2014. '"Everyone brings a piece to the puzzle": Conversations with Elaine Rosenberg and reflections on provenance research among The Paul Rosenberg Archives', in Juilee Decker, (ed.), *Collections: A Journal for Museum and Archives Professionals, From the Practical to the Philosophical*, 10 (3). New York: Altamira Press.

Stein, Laurie A. 'Provenance research at the Archives of American Art'. With Barbara Aikens, Head of Collections Processing, Archives of American Art, Smithsonian Institution and Jane Milosch, Director of the Provenance Research Initiative, Smithsonian Institution, at: www.aaa.si.edu/collections/projects/provenance (accessed 18 December 2015).

Steinberg, Jessica, 2014. 'Restitution group withdraws claims museums illegally holding looted art, wants to help'. *The Times of Israel*, 26 January 2014, at: www.timesofisrael.com/ restitution-organization-museums-jostle-over-nazi-looted-art (accessed 18 December 2015).

Task Force Schwabinger Kunstfund, at: www.taskforce-kunstfund.de/en/about_us.htm.

The Paul Rosenberg Archives at the Museum of Modern Art, at: www.moma.org/learn/ resources/archives/EAD/PaulRosenbergf.

UNESCO, 2010. 'UNESCO and the Smithsonian sign a Memorandum of Understanding for cultural and natural heritage', at: http://whc.unesco.org/en/news/663 (accessed 18 December 2015).

Vikan, Gary, 2014. 'Provenance research and unprovenanced cultural property', in Juilee Decker, (ed.), *Collections: A Journal for Museum and Archives Professionals, From the Practical to the Philosophical*, 10 (3). New York: Altamira Press.

Yeide, Nancy, 2014. 'Princes, dukes, and counts: Pedigrees and problems in the Kress Collection', in Juilee Decker (ed.), *Collections: A Journal for Museum and Archives Professionals, From the Practical to the Philosophical*, 10 (3). New York: Altamira Press.

20

'DEFINITELY STOLEN?'

Why there is no alternative to provenance research in archaeological museums

Markus Hilgert

While provenance research has been a major topic in the context of works of art looted during the national-socialist era in Germany (1933–45), systematic and comprehensive inquiries into the provenance of archaeological objects in public collections are long overdue, and form a rather embarrassing lacuna in the research profile of the pertinent museums. Given the fact that many of these collections came into being during a time when colonial asymmetries characterized the relationship between source and target states, provenance research in archaeological museums is a must in a world that strives for absolute equality and transparency in intergovernmental relations. However, apart from considerations focusing on foreign and cultural policy, there are also arguments from the point of view of recent cultural theory that favour provenance research in archaeological museums. The present article discusses these arguments and outlines a political and institutional agenda for archaeological provenance research.

'We are not accountable'

Definitely stolen? Are the holdings of archaeological museums, not only in Germany, but in the whole world, the result of unlawful appropriation, and therefore a case for law enforcement authorities? Following the long overdue admission that archaeological museums also must fully clarify the provenance of their objects, is a wave of legally constituted claims for restitution in store for us, and consequently the possibility of the overall loss of archaeological cultural goods, which by now are perceived to be indispensable to the canon of the cultural objects of our society? Do we have only an inadequate legal situation and the inflexibility of German authorities to thank for the fact that Nefertiti, the Ishtar Gate and Co. may still be shown on the Museum Island in Berlin?

The answer to all these questions is, of course, 'no': for precisely, the bust of Nefertiti from the Egyptian Amarna, as well as the Ishtar Gate from Babylon (Iraq), are perfect examples of how, as early as at the start of the twentieth century, archaeological objects could become permanent lawful property of German archaeological museums on the basis of bilateral, legally binding agreements and correspondingly with the explicit consent of the respective countries of origin.[1] Many other examples could be cited here.

The problem related to archaeological cultural property in museums and academic collections in Germany is therefore by no means that 'everything is stolen'. Rather, the problem is that we *do not know exactly* whether anything at all was 'stolen'. In other words, the problem lies in the fact that at present we do not have a comprehensive and detailed overview of how exactly these holdings of archaeological cultural property were assembled and came into being.

Putting this another way, the problem is that we are *not accountable* for the entirety of archaeological objects in public institutions in Germany: neither to the governments of the federal states and the federal republic, nor to the governments of the countries of origin; neither to the researchers who make this cultural property the object of their studies, nor to the society which, through its entry fees and taxes, enables the long-term maintenance, as well as the academic analysis, of archaeological collections in the first place, and in return may expect comprehensive information on these collections at the highest academic and ethical level.

The present article represents a passionate plea for this comprehensive accountability. It will demonstrate, through respective propositions, the following: what this accountability should relate to; through which theoretical, political and ethical arguments it may be justified; and finally, what might be the immediate consequences for the conduct and behaviour of museums and academic collections with holdings of archaeological cultural property. A repeated point of reference for this discussion will be the upcoming amendment of the Act to Protect Cultural Property in Germany, which provides for high standards for the handling of archaeological cultural property and is therefore also directly relevant to issues addressed in this article.

Most matters can merely be outlined here, but certainly with the intention of being taken up and expanded in the developing public discussion about provenance research in archaeological museums. The perspective I adopt is that of a specialist in Ancient Near Eastern Studies, who has been handling archaeological cultural property almost daily for twenty years, but has always done this in the context of university research and teaching. Additionally, since March 2014, I also carry responsibility for the collection of archaeological cultural property in the Museum of the Ancient Near East of the Berlin State Museums, which comprises roughly 600,000 objects from societies of ancient Mesopotamia and whose creation falls into the time period between the second half of the nineteenth century and the first half of the twentieth century. Against this backdrop I will attempt to examine the problem of the provenance of archaeological cultural property in public collections from different perspectives – and not least from the perspective of the affected party.

Provenance research in archaeological museums – what is it?

What must be clarified initially is what needs to happen in concrete terms in order for repositories of archaeological cultural property in Germany to become fully accountable with regard to the provenance of their holdings. The solution to this is simple, since the programme for the investigation of the provenance of archaeological objects is almost self-evident, insofar as it is in key respects comparable, in terms of methodology, with the provenance research concerning expropriated cultural property seized as a result of Nazi persecution.

The overriding goal of endeavours to comparable effect must be to clarify under which legal, political, cultural and epistemological circumstances the archaeological objects found their way into their current conditions of retention or 'property', and whether or under which conditions they may or ought to remain there. In terms of research strategy, this means researching, documenting and evaluating as comprehensively as possible the concrete processes that led to the current or last-known location of each individual object. Fragmentary results are likewise to be presented as instructive and appropriately detailed, provided that full use has been made of all available sources of information. Those documents that verify or contextualize the relevant processes must be established and processed in a scholarly manner. Finally, all sources and results of investigations ought not only to be published, but of course also to be included in the conception and design of permanent and special exhibitions of the archaeological cultural property concerned.

However, as evident as tasks and objectives are, it is equally clear that the implementation of the postulate of a comprehensive accountability in the field of provenance of archaeological objects demands tremendous resources in terms of time, personnel and finances. In this context, it is rightfully being discussed at present, and with some controversy, where the locations and who the players of such provenance research of archaeological objects ought to be. On the one hand, it is quite correct that corresponding investigations are quintessentially in the interest of repositories of archaeological cultural property, and must be one of their core tasks. On the other hand, it must be recognized that the necessary academic competencies in terms of historical, archival and museum-related research are seldom present in the museums and collections concerned. Such extensive and additional research tasks frequently cannot be undertaken with existing personnel and infrastructural capacities; furthermore, in the case of *internally* conducted provenance research, conflicts of interest can readily arise. After all, the results of such research projects will most likely only bear an examination of academic quality and have political meaning if they are verifiably conducted, and entirely independently of irrelevant official concerns – for instance, considerations of an institution's reputation, or of cultural-political constraints.

Independently of the urgent need to overcome these structural and financial challenges, it must become a matter of course, in archaeological museums as well as in politics, economics and research-funding institutions, that a methodologically solid and fully comprehensive analysis of the individual history of objects forms one of the central research tasks of the repositories of cultural property in question, and thus also provides a fundamental precondition for such institutions to appropriately fulfil other core tasks as well.

Why provenance research in archaeological museums?

Notwithstanding all that has been stated, why should public repositories of archaeological cultural property even rise to the arduous challenge of provenance research in the first place? Why *is* there no alternative to the fully extensive accountability that is laid out here? From my perspective, several different reasons may be given for this position: cultural and socio-political reasons, as well as reasons relating to cultural theory, foreign policy and, finally, ethics.

In the first instance, we must take note of the fact that visitors to archaeological museums today are increasingly interested in the cultural and socio-political topic of 'provenance', and demand information accordingly. This has not always been the case. However, in the wake of a phenomenon that I refer to elsewhere as 'Kulturisierung des Materiellen' (Hilgert 2014a) or 'culturizing material' (Hilgert 2014b), we can currently observe that objects are increasingly becoming the subject of practices and discourses that are located outside of academia and research, and by now have attracted a remarkable interest, a 'new sensitivity' (Coole 2014) within the sphere of society, politics and culture. Three overlapping complexes of problems are at issue here:

1. the 'provenance' and objects' 'appartenance' (i.e. where they belong);
2. the fundamental 'multi-perspectivity' of objects, depending on individual or collective attribution of meaning;
3. the mediating 'translation' of objects in varying contexts of transcultural reception, where the principles of mediation, 'inclusion' and 'accessibility' play a central part.

Provenance research in repositories of archaeological cultural property is directly relevant to all these topics or academic challenges. Thus it also represents a response to the increased societal and cultural interest in objects and their 'itineraries', 'biographies' or 'history'. Such research can further contribute to the clarification of concepts and terminology that are relevant to this context, yet which are frequently misused or confused in the public sphere and by the media.

From a cultural-theoretical viewpoint, an academic review of the history of acquisition of archaeological collections, as well as the diachronic itineraries of their objects, appears urgently advisable for two reasons, which are interconnected. The strands of theory generally subsumed under the term 'postcolonial theory' have not only exposed the one-sidedness of specifically European narratives of development and modernity, and essentialist cultural concepts used as discursive instruments to reinforce colonial power structures. In addition, the same theoretical work has drawn attention to the fact that the creation of collections in Europe of non-European archaeological or ethnological cultural property mostly occurred within the frame-work of *power-political and economical asymmetries*; and that such collecting also served the propagation of colonially determined and mostly derogatory perceptions of 'other' cultures and the particularities attributed to them – and precisely through museums' activities of gathering representations of 'otherness' in their collections.

These asymmetries and their consequences still have various effects to the present day, not only in the 'orientalisms' of many current narratives in Ancient Studies and in the cultural sciences, but also precisely in the worldwide systematic plundering of archaeological sites and museums in formerly colonized states for the illegal trade of cultural property in rich market states with good infrastructure. An up-to-date cultural science *of*, *with* and *as a result of* archaeological objects in historically assem-bled collections is therefore urgently dependent on academically obtaining the provenance of objects, if such scientific work wishes to avoid accusations of acting carelessly from the point of view of cultural theory, and in disregard of the post-colonial perspective on these objects.

A second argument from cultural theory for provenance research in repositories of archaeological cultural property derives from the observation that the epistemic and scientific status of objects in the humanities and social sciences has changed considerably in recent times. While objects are understood by these disciplines not only as very effective vehicles for social practices, the premise is also now accepted that *things* can never, for any person, be more than objects of one's interpretative perception. In terms of methodology and research strategy, this premise is of funda-mental significance, because it affirms that practices *of*, *with* and *as a result of* things never refer to the 'thing in itself'; only to constructed objects whose identities are multiple and variable, depending on subjective reception.

The central research strategy of object-oriented research in the humanities and social sciences must therefore, abstractly speaking, consist of *continually* document-ing the different social and practical contextualizations of an object, without distin-guishing between 'original' or 'primary', and 'hybrid' or 'secondary', 'participation' in social practices, and thereby advancing an academic evaluation and hierarchical ordering of these various social-practical 'scenarios' for objects studied. The theor-etical and practical advantage of this framework lies in the fact that it does not judge any of the various social contextualizations of an object, and therefore diversifies object-oriented research in terms of theory, method and content. The cumulative 'recontextualizations' of an object – precisely in the framework of contemporary scientific, museum and even digital practices – can thus also become the subject of object-oriented research, as can the production of such an object and its wrongful, but academically mostly privileged, 'first participations' in social practices. As an academic reconstruction of such 'object biographies' or 'object itineraries', the ana-lysis of provenance in archaeological museums is thus also *a must*, when seen from this cultural-theoretical perspective.

Yet there are, of course, also good reasons beyond cultural theory for the inves-tigation of the provenance of archaeological objects. Even in terms of relations of cultural and foreign policy between states of origin on the one hand and owner or possessor states on the other, the accountability of the latter with regard to the creation of collections of cultural property plays an increasingly important part. Meanwhile such accountability has often become even a prerequisite for bilateral cooperation in the field of museums or academia. What is at issue for the states of origin here is decidedly not simply the raising or verification of claims for restitution. Rather, they expect from a partnership on equal terms of cultural and foreign policy a responsible, transparent handling by modern states of their − as the case may be − colonial or imperial history; this naturally also entails the reviewing and publication of the provenance of archaeological cultural property in public collections. These archaeological collections, after all, were often assembled during a time when the political relationship between states of origin and owner or possessor states was decidedly not on equal terms, but rather was characterized by the asymmetry and institutionalized inequality thematized earlier in this essay.

A final ethical argument for a fully extensive academic review of the provenance of archaeological cultural property in public collections is very topical, and relates to the forthcoming amendment of the Act to Protect Cultural Property in Germany. Within the framework of this extensive revision and improvement of the act currently in force since the year 2007, the federal government wishes, among other things, to prescribe by law a compulsory certification for all archaeological cultural property that is imported to Germany. In direct reference to the legal situation in the respective countries of origin, in which the export of archaeological cultural property is mostly illegal, only those archaeological cultural assets may be imported to Germany in future that possess a corresponding valid export licence of the country of origin.

Furthermore, strict due diligence duties modelled on the Swiss Federal Act on the International Transfer of Cultural Property from the year 2005, and in consideration of the EU Directive EU 60/2014, are now to be regulated by law in Germany, particularly in respect of art dealers who trade in archaeological cultural property. These due diligence duties of the market are also to include extensive provenance research, the fulfilment of which is to be proven in writing and in a detailed manner. Not only the German law enforcement authorities, but also archaeologists as well as the institutions and professional associations relevant to this context, emphatically support this legislative initiative by the federal government.

However, according to my conviction this also implies that, as far as archaeological cultural property is concerned, we may expect the application of due diligence principles in the case of acquisition and provenance research not only from traders and collectors; rather, there must also be a legally binding requirement for the work of museums and academic collections. To this end the *ICOM Code of Ethics for Museums*[2] is already stipulating that, when acquiring an object, this should be undertaken with 'due diligence' to 'establish the full history of the item since discovery or production', as stated in Section 2.3 of the ICOM Code (ICOM 2004). In any case it is imperative that the standards for the handling of archaeological cultural property in Germany are the same everywhere, and fulfil the highest academic and ethical requirements.

Master plan: 'provenance research in archaeological museums'

Thus we reach the final issue for consideration here: namely, what consequences follow for the maintenance and conduct of museums and academic collections with holdings of archaeological cultural property, if they seriously adopt the postulate – comprehensively reasoned above – relating to an extensive accountability regarding the provenance of their holdings.

Initially, what will concretely be at issue in the near future will be defining proceedings, instruments, quality standards and examples of best practice for the academic analysis of the provenance of archaeological cultural property. Recommendations for action and infrastructures must be developed for the yet-to-be-clarified key questions concerning the temporal perspective, the institutional affiliation, as well as the regulation of this provenance research. Medium-term prognoses concerning additional expenditure in terms of personnel and material resources necessary for the implementation of this major academic project would, finally, also be politically relevant. The museums and collections in question, the professional associations, universities and extramural research-funding institutions, as well as politics, would all be called upon in the development of a suitable, and likely now inescapable, *master plan* required for ethically responsible provenance research and public interpretation of archaeological collections in the twenty-first century.

A comprehensive investigation and disclosure of the provenance of archaeological cultural property will hardly entail, as some fear, that museums and academic collections will have to return a large proportion of their holdings to the states of origin. In those cases where evidence of unlawful acquisition can in fact be provided, and a return within the framework of the current laws is required, this will evidently occur. In the cases in which this is not possible, however, an extensive accountability concerning the provenance of archaeological cultural property will launch bilateral mediation processes, which so far have not been practicable due to lack of appropriate data. In terms of foreign policy as far as Germany is concerned, this should indubitably also entail an improvement of the partially strained relations between Germany and individual states of origin.

Against the background of the forthcoming amendment in Germany of the Act to Protect Cultural Property, and the due diligence duties specified, how museums and academic collections with holdings of archaeological cultural property can contribute to the stemming of illegal trafficking in archaeological cultural property, beyond extensive additional provenance research, must be a central issue for museum policy in coming years. For instance, it is clear that in future we will have to pay closer attention, even more precisely than previously, to the following question: for which cases do we provide expert reports, or simply an assessment of archaeological cultural property? Here the greatest restraint is advisable, unless we are obliged to take action at the request of law enforcement authorities.

It would undoubtedly be worthwhile on the part of public museums and academic collections in Germany to consider a voluntary general moratorium on acquiring archaeological cultural property until the new Act to Protect Cultural Property,

with its binding regulations for the export and provenance certification of archaeological cultural property, has come into effect, and appropriate legal provisions apply
also to the entire EU Common Market. Standardized import checks for archaeological cultural property at the EU level, based on the German model, could soon be
regulated by law, since this topic has been included in the European Council's 'Work
Plan for Culture 2015–2018' on the initiative of the German federal government.

To the extent that museums and academic collections tackle the challenge of
comprehensively researching, through academic means, the provenance of the
archaeological cultural property in their care, and commit to disclosing the results
of these efforts, they will above all set an example that clearly underscores the
importance of a *responsible* handling of archaeological cultural property on behalf of
society as a whole. The shocking images that reached the world for months in 2015
from Iraq, Syria, Libya or Yemen are a powerful reminder that the *ir*responsible
handling of these objects threatens the cultural heritage of all mankind.

Note

1 In the case of the Ishtar Gate from Babylon, which can be seen in the Museum of the
Ancient Near East in the Pergamon Museum on the Museum Island in Berlin, it is
usually forgotten in the mostly very emotional debate surrounding provenance that this
structure is, strictly speaking, merely a three-storey depository for archaeological findings, the façade of which was decorated with a reconstruction of the enamel brick clad-
ding of the Ishtar Gate in Babylon. The vast majority of these enamel bricks were
produced near Berlin in the 1920s, solely for this purpose. Only the bulls and serpent
dragons carved in relief, as well as a few other segments of the façade, were reconstructed using original fragments from Babylon. These original enamel bricks were
brought to Berlin in the framework of a bilateral, excellently documented division of
finds in hundreds of boxes, and then, over the course of years of arduous, delicate work
by restorers and scholars, cleaned, conserved and finally assembled to become animal
reliefs, which were then incorporated into the reconstructed façade of the Ishtar Gate.
2 The full text of the *ICOM Code of Ethics for Museums* is provided as *Appendix I* in the
present publication. It is also available online for download from the ICOM website
(with links to translations in French, Spanish, and many other languages). The English
version is accessible at: http://icom.museum/professional-standards/code-of-ethics.

References

Coole, D., 2014. 'Die Ontologie und Politik der Materialisierung', in Susanne Witzgall and
Kerstin Stakemeier, (eds.), *Macht des Materials/Politik der Materialität*. Zürich and Berlin:
Diaphanes, pp. 29–46.

Hilgert, M., 2014a. 'Materialisierung des Kulturellen – Kulturisierung des Materiellen: Zu
Status, Verantwortlichkeiten und Funktion von Kulturgutrepositorien im Rahmen einer
"transformativen Wissenschaft"'. *Material Text Cultures Blog*, pp. 1–14, at: www.
materiale-textkulturen.de/download_werk.php?w=4000020.

Hilgert, M., 2014b. 'Materializing Culture – culturizing material. On the status, responsibilities and function of cultural property repositories within the framework of a "transformative scholarship"'. *Middle East – Topics and Arguments* 3, pp. 30–39, at: http://
meta-journal.net/article/view/2421/3124.

ICOM, 2004. *ICOM Code of Ethics for Museums*, at: http://icom.museum/fileadmin/user_
upload/pdf/Codes/code_ethics2013_eng.pdf.

21

DEACCESSIONING

Some reflections

François Mairesse

The very least one can say about deaccessioning is that it is controversial.[1] It is, of course, an issue that ICOM addresses in its *Code of Ethics for Museums*.[2] One of the paragraphs (2.16) of the Code summarizes some of the intrinsic difficulties that persist in those countries that permit deaccessioning of items from a 'permanent' institution's collection:

> Museum collections are held in public trust and may not be treated as a realizable asset. Money or compensation received from the deaccessioning and disposal of objects and specimens from a museum collection should be used solely for the benefit of the collection and usually for acquisitions to that same collection.
>
> *(ICOM 2004a)*

It is usually acknowledged that museums have been created to preserve specimens, objects and works of art that have been passed on to them while, at the same time, they extend their collections with new acquisitions. The principle of museums is based on the concept of preserving certain types of heritage; furthermore, the possibility of disposing of a part of what has been entrusted to them is usually experienced by many curators as a thwart to their vocation. For many decades it has been known that this notion is not equally addressed by museums in Anglo-American and Latin countries – for example, in France, Argentina, Italy or Spain. Nonetheless, discussions on the problem of deaccessioning seem to have shifted. In the United States, the sale of several masterworks of art from collections held previously by Jefferson University, Pennsylvania, or the Albright-Knox Art Gallery, Buffalo, triggered a significant wave of criticism within the world of museums that was widely relayed by the media (Morris 2007; Davies 2011).

The financial crisis of 2008 refuelled these tensions. Overwhelmed by debts, several museums in the United States and the United Kingdom were forced to sell part of their collections to alleviate their deficit, which annoyed, and even gave rise to a boycott from their national museum associations. A well-known case is that of the National Academy Museum, New York, which auctioned two valuable paintings and earned a two-year sanction from the Association of Art Museum Directors; but the most recent and most-discussed case was that involving the Detroit Institute of Arts, whose collections were threatened with sale to offset the city's bankruptcy (Muñoz Sarmiento 2015). In France also, a bill submitted by Lower House Representative Jean-François Mancel in 2007, to allow deaccessioning of part of the French museums' collections, as well as the preparatory work for a bill which considered a similar regulation for the federal museums of Belgium, triggered widespread outrage across the museum profession (Clair 2007; Rykner 2008).

This essay explores five lines of thought for a potential discussion of the topic of heritage *deaccession* (or *deaccessioning*) and the *cession* of collection objects.

Linguistic issues

The French and Spanish languages are not fitted to describe the process of *deaccessioning* since most of the collections of the countries that use those languages are generally considered inalienable. In its Code of Ethics, ICOM uses the terms *cession* in French and *cesión* (or the removal from collections) in Spanish to translate the English terms *deaccessioning* and *disposal*.

In French, as in Spanish, the notion of *inaliénabilité* ('inalienability') is one of the essential principles of a museum collection, for museums that are considered to be institutions (Deloche 2011). According to the ICOM definition, museums are permanent institutions and their long-lasting nature – if it arises from consensus within society – is also illustrated through the integration of museum collections into the public domain. In Civil Law countries, with laws derived from Latin legal traditions stretching back to the Roman era (and differing from English-speaking countries' legal systems based on Common Law), public property is by definition *inaliénable*. The opposite term is *aliénable*, and, therefore, the action of definitively removing an object from a collection's inventory is called '*aliénation*'. The first connotation of this term is legal: *aliénation* in French Civil Law means conveying property, an interest, etc., to someone else (*Trésor de la langue française*). The origin of the term derived from the Latin word *alienatio* dates back to the thirteenth century. Only a century later did experts start working on the second connotation of the term – namely, 'alienation of mind' or deep psychic damage. The term 'cession' is also defined in Civil, International or Commercial Law and means transferring – either at a price or free of charge – ownership of property, an interest, or right to another person.

The *Oxford English Dictionary* defines the verb 'to deaccession' as follows: 'to remove an entry (for an exhibit, book) from the accession register of a museum, a library, etc., usually in order to sell the item concerned'. Although the term 'deaccession' does not exist in French or Spanish, the term 'accession' overall means 'the action of accessing a power or dignity, a higher political or social situation'.[2] In this context, *accession* describes the transfer of an object from daily life to a museum collection by adding it to the permanent inventory. 'Accession' to the collection somehow illustrates a status that curators will define as superior, due to the loss of use of an object's use-value or exchange-value for a value of significance or *semiophore*, giving it almost a sacred status (Mairesse 2014). The term 'deaccession' is in this sense a kind of degradation, a return to daily life and use-values. If we then add the second psychological meaning of the term alienation, the delisting of an object removed from the inventory, then deaccessioned or 'dé-accédé' is not at all an enviable condition.

In this perspective, most of the terms used to remove an object from the collection seem to have a negative connotation, as also seems to be the case in German (Fayet 2010). On the other hand, the term 'repatriation', which is widely used in the same context, appears much more positive, as it celebrates the return of a beloved part of heritage to its homeland (Fforde and Turnbull 2004; Barkan and Bush 2002). So, if each deaccession procedure can be considered as a property transfer, the museum appears as the eternal 'loser', to the benefit of the 'other' whose object returns 'home'. When the museum is actively associated with the repatriation process, the benefits of the action seem to spread to both entities and sides of the action. Why could the deaccessioning and disposal process not always be considered as a global repatriation process: to another museum, to another group of people or to another private owner (even through the market)?

Practical issues

It should first be stressed that the most passionate debates on deaccessioning are focused on the art world (and usually on single works of art), which actually represents only a very small part of the museum world, but which is linked to the art market and financial issues. In general, different actors (politicians as well as museum associations) try to build general rules concerning deaccessioning, but the debate's intensity would rapidly decrease if the 'things' to sell were not financially valuable. In the alternative case, if no monetary value were at stake, the debate on deaccessioning could concentrate on more practical matters, such as reasons and outcomes.

If those who support the principles of '*inaliénabilité*' refer to a number of broad principles related to the role of the state (and underline the consequences of deaccessioning, such as the ultimate loss of an object that can no longer be consulted or experienced), most of the arguments are, above all, practical. Recent British and Dutch publications insist on the principle (currently applied to private collections) according to which the optimization of collection management, under the pressure of limited material resources, rests necessarily on a partial curtailment (see, for instance, National Museum Directors Conference 2003; Bergevoet *et al.* 2006; Museums Association (UK) 2007; Timer and Kok 2007). According to this stance, it would be advisable to preserve only those objects directly related to a museum's mission or, more specifically, to its project (as defined by its mission statement and stated in the organization's operational plans) as well as the museum's collection policy. From this standpoint, it can be noted that the problem of deaccessioning is undeniably related to that of acquisitions and collection management (Neves 2005).

According to this same rationale, undoubtedly museum resources are not endless. If the notion of inalienability is strictly respected, how will the world of museums (institutions defined as permanent) be addressed five or ten centuries from now? Even more so when the material production of our societies is considered exponential, dragging along in its wake the development – also exponential – of all those objects that have lost their use- or exchange-value (management of remains) and acquired the status of *musealized* objects.

In this regard, the problem is embedded within a paradox already summarized in 1994 by Jean-Pierre Babelon and André Chastel when they referred to heritage in the following manner: '[I]ts loss is acknowledged to be a sacrifice but its preservation is also a sacrifice' (Babelon and Chastel 1994). What sacrifices are we willing to make? To preserve collections as best possible according to the principles of *inaliénabilité* guaranteed by the State ends up by turning society into one controlled by public powers, with an associated expectation of increasing the necessary resources to preserve such collections – and obviously, higher taxes. If a curator is willing to live on less income to ensure that heritage is maintained in perpetuity, we might wonder whether that feeling is shared by society at large.

Financial matters

Although practically speaking a great number of museum professionals (in the United States, Great Britain, the Netherlands, etc.) favour, on controlled terms, the possibility of *deaccessioning*, most of them voice their fears – as overviewed also by ICOM's Code, as stated above – with regard to the potential sale of collections for non-collection purposes, and particularly with respect to the risk of such sales being used to cover potential financial deficits (van Mensch 2008). Indeed for some years now the commitment of those who are in charge of management within museums and hold a Master's degree in Business Administration has tended to favour the possibility of considering collections as real, and financially quantifiable, 'assets' (Millar 1997; Lévy and Jouyet 2006).

Financial matters, so cautiously addressed by most museum professionals, have been joyfully dealt with by neo-classical economists. These economists never show doubt in reporting museums' bad management because, unlike businesses, they refrain from considering their collections as monetarized capital assets. When analysing the development of collections and the lack of inventories, the US economist William Grampp, in 1989, argued on the basis of examples that supported his theories the case for waiving any public subsidies to museums in favour of having them operate as commercial organizations. According to Grampp, should part of the dormant collections or those not on show be sold, museums would undoubtedly gain a more evidence-based idea about the objects that the public at large most wishes to see, and would organize more popular temporary exhibitions to benefit all. Grampp's controversial reasoning is rarely followed by his colleagues. However, this has not hindered most economists from pointing out the museum collections 'stock', of unlimited growth, as being aberrant in the eyes of the market and suggesting the sale of such stock, especially when it is not very well preserved, or the storage areas remain in poor condition (Richert 2003).

Only vis-à-vis the prospects of making a purchase will a stock or pension funds manager address a potential sale. In a market-driven context, managers who cannot decide to sell the assets in their portfolio in order to purchase others would go bankrupt in the long term.

From the same financial perspective, museum managers have recently been forced to address more explicitly the question of the economic valuation of the 'stock' they hold (the collection/s), either by evaluating their economic return and impact (Hendon 1979), or by building alternative ways of using these resources (Pettersson *et al.* 2010).

The question of collection value, in this context, is essentially financial. However, a related question arises: Isn't this attitude globally echoed by attitudes of the general public?

Historical, moral and ethical dimensions

The debate on deaccessioning appears to be problematic within the universe of museums. The pertinent sections quoted earlier from ICOM's Code of Ethics are good evidence of an element of doubt about different practices around collection disposal, as is also evident in the associated bibliography prepared by ICOM (see ICOM online). Does this mean it is 'wrong' to sell museum collections and that it is 'right' to preserve and care for them? Or that it is 'necessary' to be able to dispose of collections under certain conditions? If – in a caricature of the issue – a part of the debate is based on such a stance, we must agree that the matter cannot be set forth in those terms. On the other hand, severe pressure on resources (finances) becomes increasingly a disturbing factor both for the supporters and opponents of deaccessioning.

As already stated, it is worth pointing out that not all collection items appear to have the same status as regards 'deaccession' principles. Overall, it is essential to consider the *unique* works of art and other non-renewable objects that entail real problems of potentially irreparable loss for a museum if disposal occurs. Among the great variety of objects museums preserve, works of art are the main focus of discord. In other words, specimens of natural history, multiple objects, etc. – until they become unique objects of history, and perhaps simply by chance – seem to be easier to remove from collections. This issue inevitably refers to the debate on *the original* vs. *substitutes* (or, duplicate items) and we know to what extent it is conditioned by reverence for the original, or 'authentic', object (ICOFOM 1985). Such an issue led to worshipping relics, which extended throughout the Middle Ages. In that regard, it is worth pointing out that Canon Law banned their sale and marketing at a very early stage. In this context, we could make the hypothesis that the debate on deaccessioning resonates certain kinds of conflicts that violently engulfed Protestants and Catholics in the sixteenth century (with iconoclasm and the destruction of relics). Almost five centuries later, a sort of geographical demarcation line (one that recalls religious war contexts) seems still to act as a dividing line between supporters and detractors of the principle of *inaliénabilité*.

But we do not need to go back to the Reformation to realize that from a historical point of view, *inaliénabilité* and 'deaccession' museum rules might be considered as a relatively new topic. At the end of the eighteenth century, collections were much more subject to disposal, and if museums were always seen as safe repositories and places of preservation, inalienability was not a real topic. The professional debate about deaccessioning began to emerge during the 1930s, as museums were confronted by increasing storage problems (de Forrest 1930). After long discussions, a kind of consensus started to develop among the officials of the International Museums Office (the forerunner of ICOM), who presented in 1932 a resolution to the Assembly of the League of Nations recommending the integration of the principle of deaccessioning in national legislations (Office international des musées 1933; Société des Nations 1939). The recommendation was never really followed, and the consensus disappeared after the Second World War, in a context where so many museum collections and so much cultural heritage had been destroyed.

The problem of relics, collection, destruction and iconoclasm, as mentioned above, was related to religion and morality. Yet, in a not totally dissimilar way, ICOM's Code of Ethics aims at guiding the behaviour of professionals around issues of ethical worth or *belief values* about public good. However, museal deontology (practices framing museum ethics) must undeniably be reviewed on the basis of the larger and older philosophical discipline of Ethics. This philosophical discipline (such as in the *Ethics* of Spinoza) discusses the determination of those values that guide the behaviour of museum professionals. This prompts us to ask: Which are the current principles that have shaped the formulation of ICOM standards? Worship of relics? Research? Public orientation? Democracy? Or capitalism and the cult of money? In any case, it must be recognized that these principles are conditioned by the creation and development of the neoliberal world economy in which we live and that has spread worldwide. Maybe the notion of museums is not totally alien to the principles of accumulation that provide the dynamics of all capitalist societies.

A museological outlook

The decisively pragmatic outlook that Anglo-American museology favours does not greatly differ from the notions outlined in the 1960s and embedded in Eastern European museology. When the problem of *deaccessioning* is analysed with a view to improving the quality of collections, this line of thought comes closer to the concept of an active collections policy and to the principles of *musealization* as defined by Zbyněk Stránský or Klaus Schreiner (van Mensch 1992). Musealization, which focuses on the thoughtful selection of material evidence of reality, its preservation as authentic testimonies and the *modelling* of reality (or formation of a museum collection) does not go against the deaccessioning or disposal of some objects to favour others whose specific features (museality) are preferred as superior. This position is based on the principle of *musealization*, considered to be the carrying out of scientific conduct, through the reorganization of elements of the *real*, and which can be extended on this basis across the whole of the museum field.

The collection of ICOM-produced essays that support the definition of museums, published immediately after a symposium in Calgary of ICOM's Committee for Museology (ICOFOM) in 2005 (Mairesse and Desvallées 2007; Davis *et al.* 2010), shows how broad the museum field is today, and how diverse is the museum-institution in any analysis, as well as how relatively precarious are its associated rules. Therefore, as proposed by Bernard Deloche, museums could be apprehended 'as a specific function which might be in the form of an institution or not, whose purpose is to ensure by means of a sensitive experience, the archiving and transmission of culture understood as the set of acquisitions that turn a being which is genetically human into a man' (Mairesse and Desvallées 2007). Vis-à-vis such a prospect, although collection deaccessioning can be treated from an etymological, practical, economic or ethical standpoint, it first appears as ancillary, since it does not participate directly in the museum project, focused on the development of the human aspects of mankind (or humankind). From a museological perspective, a for-profit museum that would sell part of its collections might sometimes operate in a better way than an institutional museum based on heritage *inalienability* – where everything depends on the values these museums share and people consider to be the most important of their activities. The facts are that these values are not globally shared, and they are continuously evolving and diversifying as more varied types of institutions or organizations that can gain acceptance as 'museums' seem to proliferate throughout the world.

We know that the emphasis placed on the three major museum functions – Preservation, Research and Communication – have changed considerably throughout the years. Where museums were first considered as research and/or preservation centres during the nineteenth century, they are today more often seen as communication places (if not, tourist/economic development centres). From a preservation perspective, collections are central, and *inalienability* might appear as an obvious rule. From a research perspective (which was central to Eastern European museology, as well as to Georges Henri Rivière) information prevails, and the status of the object is conditioned by its museality or documentation value. Collection refinement and disposal are not a problem *per se*, provided the result would appear more scientifically coherent. In contrast, the communication viewpoint, and focus on public experience (with the collection's status at the periphery), entails a much more flexible relation to museum objects, their conservation and/or their disposal. In theory, Preservation, Research, and Communication are supposed to be equal functions; but we know this equivalence is never maintained in reality. Roughly speaking, the museum world moved, during the 1960s, from a preservation and research-focused *place* to a preservation and communications-driven *machine*, with some institutions dedicated almost solely to the communication momentum. This transformative process has drastically differentiating influences on the attitudes of each museum towards museum objects and deaccessioning.

From this perspective, is it possible (or even clever) to conceive single rules concerning inalienability or deaccessioning for the whole museums sector? Should all museums – large or small; collection- or public-driven – follow the same line?

Although museology can be defined as the ethics of the museum field (reflecting the values that condition responses to the problems set forth in this field), analysis of either inalienability or of deaccessioning will undoubtedly cut across the fields of museum practices themselves, restlessly redefining museums and the values evoked within their functioning. Certainly, the location of objects is crucial within the museum world – their presence allows sensory apprehension, the main form of operation of modern museums – yet their preservation *ad vitam* or their authenticity are variants only recently determined (in the nineteenth century). The current museums of simulacra, copies or substitutes (for instance, on the Internet) forcibly emerge from rules that singularly move away from what has been prescribed in the field of unique object preservation. Could management of the latter have an influence on the development of the institution as a whole?

At present it is necessary to recognize that the specific role of museums as concentrations of 'masterworks', despite its being discredited or relativized by generations of museologists (from Brown Goode to Stránský, through Rivière), nevertheless continues to be an established reference model within the museum world, following the example of the Louvre or the British Museum. Such a museum model, which was recently reorganizing its position around the concept of *universal museums* (ICOM 2004b), has so far succeeded in mainstreaming the notions of inalienability (or very restricted alienability) and non-restitution. Paradoxically, these superstar museums are also the ones where a strong economic rationale prevails, and we know that the latter is strongly opposed to inalienability (Frey 1998). How long will this paradox hold?

We may at least be sure about one prediction: the momentum of normative changes in collection management *within* and *of* museums is bound to continue.

Notes

1 A previous version of this article appeared in Mairesse 2010. See also Mairesse 2009; Cornu *et al.*, 2012.
2 The full text of the *ICOM Code of Ethics for Museums* is provided as *Appendix I* in the present publication. It is also available online for download from the ICOM website (with links to translations in French, Spanish, and many other languages). The English version is accessible at: http://icom.museum/professional-standards/code-of-ethics.
3 The French term '*accession*' has no legal validity; however, in English the notion is legally defined as an 'addition to property by natural growth or by artificial improvement'.

References

Babelon, J-P. and Chastel, A., 1994. 'La notion de patrimoine'. *La Revue de l'Art*, Vol. 49, 1980. Reprint: Paris: Liana Levi.

Barkan, E. and Bush, R. (eds), 2002. *Claiming the Bones, Naming the Stones: Cultural Property and the Negotiation of National and Ethnic Identity*. Los Angeles, CA: Getty Publications.

Bergevoet, F., Kok, A. and de Wit, M., 2006. *Netherlands Guidelines for Deaccessioning of Museum Objects*. Amsterdam: Instituut Collection Nederland, at: www.icn.nl (accessed 14 December 2015).

Clair, J., 2007. *Malaise dans les musées*. Paris: Flammarion.

Cornu, M., Fromageau, J., Poli, J.-F. and Taylor, A-C. (eds), 2012. *L'inaliénabilité des collections, performances et limites?* Paris: L'Harmattan.

Davies, P. (ed.), 2011. *Museums and the Disposals Debate: A Collection of Essays*. London: MuseumEtc.

Davis, A., Mairesse, F. and Desvallées, A. (eds), 2010. *What is a Museum?* Munich: Verlag D.C. Müller-Straten.

Deloche, B., 2011. 'Institution', in A. Desvallées and F. Mairesse (eds), *Dictionnaire encyclopédique de muséologie*. Paris: Armand Colin, pp. 201–14.

Fayet, R., 2010. 'Out of neverland: Towards a consequentialist ethics of alienation'. *ICOFOM Study Series* 39: 51–59.

Fforde, J.H. and Turnbull, P. (eds), 2004. *The Dead and their Possessions: Repatriation in Principle, Policy and Practice*. London: Routledge.

de Forrest, R., 1930. 'Que doivent faire les musées de l'excédent de leurs collections?' *Mouseion* 11: 137–41.

Frey, B., 1998. 'Superstar museums: An economic analysis'. *Journal of Cultural Economics* 22: 113–25.

Grampp, W.D., 1989. *Pricing the Priceless: Art, Artists and Economics*. New York: Basic Books Inc.

Hendon, W.S., 1979. *Analysing an Art Museum*. New York: Praeger.

ICOFOM, 1985. 'Originals and substitutes in museums'. *ICOFOM Study Series*, pp. 8–9.

ICOM, 2004a. *ICOM Code of Ethics for Museums* Paris: International Council of Museums, 2006, at: http://icom.museum/fileadmin/user_upload/pdf/Codes/code_ethics2013_eng.pdf.

ICOM, 2004b. 'Universal museums – special focus'. *ICOM News*. Paris: ICOM, January.

Lévy, M. and Jouyet, J.P., 2006. *L'économie de l'immatériel: la croissance de demain. Rapport de la commission sur l'économie de l'immatériel*. Paris: La documentation française.

Mairesse, F. (ed.), 2009. *L'inaliénabilité des collections de musée en question*. Morlanwelz: Royal Museum of Mariemont.

Mairesse, F., 2010. 'The issue of deaccession: five lines of thought for reflections'. *ICOFOM Study Series* 39, pp. 13–18.

Mairesse, F., 2014. *Le culte des musées*. Brussels: Académie royale de Belgique, Académie en poche.

Mairesse, F. and Desvallées A. (eds), 2007. *Vers une redéfinition du musée?* Paris: L'Harmattan.

van Mensch, P., 1992. *Towards a Methodology of Museology* [PhD Thesis]. University of Zagreb: Faculty of Philosophy.

van Mensch, P., 2008. 'Collectieontwikkeling of geld verdienen?' *Kunstlicht* 29 (1–2): 57–59.

Millar, S., 1997. 'Selling items from museum collections', in S. Weil (ed.), *A Deaccession Reader*. Washington, DC: American Association of Museums, pp. 51–61.

Morris, J., 2007. 'A seller's market'. *Museum Journal*. London: Museums Association, July, pp. 16–17.

Muñoz Sarmiento, S., 2015. *The De-accessioning Blog*, at: http://clancco-theartdeaccessioning blog.blogspot.com (accessed 14 December 2015).

Museums Association (UK), 2007. *Making Collections Effective*. London: Museums Association.

National Museum Directors Conference, 2003. *Too Much Stuff?* October 2003, at: www. nationalmuseums.org.uk/media/documents/publications/too_much_stuff.pdf.

Neves, C., 2005. *Concern at the Core: Managing Smithsonian Collections*. Washington, DC: Smithsonian Institution.

Office international des musées (International Museums Office), 1933. 'L'activité de l'Office international des musées', *Mouseion* 21–22: 272–73.

Pettersson, S. *et al.* (eds), 2010. *Encouraging Collections Mobility – A Way Forward for Museums in Europe*. Helsinki: Finnish National Gallery; Amsterdam: Erfgoed Nederland; and Berlin: Staatliche Museen, at: www.lending-for-europe.eu/fileadmin/CM/public/handbook/Encouraging_Collections_Mobility_A4.pdf.

Richert, P., 2003. *Rapport d'information fait au nom de la commission des affaires culturelles par la mission d'information chargée d'étudier la gestion des collections des musées, n°379, session extraordinaire de 2002–2003*. Paris: Sénat de France, at: www.senat.fr.

Rykner, D., 2008. *Le spleen d'Apollon. Musées, fric et mondialisation*. Paris: Nicolás Chaudun.

Société des Nations (League of Nations), 1939. 'Recommandation de l'Assemblée de la Société des Nations du 10 octobre 1932'. *Art et Archéologie, Recueil de législation comparée et de droit international* 1: 114–15.

Timer, P. and Kok, A., 2007. *Niets gaat verloren. Twintig jaar selectie en afstoting uit Nederlandse museale collecties*. Amsterdam: Boekman Stichting.

22

FROM APOLLO INTO THE ANTHROPOCENE

The odyssey of nature and science museums in an external responsibility context

Emlyn Koster

As news stories unfold and society seeks to understand the nature and significance of events, is the museum field going to adapt to a greater role in exploring the things that profoundly matter in the world?… Although the number of exhibitions on contemporary subjects is growing, museums would perform a more valuable public service – and uniquely so given their abundance, popularity, trustworthiness and specialized expertise – if they increased attention to the issues that confront their regions and the world, now and into the future.

(Koster, 2012a: 202)

[…] it is a matter of accountability whether […] institutions opt to be part of the solution or part of the problem […] Successfully heading in this direction depends on three facets of institutional culture being in place. The first concerns mission and vision – is there a clear and firm commitment to be of value to the societal and environmental problems we face? The second concerns leadership – is there a preparedness and competence to be an activist? The third concerns strategy – is there a relentless pursuit to be more externally useful and to nurture new perspectives in funding stakeholders?

(Koster and Shubel, 2007: 119)

Timeline

In 1948, astronomer Fred Hoyle anticipated that 'Once a photograph of the Earth, taken from the outside, is available, a new idea as powerful as any in history will be let loose'.[1] This grand moment came twenty-one years later with NASA's first mission to the Moon, almost a quarter of a million miles away. Apollo's arresting view of this blue-green world with its night-time sparkle of cities spawned a profound movement which had been heralded by the renowned advocacy of Rachel

Carson (Lear, 1998). In 1970–71, national and international non-profit organiza-tions such as Greenpeace, the Natural Resources Defence Council and Pollution Probe were formed; the US Government's Environmental Protection Agency began; and the world's first Earth Day took place.

In 2000, chemist Paul Crutzen and biologist Paul Stoermer proposed that accelerating human impacts on the Earth's natural systems justified a new epoch in the Geological Time Scale called the Anthropocene (Crutzen, 2002; Robin and Steffen, 2007; Zalasiewicz et al., 2010; Vince, 2011). Over the two centuries of the Time Scale's development, this was the first instance of an interval potentially being named to highlight a dominant species. Since the Industrial Revolution – the latest nanosecond in the Earth's 4.6 billion-year history – the atmosphere, hydrosphere, lithosphere, cryosphere and biosphere have each undergone major, interrelated changes. As context since Hoyle's prediction and the Apollo mission, human population has tripled from 2.5 billion in 1948, to 3.6 billion in 1969, to 5.0 billion in 1987 (World Commission on Environment and Development 1987), to 7.3 billion today.

Apollo's photographs of the Earth have become among the world's most evocative images (Riley, 2012; Dimick, 2015). As Hoyle predicted, they catapulted 'a new idea as powerful as any in history'. First, they led to an unrelenting environmental stew-ardship movement. Second, they influenced the designation of this latest moment in Earth history as the Anthropocene to highlight, and try to mitigate, the cumulative extent of interconnected human impacts on natural systems (Gail 2016).

With intensifying news coverage, these impacts include pollution, ozone holes, climate warming, glacier and tundra melting, coastal flooding, extreme weather, ocean acidification, ecosystem damage, reduced biodiversity, soil loss and diminished non-renewable resources. Humanity as the cause of an ongoing mass extinction is the subject of the Pulitzer Prize-winning book by Kolbert (2014) and a new museum plan in New York City, which intends '[...] to move climate awareness to the center of public life'.[2] Profiled by Lewis (2009), *The Economist* (2011) and *The New York Times* (2011), the Anthropocene has quickly become a focus across a wide array of environmental disciplines spanning the sciences, anthropology, history and humanities (Koster, 2011), plus it generates more than half a million sites in a Google search. Of the seventeen Sustainable Development Goals of the United Nations last updated in 2015, eight hinge on Anthropocene-related science.[3] These are clean water and sanitation; affordable and clean energy; industry, innovation and infrastructure; sustainable cities and communities; responsible consumption and production; climate action; life below water; and life on land.

White (1987) brought to public attention the one-planet perspective from spaceflight which he named 'the overview effect'. For example, Japan's first astro-naut, Mamoru Mohri, states that '[t]he Earth is as it is, the whole being greater than the sum of its parts, and everything is connected within that whole'.[4] Mindful of this framework, the mission of Japan's National Museum of Emerging Science and Innovation is to 'understand the things happening in our world today from a sci-entific point of view, and have discussions while considering the future that awaits us'.[5] Similarly, the mission of the post-expansion North Carolina Museum of Natural Sciences is 'to illuminate the interdependence of nature and humanity' with four driving questions: What do we know? How do we know? What is happening now? And how can the public participate?'[6]

Scope

In this chapter, the quest of the nature and science museum sector for external meaningfulness is instructively viewed through the lens of the momentous period that began with NASA's mission to the Moon and continues apace with the encompassing concept of the Anthropocene. In the chapter's title, 'odyssey' is chosen to convey the complexity of options in the journeys of these institutions. The title phrase 'nature and science museums' encompasses an interrelated wide sector of the total field, including institutions engaged in the collection, research and presentation of scientific evidence related to the Earth's physical and biological diversity and processes; science-informed interactions between societies and environments; technological innovations; and, increasingly, intersections of the sciences with the arts and humanities.

This chapter reviews the evolutionary trends of nature and science museums in relevance and leadership terms as a long-view framework for how they can best navigate toward becoming valuable resources in the Anthropocene. Such journeys are regarded as this sector's new imperative of external accountability. With phrases such as 'from nice to necessary' and 'safe places for difficult ideas' becoming common, thinking in Anthropocene terms intensifies the dialogue around external meaningfulness. Going forward, it is essential that the Anthropocene be viewed through the transdisciplinary lens of humans as an ecologically inseparable part of the Earth's natural framework; that is, not to regard humanity as distinct from nature which has, in many ways, caused the challenges faced by today's world.

Nature museums

The earliest expeditionary collections were amassed at the Royal Society in London and at the Académie des sciences in Paris. The first museums included the Muséum National d'Histoire Naturelle in Paris in 1635 and the Ashmolean Museum in Oxford in 1683. In the United States, the first ones included Peale's Museum in Philadelphia with branches in Baltimore and New York City but these were short-lived, the Academy of Natural Sciences in Philadelphia in 1812, the American Museum of Natural History in New York in 1869, the North Carolina Museum of Natural History in 1879, and the Carnegie Museum of Natural History in Pittsburgh in 1896. Initial priorities were collections and research with static displays in unconnected galleries – typically of invertebrate, fish, amphibian, reptile, mammal and bird specimens and of rock, mineral and crystal specimens.

In their treatise on the evolution of natural history and science museums during the nineteenth century, Rader and Cain provide this summary:

the term conjured up quiet study, spiritual contemplation and, most important of all, collections of rare and wondrous objects [...] A museum became a physical experiment [...] a space that ordered natural objects and fostered tentative mingling between the social classes who came to view them [...] And as loose coalitions of wealthy amateur naturalists, boosters, professional scientists, and politicians joined forces to establish new museums of natural history [...] the word 'museum' came to imply a diligent middle-class respectability and civic ambition.

(Rader and Cain, 2015: 1–2)

'In a very real way and important way, museums stood on the frontier of knowledge through the century ... and contributed significantly to the creation of what we now recognize as the modern biological sciences' (Conn, 1998: 33–34). The Smithsonian's National Museum of Natural History opened in 1910, and by the mid-twentieth century most capital cities had added a natural history museum to their cultural landscape.[7] Recalling the American Museum of Natural History though the 1940s–1950s, and perhaps reflecting a rising conscience at large, its former Director opined:

[I]t seems evident that the natural history museum has reached a stage in the evolution of its relationship to society where the generally prevailing opportunistic vagueness of intentions is becoming a liability which must be replaced by a well-considered, well-integrated, and well-defined philosophy concerning the museum's place in the general research and educational system of the nation.

(Parr, 1959: 21)

Starting in the 1970s, renewal projects at natural history museums responded to new knowledge about plate tectonics and the ever-changing configuration of continents and oceans with more comprehensive storylines. Then, driven by mounting concerns over the Earth's interdependent and increasingly fragile ecosystems, Sullivan (1992) urged a new and bold approach in natural history museums. He advocated for a holistic framework of global issues with a desirable shift in the mindset of visitors from passive curiosity to active engagement. The growing educational priority of natural history museums was also noted by Han (1993).

Although collections remain the foundation of major natural history museums (Johnson, 2015), and in some quarters there are concerns about insufficient attention to collections (e.g. Kemp, 2015), these four recent international gatherings point to a broadening mindset:

- October 2007, Paris: Representatives from natural history museums and research institutes issued The Buffon Declaration:[8]

  Given that science is critical for sustainable management of biodiversity and ecosystems and, through it, survival of human populations on this planet, the vital contributions of these institutions are fourfold: a) They are the primary repositories of the scientific samples on which understanding of the variety of life is ultimately based; b) Through leading-edge research they extend knowledge of the structure and dynamics of biodiversity in the present and in the past; c) Through partnerships, and through programs of training and capacity-building, they strengthen the global capability to address current and future environmental challenge; and d) They are a forum for direct engagement with civil society, which is indispensable for helping bring about the changes of behaviour on which our common future and the future of nature depend.

- February 2012, Washington, DC: Learning-focused representatives from mainly US natural history organizations issued the following declaration:

> Humanity is embedded within nature and we are at a critical moment in the continuity of time; Our collections are the direct scientific evidence for evolution and the ecological interdependence of all living things; The human species is actively altering the Earth's natural processes and reducing its biodiversity. As the sentient cause of these impacts, we have the urgent responsibility to give voice to the Earth's immense story and to secure its sustainable future.
>
> *(Watson and Werb, 2013: 260)*

- October 2013, New York City: A colloquium titled 'Collecting the Future: Museums, Communities and Climate Change' attracted curators, educators, historians, anthropologists and others to the American Museum of Natural History 'to address and integrate the physical, social, cultural and emotional dimensions of climate change'.[9]

- December 2015, Munich: Representatives from natural history and related institutions attended a workshop titled 'Museums in the Anthropocene', organised by the Rachel Carson Center for Environment and Society, a joint initiative of the Deutsches Museum and Ludwig-Maximilians-Universität.[10] Stimulated by a pioneering exhibition to profile the Anthropocene (Möllers *et al.*, 2015), this dialogue focused on how museums can best reflect research and provide learning experiences around this major new context.

Another trend over recent decades concerning natural history museums, at least in North America, concerns the names of museums. As these institutions often ended their storylines before the anatomical and behavioural developments of humans and the rise of environmental concerns, institutional name changes to either 'nature' or the 'natural sciences' in several cities – including Ottawa in Canada, Denver and Raleigh in the USA – have enabled contemporary topics to become more readily included. However, others, old and new, such as the Museo de Ciencias Naturales in Madrid, Royal Belgian Institute of Natural Sciences in Brussels and National

Museum of Natural Science in Taichung, Taiwan – which opened in 1752, 1846 and 1986, respectively – began with broader names.

Science museums

The earliest science and technology museums were the Musée des Arts et Métiers in Paris in 1794 and the Franklin Institute in Philadelphia in 1824, each focused on scientific instruments and technological inventions. The Industrial Revolution, international expositions, national milestones and leading industrialists were influences on the development of major institutions. London's Science Museum originated with the 1851 Great Exhibition; Japan's National Science Museum opened in 1877, the Deutsches Museum in 1903, the Norwegian Museum of Science and Technology in 1932, the Henry Ford Museum near Detroit in 1929, the Museum of Science and Industry in Chicago in 1933, and the Palais de la découverte in Paris in 1937.

The 1960s saw a proliferation of science-focused museums, although not with the traditionally defining characteristic of a collection of artefacts. The Pacific Science Center in Seattle emerged from the US pavilion at the 1962 World Expo; the New York Hall of Science emerged from the New York World's Fair in 1964, and in 1968 the Lawrence Hall of Science opened at the Berkeley campus of the University of California in honour of a Nobel laureate. In 1969, coincidentally the same year as Apollo to the Moon, the Exploratorium in San Francisco and the Ontario Science Centre in Toronto both opened, becoming influential institutions. In Paris, the Cité des Sciences et de l'Industrie, which opened in 1986, and since 2010 conjoined with the Palais de la découverte to form Universcience, also became a landmark in the global science museum field.[11]

Across the USA, 'science centres' with their hallmark experience of hands-on exhibits and live demonstrations (Danilov, 1982) became influential innovators in the evolution of museums (Koster 1999) as well as frequent players in urban renewal visions. The Washington, DC-based Association of Science-Technology Centers was formed in 1973,[12] quickly becoming an international organization; Europe's similarly minded Ecsite organization began in 1989.[13] Today, these and other regional science centre networks virtually cover the world. Between 1996 and 2011, triennial science centre world summits were held in Helsinki, Calcutta, Canberra, Rio de Janeiro, Toronto and Cape Town. Having completed a worldwide circuit, a more transdisciplinary summit took place in Mechelen, near Brussels, in 2014, and the next one will occur with a sustainability theme in 2017 in Tokyo.

Building on declarations at the Toronto and Cape Town congresses and as a guide to science centre priorities, the Mechelen summit issued a declaration focused on community engagement, sustainable development, brand-building, new technologies, learning methods, citizen science and global cooperation. Science centres have, however, yet to be extensively drawn to all such aspirations. For small institutions and in regions where science centres are a new type of community resource, the purpose is commonly limited to participatory experiences about a selection of physical forces as well as some new technologies. Even in larger institutions, topics such as climate change and energy options have generally been avoided because of concerns that they may be viewed as controversial. At the same time, though, sensational exhibition topics such as plastinated human bodies have become common because of their box-office allure (Fras, 2006). For museums with giant screen theatres, there continues to be the added challenges of a diminishing choice of mission-related films and a temptation to offer adult-rated evening shows.

In recent years and especially in North America, the STEM disciplines (science, technology, engineering and mathematics) and do-it-yourself fairs have surged in popularity, creating an impression in some stakeholder circles that science museums, and science centres in particular, have reached a higher level of community relevance. An irony, though, is that commercial and other kinds of non-profit venues are also offering STEM and so-called 'maker faire' experiences.[14] Over the longer term, the evolving purpose and context of science museums and science centres have been reviewed by Friedman (1996), Kadlec (2009) and Koster (2010).

Relevance

As the following series of excerpts reminds us, to strive to be externally meaningful in the museum field is not a new calling:

- 'A good museum will always direct attention to what is difficult and even painful to contemplate' (Postman, 1989: 40).
- 'How can museums – as multidimensional, socially responsible institutions with a tremendous capacity for bringing knowledge to the public and enriching all facets of the human experience – help to nurture a humane citizenry equipped to make informed choices in a democracy and to address the challenges and opportunities of an increasingly global society?' (American Association of Museums, 1992: 9).
- [The] 'introverted focus has engendered the belief that artifactual collections are the "reason for being" for museums, rather than a tool through which we gain and disseminate knowledge' (Duckworth, 1993: 15).
- '[…] the mission statement of most museums, which often states, "Our mission is to collect, preserve and interpret fill-in-the-blank" will no longer do. Such statements do not answer the vital question of, "So what?"' (Skramstad, 1996: 38).
- 'The challenge facing the museum field […] is to create compelling experiences on subjects of importance in ways that increasingly attract society to view museums as engaging resources for lifelong learning' (Koster, 1999: 294).
- '[The] awkward matter remains that, for a variety of reasons, the museum field has never agreed – and until recently, has scarcely even sought to agree – on some standard by which the relative worthiness of its constituent member institutions might be measured' (Weil, 2006: 4).

- '[The] majority of museums, as social institutions, have largely eschewed on both moral and practical grounds, a broader commitment to the world in which they operate' (Janes, 2009: 13).

A quarter of a century ago, the global museum community convened around the aspiration that our institutions become 'generators of culture' (International Council of Museums, 1989). For this state of affairs to prevail in the new world of the Anthropocene depends on the museum field being both adequately informed about what this encompassing term entails and committed to creative, forward-looking approaches. A prerequisite is the museum's holistic orientation to public value (Korn, 2013).

Leadership and strategy

The enduring high purpose of organizational leadership has also long been stated, but easily sidetracked when faced with short-term exigencies. In an instructive recall of lessons following the Great Depression, Schwarzer quoted Harold Madison from 1933 as Director of the Cleveland Museum of Natural History:

> When the funds began to flow again, museums quickly forgot the shock of the Depression as well as their moments of innovation on behalf of the public. They slipped back into the old patterns of massive acquisition and building, sloppy financial management and marginalizing the role of educators. An opportunity to be societal role models for the wisest possible use of resources and talent was lost.
>
> *(Schwarzer, 2009: 54)*

Barker (2002) recalled Aristotle's philosophy that leadership is ideally about the harmonious pursuit of positive consequences in the world. Peniston (1999: 16) reminded us of the prescient 1909 view of John Cotton Dana that institutions should: 'Learn what aid the community needs [and] fit the museum to those needs'. Weil (2002: 192) pondered: 'If Dana's writings had become more widely available after his death, might the history of this country's museums have been different?' Dana's choice of 'needs' over 'wants', that is, of necessities over desires, is instructive because the positioning and marketing of today's museums must grapple with rapidly changing, market-driven tastes (Gelt, 2015) and with civilization 'revving itself into a pathologically short attention span'.[15]

Nanus (1992) presented a four-quadrant model for optimal institutional leadership: internal/external and present/future axes delineate the roles of coach (internal/present), spokesperson (external/present), change-agent (internal/future); and direction-setter (external/future). He emphasized that while leaders are seldom equally strong in all quadrants, allowing an imbalance to persist puts the health of the organization at risk. It follows that museum leaders, for example, who believe that their overriding task is to raise funds but whose post-campaign institutions have not become more useful to the needs of the Anthropocene might well reflect on the balance of their priorities. Directors who have candidly shared the complexity of their journeys through challenges and opportunities include Parr (1959), Weil (2002), Gurian (2006), Koster (2013), Lowman (2013) and Janes (2015). As much as 'leadership' connotes the ultimately accountable helm of the institution, more than ever this role needs to be the able facilitator of a whole-organization team effort.

There are further complications for the strategy of museums including that, in most government and boardroom circles, attendance remains the predominant, but sometimes misleading, performance measure (Koster, 2012b). To continuously augment both relevance and sustainability, two complementary institutional strategies are proposed: usefulness plus popularity equals relevance; and relevance plus renewal equals sustainability. Because each museum exists in unique circumstances, so will its pathway with this enduring approach be unique, in particular the blend of strategies that blend usefulness and popularity and that optimize the gains of renewal opportunities.

Also, progress with societal and environmental matters is inevitably punctuated by challenging and controversial moments. Public opinion around hot topics (Cameron and Kelly, 2010) can be visualized as a bell curve along the complete timeline of the controversy, which, as debate intensifies and then as acceptance grows, morphs from left-skewed to right-skewed (Koster, 2010). An instructive example of the time it takes for polarized attitudes among primary stakeholders to subside was the saga over the relative contributions of, and interactions between, Indigenous and colonial peoples in galleries at the new National Museum of Australia (Casey, 2001). Davis *et al.* (2004) discussed the challenges for museums in responding to new developments in a content area and which may make news headlines.

> Every step taken that is neutral or contrary to the greater good makes it that much more difficult for the museum to start or regain a strengthening reputation of relevance […] At what point – before, during, after, or never – does the museum responsibly become a stage for public engagement around a challenging or controversial issue? […] Should a museum that has yet to embark on a wholehearted journey of relevance plunge abruptly into the realm of controversial subject matter, it will surely do so at its public relations peril. On the other hand, for a museum that has been proactively on a journey of increasingly relating to the important matters at hand, the majority of the audience will seldom be surprised over the latest step in its zeal to address topics of a challenging or controversial nature. Indeed a consistent profile of this nature will not only incrementally affirm the museum's chosen direction but also attract funders who increasingly seek outcomes that profoundly matter.
>
> (Koster, 2010: 82, 86 and 90)

Although the Anthropocene emphasizes environmental responsibility and encourages future thinking, nature and science museums are at their most powerful when they also integrate social responsibility and unravel past-present-future trends. Indicators of institutional relevancy and several content suggestions, such as human impacts on ecosystems, and for science museums, such as the spread and impacts of the Industrial Revolution, were provided by Koster (2012a).

Through collections and research curators, museums traditionally arrived at authoritative answers to historical questions disseminated via exhibitions as the primary, if not only, type of visitor experience. Often surrounded by multidisciplinary teams drawn from collaborating institutions, today's museums are responding to broader questions in more varied ways and with audience insights about their most effective approaches. Koster and Falk (2007) delved into the marketing value of targeted connections between different experiences for different communities. Today's much expanded toolkit includes an onsite, offsite, outdoors and online menu open laboratories, films with discussions, town halls with experts and questions, science cafés, workshops and conferences, and guided field excursions. The choice of travelling exhibitions is an especially conspicuous expression of institutional intent because their short duration presents change exponentially faster than does gallery renewal. Above all, nature and science museums need new and uplifting ways to engage their communities in topics that illuminate the Anthropocene from its multiple angles. The rising popularity of citizen science – lifelong public participation in scientific research – offers a promising pathway.

In the twenty-first century, museums are also being encouraged to increase their value as civic and regional resources (Janes and Conaty, 2005; Gijssen, 2010; Scott, 2013; Koster and Pendergraft, 2015), blur their boundaries (Janes, 2015a) and infuse empathy into their core values (Gokcigdem in press). A related obligation, one of both pragmatism and conscience, is preparedness for emergency situations. While museums may be temporarily directed to close or be disabled after a disaster strikes, the immediate and long-term responses to the terrorist attacks on New York City on September 11, 2001 provided examples of positive action (e.g. Gaffney *et al.*, 2002; Gaffney and Koster in press).

Epilogue

In hindsight, the first mission of Apollo and introduction of the Anthropocene should have bracketed a period of profound introspection, reflection and inspiration across the nature and science museums sector. This was a powerful opportunity to manifest the founding *raison d'être* of 'the museum' from The Muses in Greek mythology. Arguably, this period should have galvanized nature and science museums to broaden their thinking with research insights from other fields, such as social biology and psychology which have shown that our attachment to nature (Wilson, 1986) and 'inner scientist' (Gopnik *et al.*, 1999) are instinctive.

As a branch of philosophy, ethics is about the pursuit of 'right conduct' which, despite its fundamental aura, is often regarded as an elusive concept. However, for nature and science museums, the odyssey of their evolution since Apollo's transformative photographs of Planet Earth to today's serious calling to be resources for societal and environmental needs in the Anthropocene has become a journey in which the 'right conduct' has arguably become unequivocally clear (American Association of Museums, 2011; Purdy, 2015). As a matter of external accountability, it is urgent that the talk of societal needs, institutional directions and conference declarations be matched by the holistic actions and impacts of major nature and science museums. No other sector of resources focused on the enhancement of lifelong learning about the world – past, present, future – has comprehensive expertise comparable to a progressive major museum.

Acknowledgements

I especially wish to thank public and private sector supporters, board and commission members, staff and volunteers at the North Carolina Museum of Natural Sciences for enabling its remarkable journey. Colleagues elsewhere with whom I have discussed the evolving nature and science museum field, as well as the Anthropocene, include Michael Bruton, Harold Closter, Joanne DiCosimo, Graham Durant, John Falk, Greg Fishel, Sarah George, Philip Gibbard, Elaine Gurian, Erik Jacquemyn, Randi Korn, Claudette Leclerc, Wendy Luke, Hooley McLaughlin, Mamoru Mohri, Libby Robin, Lisa Samford, Silvia Singer, Walter Staveloz, Soames Summerhays and Kirsten Wehner. Inputs to drafts of this chapter were valuably provided by Katey Ahmann, David Beaver, Roy Campbell, Jason Cryan, Donna Gaffney, Robert Janes and LuAnne Pendergraft.

Notes

1 www.spacequotations.com/earth.html.
2 www.climatemuseum.org.
3 www.un.org/sustainabledevelopment/sustainable-development-goals.
4 www.nttdata.com/global/en/insights/topics/interview/2014103101.html.
5 www.miraikan.jst.go.jp/en/aboutus.
6 http://naturalsciences.org/about/welcome.
7 https://en.wikipedia.org/wiki/List_of_natural_history_museums.
8 www.bfn.de/fileadmin/ABS/documents/BuffonDeclarationFinal%5B1%5D.pdf.
9 www.amnh.org/our-research/anthropology/news-events/collecting-the-future.
10 www.carsoncenter.uni-muenchen.de/events_conf_seminars/calendar/ws_anthropocene-in-museums/index.html.
11 https://en.wikipedia.org/wiki/List_of_science_museums.
12 www.astc.org.
13 www.ecsite.eu.
14 bn.com/makerfaire.
15 http://longnow.org.

References

American Association of Museums, 1992. *Excellence and Equity: Education and the Public Dimension of Museums.* Washington, DC: American Association of Museums.
American Association of Museums, 2011. 'The future is in the stars: An interview with Neil DeGrasse Tyson'. *Museum* (March–April): 47–51.

Aufure, M., 2015. 'Where are we going?: Considering environmental issues in developing the new Musée de l'Homme'. *ICOM News*, 3–4: 9.

Barker, R., 2002. *On the Nature of Leadership*. Lanham, MD: University Press of America.

Cameron, F. and Kelly, L., 2010. *Hot Topics, Public Culture, Museums*. Newcastle-upon-Tyne: Cambridge Scholars Publishing.

Casey, D., 2001. 'Museums as agents of social and political change'. *Curator*, 44: 230–34.

Conn, S., 1998. *Museums and American Intellectual Life, 1876–1926*. Chicago, IL: University of Chicago Press.

Crutzen, P., 2002. 'Geology of mankind'. *Nature*, 415: 23.

Danilov, V., 1982. *Science and Technology Centers*. Cambridge, MA: MIT Press.

Davis, J., Gurian, E. and Koster, E., 2004. 'Timeliness: A discussion for museums'. *Curator*, 46: 353–61.

Dimick, D., 2015. 'Hanging in the balance'. *National Geographic*, Washington, DC: National Geographic Society, p. 160.

Duckworth, D., 1993. 'Museum-based science for a new century', in *Research within the Museum: Aspirations and Realities*. Taichung, Taiwan: National Museum of Natural Sciences, pp. 13–19.

Economist (The), 2011. 'The Anthropocene, a man-made world: Science is recognising humans as a geological force to be reckoned with'. *The Economist*, 26 May 2011.

Fras, B., 2006. 'Body Worlds 2: The anatomical exhibition of real human bodies'. *Curator*, 49: 477–82.

Friedman, A., 1996. 'The evolution of the science museum'. *Physics Today* (October): 45–51.

Gaffney, D., Dunne-Maxim, K. and Cernak, M., 2002. 'Science centers as sanctuaries'. *Journal of Museum Education* (Winter): 22–27.

Gaffney, D. and Koster, E. [in press]. 'Learning from the challenges of our time: Families of September 11 and Liberty Science Center', in E.M. Gokcigdem, (ed.), *Fostering Empathy Through Museums*. Washington, DC: Rowman & Littlefield.

Gail, W., 2016. 'A new dark age looms'. *The New York Times*, 19 April 2016.

Gelt, J., 2015. 'How museums are adapting to "selfie culture"'. *Los Angeles Times*, 23 October 2015.

Gijssen, J., 2010. 'Museums in 2020: Change and connectivity'. *Muse* (November–December): 44–46.

Gokcigdem, E.M., [in press]. *Fostering Empathy Through Museums*. Washington, DC: Rowman & Littlefield.

Gopnik, A., Meltzoff, A. and Kuhl, P., 1999. *The Scientist in the Crib: What Early Learning Tells Us About the Mind*. New York: Harper Collins.

Gurian, E., 2006. *Civilizing the Museum: The Collected Writings of Elaine Heumann Gurian*. New York: Routledge.

Han, P-T., 1993. 'Foreword', in *Research within the Museum: Aspirations and Realities*. Taichung, Taiwan: National Museum of Natural Science, pp. iv–xi.

Helt, S., 2015. 'From core to cosmos: Elemental encounters at the Musée des Confluences'. *ICOM News* (September), 68 (2): 10–11.

International Council of Museums, 1989. *Museums: Generators of Culture*. Paris: International Council of Museums.

Janes, R., 2009. *Museums in a Troubled World: Renewal, Irrelevance or Collapse?* New York: Routledge.

Janes, R., 2015a. 'The end of neutrality: A modest manifesto'. *The Informal Learning Review*. 135: 3–8.

Janes, R., 2015b. *Museums without Borders*. New York: Routledge.

Janes, R. and Conaty, G., 2005. *Looking Reality in the Eye: Museums and Social Responsibility*, Calgary, AB: University of Calgary Press.

Johnson, S., 2015. 'Preserving specimen collections the goal for museum group formed at Field'. *Chicago Tribune*, 3 April 2015.

Kadlec, A., 2009. 'Mind the gap: science centers as sources of civic innovation'. *Museums and Social Issues*, 4: 37–54.

Kemp, C., 2015. 'The endangered dead'. *Nature*, 518: 292–94.

Kolbert, E., 2014. *The Sixth Extinction: An Unnatural History*. New York: Henry Holt and Company.

Korn, R., 2013. 'Creating public value through intentional practice', in C. Scott, (ed.), *Museums and Public Value: Creating Sustainable Futures*. Burlington, VT: Ashgate.

Koster, E., 1999. 'In search of relevance: science centers as innovators in the evolution of museums'. *Daedalus*, 128: 277–96.

Koster, E., 2010. 'The evolution of purpose in science museums and science centres', in F. Cameron and L. Kelly, (eds), *Hot Topics, Public Culture, Museums*. Newcastle-upon-Tyne: Cambridge Scholars Publishing.

Koster, E., 2011. 'The Anthropocene: An unprecedented opportunity to advance the unique relevance of geology to societal and environmental needs'. *Geoscientist, Geological Society of London*, 21 (9): 18–21.

Koster, E., 2012a. 'The relevant museum: A reflection of sustainability', in G. Anderson (ed.), *Reinventing the Museum: The Evolving Conversation on the Paradigm Shift*. Lanham, MD: Altamira Press, pp. 202–11.

Koster, E., 2012b. 'Broadening the reflections on science center attendance'. *The Informal Learning Review*, 113: 26–28.

Koster, E., 2013. 'New needs for new times', in R. Janes, (ed.), *Museums and the Paradox of Change*. Oxford: Routledge.

Koster, E. and Falk, J., 2007. 'Maximizing the usefulness of museums'. *Curator*, 50: 191–96.

Koster, E. and Pendergraft, L., 2015. 'Bringing the mission to the community: State museum opens a satellite in an underserved rural region'. *The Informal Learning Review*, 131: 11–15.

Koster, E. and Shubel, J., 2007. 'Raising the relevancy bar in aquariums and science centers', in J. Falk, L. Dierking and S. Foutz, (eds), *In Principle, in Practice*. Lanham, MD: AltaMira Press.

Lear, L., 1998. *Lost Woods: The Discovered Writings of Rachel Carson*. Boston, MA: Beacon Press.

Lewis, S., 2009. 'A force of nature: Our influential Anthropocene'. *The Guardian*, 23 July 2009.

Lowman, J., 2013. *Museums at the Crossroads: Essays on Cultural Institutions in a Time of Change*. Victoria, BC: Royal British Columbia Museum.

Möllers, N., Schwägerl, C. and Trischler, H., 2015. *Welcome to the Anthropocene: The Earth in our Hands*. Munich: Deutsches Museum and Rachel Carson Center.

Nanus, B., 1992. *Visionary Leadership: Creating a Compelling Sense of Direction for Your Organization*. San Francisco, CA: Jossey-Bass.

New York Times (The), 2011. 'The Anthropocene'. *The New York Times*, 27 February 2011.

Parr, A., 1959. *Mostly About Museums*. New York: American Museum of Natural History.

Peniston, W., 1999. *The New Museum: Selected Writings of John Cotton Dana*. Washington, DC: The Newark Museum Association and American Association of Museums.

Postman, N., 1989. 'Extension of the museum concept', in Anton Korteweg, (ed.), *Museums: Generators of Culture*. Paris: International Council of Museums, pp. 40–48.

Purdy, J., 2015. *After Nature: A politics for the Anthropocene*. Cambridge, MA: Cambridge University Press.

Rader, K. and Cain, V., 2015. *Life on Display: Revolutionizing U.S. Museums of science and Natural History in the Twentieth Century*. Chicago, IL: University of Chicago Press.

Riley, C., 2012. 'Apollo 40 years on: How the moon missions changed the world for ever'. *The Guardian*, 15 December 2012.

Robin, L. and Steffen, W., 2007. 'History for the Anthropocene'. *History Compass*, 5: 1694–1719.

Schwarzer, M., 2009. 'Bringing it to the people: Lessons from the first Great Depression'. *Museum* (May–June): 49–54.

Scott, C., 2013. *Museums and Public Value: Creating Sustainable Futures*. Burlington, VT: Ashgate.

Skramstad, H., 1996. 'Changing public expectations of museums', in *Museums in the New Millennium: A Symposium for the Museum Community*. Washington, DC: Center for Museum Studies, Smithsonian Institution and American Association of Museums.

Sullivan, R., 1992. 'Trouble in paradigms'. *Museum News* (January–February 1992): 41–44.

Van-Praët, M., 2015. 'Museums sounding the alarm: Challenges to museums of natural and human sciences in the face of the global environmental crisis'. *ICOM News*, 3–4: 8–9.

Vince, G., 2011. 'Geologists press for recognition of Earth-changing "human epoch"'. *The Guardian*, 3 June 2011.

Watson, B. and Werb, E., 2013. 'One hundred strong: A colloquium on transforming natural history museums in the twenty-first century'. *Curator*, 56: 255–65.

Watts, J., 2015. 'Museum of Tomorrow: A captivating invitation to imagine a sustainable world'. *The Guardian*, 17 December 2015.

Weil, S., 2002. *Making Museums Matter*. Washington, DC: Smithsonian Institution.

Weil, S., 2006. *Beyond Management: Making Museums Matter. Study Series 12, International Committee on Management*. Paris: ICOM, pp. 4–8.

White, F., 1987. *The Overview Effect: Space Exploration and Human Evolution*. Boston, MA: Houghton-Mifflin.

Wilson, E.O., 1986. *Biophilia*. Cambridge, MA: Harvard University Press.

World Commission on Environment and Development, 1987. *Our Common Future*. Oxford: Oxford University Press.

Zalasiewicz, J., Williams, M., Steffen, W. and Crutzen, P., 2010. 'The new world of the Anthropocene'. *Environmental Science and Technology*, 44: 2228–31.

23

ETHICS IN A CHANGING SOCIAL LANDSCAPE

Community engagement and public participation in museums

Sally Yerkovich

Since the late-twentieth century, museums have become increasingly concerned with broadening their audiences and more actively engaging their visitors. Efforts to do this have varied widely, with some museums simply offering entertainment (e.g. concerts, dance parties) to attract more diverse participants, and others creating mission-related exhibitions and activities that seek to appeal to people who may not normally think of museums as places to visit. In part, these efforts stem from a growing need for museums to establish that they serve a public benefit, to provide demonstrable and measurable results of how their work supports the values of society. These activities also result from an understanding among museum professionals that museums are critical to a civil society, and that they can and should be socially responsible and promote principles of equity and excellence. This essay will discuss the principles of diversity and access that underlie museums' efforts to reach out to broad audiences, review approaches to engaging audiences, briefly explore the ethical ramifications of these efforts, and examine the impact of the digital environment on community-focused engagement.

Much of the discussion about museum audiences focuses upon issues related to diversity and access. In this context *diversity* refers to the ethnic, cultural and social make-up of a museum's board, staff, volunteers and visitors. The term can also be used to raise issues related to the communities from which a museum's collections emanate as well as the subject matter of exhibitions and programmes. *Access* conventionally means the availability of a museum's resources (collections and facilities as well as its staff) for public use, reference and research. Recently, however, *access* has taken on broader connotations and it is widely understood to encompass the provision of equitable access to a museum, creating a more welcoming public space for a diversity of visitors, especially those less familiar with the institution. *Access* can refer to a museum's approachability – how easy it is for the public to enter the institution and navigate its spaces. Are the staff or volunteers that greet the public welcoming or off-putting? Are the hours of operation convenient for families, people who work during the week, people of all faiths? Does the museum provide means for people with physical and cognitive challenges to have access to its exhibitions and programmes? *Access* can also refer to affordability, especially as some museums institute entrance fees and others raise the fees they charge in an environment of increasing income disparities. And finally, *access* can encompass the ways in which a museum makes the information it presents approachable and more socially inclusive. As Mark O'Neill notes: 'Social inclusion is not about simplifying difficult things. It is about providing points of entry for people whose education or background has not equipped them to approach difficult works that they might in fact be interested in' (O'Neill 2005: 123).

Questions of diversity, access and community engagement have ethical ramifications. Six of the eight principles of the International Council of Museums' *Code of Ethics for Museums* mention access, and the remaining two address it indirectly. According to the ICOM Code,[1] the primary responsibility for a museum's accessibility rests with its governing body: 'The governing body should ensure that the museum and its collections are available to all during reasonable hours and for regular periods. Particular regard should be given to those persons with special needs' (ICOM 2004: Art. 1, Para. 4). In addition the ICOM Code of Ethics states that:

- Museums that maintain collections hold them in trust for the benefit of society and its development.
- Museums have particular responsibilities to all for the care, accessibility and interpretation of primary evidence collected and held in their collections.
- Museums have an important duty to develop their educational role and attract wider audiences from the community, locality, or group they serve. Interaction with the constituent community and promotion of their heritage is an integral part of the educational role of the museum.
- Museums utilise a wide variety of specialisms, skills and physical resources that have a far broader application than in the museum. This may lead to shared resources or the provision of services as an extension of the museum's activities. These should be organised in such a way that they do not compromise the museum's stated mission.
- Museums work in close collaboration with the communities from which their collections originate as well as those they serve.

Diversifying a museum's audience and providing access to its many resources can lead a museum to directly engage the communities it serves, including involving them in the development of exhibitions and programmes. Some early efforts to connect with community members focused upon creating community galleries, places within a museum in which local groups might mount their own exhibitions. A museum would help with the installation of the exhibition but the local group would determine what would be on display and how it would be presented. While these galleries can be effective, they tend to bring members of a particular ethnic or social community to the museum only when their own exhibition is on display, and they do little to involve community members in museum activities more generally, or to engage them to become regular visitors.

Some museums work with community members as consultants in creating exhibitions in their community access galleries. The exhibition's curator retains control over the content of the show while serving as mediator among the community voices that provide input. As Andrea Witcomb's discussion of an exhibition at the Fremantle History Museum's community access gallery about the local Portuguese community demonstrates, the show, *Travellers and Immigrants*, was not 'simply about facilitating access to representation' (Witcomb 2007: 137). Each participant in this Western Australian museum exhibition – the museum, the university for which Witcomb worked, the various members of the Portuguese community, the visitors and the show's sponsors – had a different interest in the display. In mounting the show, the museum sought to 'be seen as relevant and accessible to diverse cultural communities as well as to educate the public about cultural diversity' (Witcomb 2007: 137).

By acting as consultants to the exhibition, community members were able to tell their stories and display their objects in the museum, benefiting from the skills of a curator experienced in creating effective presentations. The university wanted to showcase the research skills of its staff, and visitors were provided with an opportunity to 'learn about the Portuguese in Western Australia and thereby understand an act of ethical self-improvement called for by the project *of* civic reform' (Witcomb 2007: 137). Working through the Portuguese Community Council, Witcomb gained access to community members and discovered that, instead of a unified ethnic community, the Portuguese in Fremantle consisted of a number of different interest groups, each with their own perspective on being Portuguese in Western Australia. Because of the complexity of the interests involved in the show and of the negotiations necessary to bring it to fruition, Witcomb noted that her curation became 'an exercise in producing a notion of community with which everyone could be satisfied', and led her to understand the role of the museum curator as *translator* among different groups, and the curatorial process as the 'result of a set of exchanges between *different* communities' (Witcomb 2007: 154).

While *Travellers and Immigrants* was a one-time, government-sponsored effort on the part of the Fremantle History Museum, an exhibition in Canada, *Souvenirs of Here: the Photograph Album as Private Archives of Chinese Montrealers*, was created by the McCord Museum of Canadian History as part of an ongoing strategy to connect with Quebec's 'cultural communities', in particular to develop a continuing relationship with the Montreal Chinese community. Originally intended to provide a local context for an exhibition of photographs by a Chinese-Canadian photographer from British Columbia, *Souvenirs of Here* quickly evolved into a major exhibition of the work of four individuals who used photography to record their families' stories. Working closely with the photographers and their families, the curatorial team built a trusting relationship that was necessary to carry out the exhibition project. According to the curator, *Souvenirs of Here* documented 'a new collective memory, a new story of families and communities', where photography 'represents a significant tool for cultural integration, a way of socializing and [...] the proof of a determination to leave a footprint in the sands of time' (Dickenson 2010: 154). The exhibition and programming it occasioned helped the McCord Museum inaugurate relationships with a range of Chinese-Canadian community groups as well as with the families of the photographers, thereby laying the groundwork for developing longer-term ties between all of them. This project demonstrates not only the necessity of building trust in the process of establishing community relationships but also the need for flexibility in a project's development. The fact that the McCord Museum recognized that this project required a fully fledged independent effort to highlight the photography of Chinese-Canadian family photographers – rather than a small display supplementing another exhibition – was undoubtedly key to the project's success. *Souvenirs of Here* acknowledged the importance of Chinese Montrealers, and their significance within Canadian history and culture, and demonstrated the McCord's willingness to be responsive to its local constituents.

For some museums, engaging with the community can become a central focus and lead to a realignment of mission and organizational values as well as organizational structure. The Oakland Museum of California transformed its operations during an institution-wide renovation project that included not just refreshing its buildings and galleries but also revisiting the relationships among the staff and with its visitors. Curators shed the role of sole authority in developing exhibitions and facilitated conversations that elicited multiple perspectives. They heard their communities' ideas about the museum, and took them into account as they renovated the exhibition galleries. The result is more effective and engaging exhibitions as well as a more welcoming museum environment. Key to becoming more integral to the community was the willingness of the museum to listen to its audiences and to respond to their interests and concerns, thereby making the museum and its exhibitions more inviting to its visitors (Henry and McLean 2010).

Listening to an organization's diverse audiences, maintaining the flexibility necessary to respond to communities' changing needs and developing strategic collaborations with community partners were essential to the New Jersey Historical Society's renewed relevance in the post-industrial, largely African American and Latino city of Newark. The Historical Society adopted collaborative practices as a mainstay of its operations – internally, its staff, which reflected Newark's diverse cultures, worked together, bridging departments and specialty areas, to create exhibitions and programmes; and externally, the staff engaged community groups and other cultural organizations to help develop the Historical Society's varied offerings and build a more cohesive social environment in the city. What the Historical Society learned from the community changed the way that it approached its work: first, by taking the needs and interests of the community into account, and then, by shaping its programmes and exhibitions around ways in which the institution's historical resources could help meet those needs (Yerkovich 2005).

One of the more dramatic instances of this approach resulted in 'Partners in Learning', a programme for 'the non-traditional, sometimes marginalized audience of adolescent parents' and their children (Ocello 2011: 193). Created to add a cultural component to a high school Infant-Toddler Centre, and to cultivate a teenaged audience for the New Jersey Historical Society, this programme demonstrated how young adults unaccustomed to frequenting cultural organizations can become regular museum visitors, using a museum's exhibitions to engage and learn individually and with their children. The Infant-Toddler Centre provided day-care for the children of high school students while they completed their classes, and also taught the students 'child development and healthy baby care'. While the Historical Society could not participate in more basic child care training, it could 'encourage [...] young mothers to pull their child away from the television and take them to a cultural institution, where they could interact with their child and promote effective learning before, during and after their visit' (Ocello 2011: 193). Outcome-based evaluation, created in partnership with the Infant-Toddler Centre, helped to demonstrate the difference that the programme made in the lives of the young parents. They learned to use cultural institutions as resources for their children on a regular basis, and testified that it also improved their communication skills so that they could interact positively with their children, 'without getting or showing him the belt' (Ocello 2011: 194).

Each of these examples demonstrates ways in which museums have elected to involve communities in their work, showing how museums implement *Principle 4* of the *ICOM Code of Ethics for Museums*, fulfilling their 'duty to develop their educational role and attract wider audiences from the community, locality, or group they serve' (ICOM 2004). In each case described, the museum worked with community members and responded to their needs, while maintaining the museum's control over the content and direction of its exhibitions and/or programmes. Yet, such collaborations and partnerships can also raise ethical dilemmas for museums. Consider the following two examples:[2]

> Example 1:
> A regional museum decided to create an exhibition about the little-known history of the internment of 'enemy aliens' in the United States during World War I. The topic is a sensitive one for the descendants of the internees but one they very much wanted to bring to light; so a group of representatives of the descendants agreed to collaborate with the museum on the exhibition. The museum's curatorial and education team worked with a small group of historians and the descendants of the internees to collect objects and to develop the exhibition narrative. The community representatives were militant and hoped to see the injustices of the internment exposed. The historians stressed the necessity of including enough information to provide a context within which to understand the internment, and the rationale behind it, without being inflammatory.
>
> After much negotiation among the curators, historians and community representatives, the group produced a closely edited exhibition narrative.

The curatorial team submitted the narrative to the museum's senior management for their review and approval. Although the senior staff did not have historical expertise and had not worked with the community, they made significant editorial changes in the exhibition text and returned it to the head of the project team, who was left with the job of finalizing the exhibition.

Because the museum made a commitment to working with the community on the development of the exhibition, moving ahead with the exhibition without again consulting with the community members and the historians involved in the project would be unethical. Consequently, the senior staff has an ethical duty to permit the project team to consider the edited text and respond. Any trust engendered by the earlier negotiations would be undermined by a unilateral management decision to move forward without further consultation. Having agreed to collaborate with the community, the museum has an ethical obligation to ensure that the community representatives have an opportunity to give their input before the exhibition opens.

Example 2:

A local history museum is creating an exhibition about a Russian community that has recently settled nearby. The curator is a specialist in Russian culture and has engaged a group of scholars to advise on the development of the project. Since the museum hopes to use the exhibition as a way to engage the local community in its activities, the curator has also enlisted members of the community as advisers. This group has been kept abreast of the development of the project. They have also introduced the curator to other community members who have loaned objects to the exhibition and participated in oral history interviews.

Working with the scholars, the curator developed an exhibition narrative that chronicles the settlement of Russians in the community and highlights their contributions. The narrative goes into detail concerning Russian customs and practices, some of which, like bribery and the underground or black market, connect elements of Soviet and post-Soviet history with the rise of the alleged Russian mafia. The scholars noted that these practices are so important to understanding *émigré* Russian community life that the museum cannot do justice to the subject without including them. Realizing that the topics might be controversial, the scholars urge the curator to provide the context within which they can be understood. When the community advisers learn of these suggestions, however, they are outraged. They threaten to withdraw their support and participation and 'go public' with their condemnation of the inclusion of these 'darker' aspects of the Russian community experience.

How should the museum react? And to what lengths should it go to accommodate the community's perspectives? If the historical relevance of the topics the historians wish to include is undisputed, the only ethical question rests upon whether, once engaged, the community has been given a fair opportunity to respond.

The content of museum exhibitions has conventionally been grounded in scholarship, presented through the lens of the curator. As we have seen in recent years, it has become common practice for museums to seek the advice and input of outside experts – both from the academy and from communities whose interests are reflected in an exhibition – to shape exhibition themes and narrative. With the development of the Web 2.0 environment of interactivity and the prevalence of social media, new avenues of communication have opened for museums. It is incumbent upon museums to understand the potential and the risks of digital engagement, and prudent to develop and issue a digital media policy to ensure that staff and volunteers understand the relevant use of these media platforms. Such policies can help avoid or ameliorate ethical dilemmas and establish a clear distinction between appropriate personal and professional uses of the internet. When guided by these policies, digital and online engagement can become an effective means for furthering a museum's overall objectives and fostering the museum's ability to engage its audiences.

An increase in the sharing of authority and community involvement in content creation through social media may be beneficial, deepening the public's involvement and broadening the diversity of voices and perspectives the museum presents. It can strengthen the museum's educational role and encourage attention to the effectiveness of a museum's communication with its audiences. As Hull and Scott point out, through the use of social media and digital curatorial practices, 'the museum can maintain its own authorial role [...] while opening up pathways for visitors to inscribe *their* stories into this history, unraveling new and unintended meaning from artifacts as they enter global spheres of circulation and appropriation' (Hull and Scott 2013: 147).

Social media commentary, however, can also create ethical dilemmas for museums. For example, the Museum of Fine Arts (MFA), Boston, loaned one of its paintings, Claude Monet's *La Japonaise* (or *Camille Monet in Japanese Costume*), to *Looking East*, an exhibition that travelled to three cities in Japan. Monet originally titled his painting *Japonerie*, a word coined in the 1870s to describe Western works that imitated Japanese objects, and the work is considered to be Monet's comment upon the vogue for Japanese culture in Paris at the time (McDermon 2015). 'Monet went out of his way to present his naturally dark-haired wife as a blonde *parisienne*, at once disguising her identity and emphasizing her difference from the exotic objects that surround her' (Museum of Fine Arts, Boston, 2013). *Looking East* included reproduction kimonos that visitors were invited to try on. This feature of the Japanese exhibition was so popular that when *La Japonaise* returned to Boston, the museum decided to introduce a similar programme for its visitors. On Wednesday evenings when the museum is free to the public, visitors were invited to don an authentic kimono, take 'selfies' with Monet's painting as a backdrop, and share the photographs on social media.

On the first night of these 'Kimono Wednesdays', there was a small protest in the museum against the cultural appropriation the protestors felt was implied in the activity. The following week three protesters returned and later counter-protestors appeared. While the protests in the museum were always modest in size, the outcry online was much more substantial, with the museum's Facebook page inundated with commentary. Although some of the posts were supportive of the activity, many claimed that it was racist. As a result, the MFA decided to discontinue 'Kimono Wednesdays'. Nonetheless it continued to display the kimonos, encouraging visitors to 'touch and engage with them' so that they could understand and appreciate the garments' embroidery and composition. The MFA also offered educational programmes to provide a deeper understanding of the historical background of French Impressionism and *japonisme*, as well as opportunities for audiences to engage in culturally sensitive discourse related to issues raised by *La Japonaise* (Museum of Fine Arts, Boston, 2015).

Should a museum respond to negative comments on social media? If so, in what way? A decision to respond depends upon how substantial these comments are considered to be. Does the number of responses matter, or are the tone and substance of the commentary the determining factors? As in the case of *La Japonaise*, all responses should be public and propose constructive resolutions. Seeking community engagement, a museum need not shunt aside its responsibility and succumb to popular attitudes or opinions, for to do so can create the impression that it is unwilling to stand by its exhibitions and programmes, and thereby call both its judgement and integrity into question.

Do these potential problems suggest that public participation is simply too risky, time-consuming and even impractical? How can museums navigate the knotty ethical problems that arise when communities are shut out? How can public participation be accomplished without museums simply shunting aside their responsibility in favour of popular attitudes? Will the content of future exhibitions be derived from crowd sourcing and participatory design rather than scholarship? These questions may challenge conventional museum practice; but – like the inclusion of community consultants in exhibitions on community-based themes – they may well be resolved through constructive dialogue between a museum and its audiences without completely devolving decision-making to the public. In particular with internet and social media platforms providing unceasing influence and opportunity for reactive comment, today's audiences can be demanding and vocal; nevertheless, establishing an intelligent and responsible dialogue with visitors and electronic constituents has become a necessity in order for museums to maintain both their reflexivity and integrity.

Crowd-sourced projects, citizen science initiatives and community curation will be important resources in the museum's continuing need to bring varied perspectives into the interpretation and presentation of cultural heritage. Engagement with community members, whether in person or through social media, can enrich the resources of a museum, providing access to new collections as well as new perspectives on existing collections (Peers and Brown 2003: 1; Srinivasan *et al.* 2010). Ultimately these activities may lead museums to become less like independent, and sometimes isolated, institutions and more like 'hubs in modern society': means for connecting people, activities and objects (Hagedorn-Saupe *et al.* 2013: 126), and fulfilling museums' potential as key institutions of civil society.

Note

1 The full text of the *ICOM Code of Ethics for Museums* is provided as *Appendix I* in the present publication. It is also available online for download from the ICOM website (with links to translations in French, Spanish, and many other languages). The English version is accessible at: http://icom.museum/professional-standards/code-of-ethics.
2 The examples given are hypothetical situations, composites of real situations and actual issues faced by museums; however, any resemblance to any particular museum is purely coincidental.

References

Dickenson, V., 2010. 'Old forms, new purposes', in O. Guntarik, (ed.), *Narratives of Community: Museums and Ethnicity*. Edinburgh: MuseumsEtc, pp. 148–75.

Hagedorn-Saupe, M., Kampschulte, L. and Noschka-Roos, A., 2013. 'Informal, participatory learning with interactive exhibit setting and online services', in K. Drotner and K.C. Schröder (eds), *Media Communication and Social Media: The Connected Museum*. London and New York: Routledge, pp. 111–29.

Henry, B. and McLean, K. (eds), 2010. *How We Visitors Changed Our Museum: Transforming the Gallery of California Art at the Oakland Museum of California*. Oakland, CA: Oakland Museum of California.

Hull, G. and Scott, J., 2013. 'Curating and creating online: Identity, authorship, and viewing in a digital age', in K. Drotner and K.C. Schröder (eds), *Media Communication and Social Media: The Connected Museum*. London and New York: Routledge, pp. 130–49.

ICOM Code of Ethics for Museums, 2004. Paris: International Council of Museums (ICOM), at: http://icom.museum/the-vision/code-of-ethics/ (accessed 12 December 2015).

McDermon, D., 2015. 'Kimono promotion yields to outrage at Boston's Museum of Fine Arts', *The New York Times*, 8 July 2015, at: http://nytimes.com (accessed 12 December 2015).

Museum of Fine Arts, Boston, 2013. *Conservation in Action: La Japonaise*, at: www.mfa.org/collections/conservation/conservation-in-action/la-japonaise (accessed 12 December 2015).

Museum of Fine Arts, Boston, 2015. *Museum of Fine Arts, Boston*, at: www.mfa.org/news/2015/july (accessed 12 December 2015).

Ocello, C., 2011. 'Being responsive to be responsible: Museums and audience development', in J. Marstine (ed.), *The Routledge Companion to Museum Ethics: Redefining Ethics for the Twenty-First-Century Museum*. London and New York: Routledge, pp. 188–201.

O'Neill, M., 2005. 'Commentary 4': John Holden's *Capturing Cultural Value: How Culture has Become a Tool of Government Policy, Cultural Trends* 14 (1), No. 53: 123.

Peers, L. and Brown, A.K., 2003. 'Introduction', in L. Peers and A.K. Brown (eds), *Museums and Source Communities: A Routledge Reader*. London and New York: Routledge, pp. 1–16.

Srinivasan, R., Becvar, K.M., Boast, R. and Enote, J., 2010. 'Diverse knowledges and contact zones within the digital museum'. *Science, Technology, and Human Values*, 35 (5): 735–68, at: http://rameshsrinivasan.org/wordpress/wp-content/uploads/2013/07/22-Srinivasanetal-STHV-RDODiverseKnowledges-final.pdf (accessed 14 December 2015).

Witcomb, A., 2007. ' "Place for all of us"? Museums and communities', in S. Watson (ed.), *Museums and Their Communities*. London and New York: Routledge, pp. 133–56.

Yerkovich, S., 2005. 'Engaging with the contemporary'. *Museum Ireland* 15: 18–29.

24

CONSERVATION

How ethics work in practice

Stephanie de Roemer

Conservation, museums and codes of ethics

Conservation's relationship with the wider museum community appears somewhat obscure yet complex. Less a matter of differences rather than of interconnectivity, the lines of what defines the museum, what is the role of conservation and the nature and extent of their relationship, are blurred.

So let's go back to 1946, the year the International Council of Museums (ICOM) was founded in Paris. The emergence of international collaboration through forums and organisations such as the United Nations Educational, Scientific and Cultural Organization (UNESCO) and ICOM were undoubtedly in response to the firm belief of nations, forged by two world wars in less than a generation, that political and economic agreements are not enough to build lasting peace but that peace must be established on the basis of humanity's moral and intellectual solidarity (UNESCO, online).

In 1959 UNESCO founded the International Centre for the Study of the Preservation and Restoration of Cultural Property (ICCROM), an intergovernmental organisation for the conservation of cultural heritage in Rome in support of ICOM to work together on cultural heritage emergency programmes in periods of conflict and natural disasters (Caple 2000). In 1967, a small group of conservation professionals created ICOM-CC, the International Council of Museums Conservation Committee, which today has over 2,600 members worldwide, making it the largest international conservation organisation and the largest committee of ICOM (ICOM-CC web).

The emergence of an ICOM committee devoted to aspects of conservation put conservation firmly at the heart of the museum, an institution involved and responsible for the collecting, display and protection of cultural heritage informing and providing best practice in all aspects of collection care and the facilitation of its access and use. To further define and allocate the function of conservation to and as part of museum practice, ICOM-CC, in 1984, specified in its Code of Ethics the activity, impact and ranking of activity, distinction from related professions, and training and education of the conservator-restorer as 'The Conservator-Restorer: A Definition of a Profession' (ICOM-CC 1984).

In 1986 ICOM published its Code of Ethics on the definition of the museum as 'an institution which acquires, conserves, researches, communicates and exhibits' and conservation as 'the activity of the conservator-restorer, consisting of examination, preservation and conservation-restoration of cultural property (Caple 2000). Amended in 2001 at the 20th ICOM General Assembly in Barcelona, Spain, and revised during the 21st ICOM General Assembly in Seoul, South Korea, in 2004, the term 'conservation' disappeared from ICOM's definition of the museum and was only mentioned as two of twenty-three activities under the Ethical Code 2 in relation to the care of collections as 'Preventive Conservation' (2.23) and 'Collection Conservation and Restoration' (2.24) (ICOM 2013: 5).

The revised *ICOM Code of Ethics for Museums* no doubt reflects the changing appearance and expansive role of the museum landscape in modern times. The image of the traditional local building structure that houses and displays collections of objects in dark storage or rows of display cases as 'treasure troves' has been largely replaced by the concept of the museum as a platform facilitating cultural creativity, circulating many new forms of knowledge, ideas, values and experience as expressions of intangible heritage.

The emergence of the recognition of the important role of intangible cultural expressions to the cultural identity of an individual, community, society and humanity as a whole has resulted in ICOM's and UNESCO's commitment to identify and manage resources on the Convention for Safeguarding Intangible Cultural Heritage, and provides the first legal framework for the support of this kind of cultural expression (ICOM, online). ICOM describes intangible heritage as:

> the living expressions like the traditions that many groups and communities worldwide have been passed down by their ancestors and will contribute to pass on to their descendants, mostly by word of mouth. Although it is the motor of cultural diversity, this heritage is fragile.
>
> *(ICOM: online)*

The term 'conservation' appearing in the codes of Ethics under activities specific to technical and practical collection care, may be indicative of a general perception of conservation as a specialist subject often carried out in restricted access studios and workshops, and thus being somewhat removed from others perception.

Conservators for various reasons may have missed opportunities to communicate conservation's purpose and value beyond the cleaning and mending of physical objects as the mean to an end, 'frozen in time' to last into the distant future.

Of greater significance, however, is conservation's purpose and value as a mechanism for Revelation, Investigation and Preservation of the intangible narratives contained and manifested through the selection, creation, assemblage, shaping and forming of the physical material culture into a physical perceivable appearance.

The physical object is a tangible coordinate, which the conservator explores and records to make accessible the associated intangible cultural expressions. Recognition and value of the importance of cultural heritage to an individual, community, society and cultures is the motivation for all conservation activity; and its various and diverse methodologies, practices and philosophies are themselves reflections of varying and changing value annotations, expressed through the nature and extent of the practice of care. The inherent variability, diversity and relativity of intangible cultural expressions themselves, and their specific value annotations over time and regions, is therefore not served well with a single approach of 'one size fits all'. Indeed, conservation methodologies, practices, training, education and awareness of the profession are equally varied, diverse and relative across cultures, regions and generations. This is reflected in the continuous growth of the International Council of Museums' Conservation Committee in membership numbers, and across forums, workshops and conferences through its twenty-one working groups around the world, culminating in seventeen international triennial meetings to date.

These conferences and meetings are by no means restricted to discussions on research, experience, skills and knowledge of technical details and practices in the documentation, cleaning, stabilisation and restoration of physical cultural heritage alone, but serve as forums for cross-disciplinary exchange and discourse, and are reflective of an active profession engaged with the changes and challenges encountered and affecting contemporary cultural landscapes.

At the 17th Triennial Conference of ICOM-CC in Melbourne, Australia, in September 2014, the presentations of examples of support provided to communities afflicted by the consequences of conflict, natural disasters and rapid industrialisation served as powerful reminders of the value of conservation as a process of providing tangible activities and practical methodologies. Facilitating training and support in retrieval, documentation and restoration of lost and destroyed physical cultural heritage as a step towards rebuilding individuals' and communities' identities, and providing practical frameworks of conservation care, serve as tangible opportunities to engage and empower the individual and community as stakeholders in the care of their past to shape their future.

Conservation's role and value in this context does not lie in the technical and practical outcome of elaborate and meticulous specialist techniques and practices carried out by one individual in hidden workshops or studios, but in its practice as the conscious act of care through facilitating and supporting connections, relationships, environments and conditions for engaged and cross-disciplinary qualitative communication. At the same conference, the revised definition of the conservator-restorer from 1984 was presented and marked a clear shift from its traditional presentation of a list of definitions in text categorising conservation/restoration actions.

The interactive navigation map, *Conservation: Who, what and why?* provides an overview of the various processes conservators are involved in and support, in addition to the roles of the various stakeholders in the wider museum landscape (Figure 24.1).

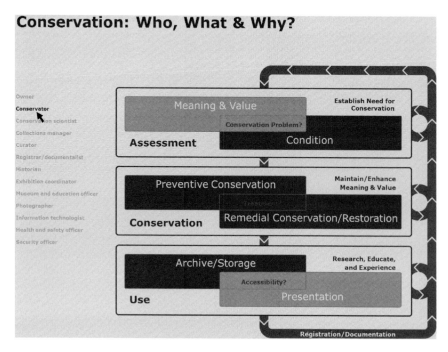

FIGURE 24.1 From *Conservation: Who, what and why?* (ICOM-CC, 2014) showing conservators role in supporting the various aims and roles of the museum. Concept and design by Andries J. van Dam.

This model allows us to trace the relational connections as 'routes' to achieving qualitative outcomes in research and education, maintenance of collections and the enhancement and retention of meaning and value.

This representation does not only highlight the shared aims and values of diverse museum professions, and their audiences, but emphasises the shared responsibility of each individual within the museum community in the care of their collections. Simultaneously this provides an accessible overview to the wider museum landscape and its stakeholders to recognise opportunity and shared interests to engage, participate, collaborate and support communication and development of new and additional practices reflective of contemporary museum ethics. The aim of this contribution is to communicate conservation as an applied philosophy, which has evolved and been shaped throughout history on the experience and expression of humanity's reverence for cultural heritage, as a practice of museum ethics, and a methodology of engagement and learning, participation and collaboration.

How conservation works

Examples of some of the varying perceptions of the 'conservator' are illustrated in Figure 24.2. All are valid if slightly exaggerated, and have one important aspect in

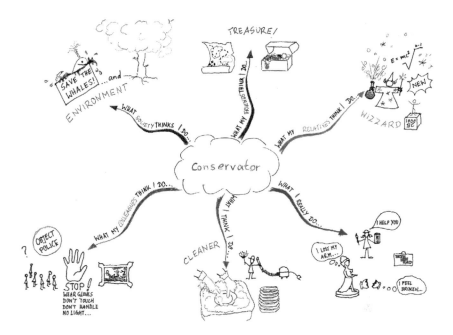

FIGURE 24.2 Mind Map – Conservator: environmentalist, treasure hunter, scientist, object guardian, cleaner, medical practitioner.

Note
Mind Map; conservator, Concept: Hannele Hentula, Conservator, Design: Stephanie de Roemer, Conservator

common; mainly that they are all care-related actions motivated by personal, professional and cultural values. (Even the illustration itself is a representation of personal, professional and cultural values by the individual who drew those images to convey a message).

Although there is a common motivation, the actions vary significantly in regard to which and whose value of protection and care they are expressing, and how these may be perceived and understood by others. Human individuality, the uniqueness of each object, the variable dynamics of environments and their conditions, and the variety of communication across individuals, communities and cultures, throughout time render values annotated to a single object relative and make it impossible to define one absolute value (quantitative). This inherent relativity of held values therefore informing the nature and extent of associated narratives will have to be identified in addition to which and whose value, appreciation and understanding its physical appearance should reflect and thereby determining the nature and extent of possible and favourable intervention.

There is a wealth of available literature and publications on the subjects of 'value', and resulting theories and philosophies in conservation: Alois Riegl's *Der moderne Denkmalkultus* (1903), Cesare Brandi's *Teoria del restauro* (1963), and most recently Salvador Muñoz Viñas's *Contemporary Theory of Conservation* (2012) to name the most prominent. Those works are essential reading for every conservator and anyone interested in the subjects. However, the accounts of perception, experience, judgement and value of an individual and the interpretation of their meaning within the practice of conservation vary between conservators, countries and cultures.

The challenge for the conservator to act in the interest of the community of stakeholders as the advocate for an object, while respecting and preserving all differing and even opposing value associations in recognition of the inherent complexities and responsibility, is the subject of the publication *Conservation Skills, Judgement, Method, and Decision Making*, by conservation lecturer Chris Caple (2000). Rather than defining the outcomes of conservation activity on various traditional philosophies and theoretical constructs alone, the author focuses on conservation as a dynamic and responsive process guided by its aims to reveal, investigate and preserve the objects' physical material culture for access and communication of the intangible cultural expressions in practice and through documentation of the experienced 'journey', which always starts with the object.

The object

Objects are preserved because of the information they contain and for what they represent (Caple 2000: 36). As a historic document and aesthetic entity, an object is not a singular absolute but presents a complex duality with opposing value associations relating to meaning, appearance and function relative to the observer.

As a historic document the conservator would seek to determine the object's composition, the decay processes at work, the form and original nature of the object, its function, who had owned and used the object and what had happened to it throughout its life (Caple 2000: 36). Investigation of an object's physical and technical aspects serves to provide information on its context, environment and conditions (Figure 24.3). Simultaneously, every object is also in part an aesthetic entity, an entity (a physical reality) which provides an aesthetic experience for everyone who senses (sees, feels, touches, smells or hears) it (Caple 2000: 36).

Consciously made or selected by a human being, it has a shape, colour and texture that that individual has created or chosen from a range of possibilities. The aesthetic entity is that aspect of the object deliberately created by the artist or manufacturer in order to communicate with the user or viewer and as such can be considered the physical manifestation of the 'artist intent', simultaneously expressing varying value and belief systems (Caple 2000) (see Figure 24.3).

Every object contains aspects that are definable as being 'documents of the past' and aspects that are 'aesthetic', and the investigation and documentation of context and narratives of the object provides a methodology to identify a rising complexity across a spectrum of opposing extremes on which differing value expressions can be explored, assessed and balanced (see Figures 24.3, 24.4, Table 24.1), informing the nature and the extent of conservation intervention (see Figure 24.5b).

Conservation investigation for analysis of the observed tangible aspects and their interpretation within context and environment also identifies potential inherent

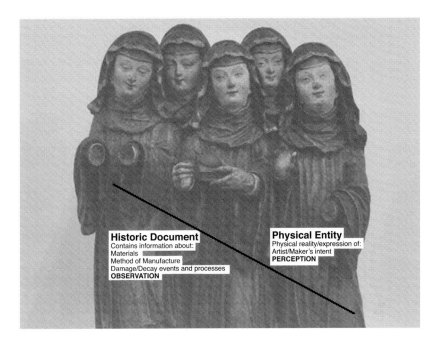

FIGURE 24.3   Schematic presentation of the object as aesthetic entity and historic document (November 2015). Photo: Stephanie de Roemer for Glasgow Museums. Design: Stephanie de Roemer.

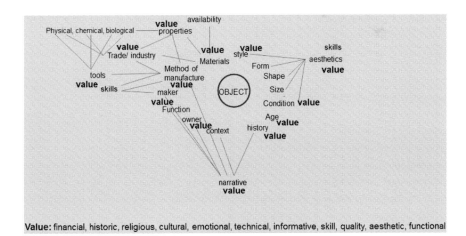

FIGURE 24.4   Visual representation of nominal and expressive aspects for conservation considerations and their potential value associations.

Note
This is not an exhaustive model.

TABLE 24.1 Overview of the conservation process of 'investigation – analysis – interpretation – value expression' on the example of medieval polychrome sculpture

Conservation investigation	of	to analyse	for interpretation of	expression of
Material identification of three-dimensional structure macroscopic microscopic qualitative and quantitative analysis of material samples (XRF, wood identification, petrographic analysis) comparative analysis of data with identified examples	**Wood species** **Stone; source quarries** **Alabaster** **Other**	source of material availability of material physical and chemical properties working properties and technologies	value of material trade workshop/industries tools and equipment quality and skills of working techniques present condition/type and extent of damage	financial value historical value investment value skill value artistic value aesthetic value
Construction of three-dimensional strucutre X-radiography comparative analysis of data with identified examples	**single block** **assemblage of blocks** **assemblage of individually prepared components** **structural fittings and fixing mechanisms**	availability of materials and skills construction techniques structural stability damage or alteration to structure age of employed fixing mechanisms: nails, screws, dowels	specific working characteristics period of construction tools and equipment quality and skills of working techniques history of physical care and maintenance, alterations	historic/artistic value age/financial value skill value artistic/investment value aesthetic/financial value
Surface decoration microscopic investigation of resin-mounted cross-sections of decorative surface layers UV light analysis fourier transform infrared spectroscopy	**extent and type of polychrome, gilding, inlay**	materials and skills employed availability of materials associated working techniques condition and extent of damage or alterations to decorative surface layers	value of materials iconography authenticity of polychrome history of care, alteration, deterioration quality and skills of working techniques industries, crafts	financial value aesthetic/historical value age/artistic/aesthetic value aesthetic/financial value artistic value historic/investment value

value associations (Table 24.1). For example, the object may conjure up childhood memories of significant emotional value to a viewer, or represent a substantial investment value in monetary terms to the owner. To the historian the object undoubtedly contains a historic and informative value, while the art enthusiast appreciates the artistic skill and aesthetic value of the work. The object may also be of religious, cultural or national significance, and therefore represent a symbolic value to an individual, community, society or culture. One person's positive value association with the object may be another's feeling of provocation to their personal, religious, political, ideological or cultural held value and belief systems, and the display of such an object may cause much conflict.

The conservator himself/herself, depending on background, education, knowledge, skills, tastes and belief, will also have his or her own opinions, values and thoughts about an object and the associated possible type and extent of care it should receive.

The remaining objective in order to place what is best for the object above personal motivations for potential intervention is what differentiates the professional conservator from the DIY enthusiast. Academic study and practical experience as part of a conservator's training instil codes of principles and practice towards sustaining physical cultural heritage as manifestations of intangible cultural expressions as defined by UNESCO, ICCROM and ICOM through ethical guidelines and concepts of 'stewardship' and 'custodianship'. The responsibility of the conservator as the custodian entrusted with the tangible care of shared cultural heritage is much the same as that of the medical practitioner, who is guided through the ethical codes of conduct and practice the medical profession abides to (see Figure 24.2, 'What I really do').

Similarly to the medical practitioner entrusted with the care of an individual's health, the conservator responsible for the care of the object has to inform, collaborate, negotiate, plan, assess and converse with various decision-makers and stakeholders not only to administer appropriate treatment but also to advise, recommend and implement appropriate actions, conditions and environments beneficial to the long-term preservation and maintenance of the object within available resources and organisational structures.

The nominal (quantitative) and expressive (qualitative) information obtained from the initial investigation and observation of the technical, scientific and art historical study of a particular object's aesthetic entity and historic document are assessed alongside other conservation considerations (Figure 24.5a) to inform and achieve the three aims of conservation: *revelation, investigation* and *preservation* providing the RIP balance (Figure 24.5b).

Establishing the RIP balance provides the conservator with a 'map' of locating and navigating between the potential irreversible outcomes of physical intervention, with potential detrimental consequences to achieving one or all aims, and conservation activities are therefore characterised as lying in the space between these extremes as a process of achieving a balance between these three activities (Caple 2000).

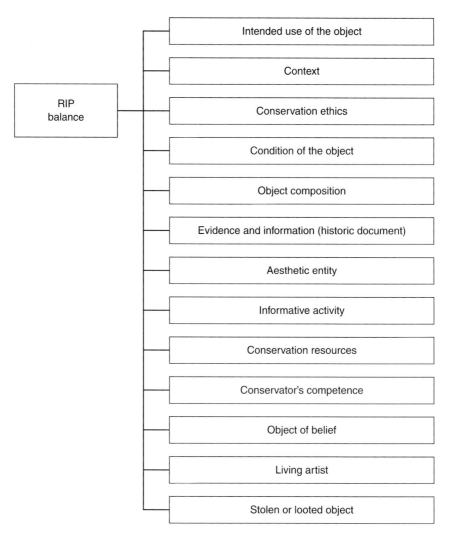

FIGURE 24.5a Overview of conservation considerations (source: Caple 2000: 34).

An archaeological metal artefact, for example, may have intricate engraved surface decoration as an expression of the artist intent (aesthetic entity) obscured by a layer of corrosion and dirt, containing evidence of the object's metal composition, associated degradation processes and environmental conditions the object has been part of (historic document). To retain both aspects of the object the conservator may carry out detailed recording and analytical *investigation* through x-radiography to *reveal* and document (*preserve*) the aesthetic value of such surface decoration as part of the object's aesthetic entity while deciding to retain the obscuring corrosion layer for future analysis and *investigation* of its informative value as a historic document (Table 24.1, Figure 24.3). This minimum intervention may simultaneously

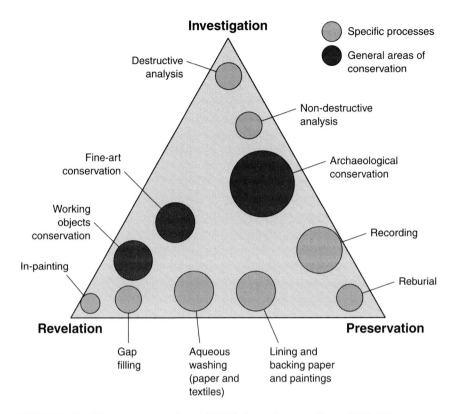

FIGURE 24.5b Visual representation of RIP balance (source: Caple 2000: 36).

be a measure of the overall *preservation* of the object, as the mechanical or chemical cleaning of the corrosion layer to *reveal* the surface decoration may pose substantial risks to the physical and chemical stability of the degraded metal shape and form. It may lead not only to the loss of information but also to the detriment of the aesthetic appreciation (Figure 24.5b).

In almost all cases conservation involves practices to achieve all three aims to a certain degree, and is hardly ever carried out to the extreme to achieve only one aim to the detriment of other aims.

Conservation is therefore the qualitative communication of ethics expressed on the values held at any point in time, and as a process of practice does not aim to achieve a specific physical appearance for the sake of intervention, but is the record of the journey of investigation, revelation and preservation communicating the narratives of past cultural expressions through the 'witness from the past' in a tangible practice of care.

The responsibility and focus of engaging with the 'witnesses from the past' as the main occupation of the conservator and the often spatial disconnect of conservation activity from management, curatorial, documentation, learning and education, and front-of-house staff's perception are likely to have contributed to the view of conservators as the 'object police' (Figure 24.2, 'What my colleagues think I do') or the 'scientist' magically reviving the decayed object back to its original condition (Figure 24.2, 'What my relatives think I do'), in both cases an incomplete and misleading understanding of conservation's true potential.

The passion, expertise and skills required for the care of objects of past and present cultural heritage should not be viewed as exclusive, technical and only relevant to the professionally trained experts for the technical care of 'difficult' objects. As a methodology of care, nurturing skills of decision-making and problem-solving to ensure best practice in achieving qualitative values and outcomes, conservation communicates itself through its practice, and is therefore a valuable tool for active engagement and participation while facilitating a tangible experience of care and learning.

As a multidisciplinary profession of art and science, practice and theory, experience and philosophy, it requires communication and collaboration across the museum and wider communities. Museums as creative places have a unique opportunity in engaging with the conservation process in many ways and on many levels: an educational workshop of object description and assessment in support of academic training courses or staff projects in assisting with display and storage maintenance, monitoring and controlling, learning and education workshops on material science for school children, provide real opportunity to engage with and support the wider role of conservation in achieving the aims as defined by the museum's ethical codes.

Conservation considerations and methodologies of inclusion of differing and opposing viewpoints and values enabling informed decision-making processes to formulate tangible solutions are by no means restricted to the protection and preservation of objects. Replacing the 'witness from the past' with a fellow 'eyewitness in the present' and adapting the process of problem-solving to conflict resolution as qualitative values for Justice, Equality and Diversity (JED), the RIP model becomes the JED balance, a map of locating and navigating between the extremes to balance activity and communication to the overall well-being (physical/tangible and spiritual/intangible) of the individual and the wider community through the practice of care.

Conservation therefore is the lubricant that ensures the dynamic museum facilitates cultural creativity, circulating many new forms of knowledge, ideas, values and experience as expressions of the intangible culture and the preservation of tangible cultural heritage in perpetuity.

Conclusion

What emerges from this discussion is that conservation is a process of navigating complexity and developing solutions while acting responsibly in consideration of the differing values of others. As a practice of engagement and participation, it is inclusive, encouraging collaboration beyond the conservation laboratory, workshop and/or studio.

Although the term conservation is largely absent from the 2013 *ICOM Code of Ethics for Museums*, its values, definitions and aims communicate the theoretical framework of what conservation practises. Conservation and museums are inter-linked; questions of which came first are, however, of less significance than the recognition of their shared purpose and values.

The visual presentation of conservation as a process and connections referenced in a navigational interactive map not only provides a qualitative revision of the 1984 definition of a profession in response to the expanding role and function of the museum, but is an invitation to the wider museum community to connect and become engaged in the processes, practices and discussions on communicating shared values in the practice of care for cultural heritage, landscapes and humanity.

References

Caple, C., 2000. *Conservation Skills, Judgement, Method, and Decision Making*. New York: Routledge, pp. 29–50.

History of ICOM-CC, at: www.icom-cc.org/250/about-icom-cc/history-of-icom-cc/#. VjyJOSvCq5I (accessed 5 November 2015).

History of ICOM, at: http://icom.museum/the-organisation/history (accessed 5 November 2015).

Introducing UNESCO, at: http://en.unesco.org/about-us/introducing-unesco (accessed 5 November 2015).

ICOM Code of Ethics for Museums, at: http://icom.museum/the-vision/code-of-ethics (accessed 5 November 2015).

ICOM – Intangible heritage – online: ICOM – Intangible Heritage – online at: http://icom. museum/programmes/intangible-heritage (accessed 5 November 2015).

ICOM Intangible Heritage, at: http://icom.museum/programmes/intangible-heritage (accessed 5 November 2015).

ICOM Partners, at: http://icom.museum/the-organisation/partners (accessed 5 November 2015).

ICOM-CC information: See 'About ICOM-CC', regularly updated and available online at: www.icom-cc.org/15/about/#.VyD7vkfETIU (accessed 27 April 2016).

ICOM-CC (International Council of Museums Conservation Committee), 1984. *The Conservator-Restorer: A Definition of the Profession*. Copenhagen: ICOM-CC, September 1984.

ICOM (International Council of Museums), 2004. *ICOM Code of Ethics for Museums*. Paris: ICOM. The full text of the *ICOM Code of Ethics for Museums* is provided as *Appendix I* in the present publication. It is also available online for download from the ICOM website (with links to translations in French, Spanish, and many other languages). The English version is accessible at: http://icom.museum/professional-standards/code-of-ethics.

UNESCO website information at: http://unesco.org/ Item: 'Introducing UNESCO', avail-able at: http://en.unesco.org/about-us/introducing-unesco (accessed 5 November 2015).

What is Conservation?, at: www.icom-cc.org/330/about-icom-cc/what-is-conservation/ conservation:-who,-what-amp;-why/#.VjyMGivCq5J (accessed 5 November 2015).

PART VI

'Torn history', reviewing, reshaping and rebuilding an integrated heritage

25

EXHIBITING CONTENTIOUS AND DIFFICULT HISTORIES

Ethics, emotions and reflexivity

Sharon Macdonald

Many exhibited histories are potentially contentious. A conventional narrative of national pride might, for example, be viewed as inaccurate or demeaning by those who are ignored or who feel themselves to have been oppressed by the national majority. Exhibited histories may also be contentious because of disagreements over facts; because of the particular emphases given; or because of the graphic content of what is displayed. In developments that gathered pace from around the 1970s, often associated with identity politics and decolonization, many countries have seen questioning of established public histories and also attempts to exhibit other histories, such as of those left out of, or represented as marginal within, established accounts. As part of a more critical approach to the past, there has also been a considerable increase in numbers of exhibitions that seek to exhibit aspects of a country's or city's history that those who identify with the country or city might have preferred to forget. Such 'difficult heritage' focuses on crimes committed by one's own nation or people, that is, what we can call 'negative self-history' for short. This history is not necessarily contentious, in that the great majority may agree upon the facts involved, but it is nevertheless difficult in that its display raises ethical issues, including over the emotions that it may provoke. In terms of negative self-history, Germany's exhibition of its World War II and Holocaust crimes has been especially extensive and has also provided some of the impetus for an increasingly widespread turn to the display of negative self-histories in many other countries. This has seen an expansion in the museological addressing of both difficult histories and contentious histories – categories that may overlap. This includes those of other wars and massacres, of colonialism, and of the subjection of Indigenous peoples and other minority groups.

In what follows below, I look first at some of the ethical issues that are raised in exhibiting troubling subject matter, such as that of war, massacre and genocide. Such subject matter is especially likely to raise strong – though also possibly varied

– emotions among visitors. A key question for museums is how they negotiate visitor emotion in relation to contentious and difficult history; and in particular how far dramatic, graphic and other emotionally arousing forms of display might contribute to or run against the grain of reflection and understanding. I then turn to the more specific case of the exhibition of perpetration by one's own country or people, which is potentially especially emotionally challenging in that it may provoke a troubling of self-identity, potentially invoking emotions of shame and guilt, or even defensive counter-reactions. Here I also look at ways in which exhibitions of difficult heritage or their visitors may engage in various forms of 'containment' or 'limitation', so that contemporary identities are less disturbed than they might otherwise be. Alongside this, I also seek to show how the exhibition of difficult and contentious history can provide important opportunities for ethical and critical reflection.

Troubling exhibitions: war, massacre and genocide

War, massacre and genocide are subjects that are likely to raise a range of emotions, dependent partly upon the position of the viewer but also upon the mode of exhibition. These emotions might include fear, revulsion, anger or shame, but also possibly excitement, pride or desire for revenge. It has been argued that classical monuments to battles and war help transcend the negative emotions that knowledge about the violence of warfare and death might produce, by avoiding reference to the horrors and instead adopting either abstract forms or depictions of valour or noble sacrifice for the greater good (Rowlands 1999). Exhibitions, too, can present warfare in ways that sidestep potential negative emotions associated with war and death, for example, by focusing upon heroism, or questions of territory, tactics or military tackle. Such approaches have merits; knowing that some have risked their own lives for others is important to remember and can be morally uplifting. A careful geopolitical analysis can provide deeper understanding of the contexts, motivations and consequences of warfare. But alone they are unlikely to help deal with existing negative emotions. Moreover, not acknowledging the human consequences of violence and death has increasingly come to be seen as a 'sanitization' or even possibly a 'glamorization' of war and violence.

How to represent the violence and horror of war, massacre and genocide within exhibitions is, however, an extremely difficult task for museums. The fact that no representation can ever fully represent atrocity has sometimes been taken to infer that it is best to not even try to do so. Given the risks also of potentially upsetting, shocking or even traumatizing viewers, it is perhaps not surprising that many public institutions, especially those with a broad rather than specialist remit, have avoided showing graphic images of the horrific consequences of warfare, massacre and genocide. Increasingly, however, this has been changing. The shift has been influenced partly by successful specialist institutions, such as exhibition memorial sites at war graves or concentration camps; by the overall expansion of sites of troubling and difficult heritage; and by the increased circulation of such images in public culture. It is, however, also part of the wider gaining of ground for the argument that not showing the horrors of warfare, massacre and genocide is a sanitization that presents an inaccurate picture, leading visitors to underestimate the awful consequences. Today, a purely heroic account of warfare is likely to be viewed as inadequate and problematically ideological and militaristic by international commentators.

Nevertheless, this still leaves awkward questions about how much suffering to show and in what way. One dilemma here concerns sites that were part of the apparatus that caused suffering – such as administrative headquarters of Fascist regimes – but in which victims were not directly present or only for relatively brief time periods (e.g. as slave labour during building construction). For some commentators, introducing images of victims is gratuitous and runs against a principle of historical accuracy that they cast in terms of only representing what happened directly in that location. For others, however, this way of thinking in part mirrors a distancing of victims that those regimes themselves engaged in. Instead, they argue that it is important to include representations of suffering caused by actions in 'sites of perpetration', even where that suffering took place elsewhere. Increasingly, this is the approach that is being taken (see Pearce 2010, for relevant discussion).

Ethical reflection and the display of suffering

As I discuss further below, the general shift in representations of warfare, especially to give more attention to the suffering involved, is also part of a broader shift from celebratory to reflective heritage: that is, to sites that also prompt people to think about ethical questions and the consequences of human actions. The growth of representations of contentious and difficult histories is part of an increased public mobilization of the past for such reflection. Daniel Levy and Nathan Sznaider (2002) have coined the term 'cosmopolitan memory' to characterize what they see as an increased tendency for pasts to be represented as universalized rather than restricted to the story of specific nations. The Holocaust, as the prime example of this, they argue, has increasingly come to be told as part of a generalized narrative of good versus evil – a story from which all should learn – rather than in terms of war between different nations or even as something specifically directed at Jews. This form of memory, or mode of relating to the past, is not, however, itself universal, even with reference to the Holocaust. Neither do all museological representations of suffering in warfare or even of massacre and genocide necessarily act primarily as prompts to the same levels of ethical reflection. As with other histories, contentious histories of suffering can also be used to nationalist and ideological ends, closing down rather than opening up questions and depicting specific peoples or nations as good or evil rather than prompting wider reflection.

The opening in China of dozens of museums of the Sino-Japanese War – or what in Chinese translates as the Anti-Japanese War – over the last two decades has, like the holding in 2014 of the first memorial day to the Nanjing Massacre of 1937, as much to do with contemporary politics between China and Japan as trying to prompt wider ethical reflection among Chinese citizens. This is not to deny that the massacre was an especially horrific atrocity. It is also not to deny that such an event should be remembered. But reminding of the horror in as much graphic detail and also drawing on such a wide range of varied exhibitionary strategies – including dioramas, models, paintings, sculptures, excavations, walls of photographs – to do so in as extensive an exhibition as the current Nanjing Massacre Museum (extended and refurbished in 2007; originally opened in 1985) seems to leave little opportunity for moving beyond the atrocity itself.[1] While this is understandable given the nature of the atrocity and China's continuing frustration with the content of Japanese textbooks and visits by Japanese dignitaries to the Yasukuni shrine, which honours some of those involved in the Nanjing and other World War II crimes, its emotional communication seems primarily oriented at arousing negative emotions towards Japan. As one of my Chinese students said to me: 'I know that I should not but after I went to the Nanjing Massacre Museum I really hate the Japanese.' On my own visit I also witnessed a couple of young men acting out machine-gunning the Japanese soldiers in a diorama, evidence perhaps of the exhibition also eliciting emotions of revenge.

This is not to say, however, that visitors are unable themselves to reach broader conclusions about the need to guard against brutality and to create a peaceful world. In an exhibition such as this, however, they may have to do so at least to some extent against the predominant grain of the exhibition's emotional communication. The fact that this is an exhibition in which the nation doing the displaying was victim is, of course, part of the operative dynamic, as is the continuing contention between the two countries.

Displaying negative self-histories

Where a nation or people exhibits crimes undertaken by those from the nation or people, either against others or sub-groups of their own, the operating dynamic – and the likely emotional constellation – is rather different. Because of the specific dynamic involved, I have suggested using the term 'difficult heritage' to refer specifically to this, and here I also use 'negative self-history'. Contentious heritage or contentious history, or dark heritage and dark history, might be used to refer to broader dynamics in which the past is, respectively, disputed or deals with unpleasant and unsettling subject matter (see, for example, Lennon and Foley 2000). As I have written before, difficult heritage – the kind in which one's own people or country are the perpetrators – is especially problematic for 'public reconciliation with a positive, self-affirming contemporary identity' (Macdonald 2009: 1). Negative self-histories raise unsettling questions about the kind of people that we might be, as well as about continuing responsibility for the consequences of those historical actions.

The move towards displaying negative self-histories – or difficult heritage in this specific sense – is fairly recent (see Macdonald 2009 and 2016). At its forefront has been Germany, with its public addressing of atrocities committed in World War II.

With roots in the immediate post-War period, this has seen a gathering pace and number of museums and exhibitions since the 1980s especially. This has included both 'sites of victims' – including concentration and internment camps – and also 'sites of perpetrators'. Although this division is not unproblematic, in that it fails to give recognition to perpetration at 'sites of victims' and vice versa, it does address some specific exhibitionary challenges as noted above. In particular, while a site in which victims directly suffered, emotions of horror, sorrow and contrition are more likely to be raised than at one in which the primary immediate aim was to stage an impressive spectacle, as at the Nazi Party rally grounds in Nuremberg. At the latter, as I have analysed in detail elsewhere (Macdonald 2009), a major challenge for exhibition-makers and also others involved in publicly communicating the site, such as tour guides, has been how to manage the likely emotions raised among visitors. As the site was purposefully designed to generate feelings such as admiration and awe, the risk is that these are what might be provoked among contemporary visitors, perhaps even giving them a positive impression of Nazism. Clearly, if this is done without any reference to the wider consequences, as noted in the discussion above, this is all the more likely in a site such as this.

The representation of negative self-histories raises particular challenges for negotiating visitor emotion (see also Simon *et al.* 2000). Of course, the question of what constitutes 'self' or 'one's own people' is also critical here. Evident from studying many examples of difficult heritage is that strategies of containment or limitation are often employed in order to draw boundaries between those who carried out the crimes and 'selves' today. So, for example, exhibitions might be framed primarily in terms of, say, 'Nazi crimes', and might focus primarily upon the actions of those in administrative and military control. This is likely to have a very different effect upon the audience from an exhibition framed in terms of 'Germans' and also looking at the everyday actions of 'ordinary' citizens that were also part of what made the Holocaust possible.

Let us take here the case of how France has represented its role in World War II in museums. As Pieter Lagrou has shown, until the 1970s the predominant emphasis was on 'effort to reconstruct the nation's self-esteem' (2007: 2). This meant that even occupation was rarely mentioned as that was regarded as detrimental to a positive self-image. In the 1970s, however, as part of a more widespread positive evaluation of victimhood, which is seen in many other countries too, this began to change and numerous museums of deportation and resistance opened (Walsh 2001). The overwhelming attention in these, however, was on the suffering that the French had endured and their acts of resistance to the German occupiers. It is only much more recently that the subject of French collaboration – self-crime – has been broached in exhibitions. Here, the recent exhibition *Collaboration 1940–1945*, which opened in December 2014 at the French National Archives in Paris, is a landmark in that not only did it tackle the subject in a prominent location, it also avoided forms of containment such as implying that those who collaborated were necessarily a criminal minority or were compelled to do so. Instead, it showed how endemic collaboration and support for the Nazi project were.[2]

This move by France has been witnessed in various other countries – such as Austria, Belgium and Poland – as well as by Germany (Macdonald 2016). Increasingly, it is undertaken not just at a national or civic level but also by companies, which have also mounted exhibitions that show the roles played by their own companies in the crimes of World War II. It has also been witnessed in relation to other difficult histories, such as that of slavery in the USA, colonialism in the UK, Belgium and Portugal, and Indigenous peoples in Australia and Canada (see Lehrer and Milton 2011). In some cases, forms of containment and distancing can be seen in the strategies employed but overall there is a clear move towards greater recognition and acknowledgment of wrongs that were committed. As this movement gathers pace it becomes increasingly accepted as the proper way of acting, such that *not* acknowledging past crimes and wrongs comes to be viewed as a failure or even as a form of covering up. In addition, owning up to crimes and wrongs of the past becomes a form of symbolic cleansing – a way of showing one's dirty laundry but also expressing contrition and in effect seeking a form of social absolution. While this might sometimes be undertaken for cynical reasons and as such act as a kind of distancing-through-acknowledgment – that is, washing one's hands of the past by saying that it has now been addressed – it can also be part of dedicated and continuing efforts to acknowledge past failings and crimes, and to use these for reflecting on ways to behave positively in the present and future, including by making amends by forms of reparations or forging new kinds of relationships. Before turning to look at some of these and at positive forms of use of 'difficult heritage', however, I first turn briefly to consider some of the challenges for visitor reception – including for emotional responses – that displaying self-crimes might face.

Distancing, identification and affect

Many exhibitions are visited by a range of people from different sectors of society and often too from other cities, regions or countries. A challenge is always, therefore, that of considering how those from different perspectives might respond to what is displayed. But the issue of how those who might be said to be the 'self' of the self-crimes being displayed raises some specific considerations. Primary among these may be a greater reluctance to engage with that history due to unwillingness to see themselves as part of the perpetrating group and discomfort with the emotions, such as guilt, that might be raised by such identification. Such reluctance is understandable and also legitimate: contemporary visitors are not those who committed the crimes. But by regarding what was done as the evil acts of some specific criminals, the potential for deeper engagement with what happened and its potential 'lessons' is limited. This is not restricted only to those who are part of groups that can be said to be part of the perpetrating 'self' in some way – if exhibiting difficult histories is to serve a broader purpose of helping people reflect more widely on the dangers of certain ways of thinking and acting, then it has to be able to speak beyond these. But taking the case of those who can be seen as 'self' helps to highlight some of the specific difficulties involved.

In particular, it shows how strong acts of containment might be. In extensive studies of World War II memory across different generations in Germany, Harald Welzer and colleagues have shown how this operates within families (Welzer 2008). Younger generations typically find ways to exonerate family members from previous generations, for example, by re-interpreting stories that they were told and filling in silences or gaps with exculpating accounts. In my own research on the former Nazi Party rally grounds in Nuremberg, I also noted a tendency of respondents to engage in various forms of 'identity-partitioning' that meant that it was always 'others' rather than 'we' who were responsible (2009: Chapter 8). Sometimes this meant talk in terms of the actions of 'Nazis', so restricting crimes to those who were part of the Nazi Party; and also for a temporal distancing, especially evident among younger people, in which they tended to refer to 'the Nazi times' as a specific and closed past period and to be less likely than older people to make comparisons with recent and contemporary events. It was also evident in the way that Germans not from Nuremberg tended to talk especially of Nuremberg; in Nurembergers' use of passive grammatical constructions; and in foreigners' references to Germans. Yet to expect identification with the crimes of that period is also affectively problematic. Studies have shown the resentment sometimes shown by young people in particular for being expected to feel shame, show sorrow and to perform contrition; and how such a sense of compulsory emotional performance can run counter to reflection or to meaningful engagement with the past at all (see Staas 2010, for reference to relevant studies).

The challenge, then, is to find ways to make the pasts exhibited 'speak' across time and generations, something that is likely to involve at least some sense of emotional identification, but to do so without making visitors feel affectively compelled to respond in formulaic ways. As Lehrer and Milton point out, just confronting people with difficult pasts is not enough (2011: 1). Instead, what is needed is the development of 'other modes, including attempts to kindle social aspirations like empathy, identification, cross-cultural dialogue, to recognize multiple perspectives, or to catalyze action' (ibid.: 1). These are issues which those involved in creating exhibitions about difficult histories are increasingly aware, resulting in expanding numbers of thoughtful and effective exhibitions. While there are undoubtedly potential pitfalls involved in the display of such histories, it is also clear that they are capable not just of maintaining memory of terrible events of the past but also of helping foster constructive ethical reflection and even of helping forge more positive relationships among those whose forbears were very differently positioned within dreadful pasts.

Reflecting upon the past

While the move towards greater display of difficult histories has various motivations, including national performance of willingness to be self-critical, it is also clear from the popularity of such sites and their increasing numbers that there is a public hunger for the display of this kind of history. Certainly, visits are often made from a sense of 'duty', that this is something that one *should* do. But that should not be interpreted to mean that visitors are only going to sites of difficult heritage out of conformity to a social expectation. It is, rather, a duty with which they agree; something that they feel morally compelled to undertake. In my visitor research at the former Nazi Party rally grounds in Nuremberg, I discussed this in part as a 'talismanic activity' of 'moral witnessing' (Macdonald 2009: Chapter 8). Making a visit entails effort – as the idea of duty partly conveys – and, as such, also shows a commitment to engage with a particular past: it is a contemporary moralized witnessing of that history. In the case of difficult and troubling histories, a key idea, as articulated by the visitors with whom I spoke, is that these histories are important to remember to help prevent the same happening again in the future. By performing their own duty and making the effort to visit they see themselves as making a small contribution to ensuring 'never again'.

In addition, however, my research with visitors in Nuremberg also made clear how visiting difficult heritage was an opportunity to engage in ethical reflection. As I put it in my summary of how visitors themselves discussed their visits:

> A good deal of this [i.e. visitors'] talk, even among those visiting for leisure, was morally inflected ... Difficult heritage prompts such ethical reflection. And this ... is what draws people to make educational visits to such sites. It provides an opportunity not only to learn about the particular histories that such places present but also to engage in broader moral consideration and self-positioning. Many interviewees did this spontaneously, without any prompting from me; and some commented on how they had already been discussing such matters among themselves. While all acknowledged that there were other information sources about the same topics, they regarded coming to an actual site – 'the place where history happened' – to nevertheless be distinctive and more effective in helping them 'grasp' it.
>
> (Macdonald 2009: 184)

What such reflection entailed in specific terms was visitors discussing questions such as the following: What might have compelled people to participate in rallies? Could such participants have seen signs of what was going on more widely? Should we always be wary of personality cults and ideological use of spectacle? Or visitors might reflect on issues of everyday life or other institutions such as the churches, asking about whether people could have known more about what was happening at the time, about ways in which individuals might 'look the other way' or how they might use the context to better their own situation. In doing so, visitors drew variously upon what they had directly encountered in the exhibition and at the site, and also upon knowledge from elsewhere, including their own families. In addition, they made connections with other histories and contemporary political events. These not only included comments about the dangers of neo-Nazism in Germany and elsewhere in Europe but also, for example, the politics of the Middle East, including Israel, or racial politics in the USA, including the legacy of slavery.

There is no reason to think that such ethical reflection would only happen at this particular site. Rather, as I have suggested, it seems likely to be a key feature of visits to sites of contentious and difficult histories, though one that is enabled or muted to a greater or lesser extent by the emotional as well as cognitive communication of the exhibition that visitors encounter.

Conclusion

The growth of numbers of representations of contentious, difficult and negative self-histories stems from a range of different impetuses and has been prompted by actions from various groups and institutions within societies. While not all representations of such histories are intended to prompt ethical reflection, there has been a clear rise in numbers and kinds of those that do so. The fact that these are attended by large numbers of members of the public shows a commitment to engaging with these pasts in forms of moral witnessing and symbolic attempts to help prevent the same happening in future.

It is also worth pointing out here that contemporary engagement with contentious and difficult pasts can help in reconciliation between those differently positioned in such histories (Lehrer 2010). As has been argued for political apologies, an important feature of these is the public and political act of recognition (Blustein 2014). Museums and exhibitions about contentious histories can also perform this role where a nation or other collective is owning up to the crimes that it committed; that is, acknowledging its own difficult heritage. But this can also potentially be the basis for greater reconciliation by bringing groups set at odds by history into contact and dialogue today. This has been part of the experience in Germany with German–Jewish dialogue opened up through activities centred upon such sites and sometimes the involvement of Jewish groups in creating these (Feldman and Peleikis 2014). It can also be seen in relation to Indigenous groups in initiatives such as exhibitions about Inuit residential schools in Canada (Iglioliorte 2011) or about the experience of 'the Stolen Generation' of Aboriginal children in Australia (Szekeres 2011). Many ethnographic museums are also investigating the contentious and difficult histories of their collections – especially but not only legacies of colonialism – to open them up for collaboration with peoples who identify with those from which they came, perhaps leading to restitution or collaborative digital or exhibitionary projects (see Coombes and Phillips 2015, especially Part II, for example; and Krmpotich and Peers 2013, for an extended case).

None of this is to say that contentious histories and difficult heritage necessarily are always used in positive ways, and neither that their display will not continue to raise difficult challenges for curators and others involved in their exhibition. Understanding how particular forms of display work emotionally, for example, remains under-researched. What we see overall, however, is evidence of more and more exhibitions that are both willing to tackle contentious pasts and negative self-histories and to explore ways to do so that can help prompt ethical reflection and even help to promote constructive forms of dialogue and engagement between those whom the past put into contention.

Notes

1 See also the analysis by Kirk Denton (2014), who shows how this was much less the case prior to the 2007 expansion and refurbishment.
2 See the French Ministry of Culture's dedicated website on the subject, at: www.culture. fr/eng/Actualites/Portrait-Dossier/La-Collaboration-1940–1945-a-travers-les-archives (accessed 7 December 2015).

References

Blustein, Jeffrey M., 2014. *Forgiveness and Remembrance: Remembering Wrongdoing in Personal and Public Life.* Oxford: Oxford University Press.
Coombes, Annie E. and Phillips, Ruth B. (eds), 2015. *Museum Transformations.* New York: Wiley-Blackwell.
Denton, Kirk, 2014. *Exhibiting the Past: Historical Memory and the Politics of Museums in Post-socialist China.* Honolulu, HI: University of Hawai'i Press.
Feldman, Jackie and Peleikis, Anja, 2014. 'Performing the hyphen: Engaging German-Jewishness at the Jewish Museum in Berlin'. *Anthropological Journal of European Cultures,* 23 (2): 41–59.
Iglioliorte, Heather, 2011. '"We were so far away": Exhibiting Inuit oral histories of residential schools', in Erica Lehrer, Cynthia E. Milton and Monica Eileen Patterson (eds), *Curating Difficult Knowledge: Violent Pasts in Public Places.* Houndmills, Basingstoke: Palgrave Macmillan, pp. 23–40.
Krmpotich, Cara and Peers, Laura, 2013. 'This is our life: Haida'. *Material Heritage and Changing Museum Practice,* 5. Vancouver: University of British Columbia Press.
Lagrou, Pieter, 2007. *The Legacy of the Nazi Occupation: Patriotic Memory and National Recovery in Western Europe, 1946–1965.* Cambridge: Cambridge University Press.
Lehrer, Erica, 2010. 'Can there be a conciliatory heritage?' *International Journal for Heritage Studies,* 16 (4–5): 269–88.
Lehrer, Erica and Milton, Cynthia E., 2011. 'Introduction: Witnesses to witnessing', in Erica Lehrer, Cynthia E. Milton and Monica Eileen Patterson (eds), *Curating Difficult Knowledge: Violent Pasts in Public Places.* Houndmills, Basingstoke: Palgrave Macmillan, pp. 1–19.
Lennon, John and Foley, Malcolm, 2000. *Dark Tourism: The Attraction of Death and Disaster.* London: Continuum.
Levy, Daniel and Sznaider, Natan, 2002. 'Memory unbound: The Holocaust and the formation of cosmopolitan memory'. *European Journal of Social Theory,* 5 (1): 87–106.
Macdonald, Sharon, 2009. *Difficult Heritage: Negotiating the Nazi Past in Nuremberg and Beyond.* London: Routledge.
Macdonald, Sharon, 2016. 'Is "Difficult heritage" still difficult? Why public acknowledgement of past perpetration may no longer be so unsettling to collective identities'. *Museum International: Museums Managing the Tensions of Change,* 67 265–268, pp. 6–22
Pearce, C., 2010. 'The role of German perpetrator Sites in Teaching and Confronting the Nazi past', in *Memorialization in Germany Since 1945.* Houndmills, Basingstoke: Palgrave Macmillan, pp. 168–77.
Rowlands, Michael, 1999. 'Remembering to forget: Sublimation as sacrifice in war memorials', in *The Art of Forgetting.* Oxford: Berg, pp. 129–46.
Simon, Roger J., Rosenberg, Sharon and Eppert, Claudia (eds), 2000. *Between Hope and Despair: Pedagogy and the Remembrance of Historical Trauma.* Lanham, MD: Rowman & Littlefield.

Staas, Christian, 2010. 'Was geht mich das noch an?' *Zeit Magazin*, 4 November 2010, at: www.zeit.de/2010/45/Erinnern-NS-Zeit-Jugendliche (accessed 7 December 2015).

Szekeres, Vivienne, 2011. 'The past is a dangerous place: The museum as a safe haven', in Erica Lehrer, Cynthia E. Milton and Monica Eileen Patterson (eds), *Violent Pasts in Public Places: Curating Difficult Knowledge*. Houndmills, Basingstoke: Palgrave Macmillan, pp. 41–54.

Walsh, Kevin, 2001. 'Collective amnesia and the mediation of painful pasts: The representation of France in the Second World War'. *International Journal of Heritage Studies*, 7 (1): 83–98.

Welzer, Harald, 2008. 'Collateral damage of history education: National socialism and the holocaust in German family memory'. *Social Research*, 75 (1): 287–314.

26

NATIVE AMERICA IN THE TWENTY-FIRST CENTURY

Journeys in cultural governance and museum interpretation

W. Richard West, Jr.

This essay overviews the subject of 'good Native cultural governance' and what it meant in law and ethical standards of practice at two institutions that have occupied a considerable part of my life in museums. The first institution reviewed is the National Museum of the American Indian (NMAI), one of the more recent components of the Smithsonian Institution in Washington, when I had the honour to be Founding Director (1990–2007). The second institution discussed enables significant comparisons through my current concerns as a museum director at the Autry Museum of the American West (Autry Museum) in Los Angeles. Finally, I will expand on a comparison of these two institutions to reflect on why 'good Native governance' in the cultural area has such deeper and wider implications for what museums are and may accomplish in the twenty-first century.

The theme of 'good Native governance' in the cultural area, notably how concepts of Native cultural governance intersect with contemporary museum policy and practice, has great resonance with my personal history. Overviewing the past century, because of the amount of Native cultural patrimony that sits in museums, I can think of no set of cultural institutions that has had more impact on Native communities. Similarly, museums' progressive responses to Native cultural patrimony have had far-reaching ripple effects, in broader philosophical and practical terms, on museums, their Native collections and the development of appropriate protocols surrounding them. I want to focus on this change-making, even transformational development of the past generation that so deeply affected museums and Native America directly, and that has everything to do with the theme of changing museum standards and ethical considerations in the complex cultural worlds for museums in their continued mission of care for heritage.

Turning first to the NMAI, created by the United States Congress in 1989: In cultural origin and intellectual spirit, it was a potent adjunct of the transformative phenomenon of multicultural change that occurred in the United States in the late

1980s and early 1990s. In the museum community, this cultural movement frequently assumed the institutional form of the 'ethnic-specific museum' – and thus
was born the NMAI. By stated mission, board policy and programmatic design, its
intentions were explicit from its beginnings: the cultural authenticity and knowledge authority of Native peoples were to be encouraged, respected and empowered. My framework for explaining how that aspiration was achieved is guided by
the inspirational spirit, piercing intellect and abundant wisdom of my first mentor
at the Smithsonian, Secretary Robert McCormick Adams, the head of the Institution and a distinguished anthropologist. In describing the NMAI, he declared the
following:

> This is a national museum ... [that] takes the permanence ... the authenticity
> ... the vitality and the self-determination of Native American voices ... as
> the fundamental reality ... it must ... represent... [W]e move decisively
> from the older image of the museum as a temple with its superior, self-
> governing priesthood to ... a forum ... committed not to the promulgation
> of received wisdom but to the encouragement of a multi-cultural dialogue.
>
> *Robert Adams*

In the ensuing years, while the NMAI, to employ a metaphor, was banging on the
door of conventional museum curation to grant entrance to Native viewpoint and
voice, several substantial and significant consequences resulted. From the standpoint of the interpretive and representational voice of Native peoples, *collections*
were important, but only part of the story. Collections were considered most valuable by Native peoples as cultural keys and cues to themselves and to the communities in which both objects and peoples lived, past and present. Accordingly,
the NMAI rapidly became in substance far more like a 'cultural centre' on the
National Mall than a 'palace of collectibles'.

'Cultural centres' by definition are very different places from traditional museums.
They are not simply one-time, single-purpose or solely cultural destinations; let
alone cabinets of curiosity for the presentation of collections of material culture.
They are broader places and wider spaces, where the institution can connect with
external interests that relate to the subject of the cultural centre in diverse ways. In
other instances, external interests may use the centre's physical and intellectual
space as a gathering place for addressing matters of import and relevance to the
community that are unrelated to the specific aims of the cultural institution. In
these instances, the cultural centre is an instrument and catalysing adjunct of the
communities – a 'community centre', however the adjective 'community' may be
defined – for engagement, conversation, debate, even controversy; but always, as
the late distinguished American museologist Stephen Weil emphasized, a 'safe place
for unsafe ideas'.

To understand the NMAI's development more broadly, reference to two crucial
pieces of legislation enacted by the United States Congress is necessary: the repatriation provisions contained in the National Museum of the American Indian Act

(NMAI Act) of 1989, and the Native American Graves Protection and Repatriation Act (NAGPRA) of 1990. The critical provisions of these two pieces of legislation can be summarized together because of their legal convergence. The Acts cover the following categories of objects and patrimony: human remains; associated and unassociated funerary materials; and sacred and ceremonial objects and cultural patrimony. Both Acts mandate the return of objects in these categories to culturally affiliated contemporary Native communities if the materials – apart from human remains and funerary objects – are essential to the conduct of contemporary life and ceremonial practice. The applicant Native community bears the burden of proof, which is a preponderance of the evidence.

The precise statutory definitions for key terms in the legislation are not extensive. Thus, the interpretation of provisions regarding what constitutes satisfaction of the burden of proof – definitions of 'culturally affiliated communities', the meaning of 'sacred' and 'ceremonial' for purposes of repatriation – remain matters of the further evolution of a 'common law' of repatriation. It is a work in progress, and each case tends to be taken up on an *ad hoc* basis within broad statutory parameters. This approach is not only statutorily prescribed but also perhaps inevitable, given the broad diversity in cultural practices among Native communities throughout the United States.

Both these external influences provided federal legislation of very real potency – they had immense impact on all museums holding Native cultural patrimony in the United States, including the NMAI. While the NMAI Act applied only to the Smithsonian Institution and its Native collections of human remains, NAGPRA by contrast, covered virtually all American museums and included collections of Native human remains, sacred objects and cultural patrimony. In particular, NAGPRA covered institutions such as the Autry Museum, which now holds the legendary collections of the former Southwest Museum of the American Indian.

In moral and practical terms, the tangibles of the repatriation legislation were seminal and substantial. They provided legal requirements that define and drive repatriation in museums with respect to Native objects. The return of human remains and funerary materials was nothing less than the confirmation of a moral imperative that corrected vast wrongs committed during the nineteenth century when the US military's battlefield sweeps sent the remains of thousands of Native ancestors to Washington, DC for 'cranial studies'. This moral imperative for remediating the injustices of history had obvious and profound ethical implications for museum standards and practices for the museum community in all its forms.

In addition, the return of sacred objects and cultural patrimony had everything to do, as a practical matter, with securing the cultural future of contemporary Native communities throughout the United States. The congressional determination, explicit in the legislative history, was that these kinds of cultural materials should never have been in a museum in the first instance. Instead, they should be returned to communities in order to sustain and, in some cases, to revive sacred and ceremonial practices.

But perhaps, in the end and of equal importance, the acts also contained 'intangibles', beyond their tangible substantive provisions, that possessed true cultural potency for future relationships between museums and Native America. These 'intangibles' preceded the internationally authoritative recognition provided more than a decade later in the UNESCO Convention for the Safeguarding of the Intangible Cultural Heritage (2003). And they might not have been perfectly understood at the time by most parties, including Native communities. The implicit message, however, was that the NMAI Act and NAGPRA forever changed the fundamental power relationships between museums and contemporary Native communities.

My point is not limited to the return of Native material and objects – important as that provision is. I always considered that requirement only the tip of the iceberg, which actually sometimes concealed below the waterline an even larger revolution in philosophy and practice for the museum community. Specifically, the definitions in the museum world of terms like 'authority', 'authenticity' and 'expertise' – questions such as 'who has knowledge and cultural authority?', 'how do museums define "interpretive expertise"?', 'who are the "experts" entitled to sit at the table of museum interpretation?' – were profoundly altered in the United States by the legislative provisions in both Acts.

So what effect did the legislation have on museum best practices and operating protocols? First, and most obviously, the legislation motivated and ultimately required museums to return tens of thousands of objects to Native communities – encompassing all the categories of objects and materials specified in the NMAI Act and NAGPRA. This provision inevitably aroused the museum community's fears of awaiting eighteen-wheel trucks that were going to demolish their collections.

I can affirmatively and emphatically state, however, that, based upon a full quarter-century of experience, these fears turned out to be completely unjustified. The NMAI, during my tenure as director, repatriated thousands of objects to federal- and state-recognized Native communities in the United States and, in addition, to First Nations in Canada and Indigenous communities in Latin America, which we were not legally required to do. I was asked routinely in the early years how the NMAI was able to survive as a museum when our collections either were being – or were at risk of being – 'gutted' by repatriation. But I kept the numbers, and my response went something like this: 'Well, we have repatriated at this point approximately 20,000 objects, and that reduction leaves us with about 980,000 still in the collection for developing exhibits and public programming – I think it is sufficient to serve the public quite satisfactorily'. At the Autry, the results were no different. The inquiring minds who needed to know finally quit asking the question – it became more than a little gratuitous.

My second broad point here is the following, and it sat at the centre of Secretary Adams' earlier quotation about the NMAI's founding vision – and is an implied message that comes from the repatriation legislation. Native peoples and communities possess legitimate and undeniable 'authority' concerning the meaning and interpretation of their objects and cultural patrimony. As stated above, by stated mission, board policy and programmatic design, the intentions of the NMAI were explicit from the beginning – the cultural authenticity and knowledge authority of Native peoples were to be encouraged, respected and empowered in the first-person voice through NMAI exhibits and public programming.

In addition, the NMAI also explored and acted upon linkages between certain international legal conventions and international standards documents and the practices of the NMAI with respect to Native cultural governance. Two such international connections merit mention here. The 1995 UNIDROIT Convention[1] – in contrast to the 1970 UNESCO Convention a quarter-century earlier – explicitly introduces a rather telling cultural precept in its Article 3. It contains a specific reference, for the first time in such international legal structures, to an undeniably non-Western cultural context: the application of a liberal statute of limitations to claims for the 'restitution of a sacred or communally important object belonging to and used by a tribal or indigenous community in a Contracting State as part of the community's traditional or ritual use'. The importance of this reference is that, alongside the usual regulation of cultural property movements between nation states, it introduces what can only be described as a compelling 'cultural' recognition, rather than more purely national or political consideration.

A second international connection for changing standards for Native cultural governance sits within the Code of Ethics of the International Council of Museums (ICOM). In the context of museum practices rather than the requirements of international legal conventions, ICOM's Code (ICOM 2004)[2] points in the same direction as the UNIDROIT Convention. With respect to the acquisition of collections, Section 2.5 of ICOM's Code, addressing 'Culturally Sensitive Material', states the following sanctions for museums' conduct:

> Collections of human remains and material of sacred significance should be acquired only if they can be housed securely and cared for respectfully. This must be accomplished in a manner consistent with professional standards and *the interests and beliefs of members of the community, ethnic or religious groups from which the objects originated, where these are known.* [Emphasis added.]

Sections 3.7 and 4.3 of the ICOM Code contain identical provisions relating, respectively, to research and to the exhibition of 'sensitive' materials or 'materials of sacred significance'.

Reviewing these provisions merited an interweaving of American federal repatriation legislation, the UNESCO and UNIDROIT conventions, and ICOM's Code of Ethics for Museums to distil them into a bottom-line legal and ethical 'wholeness' that had much to do with Native cultural governance at the NMAI. The 1989 and 1990 Acts in the United States represented a massive shift and rebalancing of the relationships between American museums and Native communities, founded, as so many Native museum collections were, on the colonial acts associated with perhaps the most shameful chapter in American history – the subjugation and attempted forced assimilation if not annihilation of Native peoples in the United States.

I wish to emphasize here that, quite apart from these legal and ethical externalities, the National Museum of the American Indian, as a matter of its own self-generated policies and practices, 'stepped up', with imagination and consistency, to affirm good Native cultural governance in concrete ways that fundamentally affected institutional organization, operations and programming. Accordingly, the NMAI established an office of repatriation, and adopted repatriation policies, prior to NAGPRA even being made applicable to the Smithsonian Institution. The Board of Trustees additionally enacted public programming guidelines that required close collaboration with Native communities and the use of their first-person voice in exhibitions. Institutional research and publications policies were adopted that required consultation with constituent Native communities where sensitive objects in the collections of the NMAI, and their use by researchers or in publications, were involved.

Let me turn now to the Autry Museum. Through a merger that occurred more than a decade ago, the Autry Museum, as indicated, is the present steward of the collections of the Southwest Museum of the American Indian, founded a century ago in Los Angeles. That Native collection is of the same rank as the NMAI, and though smaller quantitatively, is qualitatively outstanding, and in some areas perhaps even better than that of NMAI – a truth I conceded even while at the Smithsonian.

The Autry Museum is an institution that intends to generate learning and create understanding for its audiences of the vast breadth and depth of the American West. Its Mission Statement is '[T]o tell all the stories of the American West'. That beguilingly simple declarative sentence masks genuine complexity in a museum that seeks to interpret a very culturally diverse part of the United States that, more than any other, has had a substantial and enduring impact on the politics, economics and culture of an entire nation.

My purpose in discussing the Autry Museum is twofold. First, I wish to use it as a second case study (following that of the NMAI) to emphasize the breadth and depth of the new axioms of Native cultural governance in museums, many of which were given added impetus in the 1990s by the sheer magnitude of the NMAI as a new type of cultural project – and, candidly, the very name of the place where it sat: the Smithsonian Institution. Second, I want to be sure that the NMAI – or at least I as its Founding Director – do[es] not claim credit for anything and everything that has happened in the past quarter-century with respect to the progress of Native cultural governance in the museum community in the United States.

What I would like to illuminate about this second institutional setting for my work on Native cultural governance comes from answering a question that flows so naturally from the very success of the NMAI, described above, but a question now focused upon the Autry, on the opposite side of continental America. This question has the following shape: In interpreting and representing the cultural history and experience of the American West, what is the impact for museums of *already having multiple authoritative voices* at the table of conversation, discussion and debate? I believe that the results of these multiple presences are profound, as well as enlarging, enlivening and enriching for museums, for a variety of reasons.

The Autry Museum had always intrigued me because I saw it, in potentially transformational ways, as the next step: a 'third wave' to follow the NMAI's first two steps as a colonial institution when it was the old Heye Foundation Museum of the American Indian in New York, and then as an anti-colonial museum of cultural history and experience when it became the NMAI. As an ethnic-specific museum, the NMAI remains a supreme exemplar of the 'categorical' or 'vertical' cultural institution that grew up in the late-twentieth century as diverse cultural communities – Native, African American, Latino/Latina, Japanese American and others in the United States – made their way and on their own terms into museums. I believed that an institution like the Autry, however, was in fact the next logical step in this progression that began with ethnic-specific institutions. Why? Because the Autry is by contrast a 'horizontal' rather than 'vertical' model of cultural interpretation and representation. In a certain respect, it *assumes* – even though it is still a work in progress – the established presence of diverse and authoritative cultural voices at the table of interpretation, which the NMAI and other institutions like it had striven to achieve, and frequently with great success.

The Autry Museum's mission, as previously stated, is to tell not one, but 'all the stories of the American West'. That aspiration requires that the Autry attempt the complex, often nuanced and subtle task of weaving, indeed 'interweaving', these stories together by analysing and interpreting the points of engagement – sometimes harmonious and quite often not, but always important – that make up the cultural history and experience of the American West. In other words, the institution's purpose is, in an important and defining sense, 'intercultural' rather than 'multicultural'.

And why was this evolution so important as a matter of museum mission and practice at the Autry Museum? I believed it to be so for any of several reasons. First, culture interpreted in this way addresses the subject in the manner it was actually lived. We Native peoples believe correctly that we were here first among those communities constituting the cultural pluralism that is America. But the fact is that we have all lived together for the better part of five centuries – not culturally separate, but instead with full bore interactivity, both positive and negative, for the entire period. Second, using this interpretive approach to cultural history allows museum learning to reach what I believe are often the defining 'interstices' – a tricky polysyllable that simply means the 'in-between' areas – of cultural history. In those 'interstitial' areas of cultural history and associated human engagements sit multiple insights and 'truths' that not only are generally worth knowing, but more specifically, inform museum audiences far more fully and accurately about the past, present and future, the why and the whence of culture and the arts in the United States as a whole.

Repatriation also has a long history at the Autry Museum in its consolidated form with the Southwest Museum of the American Indian. Even before the enactment of the 1990 NAGPRA, the old Southwest Museum, in the 1980s, had repatriated as sacred objects a Hopi altarpiece and two Zuni war gods. Before its merger with the Autry Museum but after NAGPRA's enactment, it returned a third Zuni war god, three ancestors and a cultural item. Following the merger of the two museums more than a decade ago, the pace of repatriation quickened considerably. Since the merger, seventy-one sacred objects, forty-one ancestors, and 6,569 funerary objects have been repatriated directly and indirectly by the Autry.

The repatriations to Native community recipients are numerous, cover all categories – human remains, sacred objects and cultural patrimony – and stretch across much of Indian Country, including, among others, the San Manuel Band of Mission Indians in California, the San Carlos Apache Tribe in Arizona, the Sac and Fox Nation in Missouri and Kansas, the Kickapoo Tribe in Kansas, and the Hopi, Zuni and Acoma Pueblo communities in New Mexico and Arizona. In addition, although not required under NAGPRA to do so, ancestors and funerary items have been returned to the Tongva, a non-federally recognized tribe in the more immediate Los Angeles area. Meanwhile the Autry Museum currently has active pending repatriation claims involving the Great Basin Inter-Tribal NAGPRA Coalition, the Hoonah Indian Association in Alaska, the Central Council of Tlingit and Haida Indian Tribes of Alaska, and the Smith River Rancheria in California. The applications cover ancestors, funerary materials, sacred items and cultural patrimony.

In addition to these repatriations, the Autry has completed the process for other Native communities to benefit similarly – but, upon the tribe's request, still retains the materials. In most instances, the respective community is not yet ready to receive the objects because it does not yet have the resources to bring them home, or for other cultural reasons is not yet prepared to receive them. Communities falling into this category include the Seneca-Cayuga Tribe of Oklahoma, the Tonawanda Band of Seneca Indians of New York, and two different Paiute Tribes. Meanwhile at the Autry, as was the case with the NMAI, the repatriation legislation was a marker for wider-ranging changes with respect to good Native cultural governance and museum interpretation. The Autry begins with an inherently broad-gauge and inclusive Mission Statement indicated above – namely, to 'tell all the stories of the American West'. It also has vast collections at its disposal – some 500,000 to 600,000 objects – to match this breadth of mission.

As exemplar of how the Autry ties all of the foregoing together, let me cite as example the recent re-invention of the institution's art galleries in a core exhibit titled *Art of the West*. It opened in 2013, within months of my arrival at the Autry. Its authenticity as a genuinely intercultural approach to interpretation is evident in its departures from conventional canons of Western art history – in other words, in what it does and does not do. It does not focus on a singular category of objects or on a particular medium. Chronology has no place in any part of the exhibition, and it mixes present and past throughout. It makes no distinctions and uses no conventional Western art history hierarchies as divides among 'craft', 'low art' or 'high art'. What it does do, however, is equally affirming of important intercultural departures from Western art history norms in museum representation. Its interpretive schema is based entirely on themes – 'Religion and Ritual', 'Land and Landscape' and 'Migration and Movement' to be specific – themes relevant to all communities of art and culture in the American West. In using objects from across the deep and diverse art and cultural collections of the Autry Museum, the exhibit includes paintings, sculpture, pop art, decorative art, baskets, ceramic pots, glass art and textiles – and even a legendary Indian Chief motorcycle.

The exhibit invokes Native voice, in the first person, directly. Preston Singletary, a gifted Native contemporary glass artist, addresses visitors in holographic form in the gallery, describing what is meant culturally by his aesthetically compelling Northwest Coast 'bentwood box of glass' and the ceremonial rattle he carved that is located nearby – both of which objects sit beside equally beautiful and similar historical pieces. In Preston's words, the cultural message embedded in his art is all about cultural continuance and 'survivance', a circular hoop of cultural life and being that has only cycles with no end.

In addition to Preston's voice, the Autry Museum's curatorial interpretation in *Art of the West* represents a very compatible collaborator. As already mentioned, the exhibit is organized around themes rather than, as might be dictated by more conventional divisions of art history, chronology or categories of material or media – an approach far more consistent with Native notions of time, material culture and art. In addition, the hierarchies that have defined art in the Western world since the Renaissance are rather conspicuously absent. Brilliant pieces of basket-weaving and ceramics sit happily and meaningfully, in equality as both art and cultural material, beside two- and three-dimensional 'fine art' in the form of paintings and sculpture.

More specific examples are useful to illustrate how interpretation in *Art of the West* occurs on the ground. The first illustration appears in the 'Religion and Ritual' section of the exhibit, where the intention was to show the emergence of religious imagery in colonial New Spain, and its role in disseminating that imagery and its associated ideals. Alonso Cano's *St. Sebastian*, a seventeenth-century martyrdom painting, represents this ideal in pure and straightforward form. Responding interculturally, the contemporary artist Paul Pletka's 2008 *Tears of the Lord* shows the adaptation and appropriation of religious imagery, especially the Aztec cross and the crucifixion that are the visual centrepiece of the painting. They are powerful images that morph and take on newer, more local and empowering associations in the hands of regional and contemporary artists. But the Pletka painting reaches beyond a purely art historical framework as it gathers in broader cultural import and nuanced meaning. It well embodies a sense of cultural interactions across time and history in its portrayal of Indigenous – and pagan – Mexican masks alongside contemporary Western dress and the Aztec cross. In the indifferent response of the Indigenous dancers in Western dress at the foot of the Aztec cross to the religious vision in their midst, a sense of ambivalence, indeed tension, created by the imposition of one religion and cultural system on another, is also apparent – an ambivalence that began centuries ago and persists to this day in Native art, life and culture throughout the Americas.

A second illustration is merited, this time from the 'Land and Landscape' thematic area of *Art of the West*. These assembled objects include a classic panoramic photograph, *Dana Point*; a painting by a non-Native artist titled *Illinois Flatscape*; a

Navajo artist's painting titled *Canyon Lake III*; a Navajo weaver's contemporary weaving of a mesa landscape; and a quilt created by a member of the Hmong community in Los Angeles. These multilayered art objects speak directly, from an art historical standpoint, to the many ways that land and space may be organized within a two-dimensional surface, and how they also vary: from the photographic panorama, the non-Native artist's aerial view of landscape with its highly articulated and geometrically organized fields, roads and man-made structures; the Navajo artist's almost complete abstraction of landscape with an intensity of purely organic line and form; and the Hmong artist's narrative quilt that tells the story of a tragic and harrowing escape from war in Southeast Asia to comparative safety in Los Angeles.

A further insight, however, is far more profoundly cultural: namely, how different cultures – in this case, Native, Anglo and Southeast Asian – use contrasting methods to convey insights about the cultural community's relationship to and experience of the land itself. In short, these art objects, in addition to their dazzling aesthetic qualities, carry substantial cultural comparatives and messaging that tell us much about the abiding complexity and subtle differences in intercultural experience through time of the American West.

From my experience as the director of the NMAI and the Autry Museum, the following is what I would offer as a distillation of the impact of the past generation on 'good Native cultural governance' and museum practice. First, we have learned through the process of repatriation that certain museum practices of the past, while perhaps at least arguably defensible as a matter of Western science, are nevertheless indefensible in human, and humanistic, moral and ethical terms – that Native human remains do not belong in museum collections, nor do objects of a sacred and ceremonial nature that are essential to contemporary descendant Native communities for purposes of perpetuating Native cultures into the future.

Second, repatriation laws represented a seismic shift in museum paradigms and practice regarding 'authority' that reached far beyond the literal return of certain categories of objects from museums to Native communities. Repatriation implicitly contests that very Western notion of the 'universal museum', where art objects and cultural patrimony are assumed to transcend and leave behind their cultural connectivity to particular originating communities. It affirms the proposition that cultural authority, as a matter of the museum's social responsibility, may sometimes sit outside that institution, and in the hands of others not members of the priesthood in the temple on the hill.

Third, museums have learned another closely associated proposition concerning knowledge, and who has the authority and standing to create and speak it. The issue is not only whose stories are told in museums, but also who the storytellers are. Knowledge and truth may sit in unexpected places; and museums, correctly and steadily in the past generation, have opened the windows and permitted inclusivity rather than exclusivity, bilateralism rather than unilateralism, and outside in and bottom up rather than inside out and top down – all without an ounce of diminution in the quality of knowledge production.

I would hope that the significance of all the developments described, while focused mainly on Native cultural institutions, is evidence of a watershed in altered representation, narrative and more inclusive 'voicing' and experience of culture in the lives of museums, as they serve multiple communities and weave a broader fabric of social representation, human history and heritage. For so long, indeed the better part of a century and a half, museums could rightly be categorized as obstacles to or opponents of the legitimate connections, interrelationships and authorities of living Native communities and peoples, with the vast abundance of Native collections that still sit in these otherwise wonderful institutions called museums. As a museum director, I pray instead for our continued progress, inspired by the legal dictates and spirit of repatriation, toward the time that museums achieve, for Native America, the status of 'collaborators', 'supporters' and 'partners'.

Notes

1 The UNIDROIT *Convention on Stolen or Illegally Exported Cultural Objects* (adopted Rome, 1995) is the international treaty on the subject of cultural property protection from a private international law perspective – complementing the 1970 UNESCO Convention (UNESCO *Convention on the Means of Prohibiting and Preventing the Illicit Import, Export and Transfer of Ownership of Cultural Property*) which sits at its core. The UNIDROIT convention frames its objectives of reducing illegal traffic of cultural property by shifting the burden of proof of legitimacy of ownership to *purchasers or acquirers* of cultural property. In the case of the earlier 1970 UNESCO Convention, by contrast, a greater burden rests upon *claimants* of contested cultural property to demonstrate proof of illicit or illegal acquisition.
2 *ICOM Code of Ethics for Museums* (2004); Paris: International Council of Museums, 2006, at: http://icom.museum/fileadmin/user_upload/pdf/Codes/code_ethics2013_eng.pdf.

Reference

ICOM, 2006. *ICOM Code of Ethics for Museums* [2004]. Paris: International Council of Museums. The full text of the *ICOM Code of Ethics* for Museums is provided as *Appendix I* in the present publication. It is also available online for download from the ICOM website (with links to translations in French, Spanish, and many other languages). The English version is accessible at: http://icom.museum/professional-standards/code-of-ethics.

27

USING THE PAST TO FORGE A FUTURE

Challenges of uniting a nation against skeletal odds

Bongani Ndhlovu

After the 1994 election, the new government in South Africa focused on reconciliation, nation building and social cohesion in order to unite its different racial groups with the aim of achieving a non-racial society. Diversity was seen as the new nation's strength, and the motto adopted for a reshaped future, which, in the Khoisan language of the |Xam people, is *!ke e: |xarra ||ke*, which means '*diverse people unite*'. This crucially reorienting declaration of nationhood was enshrined in the new South Africa's national coat of arms.

To manifest South Africa's non-racial stance, a number of cultural projects were hosted under the auspices of the then Department of Arts, Culture, Science and Technology. In sport, the country did well in 1995 by winning the Rugby World Cup, and the following year the South African soccer team won the Africa Nations' Cup. These hugely followed popular events were timely and helpful in uniting South Africans behind jubilant celebrations across racial divides. Both sporting victories proved that the country was living its Khoisan-inspired motto of diverse people united in pursuit of nation building and social cohesion.

It is against this background that the call to repatriate the remains of Sarah Baartman resonated strongly among many in South Africa, and thus the country rallied behind its president, Dr Nelson Mandela, in his move to persuade France to accede to this request. Sarah Baartman was a South African woman of Khoi extraction, who was subjected to grotesque displays and use of her as a 'freak show' performer in Britain and France during the nineteenth century. After her death in 1815, her remains were held as the subject of 'scientific research' and were displayed in the Musée de l'Homme in Paris.

The call for the return of Sarah Baartman's remains culminated in the realization that South Africa's own museums – including the Iziko South African Museum – had collected, researched, exhibited and stored in their own collection the remains of Khoisan people. In addition, the museum had 'illegally' acquired a number of other cultural items from Indigenous South Africans. Realization of these practices and their consequences was soon linked to the broader politics of colonial dispossession in South Africa's history. Museums' authority and ethical standards over the treatment of human remains were called into question, and museums were severely challenged for their history and practices, and for not giving Indigenous people the respect they deserve.

The genesis of collecting human remains in South Africa

Iziko Museums of South Africa, Cape Town, has approximately 788 human remains specimens in its collection. In South Africa, the unethical collection of human remains for 'research' purposes began at the beginning of the twentieth century. This was given special impetus by a conference held in the country by the British Association for the Advancement of Science (BAAS) in 1905. One of the most influential speakers was A.C.(Alfred Cort) Haddon,[1] who founded anthropology at Cambridge University. Haddon called for a systematic documentation of South African natives, especially Bushmen and Hottentots, to gather scientific and historical records of these societies before they became 'extinct' (Legassick and Rassool, 2000).

A.C. Haddon followed his conference argument with a separate letter to the South African Museum (now Iziko South African Museum) Board of Trustees. In this letter, he made clear even more strongly his 'evolutionary paradigm' based on the idea of the 'progress' of all races along a linear scale marked by European standards: Haddon called for urgent measures to be undertaken by the South African Museum to increase its ethnological collections and displays on this subject matter before the extinction of the Khoisan 'tradition'. Haddon's pleas, according to Martin Legassick and Ciraj Rassool, were the most likely stimulus behind the collection of human remains by the Museum and other South African museums at the beginning of the twentieth century (Legassick and Rassool, 2000).

In 1906, a year after Haddon's visit, the South African Museum reported on the installation of a number of exhibitions (permanent displays from its collection), including a display case exhibiting the skeleton of the 'Strand Loper' aboriginal. This was followed by display of a plaster-cast model of a San person, reported in 1907.[2]

Conquest, missionaries and trade in human remains

At the beginning of the twentieth century, the Iziko South African Museum (ISAM), assisted by the Cape government, literally began a 'hunt' for the 'specimens' of the Khoisan people.[3] Museum officials requested magistrates to assist in this quest to find living specimens of San and Khoi people. The Museum went as far as buying the skeletal remains of Khoisan people (Legassick and Rassool, 2000). This is a classic example of a partnership between a colonizing power and its implementing instruments working tirelessly for the extinction of a race – under the guise of preserving records in the name of a conquering 'scientific tradition'.

It can be argued that during this period, Indigenous African people, and Khoisan in particular, began to form an association in their minds between museums and the cruelty of the actions and policies they carried out. Khoisan's sacred places, such as graves, were 'raided'; bodies were exhumed and stolen; and the products of museums' scientific research were displayed in museums alongside animals. Khoisan and other Indigenous people were relegated to being accessories in 'cabinets' of fauna and flora collections (Legassick and Rassool, 2000). Museums themselves thereby became a symbol of the Khoisan 'extinction', and to a highly significant degree they represented the face and actions of the colonial administration.

The long-term impact of these negative associations was to have an enduring effect of division and tensions between museums and black South Africans. However, in the democratic South Africa of the end of the twentieth century, museums were now expected, as part of their mandate, to actively participate in nation building and social cohesion projects. Inevitably the question arose: How can museums become agents of social cohesion and new nation building, given the facts that some exhibited and undertook 'scientific' research that objectified and belittled the fundamental 'humanness' of many of South Africa's diverse peoples?

The above question can be rephrased for the Iziko South African Museum or Iziko Social History Collection as follows: How can the Museum utilize the past – and all the 'evidence' of its collecting activities – to mend the relations with the community it once viewed as an object of demeaning research?

The answer to this question is particularly relevant in South Africa, because institutions that were a symbol of oppression needed to change 'from their roots' to become transformed advocates for nation building. Iziko therefore needed to transform its history and legacy 'from within', and produce affirmative strategies for repatriating unethically collected human remains to the descendants of the Khoisan people, for reburial in a manner that could at last promote nation building and lay the groundwork for a more peaceful coexistence between the museum and the Khoisan.

In doing so, and in its effort to promote nation building and social cohesion, the Iziko Museum must ask itself whether it is necessary for it to produce a public narrative of how the museum acquired such a collection. And if the museum does this, wouldn't such a narrative again rekindle painful and divisive issues that were about to be healed or perhaps forgotten? How will such action affect the relations between the museum and the descendants of its twentieth-century 'hunting' expeditions? These questions point to a need for creation of a 'cushioning' or adaptive mechanism for both the museum and the affected communities themselves to assist their transition and reformation of new relationships. And there is a further question: Should the Iziko Museum involve religious communities in its attempts to return human remains to their rightful descendants?

There is a temptation to respond positively to the last question, partly because a section of the religious community – that is, missionaries – assisted the Museum to unethically collect human remains historically. During the colonial era, it was not unusual for missionaries, government and other colonial functionaries to form partnerships against Indigenous people in pursuit of their interconnected objectives.

In 1906, a Reverend Westphal indicated his willingness to assist the South African Museum to disturb the graves and unearth remains of San people in the Pniel station. It was indicated that the missionary had previously refused such requests from other parties, but he would not object to the South African Museum's request if it had government agreement. The missionary went as far as advising a museum official on how to acquire a skeleton of a living San whose death was imminent (Legassick and Rassool, 2000, p.8).

In the democratic South Africa, some churches – like the South African Museum itself – have been struggling to dissociate themselves from past history and the cruel activities perpetuated by their predecessors against Indigenous groups. Churches are now at pains to distance themselves from these activities – wholly recognized as *unethical* in museum codes of practice, such as the ICOM[4] – mainly to protect the image of the ethical and moral position with which churches wish themselves to be identified. The stark contradiction between the unethical practices of their predecessors and the moral stance churches seek in the democratic South Africa of today places many churches in a difficult position. However, it is essential for churches to own up to the actions of their predecessors, and to reach out to the communities that were victims of those actions, if the churches are to be part of the reconciliation processes necessary to their being effective stakeholders in a transformed future for South Africa. In doing so, they could well consider partnerships with Iziko in its own nation building and social cohesion initiatives.

However, the question has a further challenging consequence. At the beginning of the twentieth century, the Museum used religious leaders, notably missionaries, to gain access to buried skulls and skeletons of the Khoisan communities, whose fate fell within the decisions of churches and their control of certain property. Are churches willing to be seen by the communities they serve today as co-perpetrators of unethical activities conducted by the Museum in partnership with major religious organizations and other instruments of colonialism at the beginning of the twentieth century? And in the twenty-first century, would an attempt to reposition religious communities today be perceived as an attempt at coercion by religious leaders: of 'forcing' communities to accept the renewed legitimacy of an institution that contributed to near-extinction policies towards a whole race in the past?

In addressing the above concerns, one option is that the Iziko Museum (and churches) might broadly interact with a full cross-section of the religious community today. This would enable spiritual leaders from various religious affiliations to mediate between the Museum and the communities that now deserve to have their wrongfully removed human remains repatriated. Through such a process the Museum might be able to regain acceptance and legitimacy in the eyes of the communities it grossly humiliated through its unethical complicity in objectifying research and illicit rendition of human remains in the early twentieth century. Furthermore, such a remedial process may give the Museum itself opportunities to affirm its new position regarding human rights, and its commitment to the human dignity of all members of the South African nation today.

Severe questions may be posed to the descendants of the missionaries: Are they willing to subject the acts of some of their forebears to searching public scrutiny today? By admitting the 'sins' of their forebears in the presence of competing religions, does Christianity stand to lose some of its membership to other faiths, at a time when all current religious leaders and affiliations would like to see an increase in the number of their followers?

These questions may be difficult and uncomfortable for some members of the churches, and for museums in particular. However, such difficulty and discomfort cannot be given greater significance than the nation-building project itself. On the other hand, are South Africa's museums, including Iziko, ensuring they are in a stronger position to play a constructive role in the social cohesion project? This is the challenge that must be addressed by all South African museums today, and they must seriously develop and publish clear strategies and policies on how to appropriately handle difficult transitions (facing and repairing the damage of the past) and moving the reconstructive process of a more integrated nation forward.

Restitution, repatriation and re-interment

Iziko was the first museum in South Africa to develop a policy to address the issue of human remains. The policy is underpinned by a spirit of respect for the dignity of all human beings, past and present. By the terms of this policy, the Museum acknowledges that in the past, 'the acquisition of human remains was often motivated by racial theories that have since been discredited as having no scientific validity' (Iziko Museum, 2005). The remains were collected unethically and as such, they should be returned to descendant communities for reburial.

The Museum sees restitution of human remains to descendant communities as one of the crucial vehicles for achieving 'closure' (Barkan, 2009). The process will enable descendant communities to have peace in knowing that the remains of their relatives were finally laid to rest with dignity. This will be carried out by the Museum through its Advisory Committee, which comprises representatives from descendant communities, the South African Heritage Resources Agency, Iziko Museum and other stakeholders.

One of the most important responsibilities of the Advisory Committee is to recommend, to Iziko and most probably to the Ministry of Arts and Culture, the appropriate forms of memorialization to be carried out (Iziko Museum, 2005). This process will also give Iziko the closure it needs on its past history, and allow it to reorient its future as one of the most influential museums in South Africa. Furthermore, it will enable the Museum to participate actively and with a clear conscience in nation-building processes thereafter, knowing that it has finally addressed the inescapable burden of unethically collected human remains through an inclusive consultative and remediation process.

Conclusion

It can be concluded that it is possible to align the Iziko Museum's past practices with current social cohesion and nation-building goals, and that it will finally have dealt with the scarred legacy of its own early history: of having studied the 'other' in order to prove a racial theory that has since been discredited; and of remediating the effects of its early research and displays that grossly violated the rights of Indigenous Khoisan people.

In modern day South Africa, the positions are reversed: the 'others' are now 'studying' the atrocities committed by the museum against their forebears, and they examine the extent to which racism was institutionalized. It is not satisfactory for museums today to argue that in the past they were influenced by government policies of the time, and that therefore it is governments that should be held responsible for the policies of their predecessors. Museums were manifestly accessories to government policies and social attitudes in the past, and those legacies can be removed today only by affirmative action in the present.

The post-1994 government of South Africa has clearly condemned inhumane practices conducted by any groups, institutions or organizations within the country's history, and has called upon South Africans today to work together for a better national future in which all social and racial constituencies have a shared future. In doing so, the government has requested all parties, including museums, to play a positive role in nation building.

Reconciliation is not an option but a necessity in today's South Africa. In the spirit of nation building and human dignity the museum – as a key social institution in modern nations – cannot forego the opportunity to reconcile with the 'other', no matter how challenging and painful the process may be. Furthermore, it is essential that the museum should become a public space for active engagements about human rights issues, and should use its experiences and considerable resources to address important challenges faced by the country today. The Iziko Museum can at least claim that it has taken a first positive step to address its difficult heritage – and this, if properly carried through, will not hamper the realization of social cohesion and nation building but can only strengthen its case ultimately as a crucial place of history and collective memory.

Notes

1 Alfred Cort Haddon (1855–1940) was an anthropologist and ethnologist who founded anthropology at the University of Cambridge. He gained fame especially for his expeditions to the Torres Strait off the north Australian coast in 1888 and 1898, and subsequent research papers and books published on Torres Strait Islander people, languages, social systems and culture, based on fieldwork and the collections he made – which were later consolidated in the British Museum and (in greater part) the Museum of Archaeology and Anthropology at the University of Cambridge. [Ed.]

2 *Report of the South African Museum*, Cape Town, 1906, p. 33; see also *Report of the South African Museum*, Cape Town, 1907, p. 21. For a discussion of the role of BAAS and its impact in influencing scientific research, Sillitoe, 2011.

3 The practice of 'hunting' human remains was well established conceptually in Europe – see Sysling, 2010.

4 The full text of the *ICOM Code of Ethics for Museums* is provided as *Appendix I* to this volume; and is also available online for download at: http://icom.museum/professional-standards/code-of-ethics.

References

Barkan, E., 2009. 'Making Amends: A New International Morality?'. In: Lyndel V. Prott, ed., *Witnesses to History: A Compendium of Documents and Writings on the Return of Cultural Objects*. Paris: UNESCO, pp. 78–94.

Iziko Museum, 2005 [online]. *Policy on the Management of Human Remains in Iziko Collections, Approved by Iziko Council on 29 September, 2005*. Available at: http://iziko.org.za/PDF/05_Iziko_SA%20Human%20Remains%20Policy.pdf [accessed 3 May 2016].

Legassick, M. and Rassool, C., 2000. *Skeletons in the Cupboard: South African Museums and the Trade in Human Remains 1907–1917*. Cape Town: South African Museum; Kimberley: McGregor Museum, pp. 1–5.

Sillitoe, P., 2005. 'The Role of section H at the British Association for the Advancement of Science in the History of Anthropology', *Durham Anthropology Journal*, Vol. 13, No. 2. Available at: https://community.dur.ac.uk/anthropology.journal/vol13/iss2/sillitoe/sillitoe.pdf [accessed 3 May 2016].

28

AFRO-DESCENDENT HERITAGE AND ITS UNACKNOWLEDGED LEGACY IN LATIN AMERICAN MUSEUM REPRESENTATION

Mónica Risnicoff de Gorgas

Introduction

In the earliest period of the trans–Atlantic slave trade, about fifteen million Africans were forced into exile and slavery. Progressively, they were made to occupy the lower strata of colonial society in the Americas. They also brought with them a strong oral tradition and, skilled artisans and artists as they were, performed all manner of tasks – rural as well as urban. Manifestations of their rich non-material heritage are evident in the monuments, the traditions and, above all, in the intangible heritage that enriches Latin American culture. It is estimated that around 30 per cent of the population in the Americas identifies itself as descendants of Africans, either as descendants of victims of the slave trade or of more recent migrants. In most countries in the region today, they constitute one of the poorer and more marginalized segments of their societies.

The present article investigates in what measure museums have recognized the cultural contribution of those whose ancestors came to these lands, in some cases more than 400 years ago. Furthermore, it will assess if the way in which this social collective has been represented in museums has influenced its current social consideration as second-class citizens. This analysis will elucidate that the subject of the trade, commercialization and workforce-use of slaves, as well as the rich cultural imprint of this populous human group, has not been reflected in their full dimensions in museums in Latin America; or alternatively has appeared only tangentially, even anecdotally, reflecting a general process of invisibility that encompasses the numerous people of African descent.

It is remarkable that, after centuries of silence, UNESCO should have launched the project 'The Slave Road', at Haiti's instigation, only in 1994. This is an intersectoral, transdisciplinary programmme that aims to break the silence about slavery, to make manifest the social transformations entailed and the cultural interactions that generated the slave trade, and to make a contribution to the culture of peace and of more peaceful coexistence among peoples.

Museums: sites of power

To situate this problem within a larger context, we must acknowledge that, although museums claim to be the sites of memory *par excellence*, they have until recently neglected to deal with a subject and a social practice present in all continents and all civilizations at huge cost to humanity: slavery. And even though seemingly no subject escapes their purview, it was not until the final years of the twentieth century, more precisely during the 1990s, that one can point to the existence of museums devoted to the history of slavery. For Carlo Celius, who offers keys to interpret this paradoxical situation, it is not merely a case of silence or fertile oblivion, but of an outright rejection or denial that finds its explanation in the very origin of the museum as an institution.

Museums, being Western institutions in origins and structure, arose as complements to the formation of European nation states. In non-European countries one finds a similar phenomenon. As early as 1973, Hugues de Varine stated that: 'starting at the beginning of the nineteenth century, the development of museums in the rest of the world is a purely colonialist phenomenon. European countries have imposed their methods of analysis of cultural phenomena and heritage upon non-European countries' (De Varine 1973: 12). Carlo Avierl Celius more recently expands upon this notion of European imposition on non-European identities:

> [T]he crystallization of these identities works in relation to the expansion of European domination around the world, one of whose necessary axes is the colonization of the New World, a colonization founded on the trade and enslavement of Black Africans [...]. The museum, insofar as it is a site of affirmation for Western identities and thus a celebration of the superiority of the White man, cannot even imagine a museum representation of the slave trade and of slavery.
>
> *(Celius 1998: 253)*

This is particularly relevant to the 'universe of museums', because what museums collect and exhibit contributes directly to the creation and shaping of social imaginations (a *social imaginary*, in psycho-sociological terms) and to the related formation of national identities.

The political and ethical dilemmas that museums face when choosing what to remember, what to legitimize – and what to 'forget' – are linked to the status of heritage as a social configuration (and again, a *social imaginary* in the realm of the social impact of cultural interactions in forming group identity, at both local and national levels). Identity and memory are susceptible to manipulation, precisely because the adjudication of senses and meanings is effected through practices that have to do with the *intangible* operations of cultural identification and indentity formation.

The system of national museums in Latin America seems to have been conceived under the syndrome of the nation that aspires to be a state, which is typical of the modern European nation states. In politically programming the public space, the new nations, in order to reassert their right to autonomy and existence, invariably adopt languages and systems of representation similar to the nations from which they have freed themselves. One way or another, Latin American museums adhere to dominant ideologies, to projects of nationhood that select the identities that should be included and repress the ones that should be marginalized, often under the inspiration of positivist theories.

The formation of nation states throughout the American continent not only coincided with the establishment (invariably conflictual and problematic) of nation state borders, but also arose from political ambitions of ruling élites that looked to Europe as the authority and source for the meting out of 'civilization'. In that sense, the geographical and symbolic frontiers of today's American nations were defined before, and continued long after, any dramatized European 'moment' of conquest and colonization. The modern states thus emerged around the inner fractures established by the dichotomies that built the idea of white and civilized – European and Catholic – nationality, excluding and denying American *indigenidad* and *africanidad* (the 'Indigenousness' and 'Africanness' throughout Latin America).

The museum that arises from a hegemonic political project remembers 'Black' identities solely to place them in the frame of a past history, thereby crystallizing their figures in history as subaltern people and slaves in the public imagination. This museological practice has persistently disqualified, through the use of negative images, citizens whose ancestors arrived in America long before others who do not need to foreground or append their ethnic origin to their condition as citizens. It is worth remarking that the transatlantic slave trade was declared a crime against humanity at the World Conference against Racism in Durban, South Africa, in 2001. Thereupon, it was also decided to adopt the term *afrodescendiente* (or 'afrodescendents' in UN terminology: people of African descent) to replace *negro*, which in most parts of the world has negative and profoundly racist connotations.

On the subject of racism, it must be considered that some official histories still represented in museums can only be questioned – for implicitly or explicitly a social imagination has been fostered that continues to support 'white' racial supremacy, from the early beginnings of the African slave trade through to the present. The social imagination that is based on the idea that the human genus is divided among several races, and that one of them (the 'white') is superior to others, was made to seem natural, sometimes even to afro-descendents themselves. As early as 1988, Tony Bennett stated this problem:

> In the context of imperial displays, subject peoples were thus represented as occupying the lowest levels of manufacturing civilization. Reduced to displays of 'primitive' handicrafts and the like, they were represented as cultures without momentum except for that benignly bestowed on them from without through the improving mission of the imperialist powers. [...]

Museums were also typically located at the centre of cities where they stood as embodiments, both material and symbolic, of a power to 'show and tell' which, in being deployed in a newly constituted open and public space, sought rhetorically to incorporate the people within the processes of the State. If the museum and the penitentiary thus represented the Janus face of power, there was none the less – at least symbolically – an economy of effort between them. For those who failed to adopt the tutelary relation to the self promoted by popular schooling or whose hearts and minds failed to be won in the new pedagogic relations between state and people symbolized by the open doors of the museum, the closed walls of the penitentiary threatened a sterner instruction in the lessons of power. Where instruction and rhetoric failed, punishment began.

(Bennett 1988: 87–88)

Paradigm changes

The acknowledgement of the museum as the site of representation and power, on the one hand, and the understanding of the social mission of the museum in the Latin American context on the other, are altogether reflected in the paradigm changes and in the valuing of non-material heritage that steadily generate critical outlooks from within both museums and museological theory. A critical stance towards museology thus emerges, which delves into specific relationships between man and a reality configured from many different worldviews.

These theoretical frameworks allow an approximation to the study of the social, political and economic environment reflected in museums, within which museums are immersed and wherefrom they promote creative strategies of action. In tune with these stances, one can affirm that:

[F]rom an ethical standpoint, if we are going to speak about inclusion, we must not only work on the problem of accessibility, but we must also start by analyzing how the groups excluded from our societies are represented in museum institutions, and if they are, which are the things included and excluded therein.

(Navarro Rojas 2011: 49–59, 57–58)

It is necessary to develop museological experiences that, from theory and practice, foster systems of interpretation and exhibition according to cultural diversity and the different ways of perceiving the time and space where they are situated. This requires providing experiences that respond to the Afro-American movements that have long been demanding the revision of dominant national histories as well as removal of the evident practices of racism and exclusion.

Thus we should highlight the experiences of some museums that feature truly innovative offerings: for example, São Paulo's Museo Afro Brasil, and its exhibition project that questions official policies concerning Afro influence on Brazilian culture; and the Museo Afro Peruano de Zaña, in northern Peru, whose main commitment is the recovery and reassessment of shared intangible heritage by the community itself. Examples from Colombia, Ecuador, Chile and Uruguay, as well as the museums in Cordoba's Estancias Jesuíticas, acknowledged by UNESCO on its World Heritage List, must also be brought to attention at this stage.

Pending matters

If the current presence of afro-descendents has been made invisible not only because *mestizaje* (mixing) has produced gradual 'whitenings', but also (and mainly) because they occupy the lower strata in the social scale, the validity of having their cultural contribution represented only in 'Afro' museums must be called into question. While processes that imply a rethinking of our history and a reassessment of the institution of the museum have indeed been gaining momentum for a while, the historical narratives that support the exhibition system in national museums still present signifying *absences*, while also repeating stereotyped images that little reflect the contributions of afro-descendents to the nation's heritage.

Nonetheless, the subject of the so-called Black slaves that is particularly mentioned – and is an ongoing subject of debate in meetings of specialists – is as yet still not present in the majority of the permanent exhibits in Latin American national museums. This situation does not arise from a lack of tangible testimony, but rather from a lack of political will compounded by internal resistance – whereby in today's society oblivion and erasure continues to be a consequence of denial. It is no easy task to reassess the value of the history of those many groups, societies and cultures whose history has been marginalized, trivialized and ignored. However, recent political changes in Latin America have kindled a debate within the national museums on the forms and formats in which the needs and concerns of the afro-descendent communities are represented: in order to enable them to reclaim their rights, and have their contributions to the nation recognized and embraced.

Some national museums have expressed these corrective themes via temporary exhibits, acknowledging, in the words of Cristina Lleras Figueroa, the curator of a temporary exhibit at the Museo Nacional de Colombia:

> [I]n what concerns the museum, as an institution it must respond to 185 years of history that still reflect in its collections the representation of official homogenization, which has been exclusionary and disrespectful – and, thus, contributes consciously or unconsciously to generalized forms of discrimination and racism.
>
> *(Lleras Figueroa 2009: 5)*

Lleras Figueroa further reminds us:

> We think it is worth pointing out that 'the histories of exclusion [and] inclusion act differently on human groups depending on whether they have implicated themselves or not as participants on the processes of nation building.

The historical dimension of political realities creates a relationship between the citizens and the national past. At the same time, they relate to the past of the nation in different ways. One is through their contribution to the national heritage. In that sense, the relationship with the heritage in the context of a national museum reinforces the feeling of having (or not) the right to belong and participate through culture. Cultural rights could be demanded in order to gain access to other rights as well.

(Lleras Figueroa 2009: 9)

Hilda Zagaglia, a visual artist and author of the exhibit *Cartographical Fragments of the Plunder*, defined the underlying ethical dilemmas such experiences have brought about. Indeed, she expressively raised the following questions:

How does one survive the memories that history flattens? How does one work within those fragments of oblivion? Or else, how does one communicate a concept, or those ideas that remove the things, the actions, of the past so that today we are being told what is worth knowing? And when the inquiries outweigh the answers, I tell myself, how does one redefine art with ethics that respond to the geographic reality, that represent the identity characteristics of this America of the plurality, where *mestizaje* and the legacy of thousands of anonymous beings seem to me more than important? How does one recover the work of intellectuals and ensure that their research does not continue occupying dark corners in dusty libraries?

(Zagaglia 2011)

Final considerations

The questions underlying these challenges are related to a conception of the museum that rests upon current political and social tendencies: Can cultural projects constitute a possible solution to society's problems? Can and should museology have an influence over the economic and social changes witnessed by our times? Can the institutions that opt for a sustainable cultural development rebuild old sites of power and change to create new, more culturally inclusive and intersocial institutions for all citizens?

From a museological perspective, this requires a high ethical and deontological commitment to document and represent the process of slavery and the histories of *afrodescendientes* in American museums. Such commitment should not continue to present those subjects as part of the past, but rather courageously venture to transform museums into agoras, wherein discussion is allowed and invited from all social constituencies. Such reinterpretation of history and representation highlights the sets of problems that we, as citizens and social subjects ourselves, must confront today, together with the imperative to incorporate the rights, needs and concerns of afrodescendents in order to represent them genuinely, and acknowledge their contributions in building up an entire nation's cultural identity throughout history.

An active memory does not solely rest upon specialists. It requires the support of a society convinced of the value of multiple identities. As for museums, premises to the debate would lie in the searching and frank acknowledgement of these institutions as sites of power. Thus could the possibility of promoting critical judgement from within be raised as an option to present resistance *to* that same power. The first step would be to document both the slave trade and slavery in order to promote the vitality of afro-descendent culture, which plays a leading role in the political formation of our societies. However, it is imperative that the issue of authority be addressed: Who should speak in the name of the communities concerned? Therein lies, ideally, the role of a transformative political power. If these are unilateral decisions by museums, however, what part then, will politicians, afro-descendent communities, researchers and museum professionals play in this process of transformation?

The need to assume ethical positions demands that institutions take an explicit stance in favour of human rights. At the same time, form and content in transformative representation ultimately depend upon the work of museums. There is inevitably much work yet to be done to attain better balance in terms of representation and power in the portrayal of history, knowledge and heritage. In this context, Latin American museums must set out concrete actions founded on critical reflections and actions that foster community participation, transforming museums' role in the construction of the concepts of nation and citizenship, together with the ideological elements that underlie the formation of their collections, and the messages or narratives that their exhibits have long conveyed.

However, the opportunity of beginning this transformative process is urgent. If it is the case that 'within the museum, ethics can be defined as the discussion process, aimed at identifying the basic values and principles on which the work of the museum relies', then the question of why certain histories are present and others absent should not only be a theoretical consideration (Desvallées and Mairesse 2009: 32–34). It is imperative that museums search for imaginative forms to repair the damage done by a stigmatizing hegemonic discourse, in order to repair a historical debt and promote social inclusion. More than ever, the cultural vitality of *afrodescendientes* and their contribution to national histories must be brought about.

References

Acondo, Aníbal, 1993. *El Ocaso de una Sociedad Estamental, Córdoba 1700–1760.* Cordoba: UNC.

Annecchiarico, Milena and Martín, Alicia, 2012. *Afropolíticas en América del Sur y el Caribe.* Ciudad Autónoma de Buenos Aires: Puentes del Sur Ediciones.

Assadourian, Carlos, 1965. *El tráfico de esclavos en Córdoba, 1588–1610. Según las actas de protocolos del Archivo Histórico de Córdoba.* Cordoba: UNC/Dirección General de Publicidad.

Bennett, Tony, 1988. 'The exhibitionary complex'. *New Formations*, 4: 73–102.

Celius, Carlo Avierl, 1998. 'L'esclavage au musée – Récit d'un refoulement'. *L'Homme*, 38 (145): 49–261.

Crouzeilles, Carlos Alberto, 2007. 'Los esclavos de la Compañía de Jesús', in *Tercer Encuentro Patrimonio Jesuítico Centro Internacional Para la Conservación del Patrimonio*, at: https://geala. files.wordpress.com/2011/03/carlos-crouzeilles-los-esclavos-de-la-compac3b1c3ada-de-jesc3bas.pdf

Decarolis, Nelly, 2006. *El pensamiento museológico latinoamericano. Los documentos del ICOFOM LAM. Cartas y recomendaciones, 1992–2005, Córdoba, Argentina, 2006.* Paris: ICOM.

De la Cerda Donoso, Jeanette C. and Villaroel, Luis J., 1999. *Los negros esclavos de Alta Gracia: caso testigo de población de origen africano en la Argentina y América.* Córdoba: El Copista.

Desvallées, André, 2001. 'Muséologie, patrimoine, changement économique et développement social'. *ICOFOM Study Series*, 33a. Paris: ICOM, pp. 32–37.

Desvallées, André and Mairesse, François, 2009. *Key Concepts of Museology.* Paris: Armand Colin, pp. 32–34.

de Varine, Huges, 1973. *Los museos en el mundo.* Buenos Aires: Salvat.

Gracia, Joaquín, 1940. *Los jesuitas en Córdoba.* Buenos Aires and Mexico: Espasa-Calpe.

Grenon, Joaquín, 1929. *Documentos Históricos.* Cordoba: Alta Gracia.

Huyssen, Andreas, 2007. *En busca del futuro perdido. Cultura y memoria en tiempos de globalización.* Buenos Aires: Fondo de Cultura Económica.

Lleras Figueroa, Cristina, 2009. 'Etnicidad, investigación y representación en la exposición Velorios y Santos Vivos. Comunidades negras, afrocolombianas, raizales y palenqueras, en Cuadernos de Curaduría'. *Museo Nacional de Colombia*, 9 (July–December), at: www-museonacional.gov.co/inbox/files/docs/ccmutis.pdf.

Mayo, Carlos, 1994. 'Las haciendas jesuíticas en Córdoba y el noroeste argentino', in Carlos Mayo (ed.), *La historia agraria del interior. Haciendas jesuíticas de Córdoba y el Noroeste.* Buenos Aires: Centro Editor de América Latina, pp. 7–16.

Navarro Rojas, Óscar. 2011. 'Ética, museos e inclusión: un enfoque crítico'. *Museo y territorio*, 4: 49–59.

Prats, Llorenç, 1997. *Antropología y Patrimonio.* Barcelona: Ariel.

Rufer, Mario, 2005. *Historias negadas. Esclavitud, violencia y relaciones de poder en Córdoba a fines del siglo XVIII.* Cordoba: Ferreyra Editor.

Todorov, Tzvetan, 1991. *Las morales de la historia.* Translated by B. Bertran Alcázar, 1993. Barcelona: Ediciones Paídos.

Torres, Félix, 1972. 'El comercio de esclavos en Córdoba (1700–1713)'. *Seminario de Investigación.* Cordoba: UNC.

Zagaglia, Hilda, 2011. 'Fragmentos Cartográficos del Despojo. Intervención (plástica + poesía)' [UNESCO Report]. Paris: UNESCO Publishing, at: www.unesco.org.uy/ci/fileadmin/cultura/2011/INFORME_MUESTRA_CARTOGRAFIA_UNESCO_2011.pdf.

29

IN SEARCH OF THE INCLUSIVE MUSEUM[1]

Amareswar Galla

The Inclusive Museum defies any definition. Defining is containing. A genuine inclusive discourse has multiple voices, multiple intersections and a complex nexus of cultural and stakeholder communities. It is not about defining or consensus. It is about the relational and processual aspects of the museum and museological discourse and acting on the symbolism present to work towards a dynamic equilibrium, bringing together people and their heritage. It is about understanding and practising shared authority. It is an open-ended project that is delineated and re-delineated by the primary, secondary and tertiary knowledge communities. It bridges the *emic* and *etic* through mutual respect. It promotes understanding of histories with both diachronic and synchronic perspectives, through digital and face-to-face participation. Several themes or pathways inform the inclusive processes of the museum. Select emerging themes are shared below as cross-cutting considerations.

Prologue

The road in search of the Inclusive Museum through professional and academic activism for the transformation of the museological discourse has been traversed from Amaravati, a rural town on the river Krishna, in South India, where I was born. It is a caste-driven ancient town of about 3,000 people who live a secluded life, with a medieval temple as the focus for all ritual purposes. *Arthanariswara*, or the non-duality of half male and half female, *Purusha/Sivam* and *Shakti* still inform the spirituality of the people in the hinterland. This non-duality valorizes the sense of place and identity of the local community groups.

The landscapes and waterscapes of the place were transformed several times throughout the past 2,400 years, resulting in layers of heritage significance. Some of the milestones are worth noting here. Buddhism was introduced by the fourth century BCE to a predominantly *Pandukal* or so called megalithic Iron Age people. The introduction of the iron ploughshare and agrarian calendar led to intensification of agriculture, lending the place its ancient name, *Dhanyakataka*, or emporium of rice. By the third century BCE, one of the largest Buddhist Stupas in South Asia was built here, inspired by Asoka, the Mauryan Emperor. The Great Stupa or *Mahachaitya* was further embellished and the monastic complexes expanded in the following centuries. It is one of the most sacred sites for Buddhism according to His Holiness The Dalai Lama. Acharya Nagarjuna, the founder of Madhyamika philosophy, the basis for Mahayana Buddhism, was born and lived here for part of his life.

There is substantial archaeological evidence of flourishing Indo-Roman trade in this area by the time of Tiberius, when apparently a pound of pepper was bought with a pound of gold from South India. Urban centres evolved at a rapid pace. While the Buddhist monks were the pioneers in the transformation of the region, it was the Brahmin priests who provided for and sustained the religious and associated domestic and community rituals. By the fourteenth century AD, Buddhism declined in the region, except for stories associated with earthen mounds. The place and its remains of the Great Amaravati Stupa impressed British colonial collectors and administrators. Apart from preliminary excavations, it was dug up and most of the sculptures were transferred to Britain. They now constitute the Amaravati Buddhist Gallery in the British Museum.

Early childhood recollections are playing hide and seek among the remains in Amaravati. The first museological encounters as an adult were in the local site museum of the Archaeological Survey of India. This was followed by studying the collections in the British Museum, inspired by the then keeper, Douglas Barrett, and my co-supervisor Raymond Allchin at Cambridge University.

In 2006, His Holiness the Dalai Lama conducted the *Kala Chakra* ceremony in Amaravati for the first time since the fourteenth century. A gilded statue of Nagarjuna marks the occasion at the entrance to the Archaeological Museum. This is in contrast to the large statue across the road of Ambedkar, unkempt and neglected. He was a Dalit from the 'dregs' of the Indian caste system, who led the mass conversion of Dalits to Buddhism in 1942 to seek dignity and equality. He was the Chairman of the Indian Constituent Assembly in 1950, when India became a sovereign republic. The new constitution included fundamental rights for all Indians, irrespective of their social and economic backgrounds, race, caste, faith, colour and class. This document is still the most significant articulation of the aspiration of India to become an inclusive society. In order to redress historical inequalities, Jawaharlal Nehru, the first Prime Minister of India, introduced legally the concepts of affirmative action and positive discrimination that are now widely used in Western democracies.

The conceptual background

The journey, championing cultural rights for all people, is punctuated by a series of negotiations of the self and the other within the dialectic of the hegemonic and subaltern discourses that permeate globalizing processes. While the tyranny of binary oppositions continues to inform popular cultures and media in its simplicity, the reality is peppered with a complexity of border crossings that transcend dichotomies (Galla 2005b). In fact, the dialectic is between and among individuals, groups, communities and their ambient contexts against the canvas of shifting sands of time and space beyond the traditional contexts.

Two significant influences guided my formative years. The first and foremost was through scholarly inspiration and a resolution to the existential dilemma of a young Indian in a post-colonial context. Romila Thapar at the Jawaharlal Nehru University, through her teaching, scholarship and supervision, became the enabler (Thapar 1975). She imparted a constructive sense of self, and more aptly self-esteem, in a conflicted world of values. It is based on an understanding of the historical legacies and politically arbitrated oppositional discourses in communalism that inform historiography and history writing. The sense of empowerment, which ethical engagement gave the strength to walk the untrodden paths of the heritage domains is embodied in her latest work, underlining the 'critical importance for the past to be carefully and rigorously explained, if the legitimacy of our present, wherever it derives from the past, is to be portrayed as accurately as possible' (Thapar 2014).

Museums and heritage agencies have often become captives of their legacies and chauvinism, rather than meaningful and constructive mediators of relevant societal issues. David Lowenthal points out succinctly that:

> Heritage is in demand. Ever more of the world's heritage is looted, destroyed, mutilated, shorn of context, hidden from scrutiny, auctioned on eBay. Why? Partly because its virtuous stewards treat nations and tribes as enduring entities with sacred rights to time-honoured legacies. Heritage is piously declared the legacy of all humanity. But the possessive jealousies of particular claimants pose huge obstacles to our global common inheritance. Confining possession to some while excluding others is the *raison d'être* of most heritage. Created to generate and protect group interests, it benefits us mainly if withheld from others.
>
> *(Lowenthal 1998)*

In this global context, the poverty of museological discourse calls for the urgent interrogation of the many issues that are central to the criticality of the museum as a relevant civic institution. The issues are: racialization of history, secularism in a post-September 2001 world of extremism, communalism in culturally and linguistically diverse societies, false nationalism, persistence of patriarchy, growth of fundamentalism in rewriting historical narratives; and the translation of the colonial legacies into neo-colonial constructs under the rubric of diversity discourse by the establishment.

Critical museologists and heritage practitioners concur that the contextual frameworks for museums are diversifying, despite the accelerated pace of all forms of globalization and homogenization. Our ability to adapt and change is dependent upon the capacity to resolve the tensions between the centrifugal forces that pull us away from our localities and the centripetal forces that keep us together through our sense of place. In this dynamic, identity formations are part of the creative tension. The movement of the self and sense of place as we transgress or transcend borders is multifaceted. One that is rooted in once 'being' and the other one of 'becoming' in a complexity (Hall 1996). At times this is also a performance of reinventing *kastom*, or 'imaginative rediscovery' (Keesing and Tonkinson 1982).

My argument is that the museum is a potential civic space to engage with the tyranny of binaries and negotiate this dialectic in a borderless world where identities have become permeable. Each one of us can affirm with confidence that 'I am many peoples'. Multiple identities, affiliations, voices and interpretations inform the call for intercultural dialogue. It is critical to cross-cultural capacity building of the museum as an agency responsive to social change, and also as an actor and *animateur* in the performance of that change. In order to address cultural diversity in museums, one needs to become a 'multicultural sophisticate' (Lowenthal, 1993). What is the capacity – organizational, professional, intellectual and emotional – of the contemporary museums or their workers to become such sophisticates?

Inclusive capitalism to inclusive museum and inclusive planning: there is widespread consensus that sustainable development pays dividends for posterity to build the 'civil paths to peace' (Sen *et al.* 2007). However, the systemic fault lines in private and public sector organizations, precluding their relevance and responsiveness to twenty-first-century concerns call for rethinking methods and approaches in museums with honesty, transparency and integrity (Janes 2009; Gershevitch 2014). The challenge is to interrogate our ethical engagement in all forms of business. To be reflective, revealing and confronting of contextual realities of our business for the 'becoming' sophisticates. In doing so it is necessary to ensure that deep research and cultural action inform the nexus between the four pillars of social, economic, cultural and environmental sustainability. Museums must be situated in the UN 2030 Development Agenda that will determine the cultural economics of the future.

New models and modalities of participation need to be scoped and developed to deliver the Sustainable Development Goals that inform the UN Agenda. Official and civil society agencies are developing organizational cultures that embed relevance and impacts in their rational, emotional and ethical engagement. For instance, World Heritage site management agencies, while focused on the central tenet of Outstanding Universal Value, are examining evidence-based benefits, qualitative and quantitative, to local communities (Galla 2012 and 2013). In this context, how do museums and heritage agencies take on the challenge and address appropriate capacity building? What are the discursive crossings and cross-cultural encounters in a culturally and linguistically diverse world? How do museums negotiate political support and will to engage with contemporary realities?

Museums and social inclusion

In the 1980s, Australia was digesting the seminal report by the Aboriginal elder, states-man and champion of cultural rights Mick Miller (Miller Report 1985). It provided the basis for my employment, through funding from the Council of the National Museum of Australia, as a migrant to lead the affirmative action programme between 1985 and 1992. The goal was to facilitate the participation of Aboriginal Peoples and Torres Strait Islanders in cultural agencies such as museums, galleries, World Heritage sites and national parks. The guidance through a committee led by majority Indi-genous Australian educationalists and select archaeologists, historians, administrators and anthropologists helped to frame the curricula with Indigenous Terms of Refer-ence (Galla 1989). Scoping and implementation were mandated and resourced to be affirmative and empowering by the Commonwealth Government of Australia.

Three axiomatic principles informed the process. The first and foremost was that Indigenous cultures are living and holistic where all heritage is intangible and per-ceived through tangible things, such as collections, sites, and conceptualizations of nature. The second is that graduates must be strong in both 'Black Fellow's Law' and 'White Fellow's Law'. Law here is understood as a knowledge system. One foot in each camp to be strong to work in a workplace where the graduate might be the only Indigenous person. Empowerment is not only about the self, but also to be able to work and flourish in the so-called mainstream museum and heritage workforce. The third was that all learning was collaborative where the learners brought their prior learning and values from the rich tapestry of Indigenous Australian nations to the classroom, field schools and laboratory-grounded applied projects.

Rethinking the museum in an inclusive frame was central to this national affirm-ative action programme. The Inclusive Museum is a response to the challenges posed by the transformations that have become imperative. If museology is the study of the science of museums then trends and approaches inform its evolution as an interdisciplinary enterprise. Critical museology and inclusive museology characterize new thinking. These are responses to the limitations of object or site-centredness and to an oppositional paradigm of people or community centredness. A negotiated balance of perspectives and prospects of all the stakeholders is necessary. The reality is the increasing pressure of economic and cultural justice imperatives on museums and heritage agencies to become relevant and responsive in the contemporary world that is diversifying across several cultural borders.

The movement of the Inclusive Museum is born out of the need to promote cultural democracy. The Inclusive Museum is an agency, aspirational in its spirit and intent, for facilitating a multisectoral and interdisciplinary dialogue for the transformation of museums into civic spaces for safeguarding tangible and intang-ible, natural and cultural, and movable and immovable heritage. It is a partnership situated within the ICOM Strategic Plan (ICOM 2007).

The unravelling of exclusion is a precondition for pursuing inclusion. This is a con-dition in addressing any form of social change including the museum as a construct. Is the museum a Western thing? It is a question that is still posed in many countries. It

FIGURE 29.1 Billy Doolan, Minya Guyu, 'Fish Spawning', 2005. In: 'Dreamtime - Lo Spirito Dell'Arte Aborigena,' MAN Museum, Nuoro, Italy, 2011 © Billy Doolan. Artist's representative, Aboriginal Exhibitions Pty Ltd.

demands a multipronged approach. One that seeks decolonization of the mind in both the host and source countries and communities where the collections are housed in museums. It is more than the collections. It is the context. The historical consciousness that is embodied in the collections. The trajectories of stories that inform them. The layers of significance, both intrinsic and extrinsic, that accumulate like the patina of time, global and yet at once local.

Recent EU elections, episodes of terrorism and the consequent apprehensions and reservations about immigration and cultural differences are evidence for urgent action by museums to address the rhetoric and reality of inclusion. No country or region is any longer monocultural. The historically diverse countries and the emerging multi-cultural nations have to address four fundamental pillars of their diverse citizenships: cultural identity, social justice, productive diversity and civic engagement. The practice of active citizenship in all sectors of museum business is warranted.

Who interprets whose heritage, and who owns whose heritage, have remained critical questions. Framers and facilitators of museum and heritage discourse often fail to understand that they consciously or unconsciously perpetuate the power relations and the hegemonic master narratives. Essentialism of the perceived other remains within the English language, a language of globalization and hence Anglo-phone writing that has become predominant. Linguists caution us through penetrating analysis of the globalizing and homogenizing impacts of dominant languages. Statistical sampling demonstrates that the predominance of academic publications in English has had a profound impact on the erosion of intangible heritage elements and living cultures, and cautions us that preserving, maintaining and sustaining living cultures requires conscious awareness of our choices, and that the cultural and linguistic diversity of the world cannot be taken for granted (Gebert and Gibson 2012). Intellectual considerations from comparative and diverse scholarship from culturally and linguistically diverse backgrounds are critical for the development of informed and inclusive museological discourse.

In this context, museums that were derived from colonial times and those that were founded in post-colonial political environments have started reinventing themselves, taking different and often challenging pathways. The twenty-first century poses relevance, participation, First Voice, multivocality and active citizenship or negotiated community engagement as indicators for the appraisal of the transformations of the institution of the museum. Partnerships are neither relevant nor sustainable in the contextual realities if they are founded in the absence of a process of psychological decolonization of museum and heritage legacies and discourses.

Contextual 'museology'

The fundamental questions about the purpose of museum work was asked decades ago: 'What is the proper business of the museum: ideas or things?' To what extent do we think that museums are in the 'service of the collections and not our fellow humans'? 'Do our museums make a real difference in, and do they have a positive impact on, the lives of other people'? (Weil 1989). These questions continue to haunt us despite efforts and demonstrated commitment to reposition museums as agents of social change.

Does an image of Krishna become an artwork in an art museum, an object illustrating religious life in a social history museum or an ethnographic object on the life of cowherds in ancient India in an ethnographic museum (Galla 2005c)? This location variable, which I have termed 'museology' (museum + locality), brings its own unique challenges of conservation and interpretation, depending on the significance ascribed to the object or collection. Few museums have openly taken on the examination of the extent to which the location of objects and artworks determines interpretations and meanings (Hodder 1992). If we acknowledge that the core function of museums is 'memory work', then to what extent do we think that museums are the means for 'creating and expressing contemporary identities, and not simply an impassive cataloguing of diverse historical cultures' (Mack 2003)?

Resolutions adopted by the Roundtable of Santiago de Chile in 1972 led to redefining the museum as an institution 'in the service of society' by the International Council of Museums (ICOM), and expanded in 2001 and 2007 to include living heritage (IBRAM 2012). The recent decades have witnessed several experiments by museums to understand, accept and accommodate this 'service' orientation. The question of service 'to whom' has been dealt with sporadically in response to the imperatives of equity and access policies. It is this momentum that has resulted in the long overdue Museum Recommendation[2] being adopted by UNESCO in the General Assembly in November 2015.

Museum leadership has been slow to respond to the challenges of inclusion. Educational and visitor management departments take on the spirit of active community engagement with minimal devolution of power and decision-making from above. Collecting and curatorship struggle to become relevant to the diverse stakeholders. Contemporary collecting and diversifying the collections with relevance to the twenty-first century continue to be sporadically addressed. Visitor studies have largely focused on museum audiences. The museum public has largely been treated as a mosaic of individual categories of identities based on class, rather than a fabric, a complexity of societal formations that are in flux, diversifying population profiles. The governing structures continue to be largely male, monocultural and elitist in many ways. Major institutions coming through unscathed during the global financial crisis have been reinventing the master discourse of museology with a focus on treasures. Innovators and bold institutions, like the Liverpool Museums in Britain, struggle financially, but in the long run continue with ethical and accountable journeys with their constituent stakeholders.

The major metropolitan museums in the West are aggressively forging entrepreneurial and commercial interests in West Asia (still called the Middle East, thus perpetuating colonial geographies), and with China and India, often reinventing the colonial discourse of elite politics, working with the establishment and reinforcing the object centredness. The colonial partnership is reinvented in a contemporary market economy. Museums have become the soft power agencies for the economic interests of established economies supported by their government agencies with the new and emerging economies. Only time will tell the extent to which the new geopolitical economic formations such as BRICS will make a difference. A major museological movement for the Dalits and highly marginalized communities in India is a long way off, as it is for the large agrarian and minority populations across Asia.

In South Africa, multiculturalism was used in the past as a basis for apartheid to keep people apart. In democratic South Africa, it has become a means to bring people together. Rasheed Araeen argues that the South African paradigm of multiculturalism reverses the question of 'self' and 'other' as perceived in the West (Araeen 1995). He says that: 'If we adopt the logic of the dominant culture in the West, whereby the discourse of multiculturalism is constructed on the basis of a division between its majority white population and its non-white minorities, turning the minority into marginal ethnic entities, would it not turn the white minority in South Africa into an ethnic entity?'

The politicization of the museum discourse has marginalized the location of the multicultural paradigm as a deficit model. It is worth noting that both Angela Merkel and David Cameron have come out in 2012 openly stating that state-sponsored multiculturalism has not worked in Europe. The reality is that providing settlement and essential services with covert policies of assimilation has not worked. Multiculturalism as a public policy to address inequalities and integration has been poorly addressed. Several countries have emulated policies from settler societies such as Canada and Australia where the immigrant groups have reduced the original populations to highly disadvantaged minorities. While there are lessons to be learnt from each other, in Europe the paradigm is different. The original populations were and continue to be the majority. The global movement of populations, the convergence of multiple stakeholder interests and the location of the museum as an institution of civil society have become far more critical to building liveable communities.

In the 'post-September-11' global environment of insecurity, coupled with a recent spate of violent disruptions across the world, understanding faith in interfaith dialogue, and locating the museum as a secular space reminds us of the dictum of Stephen Weil: that museums 'are safe places for unsafe ideas'. How do museums embrace human rights and faith in a security neurosis that is not only Western but has become global? Under the umbrella of human rights, cultural rights and freedom of religion and belief have become particularly fraught and contentious (Galla and Gershevitch 2011). It is in the areas of culture and faith that battles over ethics and domination are fought: with words and with violence.

There is considerable discussion on religious extremism. Faith-based violent extremism is best countered by justice and peace-building (Aslan 2010). The potential of the arts, whether museum or heritage-based, religiously inspired, or other forms of artistic expression, to remediate social conflict is largely neglected. There is an expanding evidence-base demonstrating that arts builds agency (collective and individual), social and emotional well-being, and reinforces social capital. Projects addressing faith to counter so called Islamophobia are funded under counter-terrorism strategies. *Muslim Women Through Their Own Eyes* at the Casula Power House museum in Sydney attempts to provide critical perspectives. There are also a small number of projects that use existing faith-related collections to promote cross-cultural understanding (Nightingale and Greene 2010).

The Arts of Islam gallery at the Louvre provides a splendid space of the Western aesthetic of the other, here Islamic art, and the casual international visitor may be lulled into a sense of comfort that France is an inclusive society. It has the potential to engage with France's Muslim population, the largest in Europe. It provides a valuable opportunity to make this iconic institution deal with inclusion for all the people who experience it. The Louvre is a financially thriving institution with increasing visitation right through the global financial crisis, and substantial partnerships with oil-rich Arab countries. In connecting communities and collections, its significant role as a cultural institution could be realised in community building. It could become a vehicle to minimise the back-lash against immigration, multiculturalism and the targeted violence against Muslims, Jews and other numerically minority communities.

Museums focusing on 'othered' identities, largely on visible minorities, have inadequately addressed the centrality of gender equality in museums. It is not oppositional between men and women, but rather a space for sharing authority, power and quality of life. The agency of women is critical for gender mainstreaming and in the making of the Inclusive Museum. It must become more than aspirational, a compliance strategy with measurable gender and diversity indicators.

While gender equity is measurable, as an outcome it is contingent on the understanding of the complexity of gender mainstreaming in strategic planning. In order to ensure evidence-based approaches, statistical data gathered should also take into consideration the intersectionality of other cultural borders, race, ethnicity, faith, colour, class, and sexuality. Strategic targets and periodic reporting mechanisms need to be scoped. Gender-sensitive research, advocacy and scholarship from both the North and South are needed in understanding the gender dimension of museums at different sites

FIGURE 29.2 The new Museum and Cultural Centre under construction in the Bamiyan Valley © A. Galla. 2009.

FIGURE 29.3 Ndebele of the Ndzundza 'tribe' redress the erosion of their self-esteem under the apartheid regime by initiating their youth as part of the Tswaing Museum project, South Africa © A. Galla, 1995.

and their safeguarding. While there is considerable analysis and literature on culture and gender in countries such as India and Nigeria, most of the academic circulation is limited to the hegemonic discourse of the North. A balanced knowledge base that takes into consideration different perspectives and approaches with the same goal is critical.

Conclusion

I have interrogated above only a few elements of museum development based on first-hand, 'fingers in the dirt' museum experience, and through various incarnations chairing ICOM committees and task forces over the past two decades. Inclusive Museum development demands integrated approaches to transformation – social, economic, cultural, environmental, digital and spiritual. The International Council of Museums began its advocacy engaging diversity in Quebec in 1992, resulting in its Cultural Diversity Policy of 1998. In 2010, ICOM adopted a benchmarking mechanism establishing a professional standard-setting soft law instrument in the form of the ICOM Cultural Diversity Charter, derived from deliberations of the ICOM Cross-Cultural Task Force (2004–10). In 2013, the ICOM General Assembly resolved to begin assessing against the Charter the extent to which inclusion and gender in museums are being addressed (ICOM Resolutions, Rio, 2013). While there is no one-size-fits-all answer, it is considered important to share and develop comparative studies in promoting inclusion in museums. The November 2015 adoption by UNESCO of the soft law instrument, as a Recommendation only but underlining the ICOM Code of Ethics,[3] is a beginning. Cooperation and coordination are a challenge across the vast operational base of UNESCO and the multitude of ICOM constitutive Committees, Alliances and Affiliates. There is no other way but to work together and embed inclusion in all its complexity in museological and wider heritage discourses and practices.

Nelson Mandela captured the spirit of the Inclusive Museum when he said that South Africa is for all South Africans, and that 'culture should be the language that should heal and transform the nation'. He concluded his Inauguration in 1994 by proclaiming: '[L]et there be food, let there be water, let there be salt for all the people [...]'. Tswaing Museum, the first museum project funded by his administration, is not only *a place of salt*; it is also symbolic of *salt for the people*, for all people.

In handing over the keys to Pietermaritzburg, where Gandhi took the early steps of the civil disobedience movement, to his grandson Gopala Krishna Gandhi, Mandela recalled Mahatma Gandhi's who said that culture is the 'authentic wisdom of human ends and means'. The Inclusive Museum Knowledge Community, a partnership of Common Ground Publishing and the International Institute for the Inclusive Museum, supported by ICOM, continues to build on the lessons learnt and ongoing discursive crossings to promote for posterity the museum – aspirational, transformational and relevant for diverse peoples. The Community maximizes the offerings and affordances of the digital domain, and meets face to face annually in different parts of the world, co-curating the Inclusive Museum discourse with local partners and guided by an International Advisory Committee where the former members of the ICOM Cross-Cultural Task Force continue to provide leadership. Themes are based on contemporary concerns, promoting museums as from civic spaces to sites of cultural freedoms. It is an open-ended means to museum development, providing for a plurality of perspectives, approaches and practices.

Note

1 This article is a revised version of an article first published only in Spanish: *MUSEOS. ES*, Numbers 9–10 (2013–14) editada por la Dirección General de Bellas Artes y Bienes Culturales y de Archivos y Bibliotecas a través de la Subdirección General de Museos Estatales, Madrid.
2 The full text of the UNESCO *Recommendation Concerning the Protection and Promotion of Museums and Collections, their Diversity and their Role in Society*, 2015, is provided as *Appendix V* in the present publication. See also François Mairesse, 'The UNESCO *Recommendation on the Protection and Promotion of Museums and Collections, their Diversity and Role in Society*', in Bernice L. Murphy (ed.), *Museums, Ethics and Cultural Heritage*. London: Routledge, 2016, Chapter 10.
3 The full text of the *ICOM Code of Ethics for Museums* is provided as *Appendix I* in the present publication. It is also available online for download from the ICOM website (with links to translations in French, Spanish, and many other languages). The English version is accessible at: http://icom.museum/professional-standards/code-of-ethics.

References

Araeen, Rasheed, 1995. 'What is post-apartheid South Africa and its place in the world?' *Africus Johannesburg Biennale Catalogue*. Johannesburg: Transitional Metropolitan Council.

Art contre Apartheid/Art against Apartheid, 1996. Cape Town. Under the patronage of Jacques Chirac, Nelson Mandela, and the United Nations.

Aslan, Reza, 2010. *How to Win a Cosmic War*. New York: Random House.

Basho, Matsuo, 1966, *The Narrow Road to the Interior*. Translated by Nobuyuki Yuasa. London: Penguin Books.

Galla, Amareswar, 1989. *Museums and Beyond*. Special Publications for the Triennial General Conference of ICOM, Den Haag, National Centre for Cultural Heritage Science Studies, Canberra.

Galla, Amareswar, 2005a. 'On being Indian: Museums and Indigenous engagement in human development', in Mark Hirsch and Amy Pickworth, (eds), *The Native Universe and Museums in the Twenty-First Century: The Significance of the National Museum of the American Indian*. New York: Smithsonian Institution Press, pp. 119–30.

Galla, Amareswar, 2005b. 'Gandhi, identity, and a search for truth: a personal journey'. *Curator: The Museum Journal*, 48 (1): 42–47.

Galla, Amareswar, 2005c. 'Krishna's dilemma: Art museums in human development', in Caroline Turner (ed.), *Art and Social Change: Contemporary Art in Asia and the Pacific*. Canberra: Pandanus Books, pp. 570–82.

Galla, Amareswar (ed.), 2012. *World Heritage: Benefits Beyond Borders*. Cambridge: Cambridge University Press and Paris: UNESCO Publishing (translation published in French, Paris, and Korean, Seoul, in 2013).

Galla, Amareswar, 2014. 'World heritage and gender: Respect and recognition for the agency of women'. *Gender Equality and Culture*. Paris: UNESCO Publishing.

Galla, Amareswar and Gershevitch, Conrad, 2011. *Freedom of Religion and Belief – Culture, Heritage and the Arts: A Brief Survey in Australia*. Sydney: Australian Human Rights Commission.

Gebert, Frieda H. and Gibson, Kevin (eds), 2012. *Sustaining Living Culture*. On Sustainability Book Series. Champaign, IL: Common Ground Publishing.

Gershevitch, Conrad, 2014. *Museums in Human Development: The Place of Museums in a Globalised and Transforming World*. On Museums Series. Champaign, IL: Common Ground Publishing.

Hall, Stuart, 1996. 'New ethnicities', in David Morley and Kuan-Hsing Chen (eds), *Stuart Hall: Critical Dialogues in Cultural Studies*. London: Routledge.

Hodder, Ian, 1992. 'The contextual analysis of symbolic meanings interpreting objects and collections', in Susan M. Pearce (ed.), *Museums, Objects and Collections: A Cultural Study*. Leicester: Leicester University Press.

IBRAM, 2012. *The Roundtable of Santiago de Chile*. Jose do Nascimento Junior Alan Trampe and Paula Assuncao Dos Santos (eds). Brasilia: Instituto Brasileiro de Museus.

ICOM Resolutions, 2013, at: http://icom.museum/the-governance/general-assembly/resolutions-adopted-by-icoms-general-assemblies-1946-to-date/rio-de-janeiro-2013 (accessed 17 December 2015).

ICOM Strategic Plan, adopted in Vienna, 2007, at: http://archives.icom.museum/strat_plan.html (accessed 17 December 2015).

Janes, Robert, 2009. *Museums in a Troubled World: Renewal, Irrelevance or Collapse?* London: Routledge.

Keesing, Roger M. and Tonkinson, Robert (eds), 1982. 'Reinventing traditional culture: Politics of Kastom in Island Melanesia'. *Mankind* (special issue), 13 (4).

Lowenthal, David, 1993. Recorded and quoted in Amareswar Galla, *Heritage Curricula and Cultural Diversity*. Canberra: Office of Multicultural Affairs, Prime Minister and Cabinet, Australian Government Publishing Service.

Lowenthal, David, 1998. *Heritage Crusade and the Spoils of History*. Cambridge: Cambridge University Press:

Lowenthal, David, 2005. 'Why sanctions seldom work: reflections on cultural property internationalism'. *International Journal of Cultural Property*, 12 (3): 393–423.

Mack, John, 2003. 'The British Museum and other theatres of memory'. *The Museum of the Mind*. London: British Museum Press, pp. 11–23.

Miller Report, 1985. *Report of the Committee of Review of Aboriginal Employment and Training Program*. Canberra: Australian Government Publishing Service.

National Aboriginal and Torres Strait Islander Education Policy: Joint Policy Statement, 1989. Department of Employment, Education and Training. Canberra: Australian Government Publishing Service.

Nightingale, Eithne and Greene, Marilyn, 2010. 'Religion and material culture at the Victoria & Albert Museum of Art and Design: The perspectives of diverse faith communities'. *Material Religion: The Journal of Objects, Art and Belief*, 6 (2): 218–35. An earlier version of this paper was presented at the 3rd International Conference on the Inclusive Museum in Istanbul by Eithne Nightingale, at: http://2010.onmuseums.com/sessions/index.html (accessed 17 December 2015).

Said, Edward, 1999. *Out of Place: A Memoir*. London: Granta Books.

Sen, Amartya, 2007. *Identity and Violence: The Illusion of Destiny*. London: Penguin Books.

Sen, Amartya. 2013. 'Opening Keynote speech'. *World Culture Forum*, 25 November, Bali.

Sen, Amartya *et al.*, 2007. *Civil Paths to Peace: Report of the Commonwealth Commission on Respect and Understanding*. Amartya Sen (Chairperson).

Thapar, Romila, 1975. *Past and Prejudice*. New Delhi: National Book Trust.

Thapar, Romila, 2014. *The Past as Present*. Boston, MA: Harvard University Press.

Weil, Stephen E., 1989. 'What is the proper business of the museum: Ideas or things?' *Muse*, 7 (1). Ottawa: Canadian Museums Association, pp. 28–32.

PART VII

Case studies, ethical dilemmas and situational ethics training

30

THE LOMBROSO MUSEUM IN TURIN

A reflection on the exhibition and scientific study of human remains

Alberto Garlandini and Silvano Montaldo

Cesare Lombroso and his museum: inception, development, crisis

In the 1870s, a young Cesare Lombroso transformed his (initially itinerant) private collection into a museum, which was institutionalized as such at the University of Turin in 1876. Born in Verona in 1835, Lombroso held a Doctorate in Forensic Medicine, and was a psychiatrist, anthropologist and criminologist. Early on, he asserted his political stance by adopting Italian citizenship at a time when North-east Italy had long been under Hapsburg reign and was still striving towards unification.

Lombroso was first a liberal critic of the new national leadership and then a key figure in development of the so-called 'socialism of the professors' in response to the young Italian State's endeavour to build a more symbiotic relationship between the scholarly elite and political leaders (see Gibson 2002; Frigessi 2003; Rafter 2008; Montaldo and Tapero 2009; Knepper and Ystehede 2013; Milicia 2014a). Lombroso continued to be interested in a wide range of topics, driven by his social commitment, materialistic convictions and the belief that only science could address the great social problems of his time.

In 1876, Cesare Lombroso founded the discipline of criminal anthropology and published *Uomo delinquente* (*Delinquent Mankind*). This new 'science' of aberrant social behaviour believed that the discovery of the natural mechanisms of crime in human society would eventually provide an effective response to one of the issues that threatened the desired unity of the new Italian State. An icon for the Positivist movement, Lombroso was at the centre of a vast network of dynamic intellectual relationships. He vowed to revitalize the culture of Italy and to promote the advent of an age of science, succeeding those of theology and metaphysics. Lombroso's most successful texts were translated into many languages, and some of the most famous exhibits in his collection were displayed to millions of visitors during international exhibitions (see Colombo 1975; Montaldo and Cilli 2015).

At the turn of the century, Lombroso's collection was elevated to the status of a university museum and installed in Palazzo degli Istituti Anatomici (the Palace of Anatomical Institutes), where it can still be seen in Turin today. The goal of the collection's maintenance was to preserve materials for intellectual study in the new 'sciences of mankind'; but also to support Lombroso's own theories, as they provoked increasing concern within the scientific community.

Lombroso's death in 1909 coincided with the decline of Positivist ideology. However, the museum he had formed actually experienced a period of growth under the leadership of Mario Carrara, who was the criminologist's son-in-law and heir to his cultural and intellectual legacy. By the end of the 1920s, the Lombroso Museum was in decline, and even Lombroso's disciples had abandoned his working theories. In 1932, the museum's fate seemed to reach a terminal point, when Carrara was banned from university teaching and removed from his post as museum director for being one of the few Italian professors to refuse to swear allegiance to the Fascist regime. After the 1930s, very little was left of Lombroso or his museum. Most people had forgotten this leading scientist of the past century and gave no thought to his collection or what had become an obsolete repository of some of the investigations of nineteenth-century social science.

There was, in addition, a deliberate political intention to erase his name from history, in particular under the Fascist regime. Following the introduction of racial laws in 1938, Lombroso was no longer simply an out-of-fashion scientist, but a candidate for complete historical erasure. His name was deleted from the street atlas

FIGURE 30.1 The main room at the Lombroso Museum of Criminal Anthropology of the University of Turin, Italy. Credit: Cesare Lombroso Museum, University of Turin (Italy). Photographer: R. Goffi.

of a number of cities, and a monument which had been erected by followers in his honour in Verona, in 1921, was removed in 1942. As for concerns regarding Lombroso's legacy within the history of science: after the Second World War, his collections were moved to a different location; their showcases were left coated in dust, with artefacts massed in disorderly array; the 'museum' dedicated to Cesare Lombroso's creation had descended into a kind of hotchpotch of contents, an object of gaping curiosity and lugubrious gossip.

The reopening of the Lombroso Museum

In the 1970s, the Museo Lombroso enjoyed an unexpected revival. Historians saw in Lombroso an exemplary figure of Positivism, and interest was renewed for his museum as an extraordinary storehouse of testimonies regarding the history of social sciences and the interconnected disciplines underpinning psychiatry. The collections and their documentation were studied anew to uncover the theoretical antecedents of a modern police apparatus, and of 'total institutions'. Artists were also interested in many aspects of the collections, which yielded rich resources for the study of new creative tendencies in modern art that reached outside of the mainstream – for example, providing antecedents for the concept and collecting of artworks under the banner of Art Brut.

Thence began the arduous task of cataloguing, researching and restoring the neglected collections, supported by intellectuals and scholars who saw Lombroso's

FIGURE 30.2 The Villella Room at the Lombroso Museum of Criminal Anthropology, University of Turin, Italy. Credit: Cesare Lombroso Museum, University of Turin (Italy). Photographer: R. Goffi.

work – in the light of new historical and cultural critiques carried forward in the work of Foucault, Goffman, Fanon and Basaglia – as an example of the relationship between 'bourgeois' science, 'class' repression and the medicalization of deviance. In 2009, with the support of Turin city council and Piedmont regional government, this collective re-examination of history led to the transfer and reopening of the Lombroso Museum. Today the Museo di Antropologia criminale 'Cesare Lombroso' is part of the University of Turin's museum system, involved in exhibitions in Italy and abroad, and provides support to the research of many scholars. Imbued with the prejudices of an era, but also yielding dazzling insights, the museum survives as the result of Lombroso's persistent, fascinating, exciting and all-embracing curiosity (Giacobini *et al.* 2010). The museum is visited by tens of thousands of people each year, and offers an intellectual excursion in the paradigms of Positivism and the history of marginality. Meanwhile, it also concentrates critical resources for diffusing effective messages contradicting racism in its historical and contemporary forms.[1]

The NoLombroso Committee's condemnation of the Lombroso Museum

After the success of its reopening, the Lombroso Museum had to cope with unexpected attacks on its existence: notably, a protest by the neo-Meridionalisti groups and the foundation of the NoLombroso Committee. The activities of this organization began in May 2010, in the days when a neo-Bourbon protest was brewing against celebrations of the 150th anniversary of Italy's Unification (see Milicia 2014b and 2015; Montaldo 2012 and 2014).

'The Museo Lombroso is obscene, inhuman, racist [...] the negation of God', declared the committee's internet press release, with an invitation to put an end to the 'disgrace' by signing an online petition. This was introduced by an apodictic premise indicating that all activity carried out by Lombroso was 'science fiction' to prove the 'genetic' inferiority of the peoples of southern Italy. According to the committee, his theories were also at the basis of the extermination of Jews and Roma people. The petition called for the removal of Lombroso's ideas from textbooks (but did not indicate which works still argue in their favour); also the removal of his name from Italian streets, and the return of every specimen of Lombroso's anatomical collection to the municipalities of origin, or – where remains are not identifiable – to a priest who has reopened the catacombs of Naples. In addition to the *damnatio memoriae* of Lombroso, whose Jewish origin the NoLombroso campaign has continued to emphasize, the committee is promoting a bill for the cancellation of any official commemoration of men guilty directly or indirectly of war or race crimes. The committee now has approximately 300 supporters, including individuals, municipal councils, music bands, tourism associations and local tourism offices.

The Motta Santa Lucia municipal council and the NoLombroso Committee lawsuit

In 2011, the Motta Santa Lucia municipal council (province of Catanzaro) and the NoLombroso Committee jointly filed a complaint in the Lamezia Terme court, requesting the 'return' of the skull of a local outlaw, Giuseppe Villella, on display in the Museo Lombroso. This relic is known internationally because it underpinned Lombroso's 'discovery', in December 1870, of the relationship between biology and behaviour. The 'cornerstone' of that intellectual formulation – despite the fallacy of its conclusions – is considered to mark the beginnings of crime science, by criminology historians and scientists investigating the relationship between mind and behaviour alike. For these reasons, the Turin museum dedicates its fourth room to the exhibition of the Villella skull. An accompanying video illustrates the coming into being of the criminal atavism theory and its later rebuttal, providing accurate information on Lombroso's research and transmitting the critical message that the results of scientific research into human behaviour are always under review (Bianucci *et al.* 2011).

On 3 October 2012, the Lamezia Terme court issued an order and established that since the *Uomo delinquente* theory had been set aside by later scientific opinion, there were no longer any 'scientific or educational reasons to justify keeping the skull of Giuseppe Villella as an exhibit in the museum'. The presiding judge did not recognize the cultural nature of the relic made famous by Lombroso, ruling that:

> [T]he right to moral redemption is the foundation of the legitimation and the interest supporting the action of Motta Santa Lucia municipal council, since the latter might garner social prestige from the recovery of the bones of a character to whom so much importance was attached by criminal anthropology and who was now being rehabilitated.

The judge then ordered that the skull be returned to Motta Santa Lucia by the University of Turin, ordering the latter to pay for transport and burial, as well as the legal costs incurred by the municipal council and the NoLombroso Committee. In his findings against the University of Turin and the Ministry of Education, the judge added: 'pursuant to Art. 4 para. 4 ICOM's Code of Ethics' but without any further explanation.

On 30 October 2012, Catanzaro's State Attorney, on behalf of the University of Turin and the Ministry of Education, presented a request to suspend the enforceability of such an order, based on ICOM's Code of Ethics for Museums,[2] the Italian *Code of Cultural Heritage and Landscape* (Legislative Decree of 22 January 2004) and the Law on Human Remains. On 8 January 2013, Catanzaro's Court of Appeals fully accepted the request made by the State Attorney, declaring that:

> [T]he conditions existed for adopting the measure of suspension invoked by the University of Turin. In fact, the arguments in the appeal – objections to jurisdiction, competence, *nonultra petita*, and merit of claims made – do not appear unfounded and deserve further review.

The Court of Appeals' decision was scheduled to be delivered on 20 September 2016.

The ICOM Italia and the ICOM Ethics Committee stance

Following a request made by the NoLombroso Committee, ICOM Italia expressed its standpoint in favour of the Turin museum:[3]

> The results achieved by Lombroso, now rejected by scientists, are a stage in anthropological research: knowledge also proceeds through errors and uses them to ensure they are not repeated.
>
> At the University of Turin's Museo di Antropologia Criminale 'Cesare Lombroso' and in the guide that accompanies it, which is the work of a group of scholars, it is clearly stated that:
>
>> the new exhibition aims to provide visitors with the conceptual tools to understand how and why this controversial character formulated the theory of criminal atavism and the errors in the scientific method that led him to found a science that was later proved to be wrong.
>
> The methods used in the study of skulls and human remains are generally part of the history of anatomical studies and medical research: in every age and in every country the fact of treating the human body as an object of science has impacted religious and secular feelings but every advance in knowledge has been an achievement [...]
>
> The collection of bones assembled by Lombroso, since it became the property of the University of Turin, actually belongs to a public museum and as such is bound to follow the Code of Cultural Heritage (Legislative Decree of 22 January 2004), in which Articles 10 and 20 state:
>
>> Cultural heritage comprises immovable and movable items [...] of artistic, historical, archaeological or ethno-anthropological interest (Art. 10, para. 1). Cultural heritage cannot be destroyed, impaired, damaged or used for purposes that are not compatible with its historic or artistic nature or be such as to impair its conservation (Art. 20, para. 1).
>
> In particular, when anatomical collections enter a museum they acquire a new status, different from the original condition of a human corpse, becoming assets to safeguard, and their dispersion would be the negation of all museum ethics [...].
>
> The example invoked by the NoLombroso Committee concerning the German authorities' return to Namibia of 20 skulls of victims of Germany's early twentieth-century colonialism, is quite a different case from the request for the return of anthropological finds located in Turin's Museo Lombroso. Many skulls have no data of origin and have not been identified, and in any case come from Italian regions. Giuseppe Villella, born in Calabria, died in Pavia's hospital in 1864 (as stated in the archives) and should be considered in

every respect an Italian citizen, namely a member of a nation that was formed with the Unification and contribution of all communities on the peninsula.

The Turin museum, which preserves the skull carefully, with all the respect and compassion due to an individual, declares in its mission a 'commitment to deny the theory of criminal atavism and highlight the errors in the method that led Lombroso to found a science later proved to be erroneous'.

The return of the remains (to bury them? to preserve them? where?), an operation which is not envisaged in the existing Code of Cultural Heritage, would lead to the loss of a memory – certainly painful – that is part of the troubled history of our country.

Following a request of the NoLombroso Committee, the Ethics Committee of ICOM 'has closely reviewed all the documentation regarding the claims against the Museum of Criminal Anthropology Cesare Lombroso of the University of Turin'. Consequently it agrees with the position of ICOM Italia:

> The scholar Cesare Lombroso is famously known for his theories in the context of positivist science. Though the work of Lombroso is currently rejected by scientists, it is considered as a stage in anthropological research. In this regard, the Museum of Criminal Anthropology Cesare Lombroso only intends to make the visitor understand the process leading to Lombroso's theories in the field of criminal atavism. Moreover, the museum insists on the incorrect scientific methods and results of Lombroso.
>
> Though scientifically wrong, Lombroso's methods in the study of skulls and human remains still belong to the history of medical research, and shall be treated as such. The role of the museum is therefore to explain to the public this part of scientific history, even though it can hurt the sensitivities of individuals or groups.
>
> The preservation of human skeletons raises many ethical issues, which are addressed by the *ICOM Code of Ethics for Museums*. In the case of the Museum of Criminal Anthropology Cesare Lombroso, ICOM and its Ethics Committee consider that the use of human remains doesn't fall under the considerations of the Code, and that the scientific legitimacy of the museum shall prevail. [selected record]
>
> Considering the scientific purpose of the Museum of Criminal Anthropology Cesare Lombroso and the non-application of the article 4.4 of the ICOM Code of Ethics with regard to its collection, ICOM and its Ethics Committee support the position of ICOM Italy concerning the claims of the No Lombroso Technical Scientific Committee.

The *ICOM Code of Ethics for Museums* and Italian legislation

The Lombroso case touches on delicate ethical issues relating to the conservation and museum display of human remains, and the *ICOM Code of Ethics for Museums* (2004) plays an important role in the case's assessment. Both the ruling of the court of first instance and the State Attorney that appealed against that judgement make reference to the ICOM Code – the former simply to cite Article 4, para. 4, without reporting the content or arguing the reference in any way. The State Attorney's judgement refers to Article 4 and quotes almost the entire opinion of ICOM Italia, in favour of the museum's claim.

Until December 2014 in Italy, the ICOM Code of Ethics[4] had no national legislative value or binding, prescriptive force. Until this date, the ICOM Code was considered a kind of 'soft law', with great moral value recognized not only by ICOM members but also by many other public and private subjects. However, the Ministerial Decree on the organization and functioning of state museums, approved on 23 December 2014, changed the legislative impact of the ICOM Code of Ethics in Italy. Article 2 of the decree stipulates that state museums should have a statute 'drafted in compliance' with the ICOM Code; meanwhile Article 7 of the Italian law states that only public and private museums 'including science, university and demo-ethno-anthropological museums [...] organized in accordance with [...] the Code of Ethics of ICOM museums' will be considered part of the national museum system.

This new regulatory importance of the *ICOM Code of Ethics for Museums* will certainly have a continuing impact on Italian case law (including that relating to the Lombroso case), and it places additional responsibility on the ICOM Ethics Committee and ICOM's National Committees, which have challenging educational and interpretive tasks of promoting education and public awareness of the Code's principles and detailed guidelines on maintaining ethical standards in the conduct of museums nationally and internationally.

Notes

1 The museum's efforts in this direction materialized in 2010, implementing a project for compulsory-level schools.
2 The full text of the *ICOM Code of Ethics for Museums* is provided as *Appendix I* in the present publication. It is also available online for download from the ICOM website (with links to translations in French, Spanish, and many other languages including Italian). The English version is accessible at: http://icom.museum/professional-standards/code-of-ethics.
3 The integral stance unanimously approved by the governing board of ICOM Italia on 8 October 2012 is available at: www.icom-italia.org.
4 The *ICOM Code of Ethics for Museums* (2004) deals with the theme under three articles (nos. 2, 3 and 4):

> 2.5 Culturally Sensitive Material. Collections of human remains and material of sacred significance should be acquired only if they can be housed securely and cared for respectfully. This must be accomplished in a manner consistent with professional standards and the interests and beliefs of members of the community, ethnic or religious groups from which the objects originated, where these are known.

> 3.7 Human Remains and Materials of Sacred Significance. Research on human remains and materials of sacred significance must be accomplished in a manner consistent with professional standards and take into account the interests and beliefs of the community, ethnic or religious groups from whom the objects originated, where these are known.

4.2 Interpretation of Exhibitions. Museums should ensure that the information they present in displays and exhibitions is well-founded, accurate and gives appropriate consideration to represented groups or beliefs.

4.3 Exhibition of Sensitive Materials. Human remains and materials of sacred significance must be displayed in a manner consistent with professional standards and, where known, taking into account the interests and beliefs of members of the community, ethnic or religious groups from whom the objects originated. They must be presented with great tact and respect for the feelings of human dignity held by all peoples.

4.4 Removal from Public Display. Requests for removal from public display of human remains or material of sacred significance from the originating communities must be addressed expeditiously with respect and sensitivity. Requests for the return of such material should be addressed similarly. Museum policies should clearly define the process for responding to such requests.

References

Bianucci, P. *et al.*, 2011. *Il Museo di Antropologia criminale 'Cesare Lombroso' dell'Università di Torino*. Turin: Edizioni Libreria Cortina.

Colombo, G., 1975. *La scienza infelice: il Museo di antropologia criminale di Cesare Lombroso*. Turin: Boringhieri.

Frigessi, D., 2003. *Cesare Lombroso*. Turin: Einaudi.

Giacobini, G., Cilli, C. and Malerba, G., 2010. 'Il riallestimento del Musep di Antropologia criminale "Cesare Lombroso" dell'Università di Torino. Patrimonio in beni culturali e strumento di educazione museale'. *Museologia Scientifica*, 4 (1–2): 137–47, at: http://museolombroso.unito.it/images/info/approfondimenti/MAC_riallestimento.pdf.

Gibson, M., 2002. *Born to Crime: Cesare Lombroso and the Origins of Biological Criminology*. London: Praeger.

Knepper, P. and Ystehede, P.J. (eds), 2013. *The Cesare Lombroso Handbook*. London: Routledge.

Milicia, M.T., 2014a. *Lombroso e il brigante. Storia di un cranio conteso*. Rome: Salerno Editrice.

Milicia, M.T., 2014b. 'La protesta "No Lombroso" sul web. Narrative identitarie neo-meridionaliste'. *Etnografia e Ricerca Qualitativa*, 2: 265–86.

Milicia, M.T., 2015. 'Noi contro tutti. Una comunità identitaria sul web'. *EtnoAntropologia* 1, TBA.

Montaldo, S., 2012. 'La "fossa commune" del Museo Lombroso e il "lager" di Fenestrelle: il centocinquantenario dei neoborbonici'. *Passato e presente*, 30 (87): 105–18.

Montaldo, S., 2013. 'The Lombroso Museum from its origins to the present day', in P. Knepper and P.J. Yshtede (eds), *Cesare Lombroso Handbook*. London: Routledge, pp. 98–112.

Montaldo, S. 2014. 'Sudismo: guerre dei crani e trappole identitarie'. *Passato e presente*, 33 (93): 5–18.

Montaldo, S. and Cilli, C. (eds), 2015. *Il Museo di antropologia criminale 'Cesare Lombroso' dell'Università di Torino*. Cinisello Balsamo: Silvana Editoriale.

Montaldo, S. and Tappero, P. (eds), 2009. *Cesare Lombroso cento anni dopo*. Turin: UTET.

Rafter, N., 2008. *The Criminal Brain: Understanding Biological Theories of Crime*. New York: New York University Press.

31

THE AUSCHWITZ-BIRKENAU STATE MUSEUM AND AN ARTIST'S CLAIM TO PORTRAITS OF HOLOCAUST VICTIMS MADE IN AUSCHWITZ FOR JOSEF MENGELE

Vojtěch Blodig

Editor's preface

In this chapter, a case study is provided that turns in subtle and complex ways on human rights issues and the rights of an artist. It also illuminates the obligations of a museum to represent historical trauma, and the fate of victims of human rights abuse, utilizing a variety of primary records and respecting varied points of view of the different 'actors' in that history and their fate – while also considering a museum's need to respect obligations to authors of primary material held by the institution, including creative works by artists.

This case was prominent in the public domain in the years 2006–09, and was covered extensively by media, especially in the United States and Canada. The case involved a claim for repatriation of watercolour sketches of inmates made at Auschwitz by a Czech-born woman who was caught up in the holocaust. Through her academic training as an artist, Mrs Dinah Gottliebová-Babbitt (who died in the USA in 2009) was enlisted – under the direction of the infamous SS physician Dr Josef Mengele – to carry out watercolour portrait sketches documenting the facial character and features of Roma people interned by the Nazi regime, prior to their later extermination in the gas chambers.

In the later years of her life, Mrs Babbitt, who had married an American and moved to the United States after the Second World War, made strong appeals for the restitution of the few watercolours painted by her that had survived the events of the liberation of the Auschwitz II-Birkenau concentration camp in January 1945. As discovered and notified to the artist by the Auschwitz-Birkenau State Museum in the 1970s – but not then arousing any claim for return – a group of watercolour portraits of Roma subjects are today in the collection of the museum, which subsequently resisted Mrs Babbitt's later claim for restitution. When supporters of Mrs Babbitt's restitution cause first approached ICOM and the Ethics Committee on her behalf in 2007, the impression of an 'artist's rights' claim seemed strong.

However, through very helpful research by colleagues in IC MEMO, the ICOM International Committee of Memorial Museums in Remembrance of the Victims of Public Crimes, who were able to study this case from a close vantage point on the historical records, and the long aftermath of the holocaust for descendants of its victims, a much more detailed and complex picture emerged of the historical facts, including the many issues involved in the later relationships offered to Mrs Babbitt by the Auschwitz-Birkenau State Museum. The research also clarified other parties' interests – such as the counter-appeals by the surviving Roma community from that area: their plea for the museum's retention of the watercolours, as primary historical records of their community's grim fate in the penumbra of the holocaust.

During the ICOM Ethics Committee's consideration of this case, it became impossible to maintain a simple 'artist's rights' argument[1] about the rightful place and 'ownership' of the contested watercolours painted by Dinah Babbitt, without consideration of other aspects. Artists' rights, and human rights arguments more broadly, turn upon questions of reciprocal status and liberty in the original situation of these 'portraits' having been commissioned. Portraiture involves mutual recognition of autonomy, free will and consent: all conditions that it is impossible to maintain were not destroyed in the Auschwitz internment camp at Theresienstadt, and especially during the scientific experiments of Dr Josef Mengele conducted in the early 1940s.

Bernice L. Murphy
Chair of the ICOM Ethics Committee (2004–11)

Status Report by ICOM's International Committee IC MEMO (2007) on the Portraits of Roma Inmates made by Dinah Gottliebová-Babbitt and retained in the Collections of the Auschwitz-Birkenau State Museum in Oswiecim.

Responding to a request of Ms Bernice L. Murphy (Chairperson, ICOM Ethics Committee), the ICOM IC MEMO Committee discussed the matter concerning the portraits of Roma prisoners that were made – at the order of the infamous SS Dr Mengele – by Mrs Dinah Gottliebová (later married Babbitt) during her imprisonment in the concentration camp Auschwitz II-Birkenau as part of the documentation serving Dr Mengele's pseudo-scientific racial research.

Mrs Gottliebová, born in Brno, now the Czech Republic, then Czechoslovakia on 21 January 1923, was first deported, together with her mother, by transport U (her own transport number: 374) from Brno to the Terezín (Theresienstadt) Ghetto on 28 January 1942, and later from Terezín by transport Dm (her transport number: 4983) to the concentration and extermination camp Auschwitz II-Birkenau, where both were placed in the camp section BIIb, called Terezín Family Camp. Since Mrs Gottliebová was a painter with adequate training (before the war she had graduated from the Academy of Fine Arts), she was selected for portraying Roma inmates

FIGURE 31.1 Watercolour portrait of a Roma woman painted in Auschwitz during World War II by Dinah Gottliebová-Babbitt. From the collection of the Auschwitz-Birkenau Museum.

who were used in the above-mentioned research by Dr Mengele. Thanks to this activity, Mrs Gottliebová saved not only her own life but also the life of her mother. As many as 3,792 prisoners, who had been deported to Auschwitz by transports from Terezín in September 1943, were murdered on the night of 8 March 1944. Only several dozens of the inmates were saved due to different reasons. Among them was Mrs Gottliebová with her mother. Mrs Gottliebová was eventually liberated at the end of the war at Neustadt-Glewe in Germany.

Only some thirty years after the war did Mrs Gottliebová learn that not all of her drawings had been destroyed. Shortly after the liberation of the Auschwitz camp in January 1945, a young man from a nearby town came to the camp for a Hungarian woman prisoner whom his parents wanted to adopt. As a sign of appreciation of this act, one of the liberated inmates gave the young man a roll containing several drawings. This included six pictures, which were then for a long time in the possession of the said family. In 1963, the adopted girl sold the drawings to the Auschwitz-Birkenau State Museum in Oswiecim. In 1977, the Museum acquired the seventh drawing from another former prisoner. As a result, all these drawings were acquired by purchase from specific persons and not through confiscation or any other irregular means. In 1969, the head of the Department of Collections of the aforementioned Museum found out that a book by Ota Kraus and Erich Kulka, titled *Továrna na smrt* (*The Death Factory*) and published in the then Czechoslovakia, contained a drawing designated 'Dinah 1944', just as the drawings acquired in the fashion mentioned above. Consequently, the identity of the author of the drawings, who was then living in the United States, could later be traced and established.

The Auschwitz Museum then contacted Mrs Gottliebová, who made use of her stay in Paris in 1973 to visit Poland and Auschwitz and its Museum where she provided her survivor report, clarifying the circumstances of the origin of the drawings of the Roma inmates. In her report, she expressed joy over staying alive and voiced her wish to acquire photographs of the portraits of the Roma prisoners, works that were in the possession of the Auschwitz Museum. For a long time (until the second half of the 1990s) this particular visit remained Mrs Gottliebová's only contact with the Auschwitz Museum. It is appropriate to add in this context that another survivor report, which is kept in the Jewish Museum in Prague and which had been recorded with Mrs Gottliebová in 1995, contains no mention of any eventual dispute with the Auschwitz Museum. There is only a remark that the drawings are kept in Oswiecim and that they had been published in books on many occasions.

According to information from the Auschwitz Museum in December 1973, Mrs Gottliebová was sent a printed version of her recollections and – in keeping with her wish – two collections of photographs of the portraits of the Roma prisoners she had drawn in Auschwitz. However, Mrs Gottliebová responded neither to this consignment nor to the following letters, which led the management of the Museum to the assumption that she no longer wanted to be reminded of those tragic moments of the past.

In the second half of the 1990s, Mrs Gottliebová – in the opinion of the officials of the Auschwitz Museum quite surprisingly – began to claim the return of the drawings, which are in the possession of that Museum. The position of the Auschwitz-Birkenau State Museum in Oswiecim is that the Museum is the lawful owner of the seven disputed portraits of the Roma inmates. At the same time, it does not question the fact that Mrs Gottliebová is, indeed, the copyrights holder. On the other hand, the Museum insists that the drawings, which are now the subject of the dispute, should stay in Oswiecim, regarding them as part and parcel of the material evidence on the Nazi crimes, which document the history of the place where the crimes had been committed. These documents, such as death announcements and prison numbers, but also works of art made by the prisoners at the Nazi's orders constitute – as part of the specific documentation – a unique testimonial to the Nazi crimes closely connected with the place where such works had been made. Some works by inmates employed in the camp's different offices, technical drawings as well as various artworks, are also signed. Former inmates who made prison photos of their fellow victims in the '*Lagererkennungsdienst*' (Camp Identification Service) are still alive. There are also many pieces of luggage brought in to Auschwitz by the prisoners and today displayed at exhibitions, which bear the names of their former owners, some of whom are still alive because they had been selected for slave labour and survived all the hardships. All these objects and documents are regarded as part of the documentation on the history of the largest Nazi camps where most victims had perished. That was also why the camp was placed on the UNESCO World Heritage List twenty years ago. Therefore, the Museum views the idea of taking any part of the collection out of the overall set as an irreplaceable loss, being well aware that Dinah Gottliebová's seven drawings constitute a mere fraction (in her request for the return in 1997 Mrs Gottliebová speaks of eight pieces; as a result the data given by the opposing parties in the dispute differ by one item) of the total. All in all, the collections contain some 2,000 works of art made by prisoners. These include works created at the orders of the SS, as in the case of Dinah Gottliebová, but also works made secretly, at the risk of certain loss of life, in an effort to document the genuine face of life in the camp.

At the behest of Mrs Shelley Berkley, member of the House of Representatives of the US Congress, a resolution was passed on 22 July 1999, supporting the claim of Mrs Gottliebová-Babbitt for the return of the drawings, and addressing in this matter the Auschwitz-Birkenau State Museum and the Polish state as well.

On 17 August 1999, the Council of Polish Roma – in its position – rejected the idea of returning the drawings because, in a sense, they constitute relics of their own kind of the Roma community imprisoned at this place of their biggest extermination, and no copy of such material evidence can ever replace such testimonials. At the same time, this position rejects the opinion expressed by Mr John Hancock, who, as a Roma living in the United States, supported Mrs Gottliebová's demand. The Council said in its standpoint that he had no authority to speak on behalf of European Roma.

For its part, the Central Council of Sints and Roma in Germany issued a statement on this matter on 15 September of the same year. It described the drawings made by Mrs Gottliebová at the order of Dr Mengele as particularly important documents on the genocide committed by the Nazis on the Roma population in Europe, and the Auschwitz camp as a symbol of this genocide. It went on to say that the author did not do the portraits voluntarily, at her own will, but was forced to do them, just as the models who had been made to sit for the portraits and were then murdered. According to the view of the Central Council, pictorial documents thus created cannot and should not be handed over into unlimited private ownership, as they represent an irreplaceable testimony. The position also demands that the pictures should, in any case, remain in the Auschwitz Museum.

In a similar vein, the position assumed by the Society of Experts and Friends of the Museum of Roma Culture, the only Roma museum in the Czech Republic, based in Brno, the native town of Mrs Gottliebová, describes her moral and legal claims as disputable, and demands that the drawings should serve the broad public for the purpose of learning about the past in a place where the greatest number of Roma perished as a result of Nazi genocide. It rejects the idea of sending the drawings to the United States, far from the places where the tragic events really unfolded.

This particular issue was discussed in September and December 1999 by the UNESCO World Heritage Committee, which noted that the matter should be considered in compliance with the local, and not international, legal norms.

On 31 September 1999, the International Board of the Auschwitz-Birkenau State Museum approved a declaration on this issue signed by Wladyslaw Bartoszewski, Poland (Chairman – former prisoner and Polish Minister of Foreigner Affairs in the 1990s), Israel Gutman, Israel (Vice-Chairman – former prisoner and head of the Research Institute of Yad Vashem Memorial Authority in Jerusalem), and Stefan Wilkanowicz, Poland (Vice-Chairman). The declaration says the Board considers that the conflict involving portraits of Roma prisoners of Birkenau is very damaging and that it only serves the interests of neo-Nazis. The Board understands the feelings of the artist who owes her survival to painting these portraits, as it understands those of the Roma brotherhood for whom they represent a precious testimonial of the martyrdom of their people. However, it cannot accept the claim that objects hand-crafted at the camp by former inmates should remain the prisoners' property to be used at their discretion. Should this principle be accepted, the collection would be depleted of articles that are indispensable for the Museum to fulfil its purpose.

Professor Jonathan Weber, UNESCO Chair in Jewish and Interfaith Studies, University of Birmingham, Member of the International Auschwitz Council, answered the question about his position in this case by saying that the Auschwitz Museum should refuse the request to return Mrs Gottliebová's drawings because it acquired them legitimately and is exhibiting them appropriately. To return the drawings would set a serious precedent and put in jeopardy the whole task of such museums to carry out their responsibilities to preserve the memory of the crimes against humanity that took place in the territories under Nazi rule. Furthermore, authentic original artefacts, held in museums at original sites of the Holocaust, are needed in order to counter Holocaust deniers now and in the future. This statement summarizes most cogently the arguments on which the Auschwitz Museum bases its position.

Unfortunately, the position of the other opposing party could not be added. The Chair of the IC MEMO Committee, as an official representing as Vice-Director the Terezín Memorial, Czech Republic, closely cooperates with the Terezín Initiative, an organization associating the former inmates of the Terezín Ghetto. That is why he has turned, after unsuccessfully asking Mrs Gottliebová-Babbitt for detailed clarification of her stance in writing, to this international association with a request for help in establishing contact. But it was found out that Mrs Gottliebová-Babbitt is not a member of the Terezín Initiative and never maintained any contact with it. That is why no new information on Mrs Gottliebová's position in this matter could be obtained. Due to the same reason, an offer of eventual mediation in the ongoing dispute has remained unanswered.

Note

1 Artists' rights claims can in many circumstances, according to an ethical perspective, take precedence over other aspects of legal ownership claims and rights. Yet legal identity itself is often a complex matter: 'Although, in accordance with copyright principles, a work of art carries the stamp of the author's personality (and also, to some extent, that of those who inspired the work), it in no way embodies its legal identity' (Cornu 2009: 329).

Reference

Cornu, M., 2009. 'The concepts of original heritage and adoptive heritage in French legislation', in Lyndel V. Prott (ed.), *Witnesses to History: A Compendium of Documents and Writings on the Return of Cultural Objects*. Paris: UNESCO, pp. 326–44.

32

THE MASK OF KA-NEFER-NEFER

The complex history of an Egyptian object

Regine Schulz

The Secretary General of the Supreme Council of Antiquities (SCA) in Egypt at the time, Professor Dr Zahi Hawass, sent a letter on 24 June 2007 to the Chair of the ICOM Ethics Committee, Bernice Murphy, to alert her to possible ethical problems related to the acquisition of the mummy mask of Ka-nefer-nefer by the Saint Louis Art Museum (SLAM) in Missouri, USA. In addition, at the meeting of ICOM's International Committee for Egyptology (CIPEG) during ICOM's General Conference in Vienna, Mr Mohamed Abdel Fatah, Head of the Museums Section in the SCA at the time, presented a statement by the SCA, dated 20 August 2007, on the protection of Egyptian cultural heritage, with a special focus on this case as an example of ethical and legal issues being faced.[1]

The Egyptian authorities were convinced that the mask was stolen and had left the country illegally. However, the disappearance of the mask was not noticed until 1973 and not reported to INTERPOL. Therefore, the Saint Louis Art Museum had no information about it, and did not know when the provenance research was done. When the SCA learned about the purchase in 2004 and realized that it was the well-known mask of Ka-nefer-nefer, they officially requested the return of the mask (see Young 2007; Gay 2015).[2] When all negotiations failed, the Egyptian government requested the support of the US federal authorities and considered filing a suit against the museum on the basis of a violation of the Traffic Act from 1930. SLAM assumed that the request had been made five years prior and was therefore forfeited.

For this reason, in January 2011 it filed its own lawsuit with a view to ensuring that the mask could not be seized by the government because the claim was too old, and that under Egyptian law, the mask was not the property of Egypt (O'Donnell 2014a). On 31 March 2012, the US District Court decided that the Department of Justice had not been able to prove that the mask was stolen. The question of forfeiture was further discussed and the Appeals Court for the Eighth Circuit was asked for an update. On 12 June 2014, the court confirmed the dismissal of the US government's attempt to seize the mask of Ka-Nefer-Nefer from the museum. Although a rehearing would have been possible, the Department of Justice decided not to take any further action in the case. However, the discussion is not over yet, and it is still possible that the Egyptian government will take legal action in the USA.

Despite the ongoing discussion, this case has been chosen for publication in this volume because it was an important topic brought before the ICOM Ethics Committee (in August 2007, October 2009 and November 2010), before an ICOM US meeting on behalf of the ICOM Ethics Committee (May 2008) and before the SCA in Egypt (October 2009 and February 2010).

What do we know?

The excavation of the burial of Ka-nefer-nefer

In 1952, the Egyptian archaeologist and Chief Inspector of Antiquities at Saqqara, Muhammed Zakaria Ghoneim, discovered during his excavation of the unfinished step pyramid of the Third Dynasty King Sekhem-khet at Saqqara, many intact burials from the Ramesside period above the royal tomb. One was the un-mummified body of a Nineteenth-Dynasty lady wrapped in a reed mat, who probably lived under the reign of King Ramesses II. A seven-row collar with falcon head terminals on the shoulders covers the chest. It is combined with two colourful rosettes with inlaid nipples on the breasts. A picture zone between the hands shows a large lotus blossom and an adoration scene inside a ceremonial barque, displaying the kneeling deceased with raised arms worshipping the god Osiris seated on his throne in front of an offering table. The arms of the mask are crossed and the hands hold a wooden *Djed-* (right) and a *Tjt*-amulet (left) symbolizing protection and stability. On the back of the right hand, there is a Hieratic inscription with one version of the lady's name: *Neferw*. Today, this inscription is no longer visible and painted over during conservation treatment at an unknown date after the discovery. Zakaria Ghoneim found, together with the mask, two pectorals, a necklace, a finger ring, several amulets and two mummy-shaped *shabti*-figures. These figures and one of the pectorals have the second version of the lady's name: Ka-nefer-nefer.[3]

What happened to the mask after the discovery and before coming before SLAM?

The history of the mask after its discovery is controversial and there are two main versions. In both reconstructions, there are gaps and until now, no one knows how to fill them in.

The Saint Louis Art Museum (SLAM) points out that it practised due diligence as far as possible with the following results:

- The findings of the excavation of Muhammed Zakaria Ghoneim were exhibited in the Egyptian Museum in Cairo directly after the discovery, but without the mummy mask. A scholar, whose name is not mentioned, confirms this in a letter from 12 December 1999 (see SLAM, online).
- The Swiss collector and dealer Charly Mathez saw the mask in a gallery in Brussels in 1952 (confirmed in a letter from 11 February 1997), but does not remember the name of the gallery any more, in a second letter from 5 October 1999 (SLAM, online, n. 2).
- In the early 1960s a Swiss collector (who wishes to stay anonymous) bought the mask from the Croatian family Kaloterna (or Kaliterna). He mentioned this in a letter (19 March 1998) to Mr Hicham Aboutaam of Phoenix Ancient Art. However, in the art law report of June 2014 on the lawsuit between the USA and SLAM on the possession of the mask, the collector is mentioned by name as Ms Zuzi (also Suzana) Jelinek (see SLAM, online).
- Phoenix Ancient Art, S.A. of Geneva bought the mask from Ms Jelinek around 1995.
- On 30 March, or in April 1998, Phoenix Ancient Art sold the mask to SLAM (SLAM, online).

The Egyptian Antiquities organization presented other facts as a result of internal research:

- After the mask was excavated in 1952 it was brought into the Sekhemkhet storage and was registered there with the number 6119. A photo of the mask was attached to the entry in the register book.
- In 1959 the Egyptian Antiquities Organization included the mask and other objects of the burial of Ka-nefer-nefer as part of a travelling exhibition to Japan. On 7 May 1959, the mask was removed from this storage and from its register. It is also mentioned in the report of the Inventory/Packing Committee from 18 July 1959. The objects, including the mask, were brought to the Egyptian Museum and have arrived there, because at the end the decision was made not to include it in the travelling exhibition.
- In 1962, the mask was sent back to Saqqara (Bradford 2014).
- In 1966, the mask travelled a second time to Cairo in a travel box with the number 54. This is the last notification of the mask in Egypt.
- In 1973, when the objects of the Ka-nefer-nefer burial were registered in the Journal d'Entrée (JE 92649) of the Egyptian Museum with new numbers, the mask was no longer part of it and appeared to be missing.

What steps were taken by the Saint Louis Art Museum to fulfil the obligations for due diligence?

- Checking the provenance information from Phoenix Ancient Art.
- Consulting several specialists in the field of Egyptology.

- On 24 October 1997 and 14 January 1998: A letter was sent from Sidney M. Goldstein, Ph, (Curator of Ancient and Islamic Art at SLAM) to the former director of the Egyptian Museum, Dr Mohammed Saleh, to ask if he knew anything about the mask. On 3 March 1998, an answer was received from Dr Saleh.
- 19 February 1998: Report from the Art Loss Register to Thomas William Alvey III.
- 16 February 1998: Letter from SLAM to INTERPOL requesting a search of their database; 23 February: response of INTERPOL to SLAM that it was stolen.
- 27 February and 4 March 1998: Request for information from SLAM to the Missouri State Highway Patrol.
- 8 October 1999: Letter from Dr Peter Lacovara (Egyptologist and Senior Curator of Ancient Egyptian and Nubian Art at the Michael C. Carlos Museum of the Emroy University, Atlanta at that time) stating that 'Egyptian nationals were allowed to keep a share of their finds, much as Europeans were given divisions' and on 27 November 2008, he gave an affidavit on this fact.

Action taken by the SCA and answers from SLAM between 2005 and 2007

- 2005: The Supreme Council of Antiquities requested the repatriation of the mask, and claimed that the mask is the rightful property of Egypt.
- From 14 February 2006 to 29 January 2007: Eight letters from Zahi Hawass (Secretary General, SCA) to Brent Benjamin (Director, SLAM) and seven direct answers.
- 5 July 2006: Additional letters by Zahi Hawass to Thomas H. Brouster (Chairman of the Trustees of SLAM).
- 24 July 2006 to 24 October 2006: Several letters between Patrick Mulcahy (President of the Board of Commissioners of SLAM) and Zahi Hawass.
- Letters between and with the legal advisors:
    - 5 January 2007: Letter from Ed Johnson (Attorney), on behalf of the SCA to Brent Benjamin;
    - 30 January 2007: Letter from Michael A. Kahn (legal counsel to SLAM), to Edward D. Johnson (legal counsel to the SCA);
    - 7 February 2007: Letter from Edward D. Johnson (legal counsel to the SCA), to Michael A. Kahn (legal counsel to SLAM).
    - After February 2007, the correspondence was on hold.

Conclusion

At the time of writing, the US court has supported the request of the Saint Louis Art Museum to keep the mummy mask of Ka-nefer-nefer. However, some questions remain: Who sold the mask in the first place? There is no record or indication that Muhammed Zakaria Ghoneim received the mask as a share in an official division of the finds between the excavator and the antiquities organization and sold it on the art market. How is it possible that there are records in register books (including a photo) and transportation records from 1952 to 1966, when the mask was out of the country in the same time since 1952? Is it not strange for someone to remember a mummy mask after more than forty years, but not the name of the gallery where he has seen it?

All speculations that the Ka-nefer-nefer mask, which was recorded in Egypt between 1952 and 1966, was another mask, are very unlikely. When the mask was discovered there was great media attention, there was a photo in the register book, and although ancient Egyptian mummy masks can look somewhat similar, each mask is different and it is unlikely that the responsible curators and conservators could mix them up. Furthermore, it was due to the mask's high quality that it was included in a special exhibition to Japan. When it left the country officially in 1952, it is strange that the responsible authorities should have forgotten this fact.

There is no doubt that the Saint Louis Art Museum attempted to practise due diligence in establishing the provenance of the mask. However, the information the museum received from Phoenix Ancient Art was ambiguous. After the letter exchange between the SCA and SLAM in 2006 and 2007, the museum was aware of the evidence the Egyptian authorities had produced. This must have caused them to question their own reconstruction of the provenance of the mask. The result we have now may be satisfactory for the museum for a while, but it is possible that Egypt will consider another lawsuit against the museum. From an ethical point of view, it is disappointing that until now no mediation or other solution has been considered. The renewed ethical codes and guidelines of the American Association of Museums (the Saint Louis Art Museum is a member of AAM) and of the Association of Art Museum Directors in 2011, as well as the *ICOM Code of Ethics for Museums*, may hopefully convince SLAM to consider fresh negotiations with the Egyptian Ministry of Antiquities to find an acceptable solution.[4]

Notes

1 In this statement, Dr Zahi Hawass pointed out that:

> We have presented the Saint Louis Art Museum with documentation of the mask's registration as the property of the Egyptian government. The Saint Louis Art Museum can produce no permits or legitimate records of any kind to support their argument that the mask left Egypt legally in the mid-twentieth century. However, they continue to deny our claim to the mask outright. We will use every diplomatic option available to us to ensure the mask's return. Furthermore, we believe that it is our right in this matter to take legal action, both civil and criminal.

2 For further details and opinions, see the Master's thesis of Laura Young from 2007 at the University of Oregon, *A Framework for Resolution of Claims for Cultural Property*, at: https://scholarsbank.uoregon.edu/xmlui/handle/1794/6575 (accessed 16 December 2015); and the article of Malcolm Gay, 'Out of Egypt', *Riverfront Times*, 15 February 2006, at: www.riverfronttimes.com/stlouis/out-of-egypt/Content?oid=2484863 (accessed 16 December, 2015).

3 *Code of Ethics of AAMD* from 2011 (section 5); *Code of Ethics of AAM* (section on Collections, point 5) and ICOM Code of Ethics, point 2.3.

4 Mentioned for the first time in an article on 7 June 1952 in *The Illustrated London News* and later published by the excavator: Goneim, M. Zakaria, 1956. *The Lost Pyramid*. New York, p. 65, pl. 15; *The Buried Pyramid*, 1956. London, pp. 54–55; *Horus Sekhem-khet – The Unfinished Step Pyramid At Saqqara, Volume 1. Excavations at Saqqara*, Cairo: Imprimerie de l'Institut Français d'Archéologie Orientale, 1957, pp. 23–27, pls. LXVII–LXIX.

References

Bradford, Paul, 2014. 'Ka Nefer Nefer, shamed US government throws in towel', at: http://paul-barford.blogspot.de/2014/07/ka-nefer-nefer-shamed-us-government.html; and opinion of Judge Autrey on the case from 31 March 2012, at: http://de.scribd.com/doc/87737286/Ka-Nefer-Nefer-Opinion (accessed 16 December 2015).

ICOM, 2004. *ICOM Code of Ethics for Museums*. Paris: ICOM (International Council of Museums). The full text of the *ICOM Code of Ethics for Museums* is provided as *Appendix I* in the present publication. It is also available online for download from the ICOM website (with links to translations in French, Spanish, and many other languages). The English version is accessible at: http://icom.museum/professional-standards/code-of-ethics.

O'Donnell, Nicholas, 2014a. 'US abandons finally its effort to seize mask of Ka-nefer-nefer'. *Art Law Report*, 29 July 2014, at: www.artlawreport.com/2014/07/29/united-states-abandons-finally-its-effort-to-seize-mask-of-ka-nefer-nefer-egypts-plans-unknown (accessed 18 December 2015).

O'Donnell, Nicholas, 2014b. 'What happens to St Louis Art Museum suit against the US over the mask of Ka-nefer-nefer?' *Art Law Report*, 16 June 2014, at: www.artlawreport.com/2014/06/16/what-happens-to-st-louis-art-museum-suit-against-the-u-s-over-the-mask-of-ka-nefer-nefer-will-museum-dismiss-its-case (accessed 18 December 2015).

33

ETHICS VERSUS LAW

The restitution of *The Miracle of St Anthony* by Giovanni Battista Tiepolo

Aedín Mac Devitt

In the days leading up to Christmas 1978, unbeknownst to Paola Modiano Ferrari di Valbona, her seventh floor apartment in the heart of Paris's Latin Quarter was being scrutinized by thieves. On Christmas Eve, seventy-one-year-old Paola had vacated her apartment on 17, rue du Petit Pont; her most valuable possession, *The Miracle of St Anthony* (*Il miracolo di Sant' Antonio*, oil on canvas, 1754/6) painting by Venetian Rococo painter Giovanni Battista Tiepolo, hung on her bedroom wall. She had inherited the work of art from her father, Jewish industrialist Ettore Modiano, following his death twenty-three years prior. On acquiring it in London in 1929, he had imported it to Italy, under temporary import regime, and it joined the family art collection in Bologna.

On returning to her apartment, Paola discovered many precious items missing from her home, including silverware, a Terracotta statue, a painting by Gerolamo Induno and the aforementioned Tiepolo painting. The latter, which depicts *The Miracle of St Anthony*, was recorded in published art historical literature on Tiepolo (Morassi, Palluchini, *et al.*) as belonging to the Modiano family. During World War II, the painting was declared a cultural asset of special importance in Italy and the country protected the Modiano family's collection from the Nazi regime. At the end of the war, this declaration was revoked given that the painting was still subject to temporary import regime.

Paola Modiano reported the theft almost immediately to the police department of Paris's fifth district through her Parisian management company (Etablissements Guibert S.L.) and then personally in February 1979. Later, with the assistance of renowned Italian art historian, Bianca Riccio, who had personally managed the division of some goods of the Modiano family, including the Tiepolo painting, she brought the theft to the attention of INTERPOL and the Louvre Museum. In a postcard sent from Rome, Riccio urged her to send the data immediately to INTERPOL, including details of the painting, as recorded in literature on the artist's work, by Antonio Morassi:

FIGURE 33.1 *The Miracle of St Anthony*, Giovanni Battista Tiepolo. Acquired in 1929 in London by Jewish industrialist Ettore Modiano.

Send all the details to INTERPOL immediately, if possible an image of the frame and a photocopy of Morassi's book. (. . .) You will definitely find it; it will be difficult to make it disappear, given that the thieves recognized it.

Translated from the Italian.[1]

The Carabinieri intervene

The police reports led nowhere, however, despite several enquiries by Paola and members of her family over the years. The painting's whereabouts remained a complete mystery. Almost twenty-two years passed before the Ferrari di Valbona family decided to take up the matter with the Carabinieri Nucleo Tutela Patrimonio Artistico, a special unit of the Italian police dealing with cultural heritage.

In November 2001 the Carabinieri paid a visit to the then elderly Paola and her family with a view to locating the work. Based on the information given by the family, together with research on art historical records, the Carabinieri succeeded in locating the painting. Their enquiries revealed that it had found its way to Germany, forming part of the collection of the Niedersächsisches Landesmuseum (Lower Saxony State Museum) in Hannover since 1985. This discovery was certainly surprising given that the painting had been identified in all catalogues since the 1920s as belonging to the Ettore Modiano collection. It later transpired that the purchase had been announced in 1986 in the French art journal, *Gazette des Beaux Arts* (Di Blasi 2010).

The Ferrari di Valbona family takes legal action

Having located the work, the family decided to engage the services of Prof. Gabriele Crespi Reghizzi, an internationally renowned Italian lawyer, to assist them in their bid to retrieve the painting. According to Cesare Ferrari di Valbona, Paola Modiano's grandson, an initial approach to the museum was rejected, with the museum showing little or no interest in taking the discussion further.

This led the family to also engage the services of Prof. Peter Raue (former Chair of the Freunde der Nationalgalerie in Berlin) and Dr Mareile Buscher of Hogan and Hartson Raue LLP, an eminent legal team in Germany, in order to file a lawsuit against the State of Lower Saxony, bringing the case before the Regional Court of Hannover. Details of the dubious circumstances surrounding the sale and export of the painting emerged during the proceeding.

The family learned that the Niedersächsisches Landesmuseum had acquired the painting in 1985 from a virtually unknown private art dealer in Paris, Ms Grati Baroni de Piqueras. In 1984, the museum's head curator met with Ms Grati Baroni de Piqueras in her Paris apartment to discuss the details of the painting and its possible acquisition by the museum. Apparently aware that the painting was Italian, and recorded in the 1920s in all catalogues (Morassi, Pallucchini *et al.*), the head curator acting on behalf of the Niedersächsisches Landesmuseum had asked the art dealer if she had duly exported the painting from Italy, obtaining all permissions necessary in this regard.

In later correspondence with the International Council of Museums, Cesare Ferrari relayed the recollection of this discussion in court as follows:

> When asked if the painting came from the Ferrari family because it had been published in many books and was known to belong to the Modiano/Ferrari family, the dealer answered 'No, a private family'. The museum replied, 'thank you'. When the museum asked how the painting arrived in France, the dealer said 'legally'. The museum replied 'thank you'.

In addition, the museum was unable to produce the export papers that would prove that the transfer of the painting from France to Germany was carried out legally. Neither was it able to prove that the required export turnover tax had been paid.

During the proceeding, Prof. Dr Jan Kelch, the former director of the Gemäldegalerie in Berlin, was commissioned by the court to prepare an expert report. The nineteen-page document provides an in-depth analysis of the requirements to be met when acquiring artworks at the time. It also examined many aspects of the case, including the Ferrari di Valbona family, their undisputed ownership of the Tiepolo in art historical records, the art dealer, the sale price, bank transfer, etc.

The aim of Dr Kelch's report was to determine whether the museum had complied with its duty to exercise due care in accordance with the international practice of museums at the time when acquiring the painting. Ultimately, Kelch criticized the museum's handling of the acquisition. His report concluded that the museum had failed to exercise due care, and to collect sufficient information required. He criticized its 'readiness to assume risk when negotiating with the art dealer' and the fact that the export formalities had 'not all been understood as a problem'.

The report also pointed to the fact that Pierre Rosenberg, Director of the Louvre Museum at the time, should have been asked to sign export permission for the painting, given its importance in the art world.

In his correspondence with the Secretariat, Cesare Ferrari confirmed that Pierre Rosenberg had declared to Prof. Dr Kelch before the court that he had never been consulted about the painting's export to Germany, and had 'never heard of that lady' (Ms Grati Baroni de Piqueras).

On 11 January 2007, the Regional Court of Hannover announced its verdict. It held that the museum had acted in good faith when acquiring the painting. The court considered that the perceived negligence was not of decisive importance given the time that had elapsed before the issue of contested ownership was raised.

In the aftermath of the verdict, the Ferrari di Valbona family issued a public press release outlining the case and the Regional Court's decision. The following excerpt illustrates their disappointment with the outcome of the four-year-long procedure:

> The Regional Court of Hannover dismissed the action of the heirs of the Ferrari di Valbona family with its judgment. The court held that the museum

had acted in good faith when acquiring the painting. With this the Regional Court provides the Landesmuseum with the right to excuse an obviously illegal transport of the painting from France to Germany.[2]

The Ferrari di Valbona family seeks the support of ICOM

On 9 April 2008, Cesare Ferrari di Valbona made contact with the ICOM Secretariat with a view to obtaining support for its case against the museum. Jennifer Thévenot, then Programmes Officer at the ICOM Secretariat, relayed the information surrounding the case, as provided by Cesare Ferrari, to the ICOM Ethics Committee, chaired by Bernice Murphy.

In a communication to committee members, Bernice Murphy expressed her great surprise at the various aspects of the case, including the museum's assumption that as a non-ICOM member, it is not bound by the *ICOM Code of Ethics for Museums*.

She suggested that the Ethics Committee consult and seek the advice of ICOM's National Committee in Germany (ICOM Germany), and that the full facts of the case, including the verdict, should be obtained before intervening.

Hans-Martin Hinz, as former Chair of ICOM Germany, confirmed that, according to the German Civil Code (Bürgerliches Gesetzbuch § 937), if an object is judged to have been acquired in good faith, and there is no intervention within a period of ten years, the ownership cannot be contested. Since the Tiepolo painting had been shown in exhibitions and discussed in journals and catalogues, he concurred that the museum would have been seen to have done everything in a professional manner according to the legislation en vigueur.

Meanwhile, York Langenstein, Chair of ICOM Germany at the time, approached the Ministry of Culture and Science in Hannover with a view to obtaining clarification on the case.

In official correspondence with the Ministry, he explained that the case had been submitted to the ICOM Ethics Committee because the circumstances of the acquisition of the painting may not have been consistent with due diligence obligations that museum experts are required to observe in the acquisition of works of art.

In terms of documentation, he requested a declaration by the State of Lower Saxony as to the legality of the acquisition of the Tiepolo painting and a copy of the judgement of the District Court of Hannover in January 2008, providing reasons for the decision.

Although the Ministry of Culture and Science in Hannover appears to have been less than forthcoming in providing substantial information on the case, ICOM Germany prepared itself to issue a public statement if lack of ethical behaviour is clearly disclosed in the case.

An appeal to the Higher Regional Court of Celle

Later that year, Cesare Ferrari di Valbona informed Jennifer Thévenot that the family had made an appeal to the Higher Regional Court of Celle, situated about 40 km north-east of Hannover, on 19 May 2008. The family was still represented by Prof. Peter Raue and Dr Mareile Buscher, with Prof. Garbriele Crespi Reghizzi as an international advisor.

In light of this new information, Hans-Martin Hinz recommended that the ICOM Ethics Committee wait for an official announcement from the Higher Regional Court of Celle before taking any further action.

Shortly after the appeal was made, the Ferrari di Valbona family nevertheless made one last attempt to settle the case out of court, by proposing a reduced payment of €300,000 for the painting. This was rejected by the museum.

On 30 October, the court issued a preliminary statement. It recognized that the Hannover Museum had been grossly negligent in its acquisition of the painting, and doubted that the opinion of the Regional Court of Hannover would withstand a legal review. However, the court would not yet overturn the previous judgement of the Hannover Regional Court and recommended that the two parties settle the dispute amicably, favouring a payment by the museum to the Ferrari di Valbona family.

In a report to the ICOM Secretariat in February 2009, Cesare Ferrari di Valbona detailed the lengthy and fruitless negotiation process with the museum as follows:

- November 2008: the museum offered the family €160,000 to settle the case. The family counter-offered a payment of the same amount to the museum in exchange for the return of the painting.
- 3 December: the museum refused this proposal, requesting an alternative.
- Mid-December: following estimates obtained by the family from auction houses Christie's and Dorotheum, who evaluated the painting at between €500,000 and €800,000, the family asked the museum to pay €400,000 by 13 January.
- 13 January: the museum requested the deadline be extended by one month pending two independent opinions requested on the value of the painting and the financial responsibility of the Niedersächsisches Landesmuseum.
- 14 January: the family agrees to extend the deadline.
- 12 February: the museum declines the family's offer of an amicable settlement, claiming to have expertise that evaluated the painting at just €150,000. (In this case a compensation payment of €400,000 would not have complied with the Budget Law of Lower Saxony.)

Following this breakdown in negotiations, the family continued to seek the support of ICOM in order to secure the return of the painting from the museum.

But in the meantime, some new evidence was brought to the attention of the Higher Court in Celle, which strengthened the case of the Ferrari di Valbona family.

A new witness, Wolfgang Gäfgen, a German painter from Esslingen, revealed that he had personally and illegally exported the painting through customs, from France to Germany. He had done this on behalf of Ms Grati Baroni de Piqueras after the museum's representatives had visited her apartment in Paris to check the painting. The court also learned that a 'fake' contract, under German law, had been signed between Gäfgen and the museum's senior curator at the time, Mr Trudzinsky, on 30 March 1985 in order to hide the French provenance of the painting. This key document had been concealed by the Niedersächsisches Landemuseum since the beginning of the case and was provided to the court by Gäfgen only. In a further twist, it emerged that Gäfgen was in fact the former son-in-law of Ms Grati Baroni de Piqueras.

In light of this new evidence, the museum was unable to demonstrate that it had acquired the painting in good faith and on 17 September 2010, the Higher Regional Court in Celle sentenced the Niedersächsisches Landesmuseum to return the painting to the executor of its original owner, Paola Modiano Ferrari di Valbona, who had passed away during the lawsuit process.

The court held that the museum had recklessly ignored suspicions when it took the art dealer for the legitimate owner of the painting.

The verdict, achieved thirty-one years following the original theft of the painting, was greeted with joy by the Ferrari di Valbona family. It was also hailed by the International Council of Museums and its Ethics Commitee as a fine example of how ethics can influence, and in some cases overthrow, legal judgements.

Notes

1 The case study has been compiled on the basis of extensive file records maintained by Bernice Murphy, former Chair of the Ethics Committee, when this case was before the Committee in the period 2008–10 until its conclusion.
2 Postcard sent from Paola Modiano Ferrari di Valbona to Bianca Riccio on 15 March 1979.
3 Correspondence between Jennifer Thévenot and Cesare Ferrari di Valbona on 16 April 2008.

Reference

Di Blasi, Johanna, 2010. 'Landesmuseum Hannover muss gestohlenes Gemälde zurückgeben'. *Hannoversche Allgemeine*, 17 September 2010, at: www.haz.de/Hannover/Aus-der-Stadt/ Uebersicht/Landesmuseum-Hannover-muss-gestohlenes-Gemaelde-zurueckgeben (accessed 18 December 2015).

34

ETHICS IN ACTION

Situational scenarios turning the keys to the Code of Ethics

Eva Maehre Lauritzen

As an ICOM member, I have always been proud of the *ICOM Code of Ethics for Museums*,[1] appreciating that it is a valid base-standards document for all museums and members, wherever they are located and regardless of what their museums collect. All members of ICOM agree to obey the Code of Ethics in joining or annually renewing their membership of the organization, so that members share a basic framework of ethical principles and guidelines in their work within or for museums, wherever this is carried out.

However, do all really know or remember in detail the contents of the Code? The Code of Ethics is not an easy text to read, even for the most positive and conscientious museum member. The more user-friendly 2004 edition, in comparison with the 1986 ICOM Code, is more clearly organized, but it is still a demanding text that needs concentration and patience to read and comprehend. Yet it is important that all museum employees know the general principles and contents of the Code and understand how to use it.

For good conduct in a museum, it is vital to understand the role of the Code as a tool guiding practice in daily work; not simply to regard the Code as a remedial authority when serious ethical problems arise in a museum. So my starting-point for training in ethics awareness for many years has been that the Code is a *tool for active use* in daily situations, and it is to be *used by all kinds of museum staff and supporters*. Ethics is not solely the responsibility of the museum's management, as some people seem to believe. All staff, members – even visitors and the museum's social community – have a stake in a museum's conduct of its ethical responsibilities. The ICOM Code plays an important role in protecting the museum objects, which are mostly unique (non-renewable objects), entrusted to public care of heritage and not to be confused with objects owned privately. It is a big responsibility for museums and museum staff to take care of their objects and other resources for heritage preservation, and the ICOM Code plays a supportive role of protecting people as well as objects from the consequences of uninformed practices, or 'wrong' decisions, that can lead to circumstances that will be regretted later.

For many years, I have been teaching museum ethics using a special workshop method. This approach arose in quite ordinary circumstances a decade ago: I was invited to present an outline of the 'new' (that is, revised) *ICOM Code of Ethics for Museums*, adopted by ICOM in 2004. This was to be provided in a non-academic museum meeting, and I was clearly told that the audience 'would not want a lecture'! So I thought about this task: 'An introduction to ICOM's Ethics Code, but no lecture!' My solution was to develop some daily-situation cases or fictional 'stories' that involved ethical issues; to invite the audience to discuss and explore questions of 'right' and 'wrong' conduct that seemed to be raised in these imagined situations; and finally to turn to the ICOM Code for study of the principles or guidelines stated – to find some solutions. It was encouraging to find, using this 'fictional scenarios' approach, that participants' interest in the themes rose intensely, and they became eager to find answers to 'situational' problems, using the Code as a resource. The evaluation of my programme was positive and convinced me afterwards that I should continue to develop this approach, as a clearly useful method for introducing ethics to a broad cross-section of museums people.

Compared to lectures, the ethics-in-action workshop method is immediately involving, interactive and engaging. It is particularly suited to multi-viewpoint learning, and it does not create an automatic division between academically and vocationally trained personnel. The workshop method is much used in different kinds of professional training, and participants gain a deeper understanding of issues or problems that are presented in daily life narratives or seemingly simple 'fables' – without relying first on any reading of texts, or listening to formal instruction.

Over some years of similar workshops, this method proved very effective as a hands-on, group-focused approach to exploring seemingly simple ethical questions that might arise casually in the activities of all kinds of staff and supporters in the life of a museum. For best success, the workshop requires a cross-section of museum staff ages, backgrounds and types of work to achieve maximum impact in spreading its ethics-in-action awareness – in direct contrast to an 'exceptional problem' attitude to ethics training, with only specialist staff in a leading role.

There were further reasons why the 'fictional tales' approach well suited colleagues from many different backgrounds. The implementation of this method enabled widest possible discussion (and elicited very frank anecdotes in some cases), precisely because the situations were fictional and non-threatening to real persons or reputations. I later found this proved its value as a methodology in varied cultural contexts – for example, when compiling 'fables' for an ethics workshop for the ICOM-ASPAC Conference in Tokyo, in December 2009 (see Mizushima 2016). Fictional scenarios helped to relieve difficulties in social contexts where open discussion of colleagues' behaviour is often a difficult matter that can arouse tension and reserve.

Utilizing an interactive method of this kind – with a broad cross-section of museums people present, including from very different types of work within museums – is now a proven, useful resource for training. Beginning with scenarios of a very informal kind, presenting awkward choices about 'right conduct', proves a strong tool for 'situational learning' – with formal codes of practice being the reference-aid used for exploring solutions to everyday dilemmas, not an 'academic tool' for the use of specialist staff.

Over some years, I have developed a set of descriptions of situations, cases or stories that I use for my museum ethics workshops – all connected to different aspects of museum work. I call them *Ethical Fables*, and their contents are easily recognized and familiar to people working in museums, especially in the smaller and less specialized museums. The fables are the results of imagining museum staff having a casual chat after work, airing their worries and frustrations among friends.

Having produced different sets of these fables, I often tailor-make them for a particular museum or a special group of participants. Sometimes a museum has a specific problem that can be brought to the surface during an ethics workshop. It might need a special situation-scenario to set off an exchange of opinions that – drawing in different people's viewpoints and experience – soon brings understanding that there is a problem needing a solution. This method provides many options and possibilities in highlighting important issues of ethical choice; meanwhile, most problems can in fact be imagined and incorporated within a fable. The main effort in workshop preparation is around good imagining of the issue in a simple narrative format; and attention to different cultural and social adaptations.

My workshops have been designed for all kinds of museum staff. They function well at various levels of training, and incorporating different experiences and backgrounds in the profession. All members of the profession have ethical responsibilities and all need to be aware of their responsibilities. The initiative for organizing a workshop most often comes from the museum management; but it is also not uncommon that it is initiated by museum employees working at a lower level of authority.

I usually begin a workshop with a general discussion of why ethics is important; why we need codes; and why learning their use and value is important. It is then time to remind participants of how useful the ICOM Code of Ethics is and a little of its background. I have called my introductory session about the ICOM Code of Ethics, 'What if…?' (What do we do if the museum receives a collection of old watches as a gift? The curator wants to get rid of some old mangles? The store rooms are too warm and too small? The janitor has a private collection?) Participants readily perceive in these simple propositions that there is a need for a Code!

Participants are then divided into groups and introduced to a prepared series of 'ethical fables', with the ICOM Code as a resource to hand. While group discussion is encouraged around any ethical problem arising, there are also some assignments with prepared questions relating to each of the fables. For example: What does the Code of Ethics say about this case? Who is responsible? How can it be solved? Who needs to be involved in implementing a solution? What actions by the museum should change in future? Are there persons outside the museum who could assist in preventing this problem occurring? Are some special training measures or new systems needed? Is there an issue that needs to be discussed with (or reported to) a person in authority?

In answering these questions, participants need to study the Code of Ethics and make notes for their presentation later in the session.

Following is an example, and the deliberately colloquial and everyday language is important to the framing of the situation:

> The head of public programmes suggested that they should try to stimulate more income-generating activities. He suggested that the museum should accept an offer from the local antique dealer to arrange an Antique Fair in the lobby of the museum. People coming could also bring their own antiques to have them valued by museum experts – 'After all, we know much more about many objects than the antique dealers do.'

In this sample, the participants soon come to a realization that it is not a good idea to arrange an Antique Fair in the museum, nor a valuation of privately owned objects. When the ICOM Code of Ethics is reached for, to provide some guidance, it turns out that sections §8.15, *Interaction with dealers*, and §5.2, *Authentication and Valuation*, provide clear guidance that museums should refrain from such practices. But these articles appear in locations, related to other statements and guiding principles, that now make these statements 'articulate' and useful, helping to guide 'real-life' decision-making. Afterwards, there is a much stronger guarantee that: (i) these situations and the guided solutions will be remembered; and (ii) participating colleagues will have gained a further understanding: that a Code is a 'living' body of guidelines, and it can be 'worked with' when considering all aspects of a museum's life and practices. While the Code is not easy to read at first, because of its abstract language, this starts to change the moment its status changes, and it is read for the purpose of trying to find an answer to a particular problem or dilemma.

Below are some of the fables I have developed. These could be used to launch a process of imagining different scenarios, capturing different problems – and using the Code as the working tool for solutions to questions about 'right conduct' that is associated with all aspects of the life and work of museums.

1. The curator had heard that a well-known artist wanted to donate to the museum a contemporary art installation. The condition was that the piece should be on permanent display in the museum. 'Personally I dislike his art,' one of his colleagues said. 'To me it is heaps of glass and wood. However, I know he is famous and sells for good prices. Do you think we can sell it?'
2. 'The Chairman of the Friends Society called some days ago and proposed that we cancel the planned graffiti exhibition,' the secretary reported. 'He insisted that the Friends don't like it and will not support any purchases or activities connected with it.'
3. The curator was very upset. The museum had recently opened an exhibition on national minorities and presented an old collection of 'type photographs' and skull models – even some human remains. The exhibition was about the strange concepts of earlier scientists concerning race, and the use of odd

techniques such as skull measuring to distinguish different peoples. Almost immediately a protest came from one of the minority groups. They found the exhibition insulting and offensive. They demanded that it should be closed, or at least that the human remains be removed. This was hard for the curator to accept. 'Our purpose was to explain what distorted ideas scientists once had, and to deal with an important part of our history. As a museum we have to be truthful when presenting our past.'

4. The secretary reported: 'The Friends of the museum want to use our meeting room for their meetings. They have also asked to be given a small office as a base for their activities. Our board of directors is sceptical and has said no. Their argument is that the museum has already declined a similar request from the local hunting and fishing club, and that there is already too little space for the staff.'

5. The young museum educator, recently employed, said that he had expected to get more information about the mission and working plans of the museum when he was appointed. One of his colleagues confirmed that he was not the only one with this problem. 'I've been here for years, and I've never heard of any mission statement or working plans.'

And finally, here are five further samples, more suited perhaps for an ethics training workshop in an academic setting. They are drawn from a chapter on ethics and ICOM's Code prepared by Geoffrey Lewis, for an ICOM–UNESCO-prepared handbook on 'Running a Museum', an initiative of ICOM's Training Committee, ICTOP, and coordinated by Patrick Boylan.

Five Sample ethics case studies

(Lewis 2004: 15)

Case Study 1

You have been planning for years to organize an important exhibition in your subject but lack of funds has always prevented this. The press and television have publicized your need for a sponsor. To your surprise a large company writes offering to bear the full cost of the exhibition, subject to their name being associated with it in any publicity. You share this good news with a colleague who tells you that the local community are fighting a campaign against this company because they wish to develop a site of scientific interest which is also sacred to the first peoples of the area. How do you proceed?

Case Study 2

You are trying to build a representative collection in your subject. There are a few gaps that you have yet to fill. You also have a number of specimens of the same type which have been given to the museum, although their associations with people and places and other material are different. A local collector has two items which would help to complete the collection and he offers to exchange these for the items you have of the same type. What do you do?

Case Study 3

You have been undertaking research on a topic to do with your collections which will eventually provide the basis for a major exhibition. Some of your findings provide new evidence which is likely to attract considerable publicity for the exhibition. Before you have had an opportunity to publish your work or prepare the exhibition, a doctoral student calls to study the same collections. What information do you make available to her?

Case Study 4

A local collector has one of the finest private collections of material relating to your subject, even though he holds unorthodox views about it. You have fostered good relations with him in the hope that your museum might benefit from this. One day he offers to lend his collection for a temporary exhibition at the museum's expense, subject to two conditions: that the exhibition only shows material from his collection and that he must be responsible for all label and publication content. Do you accept his offer?

Case Study 5

You are a specialist in your subject and your museum encourages its staff to publish academic papers. A commercial gallery, from which your museum occasionally purchases well-documented material for the collections, is now putting on a prestigious exhibition in your subject. The director of the gallery has invited you to write an authoritative introduction to the exhibition catalogue. When you see the list of items included in the exhibition, some have no provenance and you suspect they may have been obtained illegally. Do you accept the invitation?

Note

1 The full text of the *ICOM Code of Ethics for Museums* is provided as *Appendix I* to this volume; and is also available online for download at: http://icom.museum/professional-standards/code-of-ethics.

References

Lewis, Geoffrey, 2004. 'The role of museums and the professional Code of Ethics', in Patrick J. Boylan (ed.), *Running a Museum: A Practical Handbook*. Paris: ICOM/International Council of Museums, pp. 1–15.

Mizushima, Eiji, 2016. 'Ethics, museology and professional training in Japan', in Bernice L. Murphy (ed.), *Museums, Ethics and Cultural Heritage*. London: Routledge, Chapter 18.

APPENDIX I

ICOM Code of Ethics for Museums

The cornerstone of ICOM is the *ICOM Code of Ethics for Museums*. It sets minimum standards of professional practice and performance for museums and their staff. In joining the organisation, ICOM members undertake to abide by this Code.

Ethical issues that require the attention and/or consideration of the ICOM Ethics Committee may be addressed to its Chair by e-mail: ethics@icom.museum

The ICOM *Code of Professional Ethics* was adopted unanimously by the 15th General Assembly of ICOM in Buenos Aires (Argentina) on 4 November 1986. It was amended by the 20th General Assembly in Barcelona (Spain) on 6 July 2001, retitled the *ICOM Code of Ethics for Museums*, and revised by the 21st General Assembly in Seoul (Republic of Korea) on 8 October 2004.

© ICOM, 2013
ISBN-978-92-9012-407-8
II

Preamble

Status of the ICOM Code of Ethics for Museums

The *ICOM Code of Ethics for Museums* has been prepared by the International Council of Museums. It is the statement of ethics for museums referred to in the ICOM Statutes. The Code reflects principles generally accepted by the international museum community. Membership in ICOM and the payment of the annual subscription to ICOM are an affirmation of the *ICOM Code of Ethics for Museums*.

A minimum standard for museums

The ICOM Code represents a minimum standard for museums. It is presented as a series of principles supported by guidelines for desirable professional practice. In some countries, certain minimum standards are defined by law or government regulation. In others, guidance on and assessment of minimum professional standards may be available in the form of 'Accreditation', 'Registration', or similar evaluative schemes. Where such standards are not defined, guidance can be obtained through the ICOM Secretariat, a relevant National Committee of ICOM, or the appropriate International Committee of ICOM. It is also intended that individual nations and the specialised subject organisations connected with museums should use this Code as a basis for developing additional standards.

Translations of the ICOM Code of Ethics for Museums

The *ICOM Code of Ethics for Museums* is published in the three official languages of the organisation: English, French and Spanish. ICOM welcomes the translation of the Code into other languages. However, a translation will be regarded as 'official' only if it is endorsed by at least one National Committee of a country in which the language is spoken, normally as the first language. Where the language is spoken in more than one country, it is preferable that the National Committees of these countries also be consulted. Attention is drawn to the need for linguistic as well as professional museum expertise in providing official translations. The language version used for a translation and the names of the National Committees involved should be indicated. These conditions do not restrict translations of the Code, or parts of it, for use in educational work or for study purposes.

Table of contents

1 Museums preserve, interpret and promote the natural and cultural inheritance of humanity

Principle

Museums are responsible for the tangible and intangible natural and cultural heritage. Governing bodies and those concerned with the strategic direction and oversight of museums have a primary responsibility to protect and promote this heritage as well as the human, physical and financial resources made available for that purpose.

Institutional standing

1.1 Enabling documentation

The governing body should ensure that the museum has a written and published constitution, statute, or other public document in accordance with national laws, which clearly states the museum's legal status, mission, permanence and non-profit nature.

1.2 Statement of the mission

Objectives and policies

The governing body should prepare, publicise and be guided by a statement of the mission, objectives and policies of the museum and of the role and composition of the governing body.

Physical resources

1.3 Premises

The governing body should ensure adequate premises with a suitable environment for the museum to fulfil the basic functions defined in its mission.

1.4 Access

The governing body should ensure that the museum and its collections are available to all during reasonable hours and for regular periods. Particular regard should be given to those persons with special needs.

1.5 Health and safety

The governing body should ensure that institutional standards of health, safety and accessibility apply to its personnel and visitors.

1.6 Protection against disasters

The governing body should develop and maintain policies to protect the public and personnel, the collections and other resources against natural and human-made disasters.

1.7 Security requirements

The governing body should ensure appropriate security to protect collections against theft or damage in displays, exhibitions, working or storage areas and while in transit.

1.8 Insurance and indemnity

Where commercial insurance is used for collections, the governing body should ensure that such cover is adequate and includes objects in transit or on loan and other items that are the responsibility of the museum. When an indemnity scheme is in use, it is necessary that material not in the ownership of the museum be adequately covered.

Financial resources

1.9 Funding

The governing body should ensure that there are sufficient funds to carry out and develop the activities of the museum. All funds must be accounted for in a professional manner.

1.10 Income-generating policy

The governing body should have a written policy regarding sources of income that it may generate through its activities or accept from outside sources. Regardless of funding source, museums should maintain control of the content and integrity of their programmes, exhibitions and activities. Income-generating activities should not compromise the standards of the institution or its public. (See 6.6).

Personnel

1.11 Employment policy

The governing body should ensure that all action concerning personnel is taken in accordance with the policies of the museum as well as the proper and legal procedures.

1.12 Appointment of the director or head

The director or head of the museum is a key post and when making an appointment, governing bodies should have regard for the knowledge and skills required to fill the post effectively. These qualities should include adequate intellectual ability and professional knowledge, complemented by a high standard of ethical conduct.

1.13 Access to governing bodies

The director or head of a museum should be directly responsible, and have direct access, to the relevant governing bodies.

1.14 Competence of museum personnel

The employment of qualified personnel with the expertise required to meet all responsibilities is necessary. (See also 2.19; 2.24; section 8).

1.15 Training of personnel

Adequate opportunities for the continuing education and professional development of all museum personnel should be arranged to maintain an effective workforce.

1.16 Ethical conflict

The governing body should never require museum personnel to act in a way that could be considered to conflict with the provisions of this Code of Ethics, or any national law or specialist code of ethics.

1.17 Museum personnel and volunteers

The governing body should have a written policy on volunteer work that promotes a positive relationship between volunteers and members of the museum profession.

1.18 Volunteers and ethics

The governing body should ensure that volunteers, when conducting museum and personal activities, are fully conversant with the *ICOM Code of Ethics for Museums* and other applicable codes and laws.

2 Museums that maintain collections hold them in trust for the benefit of society and its development

Principle

Museums have the duty to acquire, preserve and promote their collections as a contribution to safeguarding the natural, cultural and scientific heritage. Their collections are a significant public inheritance, have a special position in law and are protected by international legislation. Inherent in this public trust is the notion of stewardship that includes rightful ownership, permanence, documentation, accessibility and responsible disposal.

Acquiring collections

2.1 Collections policy

The governing body for each museum should adopt and publish a written collections policy that addresses the acquisition, care and use of collections. The policy should clarify the position of any material that will not be catalogued, conserved, or exhibited. (See 2.7; 2.8).

2.2 Valid title

No object or specimen should be acquired by purchase, gift, loan, bequest, or exchange unless the acquiring museum is satisfied that a valid title is held. Evidence of lawful ownership in a country is not necessarily valid title.

2.3 Provenance and due diligence

Diligence

Every effort must be made before acquisition to ensure that any object or specimen offered for purchase, gift, loan, bequest, or exchange has not been illegally obtained in, or exported from its country of origin or any intermediate country in which it might have been owned legally (including the museum's own country). Due diligence in this regard should establish the full history of the item since discovery or production.

2.4 Objects and specimens from unauthorised or unscientific fieldwork

Museums should not acquire objects where there is reasonable cause to believe their recovery involved unauthorised or unscientific fieldwork, or intentional destruction or damage of monuments, archaeological or geological sites, or of species and natural habitats. In the same way, acquisition should not occur if there has been a failure to disclose the finds to the owner or occupier of the land, or to the proper legal or governmental authorities.

2.5 Culturally sensitive material

Collections of human remains and material of sacred significance should be acquired only if they can be housed securely and cared for respectfully. This must be accomplished in a manner consistent with professional standards and the interests and beliefs of members of the community, ethnic or religious groups from which the objects originated, where these are known. (See also 3.7; 4.3.)

2.6 Protected biological or geological specimens

Museums should not acquire biological or geological specimens that have been collected, sold, or otherwise transferred in contravention of local, national, regional or international law or treaty relating to wildlife protection or natural history conservation.

2.7 Living collections

When the collections include live botanical or zoological specimens, special consideration should be given to the natural and social environment from which they are derived as well as any local, national, regional or international law or treaty relating to wildlife protection or natural history conservation.

2.8 Working collections

The collections policy may include special considerations for certain types of working collections where the emphasis is on preserving cultural, scientific, or technical process rather than the object, or where objects or specimens are assembled for regular handling and teaching purposes. (See also 2.1.)

2.9 Acquisition outside collections policy

The acquisition of objects or specimens outside the museum's stated policy should only be made in exceptional circumstances. The governing body should consider the professional opinions available to it and the views of all interested parties. Consideration will include the significance of the object or specimen, including its context in the cultural or natural heritage, and the special interests of other museums collecting such material. However, even in these circumstances, objects without a valid title should not be acquired. (See also 3.4.)

2.10 Acquisitions offered by members of the governing body or museum personnel

Special care is required in considering any item, whether for sale, as a donation, or as a tax-benefit gift, from members of governing bodies, museum personnel, or the families and close associates of these persons.

2.11 Repositories of last resort

Nothing in this Code of Ethics should prevent a museum from acting as an authorised repository for unprovenanced, illicitly collected or recovered specimens or objects from the territory over which it has lawful responsibility.

Removing collections

2.12 Legal or other powers of disposal

Where the museum has legal powers permitting disposals, or has acquired objects subject to conditions of disposal, the legal or other requirements and procedures must be complied with fully. Where the original acquisition was subject to mandatory or other restrictions these conditions must be observed, unless it can be shown clearly that adherence to such restrictions is impossible or substantially detrimental to the institution and, if appropriate, relief may be sought through legal procedures.

2.13 Deaccessioning from museum collections

The removal of an object or specimen from a museum collection must only be undertaken with a full understanding of the significance of the item, its character (whether renewable or non-renewable), legal standing, and any loss of public trust that might result from such action.

2.14 Responsibility for deaccessioning

The decision to deaccession should be the responsibility of the governing body acting in conjunction with the director of the museum and the curator of the collection concerned. Special arrangements may apply to working collections. (See 2.7; 2.8)

2.15 Disposal of objects removed from the collections

Each museum should have a policy defining authorised methods for permanently removing an object from the collections through donation, transfer, exchange, sale, repatriation, or destruction, and that allows the transfer of unrestricted title to any receiving agency. Complete records must be kept of all deaccessioning decisions, the objects involved, and the disposal of the object. There will be a strong presumption that a deaccessioned item should first be offered to another museum.

2.16 Income from disposal of collections

Museum collections are held in public trust and may not be treated as a realisable asset. Money or compensation received from the deaccessioning and disposal of objects and specimens from a museum collection should be used solely for the benefit of the collection and usually for acquisitions to that same collection.

2.17 Purchase of deaccessioned collections

Museum personnel, the governing body, or their families or close associates, should not be permitted to purchase objects that have been deaccessioned from a collection for which they are responsible.

Care of collections

2.18 Collection continuity

The museum should establish and apply policies to ensure that its collections (both permanent and temporary) and associated information, properly recorded, are available for current use and will be passed on to future generations in as good and safe a condition as practicable, having regard to current knowledge and resources.

2.19 Delegation of collection responsibility

Professional responsibilities involving the care of the collections should be assigned to persons with appropriate knowledge and skill or who are adequately supervised. (See also 8.11).

2.20 Documentation of collections

Museum collections should be documented according to accepted professional standards. Such documentation should include a full identification and description of each item, its associations, provenance, condition, treatment and present location. Such data should be kept in a secure environment and be supported by retrieval systems providing access to the information by the museum personnel and other legitimate users.

2.21 Protection against disasters

Careful attention should be given to the development of policies to protect the collections during armed conflict and other human-made or natural disasters.

2.22 Security of collection and associated data

The museum should exercise control to avoid disclosing sensitive personal or related information and other confidential matters when collection data is made available to the public.

2.23 Preventive conservation

Preventive conservation is an important element of museum policy and collections care. It is an essential responsibility of members of the museum profession to create and maintain a protective environment for the collections in their care, whether in store, on display, or in transit.

2.24 Collection conservation and restoration

The museum should carefully monitor the condition of collections to determine when an object or specimen may require conservation-restoration work and the services of a qualified conservator-restorer. The principal goal should be the stabilisation of the object or specimen. All conservation procedures should be documented and as reversible as possible, and all alterations should be clearly distinguishable from the original object or specimen.

2.25 Welfare of live animals

A museum that maintains living animals should assume full responsibility for their health and well-being. It should prepare and implement a safety code for the protection of its personnel and visitors, as well as of the animals, that has been approved by an expert in the veterinary field. Genetic modification should be clearly identifiable.

2.26 Personal use of museum collections

Museum personnel, the governing body, their families, close associates, or others should not be permitted to expropriate items from the museum collections, even temporarily, for any personal use.

3 Museums hold primary evidence for establishing and furthering knowledge

Principle

Museums have particular responsibilities to all for the care, accessibility and interpretation of primary evidence collected and held in their collections.

Primary evidence

3.1 Collections as primary evidence

The museum collections policy should indicate clearly the significance of collections as primary evidence. The policy should not be governed only by current intellectual trends or present museum usage.

3.2 Availability of collections

Museums have a particular responsibility for making collections and all relevant information available as freely as possible, having regard to restraints arising for reasons of confidentiality and security.

Museum collecting & research

3.3 Field collecting

Museums undertaking field collecting should develop policies consistent with academic standards and applicable national and international laws and treaty obligations. Fieldwork should only be undertaken with respect and consideration for the views of local communities, their environmental resources and cultural practices as well as efforts to enhance the cultural and natural heritage.

3.4 Exceptional collecting of primary evidence

In exceptional cases an item without provenance may have such an inherently outstanding contribution to knowledge that it would be in the public interest to preserve it. The acceptance of such an item into a museum collection should be the subject of a decision by specialists in the discipline concerned and without national or international prejudice. (See also 2.11).

3.5 Research

Research by museum personnel should relate to the museum's mission and objectives and conform to established legal, ethical and academic practices.

3.6 Destructive analysis

When destructive analytical techniques are undertaken, a complete record of the material analysed, the outcome of the analysis and the resulting research, including publications, should become a part of the permanent record of the object.

3.7 Human remains and materials of sacred significance

Research on human remains and materials of sacred significance must be accomplished in a manner consistent with professional standards and take into account the interests and beliefs of the community, ethnic or religious groups from whom the objects originated, where these are known. (See also 2.5; 4.3).

3.8 Retention of rights to research materials

When museum personnel prepare material for presentation or to document field investigation, there must be clear agreement with the sponsoring museum regarding all rights to such work.

3.9 Shared expertise

Members of the museum profession have an obligation to share their knowledge and experience with colleagues, scholars and students in relevant fields. They should respect and acknowledge those from whom they have learned and should pass on such advancements in techniques and experience that may be of benefit to others.

3.10 Co-operation between museums and other institutions

Museum personnel should acknowledge and endorse the need for cooperation and consultation between institutions with similar interests and collecting practices. This is particularly so with institutes of higher education and certain public utilities where research may generate important collections for which there is no long-term security.

4 Museums provide opportunities for the appreciation, understanding and management of the natural and cultural heritage

Principle

Museums have an important duty to develop their educational role and attract wider audiences from the community, locality, or group they serve. Interaction with the constituent community and promotion of their heritage is an integral part of the educational role of the museum.

Display and exhibition

4.1 Displays, exhibitions and special activities

Displays and temporary exhibitions, physical or electronic, should be in accordance with the stated mission, policy and purpose of the museum. They should not compromise either the quality or the proper care and conservation of the collections.

4.2 Interpretation of exhibitions

Museums should ensure that the information they present in displays and exhibitions is well-founded, accurate and gives appropriate consideration to represented groups or beliefs.

4.3 Exhibition of sensitive materials

Human remains and materials of sacred significance must be displayed in a manner consistent with professional standards and, where known, taking into account the interests and beliefs of members of the community, ethnic or religious groups from whom the objects originated. They must be presented with great tact and respect for the feelings of human dignity held by all peoples.

4.4 Removal from public display

Requests for removal from public display of human remains or material of sacred significance from the originating communities must be addressed expeditiously with respect and sensitivity. Requests for the return of such material should be addressed similarly. Museum policies should clearly define the process for responding to such requests.

4.5 Display of unprovenanced material

Museums should avoid displaying or otherwise using material of questionable origin or lacking provenance. They should be aware that such displays or usage can be seen to condone and contribute to the illicit trade in cultural property.

Other resources

4.6 Publication

Information published by museums, by whatever means, should be well-founded, accurate and give responsible consideration to the academic disciplines, societies, or beliefs presented. Museum publications should not compromise the standards of the institution.

4.7 Reproductions

Museums should respect the integrity of the original when replicas, reproductions, or copies of items in the collection are made. All such copies should be permanently marked as facsimiles.

5 Museums hold resources that provide opportunities for other public services and benefits

Principle

Museums utilise a wide variety of specialisms, skills and physical resources that have a far broader application than in the museum. This may lead to shared resources or the provision of services as an extension of the museum's activities. These should be organised in such a way that they do not compromise the museum's stated mission.

Identification services

5.1 Identification of illegally or illicitly acquired objects

Where museums provide an identification service, they should not act in any way that could be regarded as benefiting from such activity, directly or indirectly. The identification and authentication of objects that are believed or suspected to have been illegally or illicitly acquired, transferred, imported or exported, should not be made public until the appropriate authorities have been notified.

5.2 Authentication and valuation (appraisal)

Valuations may be made for the purposes of insurance of museum collections. Opinions on the monetary value of other objects should only be given on official request from other museums or competent legal, governmental or other responsible public authorities. However, when the museum itself may be the beneficiary, appraisal of an object or specimen must be undertaken independently.

6 Museums work in close collaboration with the communities from which their collections originate as well as those they serve

Principle

Museum collections reflect the cultural and natural heritage of the communities from which they have been derived. As such, they have a character beyond that of ordinary property, which may include strong affinities with national, regional, local, ethnic, religious or political identity. It is important therefore that museum policy is responsive to this situation.

Origin of collections

6.1 Co-operation

Museums should promote the sharing of knowledge, documentation and collections with museums and cultural organisations in the countries and communities of origin. The possibility of developing partnerships with museums in countries or areas that have lost a significant part of their heritage should be explored.

6.2 Return of cultural property

Museums should be prepared to initiate dialogues for the return of cultural property to a country or people of origin. This should be undertaken in an impartial manner, based on scientific, professional and humanitarian principles as well as applicable local, national and international legislation, in preference to action at a governmental or political level.

6.3 Restitution of cultural property

When a country or people of origin seeks the restitution of an object or specimen that can be demonstrated to have been exported or otherwise transferred in violation of the principles of international and national conventions, and shown to be part of that country's or people's cultural or natural heritage, the museum concerned should, if legally free to do so, take prompt and responsible steps to cooperate in its return.

6.4 Cultural objects from an occupied country

Museums should abstain from purchasing or acquiring cultural objects from an occupied territory and respect fully all laws and conventions that regulate the import, export and transfer of cultural or natural materials.

Respect for communities served

6.5 Contemporary communities

Where museum activities involve a contemporary community or its heritage, acquisitions should only be made based on informed and mutual consent without exploitation of the owner or informants. Respect for the wishes of the community involved should be paramount.

6.6 Funding of community activities

When seeking funds for activities involving contemporary communities, their interests should not be compromised. (See 1.10.)

6.7 Use of collections from contemporary communities

Museum usage of collections from contemporary communities requires respect for human dignity and the traditions and cultures that use such material. Such collections should be used to promote human well-being, social development, tolerance, and respect by advocating multisocial, multicultural and multilingual expression. (See 4.3.)

6.8 Supporting organisations in the community

Museums should create a favourable environment for community support (e.g., Friends of Museums and other supporting organisations), recognise their contribution and promote a harmonious relationship between the community and museum personnel.

7 Museums operate in a legal manner

Principle

Museums must conform fully to international, regional, national and local legislation and treaty obligations. In addition, the governing body should comply with any legally binding trusts or conditions relating to any aspect of the museum, its collections and operations.

Legal framework

7.1 National and local legislation

Museums should conform to all national and local laws and respect the legislation of other states as they affect their operation.

7.2 International legislation

Museum policy should acknowledge the following international legislation that is taken as a standard in interpreting the *ICOM Code of Ethics for Museums*:

- *Convention for the Protection of Cultural Property in the Event of Armed Conflict* ('The Hague Convention' First Protocol, 1954, and Second Protocol, 1999);
- *Convention on the Means of Prohibiting and Preventing the Illicit Import, Export and Transfer of Ownership of Cultural Property* (UNESCO 1970);
- *Convention on International Trade in Endangered Species of Wild Fauna and Flora* (Washington, 1973);
- *Convention on Biological Diversity* (UN 1992);
- *Convention on Stolen and Illicitly Exported Cultural Objects* (UNIDROIT, 1995);
- *Convention on the Protection of the Underwater Cultural Heritage* (UNESCO 2001);
- *Convention for the Safeguarding of the Intangible Cultural Heritage* (UNESCO 2003).

8 Museums operate in a professional manner

Principle

Members of the museum profession should observe accepted standards and laws and uphold the dignity and honour of their profession. They should safeguard the public against illegal or unethical professional conduct. Every opportunity should be used to inform and educate the public about the aims, purposes, and aspirations of the profession to develop a better public understanding of the contributions of museums to society.

Professional conduct

8.1 Familiarity with relevant legislation

Every member of the museum profession should be conversant with relevant international, national and local legislation and the conditions of their employment. They should avoid situations that could be construed as improper conduct.

8.2 Professional responsibility

Members of the museum profession have an obligation to follow the policies and procedures of their employing institution. However, they may properly object to practices that are perceived to be damaging to a museum, to the profession, or to matters of professional ethics.

8.3 Professional conduct

Loyalty to colleagues and to the employing museum is an important professional responsibility and must be based on allegiance to fundamental ethical principles applicable to the profession as a whole. These principles should comply with the terms of the *ICOM Code of Ethics for Museums* and be aware of any other codes or policies relevant to museum work.

8.4 Academic and scientific responsibilities

Members of the museum profession should promote the investigation, preservation, and use of information inherent in collections. They should, therefore, refrain from any activity or circumstance that might result in the loss of such academic and scientific data.

8.5 The illicit market

Members of the museum profession should not support the illicit traffic or market in natural or cultural property, directly or indirectly.

8.6 Confidentiality

Members of the museum profession must protect confidential information obtained during their work. In addition, information about items brought to the museum for identification is confidential and should not be published or passed to any other institution or person without specific authorisation from the owner.

8.7 Museum and collection security

Information about the security of the museum or of private collections and locations visited during official duties must be held in strict confidence by museum personnel.

8.8 Exception to the obligation for confidentiality

Confidentiality is subject to a legal obligation to assist the police or other proper authorities in investigating possible stolen, illicitly acquired, or illegally transferred property.

8.9 Personal independence

While members of a profession are entitled to a measure of personal independence, they must realise that no private business or professional interest can be wholly separated from their employing institution.

8.10 Professional relationships

Members of the museum profession form working relationships with numerous other persons within and outside the museum in which they are employed. They are expected to render their professional services to others efficiently and to a high standard.

8.11 Professional consultation

It is a professional responsibility to consult other colleagues within or out-side the museum when the expertise available in the museum is insufficient to ensure good decision-making.

Conflicts of interest

8.12 Gifts, favours, loans, or other personal benefits

Museum employees must not accept gifts, favours, loans, or other personal benefits that may be offered to them in connection with their duties for the museum.

Occasionally professional courtesy may include the giving and receiving of gifts, but this should always take place in the name of the institution concerned.

8.13 Outside employment or business interests

Members of the museum profession, although entitled to a measure of personal independence, must realise that no private business or professional interest can be wholly separated from their employing institution. They should not undertake other paid employment or accept outside commissions that are in conflict, or may be viewed as being in conflict, with the interests of the museum.

8.14 Dealing in natural or cultural heritage

Members of the museum profession should not participate directly or in-directly in dealing (buying or selling for profit) in the natural or cultural heritage.

8.15 Interaction with dealers

Museum professionals should not accept any gift, hospitality, or any form of reward from a dealer, auctioneer, or other person as an inducement to purchase or dispose of museum items, or to take or refrain from taking official action. Furthermore, a museum professional should not recommend a particular dealer, auctioneer, or appraiser to a member of the public.

8.16 Private collecting

Members of the museum profession should not compete with their institution either in the acquisition of objects or in any personal collecting activity. An agreement between the museum professional and the governing body concerning any private collecting must be formulated and scrupulously followed.

8.17 Use of the name and logo of ICOM

The name of the organisation, its acronym or its logo may not be used to promote or endorse any for-profit operation or product.

8.18 Other conflicts of interest

Should any other conflict of interest develop between an individual and the museum, the interests of the museum should prevail.

Glossary

Appraisal	The authentication and valuation of an object or specimen. In certain countries the term is used for an independent assessment of a proposed gift for tax benefit purposes.
Conflict of interest	The existence of a personal or private interest that gives rise to a clash of principle in a work situation, thus restricting, or having the appearance of restricting, the objectivity of decision-making.
Conservator-Restorer	Museum or independent personnel competent to undertake the technical examination, preservation, conservation and restoration of cultural property. (For further information, see *ICOM News*, 39 (1) [1986]: 5–6.)
Cultural Heritage	Any thing or concept considered of aesthetic, historical, scientific or spiritual significance.
Dealing	Buying and selling items for personal or institutional gain.
Due diligence	The requirement that every endeavour is made to establish the facts of a case before deciding a course of action, particularly in identifying the source and history of an item offered for acquisition or use before acquiring it.
Governing Body	The persons or organisations defined in the enabling legislation of the museum as responsible for its continuance, strategic development and funding.
Income-generating activities	Activities intended to bring financial gain or profit for the benefit of the institution.
Legal title	Legal right to ownership of property in the country concerned. In certain countries this may be a conferred right and insufficient to meet the requirements of a due diligence search.
Minimum Standard	A standard to which it is reasonable to expect all museums and museum personnel to aspire. Certain countries have their own statements of minimum standards.
Museum★	A museum is a non-profit making permanent institution in the service of society and of its development, open to the public, which acquires, conserves, researches, communicates and exhibits, for purposes of study, education and enjoyment, the tangible and intangible evidence of people and their environment.

Museum professional★	Museum professionals consist of the personnel (whether paid or unpaid) of museums or institutions as defined in Article 2, paras. 1 and 2, of the ICOM Statutes, who have received specialised training, or possess an equivalent practical experience in any field relevant to the management and operations of a museum, and independent persons respecting the *ICOM Code of Ethics for Museums* and working for museums or institutions as defined in the Statute quoted above, but not persons promoting or dealing with commercial products and equipment required for museums and museum services.
Natural Heritage	Any natural thing, phenomenon or concept, considered to be of scientific significance or to be a spiritual manifestation.
Non-profit organisation	A legally established body – corporate or unincorporated – whose income (including any surplus or profit) is used solely for the benefit of that body and its operations. The term 'not-for-profit' has the same meaning.
Provenance	The full history and ownership of an item from the time of its discovery or creation to the present day, through which authenticity and ownership are determined.
Valid title	Indisputable right to ownership of property, supported by full provenance of the item since discovery or production.

★ *It should be noted that the terms 'museum' and 'museum professional' are interim definitions for use in interpreting the* ICOM Code of Ethics for Museums. *The definitions of 'museum' and 'professional museum workers' used in the ICOM Statutes remain in force until the revision of that document has been completed.*

APPENDIX II

ICOM Code of Ethics for Natural History Museums

RATIFIED 16 August 2013
Ethics Working Group of the International Council of Museums International Committee for Museums and Collections of Natural History, ICOM NATHIST

Note: The term 'natural history museum' covers all institutions that collect, display and research materials collected or extracted from 'the natural world'.

Executive summary

The *ICOM Code of Ethics for Natural History Museums* supplements, and is complementary to, the *ICOM Code of Ethics for Museums*. It was developed between December 2006 and November 2012 to address specific issues relevant to the life and earth sciences. The objective of this document is to establish a minimum standard of practice, which can be built on by individual institutions.

The document begins with a **Position Statement** that describes the purpose of natural history museums and states that all information should be accurate and with a responsible consideration of the academic disciplines concerned. Additionally, members of ICOM NATHIST should take the Committee's published position statements into account when developing policy.

Section 1 covers **Human Remains**. Although the ICOM Code of Ethics covers care and display of human remains, natural history institutions that include this in their collections can face complex and specific challenges. This section covers standards of compliance with legislation, the origin and descendants of the people represented by the material, dignity of presentation and repatriation.

The second section covers standards relating to **specimens of other extant and recent organisms, including invertebrates and plants**. The section includes collecting, displaying and storing this material, as well as its associated data.

Emphasis is placed on ensuring provenance, sharing data and dignity of display. Museums that display live specimens are covered by augmenting the standards set by the World Association of Zoos and Aquariums.

Section 3 considers **Rocks, Minerals and Fossils**. Fossil material is considered to be the traces or remains of plants, animals and other organisms preserved for geological timescales by virtue of their deposition conditions. It is argued that they should be treated appropriately within legislation. This includes minimising environmental impacts of collection.

Collecting and restitution is addressed in the fourth section. It covers ethical consideration around deposition and repatriation of natural history specimens, as well as data sharing and 'value add' activities such as object conservation and stabilisation. Section 5 gives standards for **Duty of Care for People and Objects**, which includes occupational safety and health, exchange of objects and best practice guidelines for storage and handling.

Section 6, **Publication**, is the final in the document. It sets out the need for natural history data collected to be published, fully disseminating the work to the scientific community. Appendix gives standards for **Taxidermy**.

Introduction

The ICOM *Code of Professional Ethics* was adopted unanimously by the 15th General Assembly of ICOM in Buenos Aires (Argentina) on 4 November 1986. It was amended by the 20th General Assembly in Barcelona (Spain) on 6 July 2001, retitled *ICOM Code of Ethics for Museums*, and revised by the 21st General Assembly in Seoul (Republic of Korea) on 8 October 2004.

The present draft of the *ICOM Code of Ethics for Natural History Museums* was developed between December 2006 and October 2011 to complement the *ICOM Code of Ethics for Museums*. It specifically addresses issues relevant to the life and earth sciences in greater depth than is possible in the general ICOM Code which provides base-standards encompassing different types of museums and specialised collections. The *ICOM Code of Ethics for Museums* should therefore be viewed as a parent document to the *ICOM Code of Ethics for Natural History Museums* and any perceived conflict should default to the former.

It is also recognised that while some institutions already have a code to which they adhere, the standard is not universal. Thus, the objective of this document is to establish a minimum standard of practice which can be built on by individual institutions.

Position statement

The multifaceted purpose of natural history museums is to:

- Build and store natural history collections
- Conduct research and interpret the results

- Support the process of science and biological conservation
- Enhance public understanding and appreciation of the natural world
- Collaborate with the public in deriving their own meaning from the natural heritage they encounter in the museum and in nature

While differences among cultural milieu and personal opinion are respected, all dissemination of information, whether through display, publication or other means should be well-founded, accurate and with a responsible consideration of the academic disciplines concerned. Members of ICOM NATHIST should take its published position statements into account when developing applicable policies.

Natural history collections

Natural history collections in museums are a three-dimensional archive of the natural world and relationships of societies with their environments. In many cases, they may document a world that no longer exists. As such, these collections should be treated with the care and attention merited by such an important resource.

Section 1 Human remains

Although the ICOM Code of Ethics covers care and display of human remains (ICOM Code 2.5; 3.7; 4.3), natural history institutions, which frequently include human remains and sensitive ethnographical material in their collections, can face complex challenges. Thus, an opportunity exists to explore the ethical issues in greater depth than provided by the ICOM Code. Institutions displaying or storing human remains must always observe the following standards:

a. Any legislation, both local and international, governing the use and display of human remains.
b. The origin of the material and the wishes of any descendants or other stakeholder groups must be considered in all circumstances.
c. Human remains should be stored and displayed with dignity, in appropriate environmental conditions.
d. Human remains should only be displayed or used scientifically in circumstances where the highest professional standards can be implemented. Where extant representatives of the cultural groups exist, any display, representation, research and/or deaccession must be done in full consultation with the groups involved.
e. Artefacts made from or including human remains should be afforded the same dignity as human remains. In cultures where hand-made artefacts have the same cultural and/or spiritual significance as human remains, this material should be treated similarly, with full consultation.
f. Human remains, and parts thereof, are also to be found within archaeological and ethnographical/anthropological collections and ICOM NATHIST

members should also take into account the restrictions and standards that apply within these disciplines.

g. Repatriation is appropriate where objects still confer a spiritual and/or cultural significance, or where they can be irrefutably demonstrated as being stolen. All material being considered for repatriation, even unprovenanced material, must be properly documented with respect to the repatriation process. Any repatriation that does take place must be undertaken with the full knowledge and agreement of all interested parties and comply with the legislative and institutional requirements of all parties involved.

Section 2 Specimens of other extant and recent organisms, including invertebrates and plants

Institutions collecting, displaying or storing the remains of any organisms should endeavour to store and display this material to the highest possible standards to ensure its preservation and that of its ancillary data. It should be recognised that ancillary data, for example details of the collection locality and the date of collection, add considerably to the value of any material.

In order to reach these standards the following criteria should be followed:

a. Institutions should ensure that all such material is obtained legally. Material should never be purchased, imported, collected or removed in contravention of national and international legislation or conventions pertaining to such material. It is recognised that it is sometimes difficult to establish legal acquisition. If material is acquired and subsequently discovered to have been collected illegally, the relevant authorities should be informed and further steps be taken as required by the country or countries involved. If more than one institution is involved, refer to the ICOM Code 6.2, which states that, if possible, dialogue should be established between museums in preference to government or political action.

b. Natural history material held in storage should be freely available, concomitant with the aims of conservation/preservation of those materials, for legitimate research without incurring a commercial charge, save on a cost-recovery basis. Information relating to the material should also be made available, taking into account confidentially agreements, its inclusion in on-going research projects, and species protection. Associated costs may be legitimately recovered by a holding or owning institution, but collection access should not be run as a commercial activity.

  1. For plants, the following recommendation from the International Code of Botanical Nomenclature 2006 (Recommendation 7A) should be followed: *It is strongly recommended that the material on which the name of a taxon is based, especially the holotype, be deposited in a public herbarium or other public collection with a policy of giving bona fide researchers access to deposited material, and that it be scrupulously conserved.*

2. For animals, the following recommendation from the International Code of Zoological Nomenclature 1999 (Recommendation 72F) should be followed: *Institutional responsibility. Every institution in which name-bearing types are deposited should:*
    i. *72F.1 ensure that all are clearly marked so that they will be unmistakably recognized as name-bearing types;*
    ii. *72F.2 take all necessary steps for their safe preservation;*
    iii. *72F.3 make them accessible for study;*
    iv. *72F.4 publish lists of name-bearing types in its possession or custody; and*
    v. *72F.5 so far as possible, communicate information concerning name-bearing types when requested.*

c. Photographic restrictions should normally only apply if the specific material concerned is new, unpublished, or on-going research may be jeopardised, or if the material is politically sensitive or covered by intellectual property legislation. However, museums retain the right to charge market rates to commercial entities wishing to use images for profit-making activities.

d. Animal remains should be displayed with respect and dignity regardless of the species or its origins. It is understood that 'respect' may be interpreted differently depending on the country, institution as well as the lands, cultures or peoples from which the animal material originated. Institutions should develop guidelines appropriate to their own milieu and audience and apply these consistently.

e. While a distinction is made between natural history museums and zoos, it is recognised that some museums keep animals in long-term captive display. Institutions collecting, researching or displaying living organisms should only do so if they can reach the minimum acceptable standards required for the health and welfare of the organism concerned regardless of the perceived status of the species/organism itself. The following conditions should be met:[1]
    1. The display of live animals at the museum must fully meet all legal requirements for the display of live animals.
    2. Museums keeping live vertebrates should have an ethics committee set up to approve the project, as well as monitor the animals' living conditions and care records.
    3. All staff responsible for the care and maintenance of the display animals should be appropriately trained in care and handling procedures.
    4. Contractors that undertake programs or other activities at the museum involving live animals hold the appropriate approvals under appropriate local legislation.
    5. Live animals are only used when they can be looked after appropriately, and when they can form part of a positive message about nature for our visitors.
    6. Impacts on the animals are monitored and, if any adverse impacts are detected, a museum should immediately review the display and determine whether the exhibit/activity should continue.

    7. Long-term live collections should adhere to the Code of Ethics formulated by the World Association of Zoos (WAZA) 2003, irrespective of whether or not they are WAZA members.

f. Commercial sale of animal remains or animal-derived products to the public should only come from renewable sources that do not threaten species or environments. All sales should comply with the Convention on International Trade in Endangered Species of Wild Fauna and Flora (CITES),[2] and any local or regional legislation or regulations which are in force.

g. No specimen should be collected that would threaten the sustainability of the species. Rare breeds of domesticated stock and farm or zoo breeding programmes of rare and endangered animals and birds may be acquired for display if they have to be put down for legitimate reasons such as ill health or trauma.

h. When collecting from nature only the minimum number of specimens necessary should be taken, with as little disturbance to habitats as possible. Any animal killed under the aegis of a museum should not involve animal pain or distress. Individual museums should maintain up-to-date manuals on the accepted methods by which each group of animals in its collection will be humanely killed.

i. Environmental sustainability and animal welfare should be considered in determining the sample size of collections. In determining whether an animal will be killed by a museum, the following considerations should be made:[3]

    1. *Collection should occur only after a decision has been made that it is justified, weighing the predicted scientific or educational value against the potential effects on the welfare of the species.*

    2. *Replacement: Techniques that totally or partially replace killing animals for the collection should be sought and used wherever possible.*

    3. *Reduction: Each project must use no more than the minimum number of animals necessary to ensure scientific and statistical validity.*

    4. *Refinement: Animals must be suitable for the scientific purpose taking into account their biological characteristics including phylogenetics and distribution.*

Section 3 Rocks, minerals and fossils

We consider fossil material to be the traces or remains of plants, animals and other organisms preserved for geological timescales by virtue of their deposition conditions. As such, they should be subject to applicable legislation and collection standards.

Institutions collecting, displaying or storing rocks, minerals or fossils should always endeavour to store and display this material to an acceptable standard that ensures its preservation.

a. Institutions that collect or purchase minerals, rocks or fossils for display or research purposes should ensure that the material is collected in a manner that does minimum damage to the deposits from which they are extracted. If such acquisitions are the result of large-scale commercial activities, every reasonable effort should be made to ensure that these activities do not end in the destruction of a site or deposit.

b. Geological material sold to the public under the aegis of museums should be acquired only from recognized sources or suppliers who can ensure that only limited and controlled extraction takes place under recognised conservation guidelines. Information about conservation of geologically important sites should be made available to the public at the point of sale and, where possible, certification of the specimens' legitimate collection.

c. Sale or trade of fossil material to collectors and the general public, from areas of high scientific value (e.g. locations from which the fossil fauna is not fully understood or documented) is discouraged. The commercial sales of material from known sites should also be monitored to ensure that these non-renewable sources are not over exploited for purely commercial purposes to the detriment of science as a whole.

d. Institutions that collect or purchase minerals, rocks or fossils for display or research purposes should ensure this is done following the legislation of the source country and of their own country. Guidance in Section 2 of the *ICOM Code of Ethics for Museums* should be followed whether or not such legislation exists.

Section 4 Collecting and restitution

A number of individual countries and communities have restrictions on collecting for research. Restrictions are necessary to protect vulnerable species, deposits, habitats and communities and are usually based on sound science. In some cases, however, legislation may restrict scientific requirements for environmental protection, even to the point of limiting valid scientific endeavour. Nevertheless, whether scientifically defensible or not, best practice research must always remain within the bounds of existing legislation.

a. If permits are required for the collection or export of material these should be sourced and any associated ground rules established prior to a research trip being undertaken. Collectors should follow policy and legislation for collecting both in the locality in which the collection is made and in the locality in which the museum is based. i.e. if the state in which the museum is based has more stringent animal ethics requirements than the state in which the collection is made, then the requirements of the home state should be followed.

b. Institutions and individual members should ensure, wherever possible, that information gathered in the field is made available at the earliest opportunity to the relevant authorities or institution within the country in which the material is collected.

c. The deposition of all material collected should be determined before fieldwork commences. This is important if one or more parties outside the country of origin will be 'adding value' to specimens (e.g. preparing collected fossils to a paleontological standard). If required to do so, all material collected should be shared between a local institute in the country in which the material is collected, and the initiating individual or research institute which is undertaking the work.

d. If material is already held outside its country of origin, whereupon 'value' is added (Ref Section 4.c above), it shall be deemed, except in rare cases, the property of the holding institution. Exceptions include cases in which the material was collected without a permit when one was required from the originating country, or in which the material has a significant connection to indigenous peoples. Scientific or monetary value alone is not sufficient to support restitution.

e. All natural heritage materials held within our institutions, and the related information about them, should be considered to be in global custodianship rather than the sole property of the institution in which such material resides.[4]

f. Neglect of part or all of a collection is never acceptable. In situations where capacity to care for or store collection material properly becomes limited, every effort should be made to put the material into a position of low activity or secure maintenance. Deaccession, even for transfer to another institution, should be viewed only as a last resort.

g. ICOM NATHIST actively encourages the free flow of knowledge and a minimum of restrictions while safeguarding the specimens and natural populations encompassed by collections within museums and associated institutions. Commercial interests should not prevent access to scientific datasets or bona fide research into a species, or species group, especially when their conservation is at stake.

Section 5 Duty of care for people and objects

ICOM NATHIST encourages institutions, regardless of size and location, to develop and adhere to policies for the occupational health and safety of staff, and to internationally agreed base-standards of care of objects.

a. Institutions have an obligation to ensure that their activities do not impinge on the health and safety of staff, visitors and others. This includes use and disposal of hazardous chemicals and the storage and handling of objects.

b. Exchanging or selling either biological or geological specimens that have been donated to the museum for the public good to agencies outside the museum sector is strongly discouraged and must not be done when the material is of importance to indigenous peoples and/or other cultural groups. In general, the selling of collection items should be institution-to-institution, rather than on the open market.

c. Objects should be stored and cared for according to best practice guidelines. The following publications (listed below) set out minimum standards for holding collections in the United Kingdom. ICOM NATHIST suggests that these guidelines be adhered to as minimum standards for best practice internationally.

Standards 1 in the Museum Care of Archaeological Collections 1992. Museums and Galleries Commission, UK

Standards 2 in the Museum Care of Biological Collections 1992. Museums and Galleries Commission, UK

Standards 3 in the Museum Care of Geological Collections 1993. Museums and Galleries Commission, UK[5]

d. Display of natural history objects should be undertaken in a manner that is mindful of materials conservation standards. Objects should be displayed in appropriate environmental conditions, away from harmful chemicals or other substances that may cause them damage over time. While on display, objects should be adequately supported and protected from human interference, e.g. unwanted handling or theft.

e. Collection managers are encouraged to keep abreast of agents of deterioration that might affect particular materials in their care and seek specialist advice where necessary.

Section 6 Publication

a. It is frequently the case that data collected never reach the scientific literature. Researchers are strongly encouraged to publish, or alternatively make their records available through other sources, so that other workers may benefit from their findings.

b. Publication of data should be in peer-reviewed journals that are readily accessible by the scientific community.

Appendix II

The art of taxidermy and its cultural heritage importance: code of best practice for the care of taxidermy

1. Avoid removing specimens in their original cased displays or settings. If uncased, ensure no mechanical or other physical damage can take place due to storage conditions.
2. Make accessible all associated information, including the name of the Taxidermist and the date of preparation, if known.
3. Produce and file condition reports and undertake regular inspections (at least annually) to ensure no damage or infestation has taken place.

4. Undertake any restoration to specimens or displays in sympathy with the Taxidermist's original intentions and techniques.
5. Keep a full record with photographic evidence of any conservation work, including any work undertaken on the surrounding case or display.
6. Preserve all scientifically important material and all extinct and endangered material in institutional collections, no matter how poor the material may appear to be.
7. Agree and use a formal collecting policy when deciding whether or not to dispose of a specimen.
8. Dispose of material to alternative institutions. If no local institution is willing or able to accept this material, then seek alternatives before contemplating any sale or destruction. In the case of foreign material contact institutions in the country of origin and offer them such material. (CITES REGULATIONS PERMITTING). Remember this could be an important part of their cultural heritage.
9. Dispose of material by destruction only when all other possible alternatives have been exhausted.
10. Keep a full photographic record of all material conserved, removed or disposed of, and retain copies of any documentation in the original institution.

ICOM NATHIST
December 2005

Notes

1 Modified from *Display and Use of Live Animals in Public programs at the Australian Museum*, 2004.
2 All States are encouraged to ratify the CITES Convention (1975), if they have not already done so. However as best practice, institutions in non-signatory States should adhere to the terms of the agreement.
3 Modified from the Australian Code of Practice for the Care and Use of Animals for Scientific Purposes, 2004
4 Global custodianship carries with it a presumption that disposal of material for any reason should be undertaken under the guidance of an acknowledged peer group.
5 ICOM NATHIST adheres to the standards set out in the following publications.

Code of Ethics – *ICOM Code of Ethics for Museums* 2006

Horie, C.V., 1989. *Conservation of Natural History Specimens – Spirit Collections*. BCG Publication.

Hower, R.O., 1979. *Freeze-Drying Biological Specimens: A Laboratory Manual*, Smithsonian Institution Press, Washington.

Nudds, J.R. & Pettitt, C.W., 1997. *The Value and Valuation of Natural Science Collections*. Geological Society, London.

Roberts, D.A., 1985. *Planning the documentation of museum collections*. The Museum Documentation Association.

Roberts, D.A. (ed.), 1987. *Collections Management for Museums*. The Museum Documentation Association.

Rose, C.L., Hawks, C.A., & Genoways, H.H., 1995. *Storage of Natural History Collections: A Preventive Conservation Approach* Vol. 1 SPNHAC.

Rose. C.L., & Torres, A.R. de. (eds), 1995. *Storage of Natural History Collections: Ideas and Practical Solutions* Vol. II, SPNHC.

APPENDIX III

CIMAM: Principles of Deaccession

General Principles on Conditions of Deaccession from Modern and Contemporary Museum Collections (Resolution adopted by the General Assembly of CIMAM in Mexico D.F., November 10, 2009 – revised June, 2011)

Ethical codes must evolve in response to the evolving nature of standards and practices in museums and in society, and need to be periodically reviewed, discussed and updated.

In view of recent controversial practice with regard to selling art from museum collections, CIMAM states its opposition in the first instance to the notion of deaccession. In those instances where deaccession is deemed defensible or necessary, CIMAM's General Assembly adopts the following set of principles for the conditions of deaccession, and urges the directors of member institutions to accept these principles as guidelines for their institutions.

The present General Principles have been developed to complement the *ICOM Code of Ethics for Museums*. They specifically address issues relevant to the selling of art from museum collections in greater depth than is possible in the general ICOM Code. The *ICOM Code of Ethics for Museums* should therefore be viewed as a parent document to the General Principles, and any perceived conflict should default to the former.

A Principles

I Purpose of art museums

An art museum is a permanent, educational and cultural not for profit institution, generally dedicated to collecting, preserving, conserving, documenting, scholarly studying, fostering the understanding, and exhibiting works of art.

II *Purpose of the collections*

Collections represent the world's cultural common wealth. Collecting museums hold their collections in trust for the benefit of society and its development. Inherent in this public trust is the notion of stewardship that includes rightful ownership, permanence, care, documentation, accessibility and responsible disposal★.

★ *ICOM Code of Ethics for Museums*, 2006 and *AAM Code of Ethics for Museums*

III *Deaccessioning*

Deaccessioning is the method by which a work is permanently removed by gift, exchange, sale or destruction from a museum's collection, and it is only justified to improve the quality or composition of the collection.

All institutions should adopt a policy regarding both acquisitions and deaccessions, and follow its procedures. The same deliberation and rigor applied to acquiring should be applied to deaccessioning. All institutions should also carry a register, including photographs, of all works removed from their collection.

1 *Purpose of deaccessioning*

Sound curatorial reasons for deaccession must be established before consideration is given to the removal of a work from a museum's collection. Any deaccession should be in accordance with the purpose and collecting goals set out in the museum collection's management policy; carried out solely for the advancement of the museum's mission, to enhance and improve the quality, scope and appropriateness of the collection; fully justified and the reasons recorded with care. Proceeds from the deaccession should not be used for anything other than acquisition or direct care of the collection. Expenditure of deaccession funds for operating purposes is unacceptable.

2 *Criteria for deaccessioning*

Only works meeting the criteria below should be acceptable for deaccession: redundant or duplicated, and not required for research purposes; in poor physical condition, or deteriorated beyond the institution's care capabilities; of inferior quality, or of poor quality in comparison with other works in the collection; not legitimate or illegally acquired; false or wrongly attributed; not consistent with the mission and collection policy of the institution; the mission of an institution and/ or the policies regarding the development and use of its collection may evolve over time. As a consequence, existing works in the collection may no longer be consistent with the institution's new collecting goals or appropriate to the new stated mission. Institutions contemplating deaccessioning in this situation should avoid acting in a hubristic way, thinking that their own judgement is superior to that of their predecessors, or deciding to erase the 'growth layers' of the collection.

3 Responsibility

The preservation and conservation of the collection is the responsibility of the Director, so recommendation for deaccessioning should be generated by the Director of the institution, or a member of the curatorial staff in charge of the collection. The decision should rest with the Director after full consideration of the reasons for deaccession. Any approved deaccession by the Director should be ratified by the institution's Board of Trustees or governing body.

4 What should be taken into consideration? (Legal matters, donor intent, etc.)

Deaccessioning must comply with all applicable laws. Institutions should observe all binding conditions, and only deaccession works that they fully own: works that do not belong to the museum or that the museum owns with other parties should not be deaccessioned without the permission of the owner/s; if the work was donated, it should not have any restrictions placed by the donor pertaining to its deaccession; if the work was acquired by gift, a reasonable attempt should be made to contact the donor or his/her heirs to notify the intent to deaccession; in case of a work by a living artist, it should not be sold unless to acquire a superior work by the same artist, and always with the agreement of the artist.

5 Modes of disposal: who should/should not be allowed to purchase works deaccessioned from collections?

The Director should determine the appropriate method of deaccession whether by gift, exchange, sale or destruction.

Priority should be given to retaining the work within the public domain, unless it is to be destroyed, offering it first to other museums. No member of the museum's staff, board or governing body should be permitted to acquire, either directly or indirectly, a deaccessioned work.

B Promulgation

These General Principles were adopted by the Board of CIMAM on November 8, 2009 and by CIMAM's General Assembly on November 10, 2009. To achieve maximum exposure and commitment the Principles will be translated into ICOM's three official languages, circulated to members and non members via email, and posted on CIMAM's web.

C Implemention & enforcement

1 Implementation

CIMAM expects these General Principles will be maintained by all the members of the Committee.

2 Enforcement

In order to emphasize the seriousness of these Principles and the importance to the Committee, sanctions for violations of the code may be necessary. The Board of CIMAM will have responsibility for dealing with infractions.

Amended to complement the *ICOM Code of Ethics for Museums* at the meeting of the Board of CIMAM held June 2, 2011 in Venice.

APPENDIX IV

PIMA (Pacific Island Museums Association) Code of Ethics

Preamble

The Pacific Islands Museums Association (PIMA) has existed as an Affiliated Organisation of ICOM since 1998. PIMA and its members fully endorse and support the ICOM Code of Ethics. In addition, PIMA is proud to produce this specialised code for professional museum work particularly adapted to the values of Pacific Islands museums and cultural centres.

Guiding principles

Pacific Islands museums and cultural centres:

1. are the custodians of collections of cultural resources that they hold in trust, foremost for their creator communities and the peoples of the Pacific, secondly for the benefit of people and communities elsewhere;
2. have a primary responsibility to assist communities to maintain and safeguard their continuing intangible cultural heritage;
3. build and maintain relations of cultural understanding and mutual respect with the communities they serve;
4. support the reconnection of ex-situ cultural resources, located domestically or internationally, with their creator communities;
5. are advocates for cultural diversity and sustainable, culture-centred development;
6. will advocate with governments to provide the appropriate financial and other support they require to discharge their responsibilities;
7. will advocate with governments for the effective implementation of national legislation and international conventions relating to the protection and conservation of cultural resources; and

8. encourage museums from outside the Pacific to support the repatriation of cultural resources to the countries and communities of origin.

In line with these principles Pacific Islands Museums and Cultural Centres will:

1. Relate with communities
   1.1 engage communities in all aspects of the management of museums as well as their own cultural heritage;
   1.2 assist communities to manage their own heritage by providing training, capacity-building and ongoing support;
   1.3 build the professional skills of their staff and the communities they serve;
   1.4 ensure appropriate representation of the creator communities' knowledge and beliefs in all museum activities, public programs and interpretative materials;
   1.5 maintain an active relationship with communities in the documentation and conservation of historical, cultural and natural places, which can be used in museum exhibitions and educational programs.
2. Provide access
   2.1 address their responsibilities to provide appropriate access to their premises, collections, research and public programs for all members of the communities they serve;
   2.2 support the use of local vernacular languages, where appropriate, in public programs, publications and interpretive materials (e.g., labels, wall texts, tour guiding, talks) in addition to the official languages of the respective country or territory.
3. Monitor research
   3.1 develop and promote guidelines for the undertaking of research on aspects of the cultural heritage, addressing responsibilities of both museums and others facilitating fieldwork and research ('target bodies') and the institutions supporting researchers ('sponsoring bodies');
   3.2 develop mechanisms to ensure that researchers collect for facilitating museums ('target museums') as well as for their own institutions ('sponsoring bodies').
4. Assess significance
   4.1 ensure that their personnel are knowledgeable in appropriate processes for assessing the significance of cultural resources;
   4.2 assess the significance of cultural resources on the basis of the primary importance of the cultural values that they bear for their creator communities, in addition to the secondary values of their authenticity, age or rarity;
   4.3 refrain as far as practicable from placing monetary values on cultural resources.

Please Note: this Code of Ethics was developed during a workshop as part of the *Pacific Museums in Sustainable Heritage Development Workshop*, held at the Australian

National University in Canberra in February 2006. The facilitation was expertly co-chaired by PIMA Executive Board Members, Lawrence Foana'ota (Director, Solomon Islands National Museum) and Ralph Regenvanu (Director, Vanuatu Cultural Centre) with the assistance of Bernice Murphy, (Chair, ICOM Ethics Committee) and Professor Amareswar Galla (Director of Graduate Studies in Sustainable Heritage Development, The Australian National University). It was developed in direct response to the newly published (revised) version of the *ICOM Code of Professional Ethics* (Paris, 2006), and represents the first region-specific ethics code taking its springboard from the new version of the ICOM Code.

PDF:
www.wipo.int/export/sites/www/tk/en/databases/creative_heritage/docs/pima_code_ethics.pdf.

APPENDIX V

UNESCO recommendation concerning the protection and promotion of museums and collections, their diversity and their role in society

Paris, 20 November 2015
UNITED NATIONS EDUCATIONAL, SCIENTIFIC AND CULTURAL ORGANIZATION

The General Conference,

Considering that museums share some of the fundamental missions of the Organization, as stipulated in its Constitution, including its contribution to the wide diffusion of culture, and the education of humanity for justice, liberty and peace, the foundation of the intellectual and moral solidarity of humanity, full and equal opportunities for education for all, in the unrestricted pursuit of objective truth, and in the free exchange of ideas and knowledge,

Also considering that one of the functions of the Organization, as laid out in its Constitution, is to give new impulse to popular education and to the dissemination of culture: by collaborating with Members, at their request, in the development of educational activities; by instituting collaboration among countries to advance the ideal of equality of educational opportunity without regard to race, gender or any distinctions, economic or social; and to maintain, increase and disseminate knowledge,

Recognizing the importance of culture in its diverse forms in time and space, the benefit that peoples and societies draw from this diversity, and the need to strategically incorporate culture, in its diversity, into national and international development policies, in the interest of communities, peoples and countries,

Affirming that the preservation, study and transmission of cultural and natural, tangible and intangible heritage, in its movable and immovable conditions, are of great importance for all societies, for intercultural dialogue among peoples, for social cohesion, and for sustainable development,

Reaffirming that museums can effectively contribute towards accomplishing these tasks, as stated in the 1960 Recommendation concerning the Most Effective Means of Rendering Museums Accessible to Everyone, which was adopted by the General Conference of UNESCO at its 11th session (Paris, 14 December 1960),

Further affirming that museums and collections contribute to the enhancement of human rights, as set out in the Universal Declaration of Human Rights, in particular its Article 27, and in the International Covenant on Economic, Social and Cultural Rights, in particular its Articles 13 and 15,

Considering museums' intrinsic value as custodians of heritage, and that they also play an ever-increasing role in stimulating creativity, providing opportunities for creative and cultural industries, and for enjoyment, thus contributing to the material and spiritual well-being of citizens across the world,

Considering that it is the responsibility of every Member State to protect the cultural and natural heritage, tangible and intangible, movable and immovable, in the territory under its jurisdiction in all circumstances and to support the actions of museums and the role of collections to that end,

Noting that a body of international standard-setting instruments – adopted by UNESCO and elsewhere – including conventions, recommendations and declarations, exists on the subject of the role of museums and collections, all of which remain valid,[1]

Taking into account the magnitude of socio-economic and political changes that have affected the role and diversity of museums since the adoption of the 1960 Recommendation concerning the Most Effective Means of Rendering Museums Accessible to Everyone,

Desiring to reinforce the protection provided by the existing standards and principles referring to the role of museums and collections in favour of cultural and natural heritage, in its tangible and intangible forms and to related roles and responsibilities,

Having considered proposals on the Recommendation concerning the Protection and Promotion of Museums and Collections, their Diversity and their Role in Society,

Recalling that a UNESCO recommendation is a non-binding instrument that provides principles and policy guidelines addressing different stakeholders,

Adopts this Recommendation on the 17th of November 2015.

The General Conference recommends that Member States apply the following provisions by taking whatever legislative or other measures may be required to implement, within their respective territories under their jurisdiction, the principles and norms set forth in this Recommendation.

Introduction

1. The protection and promotion of cultural and natural diversity are major challenges of the twenty-first century. In this respect, museums and collections constitute primary means by which tangible and intangible testimonies of nature and human cultures are safeguarded.

2. Museums as spaces for cultural transmission, intercultural dialogue, learning, discussion and training, also play an important role in education (formal, informal, and lifelong learning), social cohesion and sustainable development. Museums have great potential to raise public awareness of the value of cultural and natural heritage and of the responsibility of all citizens to contribute to their care and transmission. Museums also support economic development, notably through cultural and creative industries and tourism.

3. This Recommendation draws the attention of Member States to the importance of the protection and promotion of museums and collections, so that they are partners in sustainable development through the preservation and protection of heritage, the protection and promotion of cultural diversity, the transmission of scientific knowledge, the development of educational policy, lifelong learning and social cohesion, and the development of the creative industries and the tourism economy.

I Definition and diversity of museums

4. In this Recommendation, the term *museum* is defined as a 'non-profit, permanent institution in the service of society and its development, open to the public, which acquires, conserves, researches, communicates and exhibits the tangible and intangible heritage of humanity and its environment for the purpose of education, study and enjoyment'.[2] As such, museums are institutions that seek to represent the natural and cultural diversity of humanity, playing an essential role in the protection, preservation and transmission of heritage.

5. In the present Recommendation, the term *collection* is defined as 'an assemblage of natural and cultural properties, tangible and intangible, past and present'.[3] Every Member State should define the scope of what it understands by *collection* in terms of its own legal framework, for the purpose of this Recommendation.

6. In the present Recommendation, the term *heritage* is defined[4] as a set of tangible and intangible values, and expressions that people select and identify, independently of ownership, as a reflection and expression of their identities,

beliefs, knowledge and traditions, and living environments, deserving of protection and enhancement by contemporary generations and transmission to future generations. The term *heritage* also refers to the definitions of cultural and natural heritage, tangible and intangible, cultural property and cultural objects as included in the UNESCO Culture Conventions.

II PRIMARY FUNCTIONS OF MUSEUMS

Preservation

7. The preservation of heritage comprises activities related to acquisition, collection management, including risk analysis and the development of preparedness capacities and emergency plans, in addition to security, preventive and remedial conservation, and the restoration of museum objects, ensuring the integrity of the collections when used and stored.

8. A key component of collection management in museums is the creation and maintenance of a professional inventory and regular control of collections. An inventory is an essential tool for protecting museums, preventing and fighting illicit trafficking, and helping them fulfil their role in society. It also facilitates the sound management of collections mobility.

Research

9. Research, including the study of collections, is another primary function of museums. Research can be carried out by museums in collaboration with others. It is only through the knowledge obtained from such research that the full potential of museums can be realized and offered to the public. Research is of utmost importance for museums to provide opportunities to reflect on history in a contemporary context, as well as for the interpretation, representation and presentation of collections.

Communication

10. Communication is another primary function of museums. Member States should encourage museums to actively interpret and disseminate knowledge on collections, monuments and sites within their specific areas of expertise and to organize exhibitions, as appropriate. Furthermore, museums should be encouraged to use all means of communication to play an active part in society by, for example, organizing public events, taking part in relevant cultural activities and other interactions with the public in both physical and digital forms.

11. Communication policies should take into account integration, access and social inclusion, and should be conducted in collaboration with the public, including groups that do not normally visit museums. Museum actions should also be strengthened by the actions of the public and communities in their favour.

Education

12. Education is another primary function of museums. Museums engage in formal and non-formal education and lifelong learning, through the development and transmission of knowledge, educational and pedagogical programmes, in partnership with other educational institutions, notably schools. Educational programmes in museums primarily contribute to educating various audiences about the subject matters of their collections and about civic life, as well as helping to raise greater awareness of the importance of preserving heritage, and fostering creativity. Museums can also provide knowledge and experiences that contribute to the understanding of related societal topics.

III Issues for museums in society

Globalization

13. Globalization has permitted greater mobility of collections, professionals, visitors and ideas which has impacted museums with both positive and negative effects that are reflected in increased accessibility and homogenization. Member States should promote the safeguarding of the diversity and identity that characterize museums and collections without diminishing the museums' role in the globalized world.

Museum relations with the economy and quality of life

14. Member States should recognise that museums can be economic actors in society and contribute to income-generating activities. Moreover, they participate in the tourism economy and with productive projects contributing to the quality of life of the communities and regions in which they are located. More generally, they can also enhance the social inclusion of vulnerable populations.

15. In order to diversify their sources of revenue and increase self-sustainability, many museums have, by choice or necessity, increased their income-generating activities. Member States should not accord a high priority to revenue generation to the detriment of the primary functions of museums. Member States should recognize that those primary functions, while of utmost importance for society, cannot be expressed in purely financial terms.

Social role

16. Member States are encouraged to support the social role of museums that was highlighted by the 1972 Declaration of Santiago de Chile. Museums are increasingly viewed in all countries as playing a key role in society and as a factor in social integration and cohesion. In this sense, they can help communities to face

profound changes in society, including those leading to a rise in inequality and the breakdown of social ties.

17. Museums are vital public spaces that should address all of society and can therefore play an important role in the development of social ties and cohesion, building citizenship, and reflecting on collective identities. Museums should be places that are open to all and committed to physical and cultural access to all, including disadvantaged groups. They can constitute spaces for reflection and debate on historical, social, cultural and scientific issues. Museums should also foster respect for human rights and gender equality. Member States should encourage museums to fulfil all of these roles.

18. In instances where the cultural heritage of indigenous peoples is represented in museum collections, Member States should take appropriate measures to encourage and facilitate dialogue and the building of constructive relationships between those museums and indigenous peoples concerning the management of those collections, and, where appropriate, return or restitution in accordance with applicable laws and policies.

Museums and Information and Communication Technologies (ICTs)

19. The changes brought about by the rise of information and communication technologies (ICTs) offer opportunities for museums in terms of the preservation, study, creation and transmission of heritage and related knowledge. Member States should support museums to share and disseminate knowledge and ensure that museums have the means to have access to these technologies when they are judged necessary to improve their primary functions.

IV Policies

General policies

20. Existing international instruments relating to cultural and natural heritage recognize the importance and social role of museums in their protection and promotion, and in the overall accessibility of this heritage to the public. In this regard, Member States should take appropriate measures so that museums and collections in the territories under their jurisdiction or control benefit from the protective and promotional measures granted by these instruments. Member States should also take appropriate measures to strengthen museum capacities for their protection in all circumstances.

21. Member States should ensure that museums implement principles of applicable international instruments. Museums are committed to observe the principles of international instruments for the protection and promotion of cultural and natural heritage, both tangible and intangible. They also should adhere to the principles of the international instruments for the fight against illicit trafficking of cultural property and should coordinate their efforts in this matter. Museums

must also take into account the ethical and professional standards established by the professional museum community. Member States should ensure that the role of museums in society is exercised in accordance with legal and professional standards in the territories under their jurisdiction.

22. Member States should adopt policies and take appropriate measures to ensure the protection and promotion of museums located in the territories under their jurisdiction or control, by supporting and developing those institutions in accordance with their primary functions, and in this regard develop the necessary human, physical and financial resources needed for them to function properly.

23. The diversity of museums and the heritage of which they are custodians constitutes their greatest value. Member States are requested to protect and promote this diversity, while encouraging museums to draw on high-quality criteria defined and promoted by national and international museum communities.

Functional policies

24. Member States are invited to support active preservation, research, education and communication policies, adapted to local social and cultural contexts, to allow museums to protect and pass down heritage to future generations. In this perspective, collaborative and participative efforts between museums, communities, civil society and the public should be strongly encouraged.

25. Member States should take appropriate measures to ensure that the compilation of inventories based on international standards is a priority in the museums established in the territory under their jurisdiction. The digitization of museum collections is highly important in this regard, but should not be considered as a replacement for the conservation of collections.

26. Good practices for the functioning, protection and promotion of museums and their diversity and role in society have been recognized by national and international museum networks. These good practices are continually updated to reflect innovations in the field. In this respect, the Code of Ethics for Museums adopted by the International Council of Museums (ICOM) constitutes the most widely shared reference. Member States are encouraged to promote the adoption and dissemination of these and other codes of ethics and good practices and to use them to inform the development of standards, museum policies and national legislation.

27. Member States should take appropriate measures to facilitate the employment of qualified personnel by museums in the territories under their jurisdiction with the required expertise. Adequate opportunities for the continuing education and professional development of all museum personnel should be arranged to maintain an effective workforce.

28. The effective functioning of museums is directly influenced by public and private funding and adequate partnerships. Member States should strive to

ensure a clear vision, adequate planning and funding for museums, and a har-monious balance among the different funding mechanisms to enable them to carry out their mission to the benefit of society with full respect for their primary functions.

29. The functions of museums are also influenced by new technologies and their growing role in everyday life. These technologies have great potential for pro-moting museums throughout the world, but they also constitute potential bar-riers for people and museums that do not have access to them or the knowledge and skills to use them effectively. Member States should strive to provide access to these technologies for museums in the territories under their jurisdiction or control.

30. The social role of museums, along with the preservation of heritage, consti-tutes their fundamental purpose. The spirit of the 1960 Recommendation concerning the Most Effective Means of Rendering Museums Accessible to Everyone remains important in creating a lasting place for museums in society. Member States should strive to include these principles in the laws concerning the museums established in the territories under their jurisdiction.

31. Cooperation within the museum sectors and institutions responsible for culture, heritage and education is one of the most effective and sustainable ways of protecting and promoting museums, their diversity and their role in society. Member States should therefore encourage cooperation and partner-ships among museums and cultural and scientific institutions at all levels, including their participation in professional networks and associations that foster such cooperation and international exhibitions, exchanges and the mobility of collections.

32. The collections defined in paragraph 5, when held in institutions that are not museums, should be protected and promoted in order to preserve the coher-ence and better represent the cultural diversity of those countries' heritage. Member States are invited to cooperate in the protection, research and promo-tion of those collections, as well as in promoting access to them.

33. Member States should take appropriate legislative, technical, and financial measures, in order to design public planning and policies enabling to develop and implement these recommendations in museums situated in the territories under their jurisdiction.

34. In order to contribute to the improvement of museum activities and services, Member States are encouraged to support the establishment of inclusive pol-icies for audience development.

35. Member States should promote international cooperation in capacity-building and professional training, through bilateral or multilateral mechanisms includ-ing through UNESCO, in order to better implement these recommendations and especially to benefit the museums and collections of developing countries.

Notes

1 List of the international instruments directly and indirectly relating to museums and collections:

The Convention for the Protection of Cultural Property in the Event of Armed Conflict (1954), and its two Protocols (1954 and 1999);

The Convention on the Means of Prohibiting and Preventing the Illicit Import, Export and Transfer of Ownership of Cultural Property 1970;

The Convention on Biological Diversity (1992); The Convention Concerning the Protection of the World Cultural and Natural Heritage (1972);

The UNIDROIT Convention on Stolen or Illegally Exported Cultural Objects (1995);

The Convention on the Protection of the Underwater Cultural Heritage (2001);

The Convention for the Safeguarding of Intangible Cultural Heritage (2003);

The Convention on the Protection and Promotion of the Diversity of Cultural Expressions (2005);

The International Covenant on Economic, Social and Cultural Rights (1966);

The Recommendation on International Principles Applicable to Archaeological Excavations (UNESCO 1956);

The Recommendation concerning the Most Effective Means of Rendering Museums Accessible to Everyone (UNESCO 1960);

The Recommendation on the Means of Prohibiting and Preventing the Illicit Export, Import and Transfer of Ownership of Cultural Property (UNESCO 1964);

The Recommendation concerning the Protection, at National Level, of the Cultural and Natural Heritage (UNESCO 1972);

The Recommendation for the Protection of Movable Cultural Property (UNESCO 1978). The Recommendation concerning the International Exchange of Cultural Property (UNESCO 1976);

The Universal Declaration of Human Rights (1949). The Recommendation on the Safeguarding of Traditional Culture and Folklore (UNESCO 1989);

The UNESCO Declaration of Principles of International Cultural Cooperation (1966);

The UNESCO Universal Declaration on Cultural Diversity 2001;

The UNESCO Declaration concerning the Intentional Destruction of Cultural Heritage (2003);

The United Nations Declaration on the Rights of Indigenous Peoples (2007).

2 This definition is the one given by the International Council of Museums (ICOM), which brings together, at an international level, the museum phenomenon in all of its diversity and transformations through time and space. This definition describes a museum as a public or private non-profit agency or institution.

3 This definition reflects partially the one given by the International Council of Museums (ICOM).

4 This definition partially reflects the one given by Council of Europe Framework Convention on the Value of Cultural Heritage for Society.

INDEX

Page numbers in **bold** denote figures.